The AMERICAN COVENANT

ONE NATION UNDER GOD

DISCOVERY THROUGH REVOLUTION

The AMERICAN COVENANT

ONE NATION UNDER GOD

DISCOVERY THROUGH REVOLUTION

Timothy Ballard

DIGITAL
LEGEND

New York

Send inquiries to:

Digital Legend Press and Publishing
Salt Lake City UT

To see the complete Digital Legend library, visit www.digitalegend.com
For info write to: info@digitalegend.com or call toll free: 877-222-1960

ISBN: 978-1-934537-28-2

Printed in the United States of America First Printing: July 2011 (V1)

Cover design and book interior layout by Alisha Bishop

Praise for *The American Covenant*

An absorbing read into the nature of the American Covenant, how the world's history, with its many philosophical and religious movements, serves to inform and sometimes define the Restoration that crowns the Covenant. This book compels honest scholars to open their minds and hearts to the cumulative effect of history on the Restoration.... Rather than being some new religion revealed by an angel and taught by a prophet, Mormonism is actually the crowning achievement of a long historical record. By rereading American history in light of the Restoration, Ballard has given readers a clear path to follow in understanding just how God has guided history, resulting in the ushering in of the Dispensation of the Fullness of Times.

- Jeffrey Needle
Book Review Editor, *The Association for Mormon Letters*

Tim Ballard has shown great skill in compiling and researching all that has been written or spoken concerning this covenanted land of America. Many a reader has read different quotes regarding the destiny of America. The American Covenant *by Ballard brings all of this information and more together in one book. This book will be a valuable resource in every home. I highly recommend this book.*

- Vicki Jo Anderson
Author of *The Other Eminent Men of Wilford Woodruff*

Tim Ballard's The American Covenant *is an inspiring and thought-provoking work that will cause Latter-day Saints to think more profoundly about their role in America's destiny, and better understand America's place in God's plan. The* American Covenant *will stir any God-fearing patriot to reflect anew on the divine origin and destiny of this remarkable nation.*

- Mayor Mike Winder
Author of *Presidents and Prophets:*
The Story of America's Presidents and the LDS Church

For Katherine

CONTENTS

ACKNOWLEDGEMENTS

First and foremost, I acknowledge and thank my wife, Katherine. She has stood by my side throughout the entirety of this almost decade-long project. She has read every word and provided much wisdom, council, and support, all the while providing similar services to our six young children. For allowing me to be her seventh child these past ten years, I dedicate this book to her. Thanks also to my children for attending countless family nights full of American history.

There is one person who did more than any other to make sure my "best work" ended up as scratch paper on the editor's floor, exactly where it belonged. Todd Reynolds (my best friend from childhood, who somehow managed to marry my sister) read every word of my manuscript multiple times and weighed in with sometimes stinging (but much needed) criticism. I thank him for believing so strongly in the material and for being the "refining fire" that made it better. Also, his defense and promotion of my research have proven invaluable.

Others who read the manuscript and added indispensable advice and support are Dennis Ballard (my father), Craig Ballard, Brent Ballard, and Stephen Fairbanks. Other long-time heroes and helpers to my cause are Tevya Ware, Kristol Andelin, and Jerry Gowen.

Many people walked with me—at different places and in different ways—on this arduous path from research to writing to publication. Many thanks to Lance Swanson, Brandon Wood, Wes Mortensen, Shauna Reynolds, Jules and Mark Blake, Rico and Amy Zinn, Elisa and Kris Barton, Kim Ballard, Justin and Emily Evans,

Rich Ware, Susan Ballard, Dave Broberg, Dale Zinn, John Holliday, Ben Benton, Jesse Wooley, Kevin Cranney, Rhet Andelin, Christie Frandsen, Matt Hatch, Gale Tenney, Vicki-Jo Anderson, Matt Cooper, Stacy Rolfe, Rod Meldrum, Mike and Anne Tilden, and Catherine Drew (whose editing skills made me look better than I am).

Many thanks to my parents (Dennis and Melanie, and Richard and Tamra), and to my grandparents (Blain and Pat), for believing in me more than I deserved.

And finally, for the miraculous manner in which this book reached publication, I thank Skip Carlson, Jeff Needle (of the Association for Mormon Letters), and Boyd Tuttle (of Digital Legend Press)—thanks for believing!

INTRODUCTION

As I approached the Lincoln Memorial, I was impressed by the overwhelming spirit surrounding the ninety-nine foot marble edifice that houses the grand sculpture of America's sixteenth president. I walked up the majestic stairway leading to the entrance hall and was overcome by the building's radiant glow against the backdrop of night. I found myself mesmerized as I gazed at the sculpture representing this great man and pondered his profound words as they appeared memorialized within the walls of the structure. Though I understood this memorial building was often referred to as a *temple,** the idea took on a whole new meaning for me that night.

Yet it wasn't the words on the walls—the Gettysburg Address and Lincoln's Second Inaugural Address—that struck me the deepest; nor was it the edifice or sculpture alone that created the lasting effect. As meaningful as these were, it was the profound spiritual manifestation I received that night, testifying to me that the United States of America is truly *one nation under God*, set apart as a choice land and commissioned with a divine purpose. I believe similar manifestations fill our hearts in certain moments when, for example, we watch our flag waving in the air, sing the *National Anthem* with our church congregation, or ponder the words of that powerful hymn: *God Bless America*.

Days before my experience at the Lincoln Memorial, I had moved to the Washington D.C. area with my wife and baby son to fulfill an assignment at the Central Intelligence Agency. Little did I

---

* Within the memorial, above the famous statue of Lincoln, there is an inscription that describes the grand edifice as a "temple."

know that accepting this position and relocating across the country would lead me to this personal revelation, which, in turn, would inspire the writing and publication of this work. Indeed, this singular experience pulled me into an in-depth study of God and country, as I yearned to fully comprehend the connection. What I found both astonished and delighted me. I discovered compelling evidence of an America founded by the Almighty, embedded in divine purpose, and deeply rooted to that which I hold most sacred —the restored gospel of Jesus Christ as manifested by and through The Church of Jesus Christ of Latter-day Saints.

I had always considered America to be a special place, as it was the host country of the Restoration. However, I had never before known how profound that connection was. This study presents the details of that connection by showing how God, in an effort to further His ultimate design for His children, created and offered up America by and through a *national covenant*. It is a covenant between God and the people of our nation, and it comes complete with specific obligations, promised blessings, and divine instruction. It is a covenant whose principal fruit is the development, defense, and distribution of three very specific socio-political blessings: 1) Liberty, 2) Protection, and 3) Prosperity. It is a covenant that, through imparting such blessings, enhances and maximizes God's gift of agency unto personal salvation. It does so, first, by providing an environment where God's children might choose freely, becoming who and what they desire to be, thus enabling their personal progression. And it does so, second, by providing the environment in which the restored gospel, with its saving principles and ordinances, might thrive both at home and abroad, thus enabling God's children to not only progress, but to specifically progress unto eternal life. It is *The American Covenant*.*

---

* As will be shown throughout the length of this book, the covenant referred to is as real as the scriptures that define it. That said, I do not pretend to have the authority to give this covenant a specific name. However, for convenience in navigating through the story of this covenant, I will refer to it as *The American Covenant*.

We are familiar with certain scriptural representations of this American Covenant, such as the popular declaration found in the Book of Mormon that America "is a choice land" to "be free from bondage," as long as we "serve the God of the land" (Ether 2:12). And yet, too often we have not recognized the deeper significance of what such declarations have yearned to tell us. Too often we have not seen the overwhelming evidence of this more powerful meaning —derived from a myriad of both scriptural and historical documentation—which enables us to better understand and participate in the American Covenant.

This study, then, invites you, the reader, to dig a little deeper in order to fully comprehend the most profound and truest meaning of this covenant. Such comprehension will not fully congeal through reading a few lines of scripture or reciting the Pledge of Allegiance per se; for the American Covenant transcends verse and text. Its fullness is a puzzle with pieces scattered among various places, people, prophecies and prose. For not only has the covenant been revealed to a multiplicity of religious and political leaders, its effects have been made manifest in countless historical occurrences. While a complete assemblage of this scattered evidence may appear daunting, there is good news. With a little effort in gathering sources and stories, we can assemble enough of the puzzle to learn of the covenant and feel the power of its divine purpose.

As we now commence an exploration of the evidence, a story will begin to unfold. It is a familiar story of a nation that has struggled through bloody conflicts, glorious victories, devastating scourges, healing redemptions, long silences, great proclamations, deep tragedies, and phenomenal miracles. Laced throughout this story are unlikely combinations of varied people, events and experiences—combinations we often segregate and view as independent variables. We tend to label some variables as "religious" and others as "secular" (i.e. political, historical, social). This story brings them together and, in so doing, introduces us to amazing insights and revelations.

For example, we will learn that ancient prophets saw the discoverer Columbus and that Columbus knew he had been seen; that the first settlers and founders willfully received the land and nation under covenant, and that they knew something of the religious restoration to follow; that George Washington's scripture of choice was an ancient prophecy about the gospel destiny of latter-day America, and that the General *knew* the many battlefield miracles he witnessed were connected to a covenant with the Almighty; that Thomas Jefferson testified of a forthcoming restoration of Christ's church; and that the Declaration of Independence and the Constitution profoundly reflect and codify the American Covenant. Furthermore, we will learn why the Book of Mormon deals not only with purely religious instruction, but also overflows with wisdom concerning government, politics, and warfare; why the Prophet Joseph Smith *really* ran for the presidency of the United States; and how Abraham Lincoln fulfilled some of the greatest prophecies related to God's Kingdom (and why he perhaps felt compelled to seek out a Book of Mormon during the darkest days of his presidency). Additionally, we will learn of the astonishing and miraculous relationship (forged in life and death) between the founders of this nation and the temple of God. As we now journey from America's discovery all the way through to the present day, we will stop at every step to internalize the details of these—and many other—miracles, revelations, tokens, and symbols of God's work throughout our history.

But how can we possibly bring such varied and seemingly unconnected people and experiences together in an orderly way? In other words, is there a single context that makes sense of it all? Yes, the puzzle into which all these pieces connect *is* the American Covenant. So the purpose of this study is to provide the story of this covenant.

We will assemble this story through the words and deeds of America's prophets, presidents, citizens, and soldiers. As it comes together, we will clearly see that this covenant is real, alive, and complete with heavenly ordained obligations and blessings. And we will observe that it is administered directly by the Almighty to provide the socio-political foundations that maximize and enhance the power of agency—a requisite for mankind's eternal salvation.

To the skeptic, we concede that there exist valid questions and concerns pertaining to this "theory" we call the American Covenant. When exactly was this covenant made? Where might we find the details explaining its obligations and blessings? How do such obligations and blessings really tie into God's work? By what authority was this covenant offered and received? What proof really exists that such a covenant was, in fact, given by God and accepted by latter-day Americans? How can we be sure that whatever connections we find in the historical record are not just coincidences? If God made such a covenant, where is the divine "stamp of approval"?

In an effort to answer these and other related questions, this book is organized into two volumes. Volume I tells the covenant story from the time of America's discovery through the Revolutionary War. Volume II picks up at the end of the Revolution and takes us through the creation of the Constitution, the tragedy of the Civil War, and on through to the present day. This first volume, Volume I, is composed of two parts. Part I: *Defining the American Covenant*, will lay out the conceptual foundation. Through ancient prophets and prophecies, we will come to understand the covenant and the people responsible for it. We will also come to understand the blessings and obligations of the covenant and how they serve God's ultimate purpose—"to bring to pass the immortality and eternal life of man" (Moses 1:39).

Part II: *Living the American Covenant*, makes up the overwhelming majority of this study. Here we will see how American history fulfills the ancient prophecies concerning the American Covenant. We will see this inspiring fulfillment through America's unique, yet undervalued, spirituality—a spirituality that has been the primary asset in its eternal struggle against adversarial attacks on man's agency and thus on God's plan of salvation. Most importantly, we will learn how every victory we have achieved as a nation in this eternal struggle has been contingent on our ability to live the American Covenant. This study will provide insight into such national lessons and will deliver practical instructions on how we can better live the national covenant, thus allowing us to more fully assist God in His work and glory.

Along the way, we will be introduced to many surprising connections between prominent historical experiences and God's true gospel—connections linked by the American Covenant. Through it all, we will begin to internalize why the spiritual feelings ("fruits of the Spirit") we feel in connection with the gospel are so often the same spiritual feelings we experience upon witnessing or pondering events related to the greatness of our country. Indeed, we will internalize the Book of Mormon declaration that "the Spirit of God...is also the spirit of freedom" (Alma 61:15).

★ ★ ★ ★

As we now approach this study, we would do well to remember that the American Covenant is as relevant today as it ever was. Consider the following warning from President Gordon B. Hinckley—a prophet not only to the Church, but to the nation and world—which he gave specifically to our American generation:

> For a good while, there has been going on in this nation a process that I have termed the secularization of America. The single most substantial factor in the degeneration of the values and morals of our society is that we as a nation are forsaking the Almighty, and I fear that He will begin to forsake us. We are shutting the door against the God whose sons and daughters we are....Future blessings will come only as we deserve them. Can we expect peace and prosperity, harmony and goodwill, when we turn our backs on the Source of strength? If we are to continue to have the freedoms that evolved within the structure that was the inspiration of the Almighty to our Founding Fathers, we must return to the God who is their true Author....God bless America, for it is His creation. [1]

ENDNOTE

[1] Gordon B Hinckley, *Standing for Something* (New York: Times Books, Random House, Inc., 2000), xviii, xxiii, xxv

PART I

★ ★ ★ ★

Defining the American Covenant

* Note to reader: Part I (composed of Chapters 1 and 2) lays a foundation, which gives power and meaning to the miraculous stories laced throughout Part II. Part I is a bit more analytical than the rest of the book, but without an understanding of it, the narrative in Part II will merely tickle your intellect. *With* an understanding of it, however, that which follows has the potential to penetrate your very soul.

Moroni Burying the Plates, Tom Lovell
Courtesy of Intellectual Property Division, LDS Church

CHAPTER 1

THE COVENANT

*[I]f it so be that they shall serve him according
to the commandments…it shall be a land of
liberty unto them; wherefore they shall never
be brought down into captivity.*

—2 Nephi 1:7

The story of the American Covenant begins with the God of
Abraham directing chosen people to a promised land, known today
as America. His purpose behind this new nation and its covenant
was to establish a socio-political foundation whereupon His children
might fully exercise their agency to choose Christ and His gospel
and thus qualify themselves for eternal life. If we are to fully grasp
the meaning behind all of this, we must first understand certain
basic concepts. What is a "national" covenant? Why is it important?
Why should we think to apply such a covenant to the United States
of America? And finally, what do the scriptures teach us about the
stated promises and obligations of this proposed covenant in
America? Though it will take the length of this book to fully develop
these foundational concepts, it is the purpose of this chapter to
introduce them.

What is a National Covenant?

W hen we consider what a *covenant* is, our minds rightly reflect upon personal promises made with our Heavenly Father through His priesthood power, such as at baptism or in His sacred temples. We promise to keep His commandments and He promises us great gifts, such as His Holy Spirit, the power of His holy priesthood, and, ultimately, eternal life. These are far and away the most significant covenants, as they directly fulfill the purposes of God by assisting His children to fill the measure of their creation.

National covenants, such as the American Covenant, are different. They are made with *nations*, not individuals, and exist as a support mechanism to the more important gospel covenants (those made at baptism and in the temple). National covenants provide the framework, foundation, and environment in which these most important priesthood covenants might be made and lived unto eternal life. And so, though national covenants serve as lesser covenants—and certainly are not requisite for individual salvation— they do carry the same eternal purposes of God.

The most prominent example of a national covenant is that covenant made with the Hebrew nation. It is detailed throughout the Old Testament: "For I will have respect unto you...and establish my covenant with you...And I will walk among you and will be your God and ye shall be my people" (Leviticus 26:9, 12). This is but one of many such Old Testament verses which describe this national covenant made, not with an individual, but with an entire people (known as Israel). The familiar blessings offered to Israel as part of this covenant were liberty, protection, and prosperity. We see the blessings of *liberty*, for example, distributed when the Lord liberates Israel from Egyptian slavery, as manifested in part by the miracle of the parting of the Red Sea (Exodus 14:13-16). We further witness these blessings when God establishes this chosen people under a sound system of government that protects these liberties.[1] We see the blessings of *prosperity* distributed when the Lord provides Israel with a promised land in which it could thrive economically, even a land "flowing with milk and honey" (Exodus 3:8). And we see the blessings of physical *protection* distributed when the Lord provides defenses against foreign powers, such as the Philistines, who sought to destroy God's work among Israel (1 Samuel 17:45-47). If His people would but listen and obey, all this would be theirs.*

Though we accept this covenant relationship, we often times fail to ponder why it was, exactly, that the Lord provided these temporal blessings of *liberty, protection,* and *prosperity* to ancient Israel. Did He do this solely because He wanted to help a group of people overcome certain hardships of mortality? If so, what about the millions of others at this time, and at other times, who never received such an offer? The truth is, there was and is much more to it. From the day God covenanted with Abraham, the father of Israel, promising him that the ultimate gospel purpose—to bring to pass the eternal life of man—would be worked through him and his posterity, God has continually offered Abraham's posterity this national covenant. He did so because it was through the blessings of this national covenant—the *liberty, protection,* and *prosperity* provided—that the greater gospel purposes and priesthood covenants made with Abraham, as revealed and provided in sacred temples, could be secure enough to bless the world and fulfill God's work and glory. Would the Lord have, for example, set up his sacred temple and ordinances for His people while they suffered under the distrustful eye and brutal tyranny of the Egyptians? Could His temple and ordinances have remained undefiled in a land of overwhelming poverty and crime? Or in a land riddled with conquering invasions? Could God trust that His gospel and His temple would be secure in a land of overbearing oppression and wickedness? Trying to establish God's work on earth without a national covenant to fight against these obstructions would be like tossing a handful of seeds into a pot filled only with concrete— doomed from the start. Conversely, instituting a binding covenant

---

* See Leviticus 26 for a detailed description of Israel's national covenant, complete with obligations of obedience, and blessings of liberty, protection, and prosperity.

that carried protective promises would be like filling the pot with rich soil and then carefully planting the seeds.

In sum, national covenants serve to secure and enhance the social, economic, and political situation of God's children, thus maximizing their ability to safely, securely, and freely access His greater priesthood covenants unto eternal life.

Why a National Covenant Today?

Without the social, political and economic security provided by national covenants, the gospel in its fullness would struggle to survive. Had ancient Israel been faithful until the end, their national covenant might have remained intact until the present. This would have allowed God's eternal purpose for His children to thrive continuously through Israel, from their day to ours. However, as a result of broken covenants, not the least of which was its failure to worship the one true God, Israel lost the power of its promised land —it lost the covenant blessings of its promised land. Slowly but surely, Israel's *liberty, protection* and *prosperity* faded away, causing it to be destroyed, swept off and scattered throughout the world. General apostasy from truth then pervaded the earth (Deuteronomy 4:26-27, Ezekiel 11:16; Amos 8:11). It was during this dark period that the Savior came into mortality. Clearly, there was enough freedom still left in Israel to allow Christ to teach the people, restore His gospel and organize His church. (This was mostly due to Rome's initially tolerant stance on religious freedom within its commonwealth, of which Israel was a part). But after He completed His mortal mission, the most important part of which was His atoning sacrifice, His church had little time to develop and congeal. For, with the lack of any strong national covenant that would support the existence of Christ's gospel, the church collapsed almost entirely by the end of the first century AD. The political foundations (both Roman and Israeli) that could have and should have protected it, ultimately came down upon it and destroyed and/or exploited precious truths and sacred priesthood. The Great Apostasy had fully commenced. Christ Himself recognized in mortality that His nation would not adhere to its national covenant and that His gospel would, as a consequence, be taken from the earth in short order (see Matthew 21:43; 23: 37-38). His gospel would not return in its fullness until God could first re-establish a strong national covenant to support it.

★ ★ ★ ★

Though this glimpse into history reveals our need for a national covenant today, to fully understand the most significant reasons such a national covenant would be needed in the latter-day era (or any other era), requires us to reach eons before the establishment and failure of ancient Israel, and takes us all the way back to our pre-earth life and to that infamous War in Heaven. According to the scriptures, "Michael and his angels fought against the dragon; and the dragon fought and his angels, and prevailed not" (Revelation 12:7-8). "Wherefore," stated the Lord, "because that Satan rebelled against me, and sought to *destroy the agency of man*...I caused that he should be cast down" (Moses 4:3-4, emphasis added). During the pre-mortal existence, Satan proposed a "plan of salvation" for God's children that would take away agency and replace it with forced obedience. Satan was so adamantly against any opposing plan that included agency, that when his own plan was rejected, he responded by waging a war in heaven, which he would ultimately lose.

The relevant question in all this is, *Why would Satan work so hard just to deny us our agency?* The answer is simple: Satan understood that free agency in its fullness was the only way to achieve eternal progression in its fullness—and he certainly did not want God's children to progress beyond his self-perceived grandeur. And so he would fight for a system of governance that oppresses, compels, and makes choices for its subjects, thus making the true steps of eternal progression impossible to achieve. Indeed, his system would deny us the liberty to be tested, to face adversity, to fail, to learn from mistakes, to find and employ faith, to fully repent, to seek and find truth, to change within, to longingly make and keep covenants, to succeed, then to grow, and thus "work out [our] own salvation" (Philip 2:12), as God has outlined it (2 Nephi 2:11; Alma 62:41; D&C 122:1-9). If Satan forced us into taking these steps, our personal drive and righteous desires necessary for their fulfillment would be dissolved, thus rendering void the entire process. If he simply withheld aspects of this process, such as true principles of faith, repentance, covenants, etc., the effect would be the same. Either way, his choice-impeding, freedom-less plan of governance would deny us the gospel as we know it and thus withhold from us our fullest potential. In short, though Satan's plan would offer some sort of "salvation," without the invaluable environment provided by a fullness of agency, man—mired in a stagnant state—would, as Satan devised, lack the resources to become worthy of exaltation with the Father.

On the other end of the spectrum was Jesus Christ, whose plan glorified the Father and allowed mankind, through agency, to be "free to choose...eternal life through the great Mediator" (2 Nephi 2:27). This freedom would ultimately allow God's children the ability to employ all the above-outlined essential steps of faith unto eternal life, including, most importantly, the opportunity to choose Christ and thus, through His atoning power, perfect themselves and ultimately share in His glory. In the end, God's plan based on agency would be so important to Him that He was not only willing to fight a war in heaven over it, which would cause the eternal expulsion of one third of His pre-mortal children (D&C 29:36-37), but was also willing to sacrifice His Only Begotten Son over it. For if He were to allow His children the agency necessary for full salvation, sin would naturally result in everyone, thus requiring an atoning sacrifice by His only perfect Son. Rather than spare His Son unspeakable agony, God chose agency for His children, so that eternal life and exaltation might be possible for them. Of such is the importance of agency to the Father.

The righteous children of God who accepted and fought for His plan of agency in the pre-mortal existence are now on earth. However, their opponents in that fight, even Satan and his followers, are also here, albeit without physical bodies (see Moses 4:1-3; D&C 29:36-37; 76:25-38). With these two forces for good and evil together again—this time in mortality—it naturally follows that the same war over agency unto salvation would continue to rage. Satan and his followers, once "cast down" to earth, would certainly continue to employ their *modus operandi,* and do all in their power to influence those they could—from kings and their armies to tyrants and their navies—to reign and oppress with blood and horror on the earth. They would attempt to control man, thus limiting his choices and thwarting his God-given agency. This would allow them the opportunity to frustrate man's eternal advancement. Of course, Satan would disguise his evil intentions, even permitting the use of some semblance of truth and scripture; but this scripture would merely be mingled with the dominating and oppressive philosophies of men. For, no matter how he presents it, we have been warned that his evil plan will always have at its root a malicious attempt to "lead them captive at his will" (Moses 4:4). As President Gordon B. Hinckley declared (quoting President Wilford Woodruff), "There are two powers on the earth and in the midst of the inhabitants of the earth—the power of God and the power of the devil…when God has had a people on the earth, it matters not in what age, Lucifer, the son of the morning, and the millions of fallen spirits that were cast out of heaven have warred against…the work of God."[2]

Commenting on such adversarial ploys, Brigham Young University religion professor Andrew Skinner points out that "[t]emple teachings expose Satan's tactics: rebellion, ignorance, violence, tyranny, and the destruction of agency in this world."[3] Again, Satan knows now, like he knew then, that it is only through freedom and agency that man might experience exaltation. Therefore, in an effort to obstruct such exaltation, the adversary has always (and will always) fight to destroy freedom and agency—whether in the pre-mortal existence or right here on earth. President David O. McKay identified this trend when addressing the satanic and oppressive system of government that Americans were fighting against during World War II. "Think of it now —the value of freedom of choice! That was the great principle involved when the war arose in Heaven when Lucifer would have deprived God's children the right to choose." The Prophet continued: "Your sons and mine are out fighting for that principle [of free agency]. In the last analysis that is the great question in this war so far as the Allies are concerned—whether we shall have the right to think as we please." President McKay knew that "even God could not make men like himself without making them free." [4]

Today we stand on earth, witnessing Satan's promises and intentions. A mere glimpse into latter-day history (say, the last couple hundred years) reveals the Evil One's influence over governments. Backed by armies and navies, men susceptible to Satan's influence have undoubtedly turned to tyranny and have attacked precious freedom and liberty. Such attacks have invited ignorance, violence, and the near destruction of agency, and thus the near destruction of personal progression towards eternal salvation. Consider, for example, the monarchical systems of Europe, the oppressive Confederate system/culture that once existed in the United States, fascist regimes like Nazi Germany, dictatorial regimes such as those the world witnessed under the Soviet Union, or the tyrannical systems of the Middle East we still see today. Though, admittedly, no such system of wicked governance could ever completely destroy agency and progression, (man does, after all, always maintain his thoughts and intentions, which allows for at least limited progression), these examples of bad government come dangerously close. For they have allowed Satan to have his way; depending on the firmness of his evil grasp, sometimes this means the ability to control and oppress almost every aspect of man's life. Other times, it means less control over man's every choice, but still a full ability to deny the freedom required for God's true church to establish itself within the borders of the infected nation-state. Either way, through denying a fullness of agency, the adversary has, through time, maintained a choke-hold on mankind's progression.

And this is where the national covenant comes in. For, as this adversarial influence created a very real and *physical* affront to God's plan for the full salvation of His children (again, we are talking about the adversary's influence over literal armies and navies, etc.), a very real and *physical* response from Heaven would be required. To be sure, if God could counter Satan in the latter-days, as He had done in earlier days (like He did with ancient Israel), by forming a government, set forth on a new national covenant complete with the necessary *liberty, protection,* and *prosperity,* then this new nation could, under the guidance of Heaven, fight and destroy these kings and tyrants, these armies and navies, and thus enforce and maximize the divine agency of man. Only then could all mankind receive the opportunity to fully and freely worship the one true God and thereby find salvation. The members of God's Church, who would administer the gospel upon the earth, could not alone defeat such a physical threat. But a righteous nation, of which they were a part, certainly could. Once such a nation and government under God was in place, with agency unto salvation enhanced, the eternal progression of God's children would be facilitated and the Kingdom of God, even the Church of Jesus Christ, could exist and prosper.

It should be noted, however, that though the gospel in its fullness is the crowning purpose of God's national covenants, this does not exclude non-Church members as beneficiaries of it. As implied above, these national covenants, which provide and enhance agency, benefit *all* children of God by allowing them to choose freely, employ personal responsibility, and thus learn and grow from their successes and failures—whether in or out of the gospel. As any positive progression brings these children closer to God and His eternal plan for them, they too have claim and interest in the national covenant. Indeed, the eternal outcome of all God's children is attached to this national covenant, which is why we need a national covenant today and always.

Why the United States of America?

Though we might acknowledge our need for a national covenant today, why the United States of America? What proof exists that the United States is the latter-day nation God has established and set apart under this covenant? What evidence is there that America is His instrument in developing, defending, and distributing the socio-political system that would promote agency? Answering this question in full will require the length of this book. However, there are certain immediate evidences that place the United States in this high position.

For example, if there is such a thing as a modern national covenant, it certainly would have been established within the host-nation of the Restoration in order to lend support to God's work and glory against the inevitable attacks from the adversary.

But beyond this obvious suggestion, we might also consider how even a cursory review of American history reveals a consistent pattern: where goes the adversary's political and military tools of oppression unto spiritual obstruction, there goes America to confront and defeat it; and where goes America to confront and defeat it, there follows the heavenly influence of the constitutional principles of liberty and free agency; and where go these divine principles, there follows man's opportunity for personal growth and his introduction to (and advancement in) God's restored gospel.

We recently identified several such adversarial regime-types in the latter-days that have thwarted or at least severely hampered liberty and agency and have thus been responsible for obstructing the eternal progression of millions upon millions of God's children. And in every case, it was America who led the fight back at them. It was America who first took on the monarchical system of the Old World by defeating Great Britain and thus securing the freedom that would become the fertile ground for the Restoration. The American Union would likewise take on wicked elements from within (like the Southern Confederacy), thus purifying this fertile ground. America has also successfully attacked both fascist and communist dictatorships—for example: Nazi Germany and Soviet Russia—along with Middle Eastern tyrants and other wicked regimes. As liberty has thus spread, so have the effects of enhanced agency. And in almost every instance, once America's victory is secured—whether at home or abroad—America moves on, leaving God's temples gloriously in its wake. So it has been, and so it shall be. Indeed, the war that started in heaven continues on earth. As a covenant nation, America has been (and will continue to be) the driving force for the work of God on earth in this last dispensation.

In light of this historical glimpse, it should be of little surprise that it was God Himself who declared that He "established" the American nation for the very purposes outlined above: for the "rights and protection of all flesh...that every man may act... according to the moral agency which I have given unto him" (D&C 101:77-80). And these verses are convincingly corroborated by America's founding documents, which, as we will discuss later, are the first of their kind, in both their inspired content and the miraculous manner in which they came to exist. The documents referred to, of course, are the Declaration of Independence and the Constitution, which declare that it is the responsibility of America to "secure" certain "inalienable rights," which have been "endowed [to man] by their Creator," and which include the gifts of "Life, Liberty, and the Pursuit of Happiness," and promote as their ultimate goal, "the blessings of liberty."

Furthermore, the United States has, for reasons not fully explicable to the secular mind, developed into perhaps the only country in world history blessed with the resources necessary to fulfill this divine purpose. What other nation has possessed the ability to not only provide and enforce such liberty at home, but also —through example, diplomacy, economic incentive, and even war (if necessary)—provide and enforce this same liberty abroad? And more amazing still, America only began to fulfill such a divine mandate mostly *after* both the founding documents and the D&C scriptures, cited above, set America's divine course. It is certainly significant that God and the Founding Fathers declared this "freedom promoting" intention for America, and then America proceeded to fully fulfill this divine mandate in ways no other nation could. In fact, what we witness here is more than just significant. It borders on the prophetic. Like ancient Israel, America's God-given abundance of *liberty*, *protection*, and *prosperity* has certainly been put to effective use for the ultimate purposes of Heaven.

America may ask, *Why me?* The reply: *Because God created and prepared you specifically for this mission at this time; This is your burden and your blessing.* And to bind her to this divine mission, the Lord instituted a covenant.

How Does the American Covenant Work?

Questions that follow the assertion of an American Covenant include: How does it function? What are the promises and obligations? How do the people work within the structure of the covenant? Answers will be given throughout this book. However, a summary would be helpful here.

First, given Heavenly Father's propensity to make covenants with His children, it is safe to assume it is an effective method. He will not compel His children, but of all the forms of influence, it seems covenants work best. Not only do they constantly remind us of the desired blessings or the feared scourges that await our decisions in mortality, thus prompting us to choose the right, they also unite us with our Father in Heaven, as individuals, as families, and even as nations.

That said, whereas we are clear on where we might find instructions for our personal priesthood covenants, thus enabling us to learn our obligations and blessings associated with them, where might we find the rules that govern this national covenant? Ancient Israel's national covenant is laid out fairly clearly in the Old Testament (see, for example, Leviticus, Chapter 26). Similarly, the American Covenant is appropriately, and quite clearly, laid out in the Book of Mormon—for it was established in Book of Mormon history amongst at least two separate groups of ancient Americans.

To the first group of ancient Americans, known as the Jaredites, the Lord declared, "This is a choice land, and whatsoever nation shall possess it shall be free from bondage, and from captivity...if they will but serve the God of the land, who is Jesus Christ" (Ether 2:12). To a second group, known as the Nephites, the Lord made the same promises through the Prophet Lehi, calling the land "choice above all other lands", which land He "hath covenanted" to both the Nephite posterity and "all those who should be led out of other countries by the hand of the Lord...[and] none shall come into this land save they shall be brought by the hand of the Lord" (2 Nephi 1:5-6). Furthermore, as part of this national covenant, the Lord promised the Nephites, as he had the Jaredites, that "if it so be that they shall serve him [the Lord] according to the commandments...it shall be a land of liberty unto them; wherefore they shall never be brought down into captivity" (2 Nephi 1:7). And finally, within this chapter, wherein is outlined this national covenant, the Lord adds this familiar refrain for the new nation: "Inasmuch as ye shall keep my commandments, ye shall prosper in the land" (2 Nephi 1:20).*

★ ★ ★ ★

In the pages that follow, we will analyze the meaning of this national covenant language in the Book of Mormon; but before doing so, we will first pause to address those critics who would question both the inclusiveness and the modern application of this ancient covenant. In reference to the verses cited above, critics will argue that the Lord was speaking exclusively to His church, as opposed to the entire American nation, and that He was speaking only to the *ancient* American inhabitants, as opposed to His modern ones. Such arguments, however, are in error, as it is clear the Lord was speaking to the entire American nation, regardless of one's status in or out of the Church; and it is clear that He was, in addition to the ancients, speaking to His American nation in the *latter-days*. We know this in part by simply analyzing the very scriptures cited above.

First, the scripture clearly states that the land would be "covenanted" to "all those who should be led out of their countries

---

* The Lord makes continuous references to these blessings and obligations throughout the Book of Mormon. Examples of such include, but are not limited to, 1 Nephi 13:16, 2 Nephi 10:10-12, 1 Nephi 13:15, 1 Nephi 13:19, and 1 Nephi 22:7.

by the hand of the Lord…[and] none shall come into this land save they shall be brought by the hand of the Lord" (2 Nephi 1:5-6). Considering the enormous number of people of different religious backgrounds brought to this land since the time this promise was made, attempting to limit this covenant exclusively to Church members is absolutely futile. Furthermore, these peoples have continued to come in post-ancient times, refuting the claim that such a covenant lived only in the past.

Second, the scripture cited above describes the covenant-makers as "whatever *nation* shall receive it [the land]" (Ether 2:12, emphasis added), again opening up participation to vast amounts of people with differing religious views.

Third, as will be detailed in coming chapters, the founding generations of latter-day Americans, who obviously included non-Church members and who were obviously post-ancient, outwardly and repeatedly acknowledged the national covenant described in the Book of Mormon. The fact that the same national covenant found in the Book of Mormon was clearly written in the hearts of these modern-day Americans corroborates the idea that the same ancient national covenant in the Book of Mormon still applies to modern-day and is not exclusive to any one religion.

Fourth, as the Book of Mormon was clearly written and reserved for the latter-days, it is senseless to assume that this national covenant language—so prominent amongst its pages—was never intended for us today. Many of the Book of Mormon scriptures that deal with the American Covenant even specifically make reference to its application in the *last days*. For example, 2 Nephi 10:7-14 discusses how *latter-day* America "shall be a land of liberty," complete with fortifications "against all other nations," and that these blessings will be given by covenant. (There are no less than three references within these short verses that credit God with giving these national blessings as part of a covenant or promise.) Jacob, Chapter 5 discusses allegorically how *latter-day* America will be set up to serve as the venue for God's ultimate gospel purposes in restoring Israel and the gospel. And 3 Nephi 21:4 quotes Jesus Christ

Himself who prophesies of the same, declaring that *latter-day* America will "be set up as a free people by the power of the Father...that the covenant of the Father may be fulfilled."

Fifth, do our priesthood covenants offer promises of a land of liberty, physical protection of our nation against oppressors, and economic prosperity? Are these promises spelled out at baptism? Are they articulated in temple ordinances? No, not directly. The Book of Mormon refers here to a different type of covenant, available outside the sacred structure of God's church. It refers to a more inclusive, national covenant.

Finally, even after accepting these Book of Mormon covenant promises as pertaining to a modern nation-state, there are those who might question how we know for certain that it is the United States. After all, when the ancients revealed these prophecies and promises about the future of their land—what they repeatedly called "this land"[5]—they were residing in any number of locations across the Americas (the Church has never confirmed a precise geographic location for a Book of Mormon setting). As the ancients did not have the advantage of living within modern-day borders and boundaries, many believe it is reasonable to assume they were speaking inclusively about "this land." In other words, they were distinguishing "this land," even the entirety of the New World, from "*that* land" or the land of their fathers, even the Old World from whence they had come. Therefore, no matter where ancient American prophets had been residing within the New World, this theoretically places any modern nation-state in North, Central, or South America in a position to be the chosen one of the prophecies.[6] That it was the United States, however, is clear and convincing. We have already touched on this above, when outlining how the United States, more than any other nation, fulfills the covenant's purposes and promises. Furthermore, there is only one nation in the Americas (or in the entire world for that matter) whose divine discovery, creation, and founding was foreseen and prophetically described in the Book of Mormon (see 1 Nephi 13). There is only one nation that has received a scriptural approbation directly from the Almighty (see D&C 101: 80). There is only one nation that has been recognized by latter-day prophets and apostles as the rightful latter-day heir of the national covenant referenced in the Book of Mormon.[7] And there is only one nation that has been given the divine right and mandate to house the city of Zion, even the New Jerusalem, and host the Restoration (see D&C 57: 1-4; 45: 66-67).

And so, though much more evidence will be produced in the coming chapters, there is sufficient reason, even at this early point in our study, to accept that the covenant promises from the Book of Mormon (as cited above) are directed to a modern nation-state, and that this modern nation-state is the United States of America.

★ ★ ★ ★

Now that we have established that the Book of Mormon covenant pertains to the United States of America, we will delve deeper into the above-cited Book of Mormon references to this modern, national covenant. For, not only do these verses indicate who the heirs of the covenant were to be, but they also outline how the covenant was to work. Indeed, they outline the meanings of the covenant's blessings, obligations, and general functionality.

According to the above-cited verses, as long as we, as a nation, "keep [His] commandments" and "serve the God of the Land", then we will have at least three things: 1) "a land of liberty" (enhanced agency), 2) protection against those who would rob us of this liberty—that we "shall never be brought down into captivity," and 3) the ability to "prosper in the land." It is noteworthy that these blessings of *liberty, protection,* and *prosperity* are identical to those given by covenant to ancient Israel, as discussed earlier. It follows, then, that the American Covenant has a purpose that is similar, if not identical, to that ancient national covenant. It is to this purpose that we now turn our attention.

The Lord is clearly purpose-driven in His actions, and it is therefore important for us to recognize that the blessings and obligations given under this or any other covenant have a direct and powerful purpose. In living our more familiar baptismal covenants, we see how this principle plays out. If we live up to our baptismal obligations, the Lord promises us His Spirit; but this powerful gift is not given just for fun, nor is it given to simply reward us with something. It is a gift that serves the purpose of supporting us in our quest to help ourselves, and those we serve, to achieve eternal life. It is a blessing given by covenant to further the work and glory of God. The American Covenant functions in the same way. As we discuss both the blessings and obligations of the American Covenant below, and throughout this book, we will recognize that the divine purpose behind these blessings and obligations is to provide a tool in the eternal fight against the adversary. It is to provide a tool in the development, defense, and universal distribution of freedom unto salvation.

Blessings of the American Covenant

If God gives blessings in furtherance of His ultimate purposes in bringing to pass the eternal life of man, then it follows that the three prominent American Covenant blessings of *liberty*, *protection*, and *prosperity* were given for this same eternal end. Not surprisingly, the Book of Mormon defines these national blessings with just such an eternal perspective. And as these covenant blessings were originally given in a Book of Mormon context, we must understand them today within this context.

For example, a full read of the Book of Mormon makes it very clear that the *liberty* promised was generally in reference to the people's ability to possess a land and government that permitted it to believe and worship freely, and thus progress unto eternal salvation. In the Book of Mormon account, we witness how God provided such liberty through inspired proclamations, laws, and decrees. For example, God placed the Jaredite king, Shule, in position, that he might "execute a law throughout all the land, which gave power unto the prophets that they should go whithersoever they would" without fear of persecution or oppression (see Ether 7: 25). God inspired the Nephite king, Mosiah, to do away with the throne and replace it with a system of elected judges, putting the power with the people, and thus establishing "a land of liberty" where "every man may enjoy his rights and privileges alike" (see Mosiah 29: 25-32). God similarly inspired the Lamanite king, Lamoni, to provide the "liberty of worshiping the Lord their God according to their desires" (Alma 21:22). The Nephite chief judge, Paharon, followed the same inspired pattern by issuing a decree to keep "the freedom of the people, and to grant unto them their sacred privileges to worship the Lord their God" (see Alma 50:39). And then there was Captain Moroni's Title of Liberty, which also reflected the American Covenant: "Behold, whosoever will maintain this title upon the land, let them come forth in the strength of the Lord, and enter into a covenant that they will maintain their rights, and their religion" (see Alma 46:20).

The promises of *protection* were given in the context of God protecting such institutions of liberty against those enemies who would destroy them. This blessing included divinely induced defenses against bondage and captivity—against the threat of those evil forces represented by wicked kings, Lamanite armies, Gadianton Robbers, and others who would oppress. Such tyranny frustrated precious agency unto salvation, and usually came about through things like obscene taxes, the disallowance of private worship, or full-scale enslavement (see Mosiah 24:11; Alma 43:10). But when the ancient American Covenant-makers were worthy, God's *protection* saved them, their liberty, and their gospel cause. One of many such examples is the story of the young Army of Helaman, which had "entered into a covenant to fight for the liberty of the Nephites." And, being a righteous army that had kept the commandments of God and "walk[ed] uprightly before him," they knew that "God would deliver them." In the end, though they were young and inexperienced, they defeated the Lamanite foe, having fought "with the strength of God," even with "miraculous strength" (see Alma 53: 1, 21; 56:47, 56).

And finally, in order to ensure these heavenly ideals of the covenant were further applied, the covenant blessing of *prosperity* was also provided. This blessing, as referenced in the Book of Mormon, is clearly counted in terms of economic gain. For, as the people kept the commandments, the Lord, honoring His end of the national covenant, prospered them so that they could (for example) build beautiful temples and other places of worship. Their financial blessings also enabled them to establish armies and fortifications in defense of the liberty required to build, maintain, and utilize these temples. That this blessing is in fact counted in terms of economic gain is further supported by the oft-referenced social trend known as the "Nephite Pride Cycle." Through this trend, we see how the financially struggling and thus humbled people repent of wickedness and become righteous, allowing the Lord to prosper them economically as a people (see 4 Nephi 1:7-8), until their wealth turns them to pride, which turns them to wickedness, after which the Lord places them back into a declining economic state (see 4 Nephi 1:24-49). And so, the Book of Mormon leaves no doubt in our minds that the *prosperity* offered by covenant to the ancient Americans was in large part counted in terms of national wealth.

The Book of Mormon further helps us understand our blessings under the American Covenant by distinguishing them from the more important blessings we receive under our priesthood covenants. For example, when the Book of Mormon speaks of gifts like the Holy Ghost and eternal life, these gifts are connected with gospel covenants we begin making at baptism (see 1 Nephi 31:12-13,18; 3 Nephi 26:17). But these higher priesthood covenants made at baptism or in the temple, as put forth in the Holy Scriptures and elsewhere, do not necessarily offer us a land of liberty, physical protection against tyrants, and economic prosperity. Though the Lord may bless anyone on a personal level with any gift He chooses, including things like economic prosperity, we still would have little basis to recognize such a blessing as necessarily stemming from baptismal or temple promises (again, the promised blessings of our baptismal and temple covenants simply do not include such things).

I remember hearing the confusion of a very active member of the Church who, despite her genuine efforts and general success in keeping her temple covenants, was not enjoying the economic "prosperity" that was clearly offered to the righteous Nephites and therefore "promised" to her through the Book of Mormon. She was making the common mistake of confusing priesthood/temple covenants (guaranteed to individuals), with national covenants (guaranteed to people in the aggregate, and not necessarily to individuals). It must be understood that a nation can be wealthy for the purposes of God, without every individual directly enjoying this wealth. If we are to understand and apply these blessings *as a nation*, we must see them as coming from our *national*, and not our priesthood, covenants.

And so, with the Book of Mormon perspective, as outlined above, we not only get a definition of what *liberty, protection,* and *prosperity* mean under the American Covenant, but also gain an understanding of how these national covenant blessings, though not directly associated with our priesthood covenants, clearly work to support these greater priesthood covenants and to support God's plan of salvation. With this knowledge, we can easily apply the American Covenant, as the Book of Mormon intends, to our American nation in the latter-days.

For example, just as the Nephites relied upon their national covenant to receive the blessings of *liberty,* that they might work out their salvation freely, so did modern Americans. As will be seen in the coming chapters, the Founding Fathers indeed relied on the same covenant in both word and deed as they discovered, settled, and developed their new land for the purposes of the gospel. Like the Nephites, they, too, invoked God and covenant on a regular basis, and were thus blessed with the freedom they sought. As both groups strove toward righteousness, they were inspired from on high to conceive precious documents, laws, and institutions, whether issued anciently through the Title of Liberty or presently in the U.S. Constitution. And thus we see the American covenant blessing of *liberty* provided to the United States.

The same can be said for the covenant blessing of *protection*. Just as the Nephites relied upon their national covenant with the Lord to prevent the Lamanite armies (and other oppressors) from threatening their national laws and institutions of freedom—to protect themselves from being "brought down into captivity"—so American Covenant-makers in the latter-days have done likewise. Even in its days of youth and inexperience, the latter-day nation, like the young Army of Helaman, found victory (often times in miraculous ways) against mightier foes because its God fought its battles per the promises of the covenant. History is clear that it was America's reliance on God and the American Covenant—a reliance reflected in national prayers, national religious acts, and other national efforts at righteousness—that enabled her to push back the British threat to the New World in the eighteenth century, the American-Southern/Confederate threat to the new nation in the nineteenth century, the fascist and communist threat to the world in the twentieth century, and the terrorist threat to mankind in the twenty-first century. Notably, all of these foes of America, like those foes of the Nephites, were and are following the same adversarial stratagem. They thus presented (and continue to present) a grave threat to agency and, by extension, to man's opportunity for eternal progression. In both the ancient and modern cases, the national covenant brings God in to wield the sword of truth and justice. Through the covenant, He protects and enhances agency, that man might be able to progress—however, or in whatever religion, he chooses—and that Christ's true Church, along with its principles and ordinances unto eternal life, might exist and prosper. And thus we see the American Covenant blessing and purpose of *protection* fulfilled in the latter-days.

As far as the national covenant's promise of "prosper[ing] in the land" is concerned, the same applies. The Lord has proven that He does offer wealth as part of His national covenants, as far as it serves His ultimate designs. Just as the Lord blessed the Nephites with wealth for such higher purposes, so He does today with the United States of America. The wealth provided to the nation (again, this is aggregate and not individual) positively affects God's gospel plan in multiple ways. We will outline some of these ways below. As we do so, we would do well to remember that this particular blessing must be received with warning, for it can lead to pride and destruction (as the Book of Mormon incessantly teaches). Also, as we recognize how national wealth can be imperative to God's plan, we might also consider that the adversary's assault on nations includes an intent to impoverish them, so that an oppressive financial burden might conflict with the ability to worship and progress freely and unimpeded.

First, wealth in the United States generates significant government revenues, which in turn pay for the many institutions— including military, law enforcement, and diplomatic entities— necessary to protect God's children both at home and abroad from the constant threats to their freedom and agency. We see how this covenant blessing works in conjunction with the covenant blessing of *protection*.

Second, wealth in America frees up time for good men and women to work on projects that keep our nation strong, virtuous, and free under God. For example, if the Founding Fathers had to scavenge for food, who would have written the Declaration of Independence or the Constitution? And without the divine principles stemming from such documents, how would the Church be doing today?

Third, American wealth has encouraged the invention, development and/or the massive distribution of priceless technologies. Consider the wonders of radio, television, air transportation, or the Internet—to name a few. Consider how much faster and stronger the Church has grown and spread from Zion as a result of the prosperity that has offered these technologies.

And fourth, the wealth generated in America directly and positively affects the tithes and offerings to the Church, which affects the ability of the Church to function in its mission under God. Based on the demographics of Church membership, we can assume that at least half, though probably much more, of Church tithes and donations have flowed from America. (And many of those foreign economies that generate other tithes and donations to the Church are dependent on the U.S. economy for their stability.) And so, the general blessed state of the U.S. economy, provided under the American Covenant, significantly supports the Church's financial success, and thus forwards God's work in significant ways. It is, after all, financial success that contributes to the spreading of gospel principles (through, for example, the publication and distribution of the Book of Mormon), and which permits priesthood ordinances to be made available (through, for example, the building of temples around the world).

It is clear that in order for our agency unto salvation to be maximized, we must be able to overcome the oppressive burden sometimes posed by financial despair. The covenant blessing of financial success in America largely eliminates this burden. And thus we see the power and purpose of the American Covenant blessing of *prosperity* fulfilled in the United States.

These American Covenant blessings of *liberty, protection,* and *prosperity* benefit us as a nation, as families, and as individuals in ways too numerous to list, thus making America the hope and example of all nations. But of all the benefits we as Americans receive as heirs of the national covenant, the most important and eternally significant benefit is the ability and privilege given to us to utilize these blessings of the covenant in supporting and enhancing God's gift of freedom and agency. And thus we assist the Lord in furthering His work and glory.

Obligations of the American Covenant

"There is a law, irrevocably decreed in heaven before the foundations of this world, upon which all blessings are predicated—and when we obtain any blessing from God, it is by obedience to that law upon which it is predicated" (D&C 130:20-21). The American Covenant bears no exception to this eternal principle. And so, the question that remains is as follows: What are we, as a nation, required to do under this covenant to retain its lofty blessings? Returning to the national covenant scripture verses cited above, it is clear we will continue to receive our national blessings if we "keep [His] commandments" (2Nephi 1:20) and "if [we] will but serve the God of the land" (Ether 2:12).

The first national obligation is to keep the commandments. As the nation has not been placed under the strictest of priesthood covenants, such as those made in the temple, the loftiest standards are naturally not required for the nation to gain access to the blessings of the national covenant. However, the "Spirit of Christ [Light of Christ] is given to every man that he may know good from evil" (see Moroni 7:13-16). As such, the people of the American Covenant can certainly be expected to at least live the basic tenants of the Ten Commandments, to include recognizing and worshiping God, avoiding idolatry, honoring parents, not killing, not committing adultery, not stealing, not lying, etc. Religions the world over may disagree on doctrine, but almost all of them maintain the basic moral codes of these basic commandments. Such codes are so basic that they even provide the foundation for most laws that govern most lands. In a symbolic gesture of this fact, there are several engravings of Moses and the Ten Commandments throughout the U.S. Supreme Court building.[8] They represent a minimum standard which does not require membership in, or endorsement of, any particular religion. There is no excuse for their violation.

The Lord has, after all, made His position on this matter clear within the context of the national covenant. He made it clear with the recipients of ancient Israel's national covenant: for "righteousness exalteth a nation: but sin is a reproach to any people" (Proverbs 14:34); He made it clear to his national covenant bearers of ancient America: for "if the time comes that the voice of the people doth choose iniquity, then is the time that the judgments of God will come upon you...he will visit you with great destruction" (Mosiah 29: 27); And His principles still apply today: "I the Lord am bound when ye do what I say; but when ye do not what I say, ye have no promise" (D&C 82:10).

The people of the national covenant must indeed be clean and pure in order to continue to receive the promised blessings and to carry out the divine mandate. It should be enough to accept this principle without question, based alone on the scriptures that declare that all blessings from God are predicated on obedience to His commandments (see D&C 130:20-21). But in addition to simply accepting it as God's law, there are actually very practical and comprehensible applications of this principle in terms of the covenant. For example, if the people are not willing to adhere to a certain basic moral behavior and to certain basic commandments, how can the Lord trust that this people will be willing to do anything in forwarding His work under the covenant? The commandments, and the people's reaction to them, thus become a preliminary indicator for the Lord to determine if the nation is willing and ready—to determine if the covenant blessings and purposes will be placed into the people's hands.

Furthermore, the work under the covenant may require that certain actions, even specific actions, be performed by the nation in furtherance of God's cause. (We will see examples of these specific required national actions in the chapters that follow.) But in order for this to occur, the people must be privy to God's inspiration so as to receive and carry out His divine instruction. And in order for the people to be worthy of this inspiration—in order for them to be clean receptacles for God's revelations—they must be sanctified through keeping the commandments. If the nation maintains "an eye single to [His] glory," then it "shall be filled with light, and there shall be no darkness in [it], and that body which is filled with light comprehendeth all things." And so God issues the command to "sanctify yourselves" (D&C 88:67-68). God needs a people who can receive and comprehend His designs, which underlines the necessity for the covenant people to obey the commandments and thereby be privy to the light. And so again, per the covenant, if America is not willing to obey the commandments, God has neither reason nor obligation to bestow the covenant blessings.

The importance of the people's general righteousness under the covenant especially applies to a republic, like the United States. Under a republic, the policymakers and administrators, who possess the power of government to be a force for good, are directed and influenced by the people. As such, the *people* hold the power and influence, and *their* righteousness and light—or conversely, *their* wickedness and darkness—flows upwards to those in power. Therefore, when the people are righteous and living the commandments, then God can be confident His designs for the nation will be accomplished. The Lord has certainly invited and allowed us to use our righteousness within the republic by declaring that we "do [our] business by the voice of the people," as it is "not common that the voice of the people desireth anything contrary to that which is right" (Mosiah 29:26). The Lord has even been so specific in this commandment as to require us to elect and uphold "honest men and wise men" into government positions (D&C 98:10). But again, our success in this divinely appointed endeavor begins with, and hangs upon, our ability as a nation to obey the commandments.

The need for the covenant nation to obey the commandments, then, is paramount. And American history proves it. As we will see, only general righteousness brought the covenant blessings and fulfilled the covenant purposes.

The second obligation we have as a nation under this covenant is to "serve the God of the land." As individuals, we can obviously improve national worthiness by serving God in whatever way we can in our own lives. However, there is also a very specific way we can "serve the God of the land" *as a nation*: by appropriately maintaining and developing the tools and institutions the Lord has provided us through the Constitution—tools and institutions that support and promote agency. As God established America for such a purpose (D&C 101: 76-95), what does it profit Him if we run the country into the ground and render it useless to His plan? What does it profit Him if we squander His covenant blessings? Captain Moroni, working under the ancient American Covenant during wartime, understood this point and made sure his nation's leader understood it as well. In an epistle to the Nephite governor, Moroni rhetorically asked: "[D]o ye suppose that the Lord will still deliver us, while we sit upon our thrones and do not make use of the means which the Lord has provided for us?"(Alma 60:21). Surely this sort of neglect and abuse would constitute a breach in our national covenant, making it invalid, and keeping its blessings out of our grasp. Therefore, America must ensure that the three branches of government, along with critical agencies and departments, continually support and protect agency—or as the Constitution promises, "secure the blessings of liberty." Americans must direct their government (both state and federal) to seek and appropriately apply—under the inspiration of heaven—those blessings that support, protect, and enhance agency, even the blessings of *liberty*, *protection*, and *prosperity*. This applies not only to our righteous efforts at home, but also to those abroad. Doctrine and Covenants 101:77, after all, points out that God inspired the Constitution of the United States for "the protection of *all* flesh" (emphasis added)—and this He did that *all* mankind might enjoy eternal progression.

The most basic understanding of a commandment to "serve the God of the land" might take us to the familiar Book of Mormon scripture that declares that "when ye are in the service of your fellow beings ye are in the service of your God" (Mosiah 2:17). The American quest to bring liberty and light, even at great sacrifice, to those suffering oppression certainly constitutes a powerful example of rendering service to our fellow human beings. And so we further see how preserving and promoting the institutions of free agency place the nation squarely in compliance with the covenant obligation to "serve the God of the land."

There is another noteworthy aspect of this particular obligation. As we serve the God of the land by preserving and promoting the inspired institutions of free agency, blessings will flow from God in more than one way. First, as we act to fulfill this national duty, God recognizes our efforts in obedience and thus blesses us with the covenant blessings—blessings that often come about through miraculous measures. And second, the very act of seeking and applying those covenant blessings that support agency is in some ways a self-fulfilling blessing. In other words, the very thing God requires us to do, if we do it, will *naturally* provide the covenant blessings that support agency. As we, for example, work to elect leaders that respect the First Amendment, we can expect that, as a natural consequence, our First Amendment rights—which include the covenant blessings of *liberty*—will be preserved. The Lord is obviously deliberate and purpose-driven when deciding which obligations will fulfill His covenants. He has always worked this way, even with our priesthood covenants. For example, He commands us to live a strict law of health, for which He blesses us for our obedience in whatever way He sees fit. But also, our very acts in obedience to this law (eating well, rejecting alcohol, etc.), *naturally* provides us—in addition to whatever blessings He might give us—with the great blessings of health. Though God will allow us to sacrifice greatly in our efforts to comply with the national covenant obligations, this is not to say we are ever alone in fulfilling them. For with the adversary ever on the attack, our efforts alone to secure the covenant blessings will never be enough. But as long as we are striving toward this goal, the Lord will back our efforts and always provide the full measure of the promised blessings after we have done all we can do. When it comes to His covenants, there is certainly truth to the adage, *"God helps those who help themselves."*

And finally, by applying the first national obligation—to keep the commandments—the nation will more easily fulfill the second. For, an obedient nation is sufficiently sanctified, and will, therefore, have the light, knowledge, and divine assistance it needs to "serve the God of the land" through preserving and promoting the ideals and tools of agency unto salvation. As we manifest righteousness, God will more easily lead our efforts. Only then will the world have the assurance that the vision set forth by our founding documents will continue to be realized. Only then will the world know that the nation will continue producing leaders that understand America's divine role and will carry out this vision—leaders like George Washington, who recognized that America, under the "smiles of Heaven," had created a "sacred fire of liberty."[9] Or leaders like Abraham Lincoln, who understood that it was America's divine calling to establish, "under God...a new birth of freedom."[10] Or John F. Kennedy, who declared to the world, and issued caution to the tyrant, that "the rights of man come...from the hand of God," and that America "will pay any price [and] bear any burden...for the success of liberty."[11] Or leaders like Ronald Reagan, who declared that "America as a place in the divine scheme of things...was set apart as a promised land" intended for "people who had a special love of freedom," and that "we were preordained to carry [this] torch of freedom to the world."[12]

As the nation commits to keep His commandments and to serve Him, it must be ever mindful of a general requirement underlying both these obligations, and that is to publicly and regularly invoke God and the covenant. Specifically, the United States government must do what it has done since its founding, by officially issuing, in the name of the people, public recognitions, proclamations, acts, and prayers—all unto God. Examples of these include the Pledge of Allegiance taken "under God," national days of prayer, the issuance of the national motto: "In God We Trust," and other like-minded actions. These national actions represent tokens and sacraments of the American Covenant. Their overall effect is to encourage—though never compel—the people to live righteously and serve God. In other words, they remind and influence the people to turn to the Lord and fulfill the obligations of the American Covenant, making them worthy to receive the covenant blessings and worthy to participate in God's work. Furthermore, these national invocations in and of themselves represent a powerful offering to God, which will result in added blessings from Him. Altogether then, these national actions performed for God bring an added measure of the covenant blessings, and thus propel God's work to higher places. Such has been the covenant pattern throughout American history.

The modern-day critic will, of course, balk at the suggestion that government involve itself in such spiritual encouragement, interpreting the great American principle of "separation of church and state" as being in conflict with such ideals. However, the ultimate conclusion of this study fully supports, and even promotes, the principle of "separation of church and state." For this constitutional principle protects our agency unto eternal progression from the threat of a meddling and potentially tyrannical government. Indeed, it prevents the government from favoring, rejecting, or in any way influencing any particular religious denomination. It keeps the government's hand out of our personal religious preferences, allowing God—not imperfect man—to influence the personal religious upbringing of His children. What the critic does not understand (and what this book will hereafter show) is that there is a great difference between "separation of church and state" and "separation of God and state." The former allows us to pursue our personal religious goals unmolested unto progression, while the latter does the exact opposite. For, the latter leaves us without a source of protection—without a guardian and deliverer of our longed-for and indispensable agency. More than anybody, it is God who desires all to be free to choose any religion or no religion; so why would we not want Him involved in our affairs? Why would we, as a nation, not invoke His name and covenant as much as possible? As ancient Israel and as ancient America painfully learned time and again, the only way to guarantee the blessings of the national covenant—even the cherished gift of agency—is to invite God in and allow Him room to wield the sword of truth and justice. To put it simply and concisely (but in a phrase that for the secularist is too ironic to grasp), *we are indeed for "separation of church and state"—under God*. The Founding Fathers understood this, as their history clearly reveals. But somewhere along the line, many of us have begun to forget it.

Let us, therefore, redouble our efforts to live all the covenant obligations. For, as we succeed in so doing, the national blessings of *liberty, protection,* and *prosperity* will flow in greater measure. If we fail, however, we will, as President Hinckley warned, suffer the tragic loss of our great American blessings under our great American Covenant, even the loss of "peace and prosperity, harmony and goodwill" and the loss of "the freedoms that evolved within the structure that was the inspiration to our Founding Fathers."[13] After all, if we don't prove ourselves worthy of these blessings and/or if we refuse to use these blessings for the purposes they were given, why would God continue to give them at all? Such a warning is especially powerful when pondering the fate of earlier nations, such as ancient Israel and ancient (Jaredite/Nephite) America, who at one time possessed the national covenant, but who failed to adhere to the prophetic warnings concerning it, and were thus "forsaken" and "swept off" (Jeremiah 4:29; Ether 2:8-10). The United States of America is certainly no more indispensable to God's plan than was ancient Israel or ancient America. It follows, then, that even though the Lord is utilizing the United States in these latter-days for His purposes, if we as Americans fail Him, we will lose our place in His plan, as He turns to another method to carry out His purposes. But what a tragedy it would be for this nation to squander this divine privilege, blessing, and responsibility!

Conclusion

In an effort to summarize the validity and functionality of the American Covenant, we will review one of the greatest American Covenant scriptural references, found in 2 Nephi 10:7-17. After Jacob prophesies about the devastating effects of the Great Apostasy (to follow Christ's death), the Lord reveals how He will counter such darkness in the latter-days by first establishing a national covenant, even the American Covenant, as described above. These prophetic verses (with the addition of my commentary included in the brackets) begin: "But behold, thus sayeth the Lord God:"

When the day cometh that they shall believe in me, that I am Christ [probably referring to the day when certain inspired ones at last break through the religious darkness of the Apostasy and inspire a truer Christianity, which the earliest American settlers would bring with them to their new land], then have I covenanted [the American Covenant] with their fathers that they shall be restored in the flesh, upon the earth, unto the lands of their inheritance. And it shall come to pass that they shall be gathered in from their long dispersion...to the lands of their inheritance. [That this land of their inheritance is America is detailed in 3 Nephi 15:12-13.]

....and the Gentiles [referring to those chosen covenant-makers to inhabit latter-day America] shall be blessed upon the land [referring in part to the promised *prosperity*]. And this land shall be a land of liberty unto the Gentiles [referring to their promised *liberty* and agency unto salvation], and there shall be no kings upon the land, who shall raise up unto the Gentiles. And I will fortify this land against all other nations [referring to the promised *protection* of agency unto salvation]. And he that fighteth against Zion shall perish, saith God. For he that raiseth up a king against me shall perish, for I, the Lord, the king of Heaven, will be their king, and I will be a light unto them forever, that hear my words [meaning all national blessings are contingent upon America's ability to live its national obligations and accept God as their "king" and "hear [His] words"].

Wherefore, for this cause, that my covenants may be fulfilled which I have made unto the children of men, that I will do unto them while they are in the flesh, I must needs destroy the secret works of darkness, and of murders, and of abominations. [That is, in order for God's greatest covenants unto eternal life to be fulfilled, He will use America and her covenant to "destroy the secret works of darkness," which have—from the war in heaven on into mortality—attempted to thwart man's agency unto exaltation.]

Wherefore, he that fighteth against Zion, both Jew and Gentile, both bond and free, both male and female [perhaps indicating that these enemies may come from anywhere, foreign or domestic], shall perish; for they are they who are the whore of all the earth; for they who are not for me are against me, saith our God. For I will fulfill my promises which I have made unto the children of men.

As we continue to live the American Covenant today by fulfilling our obligations to God, the blessings of *liberty, protection,* and *prosperity* will be ours, and the ultimate purpose of God—to bring to pass the eternal life of man on principles of agency—will go forward. With such important goals hanging in the balance, it is no wonder that President Ezra Taft Benson, who not insignificantly sat in the highest offices of both church and state, revealed that the United States of America is "the Lord's base of operations"[14] in these latter days.

ENDNOTES

[1] Ancient Israel's government promoted policies such as "Proclaim liberty throughout the land" (see Leviticus 25:10). Small, manageable units of government were also established, allowing participation amongst the citizenry (see Exodus 18: 13-26). Furthermore, leaders were elected and laws were approved by consent of the people (see Samuel 2:4; 1 Chr. 29:22; 2 Chr. 10-16; Exodus 19:8). For more, see W. Cleon Skousen, *The Five Thousand Year Leap* (Washington D.C.: The National Center for Constitutional Studies, 1981), 15-17.

[2] Wilford Woodruff, as quoted by Gordon B. Hinckley, "An Unending Conflict, A Victory Assured," *Ensign,* June 2007, 7.

³ Andrew C. Skinner, *Temple Worship* (Salt Lake City: Deseret Book, 2007), 132.

⁴ David O McKay, as quoted by Gregory Prince and Wm. Wright, *David O. McKay and the Rise of Modern Mormonism* (Salt Lake City: The University of Utah Press, 2005), 41-42.
⁵ That ancient Americans described the promised land of the future heirs of the covenant as "this land," is documented in 2 Nephi 1:5-9, 2 Nephi 10: 10-12, and Ether 13:8 (among other places).

⁶ The scope of this study does not include any determination about the precise ancient geographic location of Book of Mormon events. Some LDS scholars promote the "Heartland Model," which theorizes that the ancient Book of Mormon lands included the very land in North America upon which the United States of America was later established. See Bruce Porter and Rod Meldrum, *Prophecies and Promises, the Book of Mormon and the United States of America* (Mendon: Digital Legend, 2009). If this theory is correct, then the ancients' reference to "this land" as being the future modern nation-state to fulfill the promises certainly fits well; for they would have been physically standing precisely upon "this land" of the prophecy. The more prominent theory for Book of Mormon geography includes a Mesoamerican setting, which proposes that ancient Book of Mormon events occurred in what is now the Southern Mexico / Guatemala region. See John L Sorenson, *The Geography of Book of Mormon Events,* (Provo: FARMS, BYU, 1990); John Lund, *Mesoamerica and the Book of Mormon* (The Communications Company, 2007). If this theory is correct, it does little to dissuade us to believe the modern nation-state referenced by the ancients is the United States. When the ancients referred to "this land" they did not necessarily have in mind any concept of modern-day geographical boundaries. All they knew was that they had discovered a new land consisting of the New World unknown to the Old World. Therefore, if they stood in what is now Guatemala and described the chosen future modern nation-state as pertaining to "this land," it is completely reasonable to assume they meant that this modern nation-state would emerge somewhere upon "this land," meaning this new continent, this New World, this new land, which is not "*that* land" of the Old World from whence they had come. In this light, the United States of America can also be included as part of "this land," even in a Mesoamerican setting. Either way, per the evidences put forth in this study, once the latter-day era began upon the New World, it soon became obvious that the ancient prophecy was, in fact, made in reference to the United States of America. As far as the opposing viewpoints for the ancient geographical setting are concerned, both arguments have merit and are interesting. It is left to the reader to study the issue and make the determination.

⁷ Among other Church authorities, President Ezra Taft Benson, President Marion G. Romney (of the First Presidency) and Elder Mark E, Petersen (a member of the Quorum of the Twelve) all made it abundantly clear that the Book of Mormon promises made to modern-day America were specifically directed toward and fulfilled by the United States of America. Their addresses that detail this conviction, which include addresses in General Conferences, are quoted in Bruce Porter and Rodney Meldrum, *Prophecies and Promises, The Book of Mormon and the United States of America* (Mendon, NY: Digital Legend, 2009), 64-67.

⁸ Newt Gingrich, *Rediscovering God in America* (Nashville: Integrity House, 2006), 87.

⁹ From George Washington's First Inaugural Address, April 30, 1789, available at www.nationalcenter.org/washigtonfirstinaugual .

¹⁰ Lincoln, as quoted by William J. Bennett, *America, the Last Great Hope, Volume II, From a World at War to the Triumph of Freedom* (Nashville: Thomas Nelson, 2007), 368.

[11] From John F. Kennedy's Inaugural Address, January 20, 1961, Washington D.C., available at www.jfklibrary.org.

[12] Ronald Reagan, as quoted by Paul Kengor, *God and Ronald Reagan* (New York: Regan Books, 2004), 95.

[13] Gordon B Hinckley, *Standing for Something* (New York: Times Books, Random House, Inc., 2000), xviii, xxiii. See Introduction of this book for full quote.

[14] Ezra Taft Benson, "The Lord's Base of Operations." Talk given at the 132nd Annual General Conference of the Church of Jesus Christ of Latter-Day-Saints, 8 April. *The Improvement Era* 65, no.6 (1962): 454-56.

Washington's Inauguration-1789, by Allyn Cox.
Courtesy of the Architect of the Capitol.

CHAPTER 2

THE COVENANT-MAKERS

Joseph is a fruitful bough, even a fruitful bough
by a well; whose branches run over the wall....

—Genesis 49:22

If the American Covenant exists as proposed, it follows that there is, and has been, a chosen people responsible for accepting and carrying it out to fruition. This chapter will show that the American Covenant was so important to the Lord that He did in fact designate through prophecy certain peoples, even thousands of years ago, to be His chosen ones of this covenant. As we trace these prophecies—stemming from prophets like Jacob, Moses, Jeremiah and others—from antiquity and connect them to modernity, we will be driven to accept astonishing conclusions. We will begin to see familiar scriptures in a different light and, thus, be convinced to consider that these powerful prophets of old not only understood the American Covenant, but had visions of its carriers—visions of America's settlers and founders, even visions of people like George Washington, John Adams, Thomas Jefferson, and Benjamin Franklin. As we review these exciting connections concerning the people of the covenant, we will lay the foundation whereby we can effectively explore the story of this covenant. And we will come to more fully comprehend the preeminent role and divine responsibility America and its inhabitants have always had, and still do have, in God's ultimate designs.

From Abraham to America

As discussed in the previous chapter, the most prominent *national* covenant was that associated with ancient Israel—even that covenant which is connected and subservient to the greater priesthood covenants made with, and brought to the world by, Abraham and the House of Israel. What we did not discuss, however, was the idea that these ancient covenants are directly linked to the American Covenant. This connection is highly significant; for if we can link the American Covenant to God's renowned Old Testament covenant, then surely the American Covenant gains enormous credibility as a preordained and carefully arranged tool created and used by the Almighty for His ultimate purposes.

To fully understand this connection, we will begin with a brief analysis of the greatest of all covenants: the Abrahamic Covenant. The Abrahamic Covenant is called such because it was initially made with Abraham, the father of the House of Israel. It is the greatest of all covenants because it is through it that the greatest gifts and blessings of eternity are offered. Indeed, this covenant's promises and obligations (whose fullest comprehension may only be achieved through temple worship) produce the greatest blessings of the priesthood and gospel, to include celestial marriage and eternal increase—even eternal life with the Father. And those who participate in receiving, and those who assist in distributing, these blessings must be members of the House of Israel, which is realized at birth and/or by adoption through baptism (see Abraham 2:7-11).[1]

So, what does this have to do with the American Covenant? It has *everything* to do with it because the American Covenant flows out of this Abrahamic Covenant. While the eternal blessings of the Abrahamic Covenant, as just outlined, are the most important (and therefore rightly receive most of the attention), there are other elements of the Abrahamic Covenant that lend support to the greater ones and are, therefore, significant. Many of these other elements are distributed and promised through one of twelve designated great-grandchildren of Abraham, collectively known as the Twelve Tribes of Israel. *The LDS Bible Dictionary* supports this concept by defining the Abrahamic Covenant in terms of "portions." According to the *Bible Dictionary*, some of these other portions include promises pertaining to Christ's mortal lineage and to "certain lands" that were to be given to Abraham's posterity as an "eternal inheritance."[2] More specifically, one portion of the Abrahamic Covenant, which comes through the Tribe of Judah, is that the Messiah would enter mortality through that line. And another portion, which stems from another prominent great-grandson, Joseph, is the promise of the American Covenant!

Indeed, the Tribe of Joseph was foreordained thousands of years ago to house the American Covenant. This portion of the Abrahamic covenant becomes ever more significant in light of the fact that the national covenant originally given to the ancient Hebrew nation would fail, thus leaving a void that the American Covenant was destined to fill.

Though it is plainly asserted that through Abraham, the Lord would "make nations" (Genesis 17:6),* most Biblical scholars of the world would admittedly scoff at the idea that Abraham's covenant —extended through the posterity of his great-grandson Joseph— included America as one of these nations. However, thanks to the enlightenment provided by the latter-day Restoration, such a concept leaps out of the pages of the Old Testament. The most powerful Old Testament affirmation that the Lord had America in mind when He was organizing His Kingdom and its future through Abraham and the House of Israel, is revealed in a patriarchal blessing given by Abraham's grandson, Jacob (or Israel), to Abraham's great-grandson, Joseph:

---

* See also Abraham 2; Genesis 22:15-18; and Galatians 3.

And Jacob called unto his sons, and said....Joseph is a fruitful bough, even a fruitful bough by a well; whose branches run over the wall. The archers have sorely grieved him, and shot at him and hated him: But his bow abode in strength, and the arms of his hands were made strong by the hands of the mighty God of Jacob...[T]he Almighty...shall bless thee with blessings from heaven above, blessings of the deep that lieth under, blessings of the breasts and of the womb: The blessings of thy father have prevailed above the blessings of my progenitors unto the utmost bound of the everlasting hills: they shall be on the head of Joseph, and on the head of him who was separate from his brethren (Genesis 49: 1, 22-26).[3]

So important are these blessings that they are repeated in almost identical language in a similar blessing given by the Prophet Moses to the same Tribe of Joseph (see Deuteronomy 33:13-17).

And finally, as an extension to this blessing, it is recorded that Jacob also blessed Joseph's posterity to be "a light unto my people, to deliver them in the days of their captivity, from bondage; and to bring salvation unto them" (JST Genesis 48:11).

So what does this blessing imply? To begin with, it clearly prophesies of several blessings that are to accompany Joseph's posterity. First, it speaks of Joseph's ability to thwart his enemies, even "the archers" that "shot at him and hated him," and suggests that Joseph would defeat them with his "bow [abiding] in strength." This promise implies that Joseph will possess effective machines of war and defense. Furthermore, it is made clear that this defense is made possible through the strength provided "by the hands of the mighty God of Jacob." And so we see that Joseph's posterity would defeat its enemies through the *protection* of the Lord.

The second blessing mentioned are those things connected to being "fruitful," even blessings of the "breasts" and "the womb" (a strong posterity) and "blessings of the deep that lieth under." Moses' version of this particular blessing includes the promise of "precious fruits brought forth of the sun," and "the chief things of the ancient mountains," implying the richness of resources to be made available (Deuteronomy 33:14-16). It appears Joseph's posterity would be offered a blessed land. So great and abundant would be the blessings of this land that Jacob describes them as having "prevailed above the blessings" of his own powerful ancestry. It is clear then that Joseph's posterity would be large, enduring, and would not want materially in their promised land. They would be provided with health and strength through material goods that would bless their lives. They would enjoy *prosperity*.

And finally, it naturally follows that this protection and prosperity would provide Joseph's people with freedom. As cited above, the blessing even specifically states that they would be free "from bondage" and that this freedom, even this free agency, would "bring salvation unto them." In short, Joseph's land of *protection* and *prosperity* would also be a land of *liberty*.

The reader will recognize these stated blessings—the *liberty, protection,* and *prosperity* unto salvation—as a precise match of those blessings of the American Covenant, as defined in the Book of Mormon. Perhaps at first glance we could write off such a connection as coincidence. However, a more thorough read of Joseph's promises above offers compelling evidence that this patriarchal blessing is nothing less than a direct reference to the American Covenant itself.

Jacob's blessing indicates that Joseph's "branches" (posterity) would "run over the wall." Exodus 14:22 uses the word "wall" to mean great waters. As such, it can be implied that the above-referenced promises to Joseph's posterity were connected to a land across the seas from the Old World. Jacob's concluding words to his son substantiate this by indicating that Joseph's people would be "separate from [their] brethren." And finally, in addition to being located far across the sea, the blessing suggests that this new land would contain "everlasting hills." The longest mountain range in the world stretches over 4,500 miles and runs through at least seven countries. It is called the Andes and it resides in the Americas.

With an exact description of the American Covenant, as the Book of Mormon defines it, together with the geographic clues laced throughout, there is little doubt that Jacob's Old Testament prophecy/ blessing indeed speaks of the American Covenant. And, as Joseph is clearly to be the predominant bearer of this covenant, his posterity naturally becomes our American Covenant-makers.

In order to confirm that this prophecy is in fact related to the American Covenant, we should seek for evidence of its fulfillment—evidence that Joseph's posterity inherited the lands of America and enjoyed the covenant blessings therein. The problem is that the Bible, from whence the prophecy is derived, is silent as to its fulfillment. There is, however, an Old Testament reference to a separate book which may contain such information:

> Moreover, thou son of man, take thee one stick, and write upon it, For Judah, and for the children of Israel his companions: then take another stick, and write upon it, For Joseph, the stick of Ephraim, and for all the house of Israel his companions: And join them one to another into one stick; and they shall become one in thy hand (Ezekiel 37:16-17).

It seems clear from this passage that the posterity of Joseph has a separate record or "stick" (scroll or tablet on which the ancients wrote)* from that of Judah, or the Jews. Clearly the Jews offered what is now the Bible. And it can be assumed that if Joseph's record existed, it would certainly include a fulfillment of his great promises. Indeed, this additional record should include the story of Abraham's posterity, through the line of his great-grandson Joseph, leaving the Old World, crossing "over the

---

* According to Matt Brown, *All Things Restored*, (American Fork: Covenant Communications, 2000), 187-188, many Biblical scholars believe that the word "stick" in this passage refers to the ancient wax-filled tablets utilized in the Near East during the days of Ezekiel to keep records. After the discovery of these tablets in 1953, the New English Bible changed the word "stick" in this passage to "wooden tablet."

wall," discovering a new land with "everlasting hills," and enjoying the blessings of *liberty, protection,* and *prosperity*—all for the gospel purposes of God.

Through the restored gospel, we know where we can find this marvelous work "[f]or Joseph," even this "stick of Ephraim" (Joseph's son and preeminent heir). We know it is in fact the Book of Mormon, and we know that this great book of scripture does nothing less than fulfill Joseph's grand promises in every particular. Furthermore, we know that this book has indeed been "join[ed] one to another" with the Bible;[4] and together they truly have become "one in [our] hand." The Prophet Nephi uses almost identical language in 2 Nephi 3:12 to confirm the claim that the Book of Mormon is in fact this second "stick," even *another* testament of Jesus Christ. As we now discuss the details concerning how—particularly through the Book of Mormon—the American Covenant represents a fulfillment of Joseph's promises of old, we would do well to recognize the significance of such a suggestion. For, if it is true, not only do we connect the American Covenant to Abraham, but we witness how this covenant was foreseen thousands of years ago by the Lord's most chosen servants. Certainly this lends powerful credibility to our national covenant.

The American Covenant connection to Abraham and the House of Israel becomes even more fascinating when we consider the fact that the American Covenant has been established in America in at least two separate eras. First, it was established in ancient America, through the Jaredites and Nephites; and second, it was established among the founders and present citizenry of the United States of America. In a string of even more exciting scriptural connections, we will now see how both of these American Covenants stem from the same scriptural base established above. That is, the American Covenant promises outlined above from Abraham, through Jacob and Joseph, and which are later substantiated and detailed in the Book or Mormon, provide the foundation and launching ground from which both these American Covenants originate. Though we have already detailed how Book of Mormon references to the American Covenant apply equally to the ancient and modern forms of it (refer to Chapter 1), we will now focus on how Joseph's seed does the same. That is, we will discuss how Joseph's posterity, even that group of chosen Israelites responsible for carrying this great American national covenant, represents those chief American Covenant-makers in both ancient and modern American settings.

Jacob Blessing the Sons of Joseph, Rembrandt.
Displayed in Staatliche Museen Kassel, Germany

As an introduction to this next wave of scriptural foundations for the American Covenant, we should understand that Joseph had two sons inducted into the House of Israel: Ephraim and Manasseh. So important was their induction, that Jacob also laid his hands upon them and transferred the blessings to them and their posterity, declaring that their seed shall become a great people and "a multitude of nations" (see Genesis 48:9-20). As they were both direct descendants of Joseph, it follows that they both were to carry the same general responsibilities regarding the American Covenant (not to mention, again, the more prominent and important priesthood covenants of Abraham). As we will see, Manasseh's posterity would predominantly carry the American Covenant to ancient America, while Ephraim would establish it in modern America. Though this study is obviously focused on the modern American Covenant, we will first briefly address this national covenant as it was given to ancient America. Not only will this initial analysis of the ancient American Covenant lend credibility and understanding to its modern counterpart—as they are, in fact, closely connected—but it will also establish the validity and longstanding, foreordained importance of America, her covenant, and her covenant-makers under God.

Prophecies Fulfilled: Ancient American Covenant-makers

Scriptural evidence proves that it was Joseph's posterity through Manasseh that was to establish the Abrahamic Covenant—and by extension, the American Covenant—in ancient America. This fact is evidenced by and through the first mentioned Book of Mormon prophet, Lehi, who was directed by the Lord to leave the Old World of Israel and travel to the New World, known today as America. The genealogical connection is revealed in Lehi's own confirmation that he was a descendant of Joseph of Egypt (2 Nephi 3:4-5, Jacob 2:35, Alma 26:30). This lineage from Joseph to Lehi was so important, that Christ Himself confirmed it during His visit to the Americas (3 Nephi 15:12). Furthermore, the scriptures tell us that Lehi—and by extension, his posterity—was connected to Joseph predominately through the branch or tribe of Manasseh (Alma 10:3).* This would explain why so many

---

* It is reasonable to assume that other tribes were also among those that inhabited the Book of Mormon lands. For example, according to Brigham Young, Joseph Smith proclaimed that Father Ishmael, whose daughters married Lehi's sons, and traveled with the group to ancient America, was from the Tribe of Ephraim (see Brigham Young, *Journal of Discourses*, 23:184). However, the only claim in the Book of Mormon concerning the lineage of its people to Joseph is through Manasseh. Most Book of Mormon references to Ephraim deal with the prophecies of Isaiah concerning the restoration of the gospel in the last days.

Latter-day Saints of Native American ancestry (which ancestry we believe is connected to Lehi's posterity) are declared in their patriarchal blessings to be from the Tribe of Manasseh.[5]

In light of the blessing Jacob gave to his son, Joseph, concerning his posterity inhabiting a new world, Lehi's great interest in this genealogical link to Joseph begins to makes sense. Before embarking by sea to the New World, Lehi sent his sons back to Jerusalem to acquire the Brass Plates (which today we would call the Old Testament) from Laban. Lehi did not say he was doing this for the sole purpose of acquiring the needed gospel principles found therein—though this is the most prominent explanation generally given. To be sure, his intention was also focused elsewhere. Lehi told his son Nephi: "The Lord hath commanded me that thou and thy brethren shall return to Jerusalem. For behold, Laban hath the record of the Jews and also a *genealogy of my forefathers*" (1 Nephi 3:2-3, emphasis added). But why would Lehi risk his sons' lives at the hands of the wicked Laban to possess this genealogy? Because he understood himself to be a significant part of Joseph's blessed "branch" that would "run over the wall." He understood the profundity of who he was in relation to Joseph and the covenant of the Promised Land, complete with the promises of *liberty*, *protection*, and *prosperity* for the eternal purposes of God. Lehi had surely read what information was contained on those desired Brass Plates, which no doubt contained the promises from Jacob to Joseph as we have recently read them (and, most probably, contained even more detail than we have today). Surely those records would serve him and his posterity for generations to come, if only to provide knowledge of who they really were and what their lineage really meant. Said Lehi:

> I am a descendant of Joseph who was carried captive into Egypt. And great were the covenants of the Lord which he made unto Joseph. Wherefore, Joseph truly saw our day. And he obtained a promise of the Lord, that out of the fruit of his loins the Lord God would raise up a righteous branch unto the house of Israel (2 Nephi 3:4-5).[6]

While Lehi certainly understood such "covenants of the Lord" to include those administered by the priesthood unto eternal life (like those made in sacred temples), he most certainly understood them also in the context of that supportive national covenant, even the American Covenant. Again, Lehi had the Brass Plates, which, as we have concluded above, outlined the American Covenant via Jacob's blessing to Joseph. Furthermore, when Lehi read the passage concerning such national covenant blessings being connected to a part of Joseph's seed that would travel "over the wall" (even over the great waters) to the land of "everlasting hills," he certainly pondered his own powerful connection. For he had in fact crossed great waters; and when he landed on the coast of the Americas, he quite possibly witnessed (or perhaps only his posterity would witness) the largest mountain range in the world, even the "everlasting hills" known today as the Andes.* And it certainly would not take him long to recognize the other obvious promises from Joseph's blessing, to include the rich resources found within this Promised Land.

If this is not enough to convince us that Lehi and his people understood themselves to be American Covenant-makers in fulfillment of the blessings and prophecies given to Joseph by his father Jacob, then the following reminder will: It was Lehi himself who spelled out the very blessings given by Jacob to Joseph, and framed them within the bounds of a national covenant. As detailed in the previous chapter, Lehi expounded on this same national covenant, with its obligations of obedience and blessings of *liberty*,

---

* Some scholars point to certain historical records of the Church which seem to indicate that Joseph Smith supported the idea that Lehi landed on the western coast of Central/South America. Some say he indicated Panama, while others say he pointed to northern Chile. This is discussed in John L. Sorenson, *An Ancient American Setting for the Book of Mormon* (Deseret Book Company, 1985), 1-2. Interestingly, the Andes Mountain range begins in Panama and ends in Chile. This idea is brought up as nothing more than a point of interest, as the scope of this study includes no determination about the geographical setting for the Book of Mormon.

protection, and *prosperity* (refer again to 2 Nephi 1:5-6; 2 Nephi 1:7; and 2 Nephi 1:20). Then, as the saga of Lehi's descendants is told over hundreds of years, we actually see this American Covenant at work, as God does fulfill His promises to Joseph, as defined by Jacob (in the Old Testament) and by Lehi (in the Book of Mormon). We do, after all, witness throughout the Book of Mormon narrative how the people retain their blessings of *liberty, protection,* and *prosperity* when they obey, and they lose these blessings when they do not. Lehi and his posterity truly were covenant-makers of and for what would be the land America. God truly led him and his family to that land for a divine purpose, as He had done for others before and would do for others again.

Tragically, Lehi's descendants in the Americas, after more than a thousand years of spiritual ups and downs, eventually fell from the light, broke the covenant, and lost the blessings. (The aforementioned Jaredite nation shared the same fate for the same reasons.) God's *liberty, protection,* and *prosperity* were thus withdrawn, leaving a void in which no inspired government could function. History books today that document what little we know about Pre-Columbian America all agree that whatever had been of the ancient Americans, they had most certainly declined into a warlike people with little regard for things like human rights.[7] Without a national covenant to provide any sort of secure or benevolent political structure—without the institutions to support agency—oppression and bloodshed had driven the prophets, their truths, and their priesthood into oblivion. Just as it happened in ancient Israel, with the national covenant in breach, the gospel/priesthood blessings lost their support and thus faded away. The divide between sin and salvation grew wide and deep, and the purposes of God were temporarily frustrated. Fortunately, the Lord has blessed us in these latter-days with the sacred records of these ancient Americans, so that we might learn from their mistakes. As a nation, we must live the American Covenant if we want to avoid a similar fate.

The last Book of Mormon prophet buried the sacred record in about 400 A.D., marking the end of truth and light in ancient America. During this same time on the Eastern Hemisphere, the truth had also been lost. The entire world had entered the Dark Ages, even a universal famine

—"not a famine of bread, nor a thirst for water, but of hearing the words of the Lord; And they shall wander from sea to sea, and from the north even to the east, they shall run to and fro to seek the word of the Lord, and shall not find it" (Amos 8:11-12). The tragic day of apostasy, foreseen by Old Testament, New Testament, and Book of Mormon prophets, had arrived: for the world had "transgressed the laws, changed the ordinance, broken the everlasting covenant" (Isaiah 24:5).*

But as these same prophets assured, the truth, priesthood, and covenants would return in the last days.** After John the Revelator revealed his vision of the Apostasy (Revelation 13:1-8), he immediately presented what would be the Lord's solution to this world-wide spiritual famine: "And I saw another angel fly in the midst of heaven, having the everlasting gospel to preach unto them that dwell on earth..."(Revelation 14:6-7). But to what land and to what people would this angel descend upon initially? Who would these new covenant-makers be? Where would they carry out their work? Considering the magnitude of a final gospel restoration complete with visitations from heaven, divine transfers of authorities, and the reception of eternal truths, naturally, answers to such questions were pre-conceived and even foreordained. And naturally, the first step in such a restoration, especially one that was to endure until the Second Coming of the Lord, would be preceded by a national covenant that would set the stage and provide the needed social, political, and economic infrastructure.

As such a national covenant mandate had been promised from Abraham through Jacob's blessing upon the posterity of Joseph, we might naturally look to this lineage for the development of this modern American Covenant. Though Manasseh had ultimately failed to endure anciently, Joseph's other son and heir of

---

*Additional prophecies of the Apostasy: 2 Timothy 3:1-6, Matthew 24:4-5, Acts 20:29-30, 2 Peter 2:1-3, 2 Thessalonians .2:1-5, Alma 45:10-12, 1 Nephi 12:19-23, 2 Nephi 26: 19-22

** Bible prophecies of the Restoration: Acts 3:19-21, Malachi 4:5-6, Isaiah 29, Micah 4:1-4.

the same covenant, Ephraim, would now have his chance to extend the national covenant in the last days. The posterity of Joseph was not finished providing the American Covenant!

Prophecies Fulfilled: Modern American Covenant-makers

The angel foreseen by John the Revelator was indeed bound for Joseph's seed through Ephraim and modern America. Though most Latter-day Saints recognize the preeminent role Ephraim would play in the restoration of the gospel covenant, we fail to always identify the precursor covenant, even that national covenant, which would also be brought and established by Ephraim. The Book of Mormon establishes this covenant pattern clearly through Lehi and his family. We will recognize that before churches and temples were built up for the ancient Nephites' eternal salvation, the Lord first established His national covenant with Lehi and His other new American Covenant-makers in order to secure these greater priesthood blessings to follow. (There is, after all, a reason that the major Book of Mormon descriptions of the American Covenant, as detailed in the previous chapter, are found in the very beginning of the Book of Mormon narrative.) As such, we should expect this same covenant pattern to hold true for the modern day gospel narrative of America. To be sure, we will now see how Joseph, through Ephraim, would in fact establish the modern American Covenant before bringing the greater Priesthood blessings through the restoration of the gospel.

A Foreordained Lineage

If Joseph's posterity through Ephraim really was responsible for so much in latter-day America, then perhaps we should examine what is historically known about Ephraim, that we might follow his genealogy from ancient Israel to modern-day America. From a Biblical perspective, the last time we hear from the Tribe of Ephraim is when—as narrated in the Old Testament—it leads a rebellion against the rest of ancient Israel and separates itself from the others of the House of Israel. Ephraim thereafter becomes known as the Northern Kingdom or Israel. (The Southern Kingdom becomes known as Judah.) Ephraim and his ally tribes live independently until their wickedness and disobedience allows the Assyrians to conquer and carry them off to a land north of Nineveh. From there, they eventually gain a new spirit of independence and migrate to unknown lands to the north—thus becoming the "Lost Tribes of Israel."[8]

Little more is said about Ephraim until Joseph Smith begins revealing this tribe's preeminent place in the latter-days. However, the few ancient references that are made reveal something about the prophecies and promises of Ephraim's destiny. For example, whereas the Lord could have destroyed them for their wickedness (as He had done with other peoples who had failed Him), He instead chose to hide them away and preserve them for a later mission in a later day. As the prophet declared, though "Ephraim is smitten", the Lord would only "cast them away" to be "wanderers among the nations" (Hosea 9:17). Furthermore, and in spite of their wandering state, they were to strongly present themselves again. Said the Lord: "I will save the house of Joseph, and I will bring them again to place them...and they shall be as though I had not cast them off...And they of Ephraim shall be like a mighty man, and their heart shall rejoice...And I will sow them among the people: and they shall remember me in far countries" (Zechariah 10:6-9). "Is Ephraim my dear son?" declared the Lord, "I will surely have mercy upon him" (Jeremiah 31:20). In light of these and related prophecies, one might surmise that Ephraim was carried to "far countries" in order to support and build up such lands unto God. After all, it was given anciently to Ephraim, through his lineage from Abraham and Joseph, to "make" and "bless" nations (Genesis 17:6; 22:18). And let us not forget that Ephraim's blessings were to supersede even those of Manasseh (Genesis 48:19). So, if Manasseh was delivered to set up an ancient promised land in the New World for God (as detailed in the Book of Mormon narrative), might we expect Ephraim to do the same in his appointed time?

One fascinating clue sheds some light on this question. Elder George Reynolds of the Quorum of the Seventy, in his book *We Are of Israel*, explains how ancient writings indicate that a large portion of the Lost Tribes of Israel, particularly the Tribe of Ephraim, settled in what is now Europe. Elder Reynolds quotes the apocryphal writer Esdras, who describes the Lost Tribes' trek northward, showing that by geographic necessity they swung near or through modern-day Europe.[9] Elder Reynolds then explains:

> Is it altogether improbable that in that long journey of one and a half years, as Esdras states it, that from Media the land of their captivity to the frozen north, some of the backsliding Israel rebelled, turned aside from the main body, forgot their God, [and] by and by mingled with the Gentiles? The account given in the Book of Mormon of a single house, its waywardness, its stiffneckedness before God, its internal quarrels and family feuds are, we fear, an example on a small scale of what probably happened in the vast bodies of the Israelites who for so many months wended their tedious way northward. Laman and Lemuel had, no doubt, many counterparts in the journeying Ten Tribes. And who so likely to rebel as stubborn, impetuous, proud and warlike Ephraim? Rebellion and backsliding have been so characteristically the story of Ephraim's career that we can scarcely conceive that it could be otherwise...Can it be any wonder then that so much of the blood of Ephraim has been found hidden and unknown in the midst of the nations of northern Europe...until the spirit of prophecy revealed its existence?[10]

It is quite possible that the apocryphal writings of Esdras, from which Elder Reynolds made these conclusions, were true; for the Lord declared to Joseph Smith that "there are many things contained therein [referring to the Apocrypha] that are true" (D&C 91:1). So, assuming that Esdras' and Elder Reynolds' conclusions are correct, what does it reveal about the modern American Covenant? By virtue of the fact that it was predominantly Europeans who established North America, it can safely be said that an overwhelming share of the U.S. population, particularly during the era of its founding, descended from the Tribe of Ephraim: from explorers to settlers, revolutionaries to founders, presidents to patriots, and prophets to congregations across the land. This would theoretically imply that the Founding Fathers—to include Washington, Adams, Madison, Jefferson, Franklin, and thousands of others from those early latter-day American generations—were the original modern-day American Covenant-makers, not only through their words and deeds, but also by virtue of the authority bestowed upon them by their birthright through Ephraim.

Other indicators that these latter-day American founders were connected to Ephraim and his pre-ordained mission are revealed by prophets who knew something about this lineage. For example, Brigham Young stated that "[Joseph Smith's] descent from Joseph that was sold into Egypt was direct, and the blood was pure in him....Joseph Smith was a pure Ephraimite."[11] Joseph of Egypt himself concurred; for, after seeing Joseph Smith in vision, he recognized the latter-day restorer as a "fruit of my loins....his name called after me." He further stated that "by the power of the Lord [Joseph Smith] shall bring my people unto salvation"(2 Nephi. 3: 6,15). The point is that Joseph Smith is a literal Ephraimite, and we know through genealogical research that his lineage stems from Europe.[12] Therefore, it may be presumed that those with similar ancestral ties also share such Ephraimite heritage. Such a presumption is not only consistent with the aforementioned prophecies, but is confirmed by the hundreds of thousands (possibly millions) of patriarchal blessings that declare such Ephraimite lineage to Americans of European descent. If Washington, Adams, Madison, Jefferson, Franklin, and their founding generations were to have received their patriarchal blessings, it is likely they too would have been pronounced members of the Tribe of Ephraim. If that is the case, their inspired work during mortality is connected to an ancient birthright and a foreordained responsibility.

It is also interesting to observe that many of the American founders share personal preferences and attributes with Ephraim—a love of justice, freedom, and independence (and a willingness to rebel against tyranny in order to preserve these gifts). As the ancient scriptural account in 1 Kings 12 details, it was, after all, Ephraim who led a violent and successful revolt on behalf of the Northern Kingdom against Judah and the Southern Kingdom. And what started this revolution? Unfair and unauthorized taxes levied by the Southern Kingdom.

Jacob's Promises to Joseph Reconsidered

In light of evidence connecting modern-day American Covenant-makers to Abraham through Joseph, we might reconsider Jacob's promises to Joseph to see if there exist any hints of a modern-day application. To that end, we will briefly reexamine this blessing found in Genesis 49. We have already established the idea that this blessing flowed from Abraham to Joseph to Manasseh to Lehi, and on to his posterity. We will now see how those covenant blessings would equally flow from Abraham to Joseph to Ephraim, and then to the Europeans who settled and founded modern-day America. It is logical that the prophecy regarding Joseph's seed crossing "over the wall" to the land of "everlasting hills" is as equally applicable to the second "founding" of America as it was to the first. God offered the same blessings to Lehi, Nephi, Alma, and Mosiah (through Manasseh) as He did to Christopher Columbus, George Washington, John Adams, Joseph Smith, and Brigham Young (through Ephraim).

We might even argue that this time around the description of "everlasting hills" was in reference not only to the Central/South American Andes (as it may have been in the account of Lehi), but also to the North American Rocky Mountains. This mountain range has, after all, been identified as a landmark that served as a gospel marker for where the second and final covenant would be established. Church leaders have confirmed that Isaiah saw these mountains as part of his vision of the great latter-day Restoration. More specifically, Isaiah saw the Salt Lake Temple residing among these mountains, and so he prophesied that the "Lord's house shall be established in the top of the mountains; and shall be exalted above the hills" (Isaiah 2:2).[13]

That Jacob's promises to Joseph were also intended for Ephraim in *latter-day* America is further established by the fact that when Jacob brought Joseph and his sons to pronounce these blessings, he clearly stated that these blessings would "tell you that which shall befall you in the *last days*" (Genesis 49:1, emphasis added). Furthermore, in Moses' aforementioned version of the same blessings, he refers to the posterity of Joseph as "the ten thousands of Ephraim" and the "thousands of Manasseh," implying that Joseph's American Covenant blessings would fall predominantly on Ephraim. As Ephraim's prominence is clearly positioned in the latter-days, its seems these American Covenant blessings from Jacob to Joseph predominantly look forward to the latter days. [14]

The Stick of Joseph Reconsidered

We discussed above how Ezekiel's vision of the Stick of Joseph represents a powerful prophecy of the Book of Mormon. We further described how through this Book, the fulfillment of Joseph's blessings have been recorded—his seed (through Lehi) discovered the new land and received the covenant blessings just as Jacob foresaw. But if Joseph's promises were projected to be fulfilled predominately in the last-days, should not the Stick of Joseph, even the Book of Mormon, also emphasize this second fulfillment? It should; and it does. For example, an entire chapter in the Book of Mormon is dedicated to a prophecy outlining how this second fulfillment would occur. In 1 Nephi 13, we see the latter-day heirs of America crossing "over the wall" to their new land; we see them fight and win a war for independence; and we see them create a land and country under covenant in preparation for the Restoration. Not only does he tell their story, but Nephi also makes it clear that these latter-day heirs would be working under the covenant—they would be carried "out of captivity" (verse 13), they would have the "power of God" which would fight against "all those that were gathered together against them to battle" (verse

18), and they would "prosper in the land" (verse 20). Not only are these covenant blessings of *liberty, protection,* and *prosperity* clearly to be offered to the latter-day Americans, but we are told that these new heirs of the land would only be worthy of these blessings as they "humble[d] themselves before the Lord" (verse 16). Nephi knew it was to be a renewed national covenant.

A vision of this second fulfillment of the covenant is also seen in other places throughout the Stick of Joseph. Indeed, there are several additional scripture references which appear to indicate that modern America's founding generations sprung out of Israel and were brought to the New World under the covenant of old— even the American Covenant—for the purposes of God in the latter-days. One of these scriptures is 2 Nephi 10:7-17. In this scripture the Lord explains that in response to the Great Apostasy, He would lead a group of His latter-day chosen ones to a new land of their inheritance, and provide for them, by a covenant He made with their fathers, the *liberty, protection,* and *prosperity* of the Lord— even those same promised blessings Jacob promised to the seed of Joseph.[15] Furthermore, consider the Savior's prophecies regarding latter-day America: "For it is wisdom in the Father," declared a resurrected Christ, as he stood upon the very American ground over which he spoke, "that they [referring to the latter-day inhabitants of America] should be established in this land, and be *set up as a free people* by the power of the Father, that *the covenant of the Father may be fulfilled* which he hath covenanted with his people, *O house of Israel*" (3 Nephi 21:4, emphasis added). Here, the Lord speaks of a covenant made with the House of Israel, a covenant which will be fulfilled in latter-day America, and whose fruit includes the blessings of freedom and liberty. How can we deny that this is an exact description of the American Covenant? That Christ was revealing such a *national* covenant element in His prophecy is perhaps corroborated by His earlier statement to Judah: "[T]he Kingdom of God shall be taken from you, and given to a *nation* bringing forth the fruits thereof" (Matthew 21:43, emphasis added). Again, Christ implies a *national* element by indicating that another *nation* would receive the kingdom. The LDS King James Bible cross-references this scripture with 1 Nephi 13:26 and D&C 90:1-5, both of which support the claim that the new "nation" Christ was referring to was, in fact, America.

Another scriptural reference from the Stick of Joseph that perhaps includes elements of our American Covenant, and its connection to Israel, is Jacob, Chapter 5. Here Jacob discusses (through the allegory of the tame and wild olive trees) how latter-day America will be reserved to support and at times replace Israel as the venue for God's ultimate gospel purposes. Similarly, in Ether Chapter 13:1-8, we witness the Prophet Ether, foreseeing latter-day Americans, as he declares that "the remnant of the house of Joseph shall be built upon this land; and it shall be a land of their inheritance." These many references to the national covenant in latter-day America should also compel us to reconsider what the Prophet Moroni wrote in his introduction to the Book of Mormon. He clearly wanted his latter-day readers to know that the Book was written "to show unto the remnant of the House of Israel the great things the Lord hath done…and that they may know *the covenants* of the Lord, that they are not cast off forever."[16]

All together, it is abundantly clear that the Stick of Joseph was not only intended to fulfill Joseph's promises through the telling of the ancient story of Joseph's posterity through Manasseh and Lehi, but also through the telling of a modern day story—the story of his posterity through Ephraim, even the latter-day heirs of the land. That this latter-day fulfillment of Joseph's ancient covenant promises was intentional and predominant perhaps explains why, when Ezekiel described the Stick of Joseph, he also called it the "Stick of Ephraim," even though Manasseh played a more prominent role in the Book of Mormon narrative. Of such is the significance of the American Covenant and the American Covenant-makers in the latter-days.

The significance of the latter-day national covenant was certainly not lost on ancient American prophets. We have already discussed how Book of Mormon prophecies made it clear that not only would Lehi's direct lineage enjoy the blessings of *liberty*, *protection*, and *prosperity*, but that these same blessings would be given to latter-day heirs of the New World as well (see Chapter 1). This must have been comforting to these ancient American prophets, as they considered the prophecies concerning their own people, even the children of Lehi. For it was clear to them that their posterity would eventually break the covenant, lose their blessings, and be destroyed.[17] This must have been especially comforting to the Nephite prophets who actually witnessed this final and tragic end.

One such witness was the Prophet Mormon. Before giving the Gold Plates to his son, Moroni, that he might bury them up, Mormon indicated his knowledge that the blessings, though taken from the earth, would return in the latter-days. "[T]he Lord," declared Mormon, "hath reserved their [the Nephites'] blessings, which they might have received in the land, for the Gentiles [latter-day Americans] who shall possess the land" (Mormon 5: 19).* Mormon knew that God had "been merciful unto the seed of Joseph." And he knew, despite the fact that Joseph's seed had fallen, that there would be another chance. Mormon declared, "surely shall he again bring a remnant of the seed of Joseph to the knowledge of the Lord their God." God would fulfill these promises, declared Mormon, "unto the restoring all the house of Jacob unto the knowledge of the covenant that he hath covenanted with them" (see 3 Nephi 5: 21-25).

---

* It should be noted that there is no contradiction in using the term *Gentile* to describe latter-day Americans who are descendants of Israel. For, as the *Bible Dictionary* states, the term *Gentile*, "as used throughout the scriptures…has a dual meaning, sometimes to designate peoples of non-Israelite lineage, and other times to designate nations that are without the gospel, even though there may be some Israelite blood therein. This latter usage is especially characteristic of the word as used in the Book of Mormon." See "Bible Dictionary," *The Holy Bible, King James Version* (Salt Lake City: LDS Church, 1986), 679.

These ancient American prophets did not just record the many above references to latter-day America, including their foreordained position as future covenant-makers, just for fun. They understood the deeper meaning: their covenant was to be transferred to a later generation of Americans. This fact alone sheds much light on the latter-day Americans who would be the heirs of the covenant. For as Joseph's national covenant blessings (given through Jacob) are clearly linked to Lehi's national covenant blessings, which are clearly linked to latter-day America's national covenant blessings, we have additional proof that the modern American Covenant and its participants stem firmly from Abraham, Jacob and Joseph—even from the blood and covenants of Israel.

Inasmuch as the ancient Americans understood how their own national covenant blessings stemmed from Abraham through Joseph, surely they considered that the latter-day heirs of the covenant would be from this same family. Indeed, if it was the same covenant resurfacing again in America, this time in the latter-days, it only makes sense that it would stay in the family whose right and authority it has always been to participate in it. And based on all of the above, it must be Ephraim that becomes the national covenant-maker in the latter-days. Whereas Joseph's descendants through Manasseh would be prominent among the American Covenant-makers of the Book of Mormon era, so would Joseph's descendants through Ephraim—after receiving a sort of transfer of covenant—carry that blessing and burden in the last days. Certainly the Lord would once again seek out Joseph's descendants (this time through Ephraim) and bring them back across the sea to America, where they would again covenant to lead the establishment of a government that would serve His eternal purposes.

This covenant transfer takes on an almost literal air as we consider that upon Manasseh's failure to live the American Covenant anciently, his posterity (in this case the Prophet Moroni) deposited the detailed language of the covenant in the ground on gold plates, so that his brother Ephraim (as represented by the Prophet Joseph Smith), once fully prepared, could receive it at a later date and thus reveal its important contents.

The Stick of Joseph most certainly provides a powerful witness, not only concerning the existence and foreordained role of the latter-day American Covenant-makers, but also concerning who these latter-day American Covenant-makers *really* were.

Prophecies of Jeremiah Reconsidered

Jeremiah, in his famous Old Testament prophecies regarding the gathering of Israel in the latter-days, also foresaw the American Covenant and its participants. Though his prophetic emphasis mostly points to the Restoration, as pointed out by Elder LeGrand Richards and others,[18] it is difficult to miss how his ancient prophecies also reflect upon the earliest founding generations of latter-day Americans/Ephraimites. For Jeremiah speaks of the latter-day "Children of Israel" being brought by the Lord from the "land of the north and from all the lands whither he had driven them" into "their land that I gave their fathers" (Jeremiah 16:15). He further details this migration, stating that "Ephraim shall cry, Arise ye, and let us go up to Zion" (The LDS Bible Dictionary defines Zion as "all of North and South America").[19] Jeremiah then foresees them traveling from the "north country" (Europe) and into this new land (America), saying they will come "with weeping, and with supplication" (the historical record is clear on the difficulties faced by our American founders during their early migration and settlement).* But, as Jeremiah points out, the Lord would also bless them with the very blessings of the national

---

* The obvious perils the early American settlers faced—from sea travel, to disease, to attacks from the Native Americans—is reflected in the fact that during the first decade or so of certain American colonies, the mortality rate approached 80 percent. See Matthew S. Holland, *Bonds of Affection* (Washington D.C.: Georgetown University Press, 2007), 29.

covenant. God would indeed "lead them" and protect them "from the hand of him that was stronger than [them]." The Lord further promised to provide for them that they might "come and sing in the height of Zion" and receive "the goodness of the Lord," even "wheat", "wine", "oil", "the young of the flock and of the herd," and thus sayeth the Lord, "my people shall be satisfied with my goodness" (Jeremiah 31:6-14). It should be noted that at the time Jeremiah made these prophecies, Israel, to include Ephraim, was in Assyrian captivity and had been for well over one hundred years.[20] This would suggest that the blessings would be restored to Ephraim at some future date—even at some *latter-day* date. In summation, and in light of all the evidences put forth in this chapter, these unambiguous references about Ephraim migrating during a time that points to a latter-day setting, to a land that provided the very same blessings offered through the American Covenant, make it appear as though Jeremiah was in fact tuned in to latter-day America and her covenant.

But Jeremiah was not finished commenting on this subject. In the Book of Jeremiah, Chapter 31, he defines the relationship between God and Ephraim as the "new covenant" (verse 31). He also points out that on an earlier occasion God made this covenant with Israel when He "took them by the hand to bring them out of Egypt," but that they had broken that covenant (verse 32). And finally, he states that in the latter-days the Lord would bring this covenant back and "put my law in their inward parts, and write it in their hearts; and [I] will be their God and they shall be my people" (verse 33).

Again, the most prominent message from these and other similar verses most certainly has to do with the Restoration and the individual priesthood covenants that offer eternal life. However, several points about these verses compel us to believe that Jeremiah was also foreseeing the American Covenant. For example, the "new covenant" he referred to has been defined in latter-day revelation as "the Book of Mormon and the former commandments [the Bible]" (D&C 84:57). While these scriptures no doubt make reference to our most important priesthood covenants, we must remember that also included in these books of scriptures—as argued above—are the promises of the American Covenant. Furthermore, by comparing this new covenant to what was clearly an ancient *national* covenant—even that covenant made with the children of Israel on their exodus from Egypt—implies that this new covenant is but another attempt at a *national* covenant. And finally, the fact that this new covenant must be "writ[ten] in their hearts" perhaps implies that these early national covenant-makers would *feel* their responsibility under the covenant more than they would actually learn of it in a scriptural or even an academic sense. In that our earliest latter-day American Covenant-makers (the Founding Fathers) predated the fullness of the Restoration, and in that many of our current national covenant-makers do not yet count the Book of Mormon as scriptural, their comprehension of the national covenant and their actions related to it was and is based largely on something they felt/feel inside more than anything else. The American Covenant was and is, as Jeremiah implied, "written in their hearts."

Jeremiah truly saw the American Covenant-makers. He knew they stemmed from Ephraim and Israel. And he knew theirs would be a divine mission.

Latter-day Evidence of the Fulfillment

Perhaps some of the greatest evidence for our claim that these ancient covenant blessings apply to modern America and its early founders through Ephraim, comes to us from reviewing again what these blessings were. These blessings to Joseph and Ephraim included the promises of *liberty, protection,* and *prosperity*. And these blessings are reiterated and projected toward latter-day America through the Book of Mormon and through ancient prophets, like Jeremiah, as recently noted. The evidence lies in the fact that these three gifts are so abundantly reflected in latter-day America. What's more, we can easily see how these American blessings have directly supported and sustained God's restored gospel in the latter-days. In light of all the supportive evidence given above about how Joseph's seed through Ephraim wandered and settled in latter-day America, could an exact match of Joseph's promised blessings to that seed with those blessings we see today in latter-day America, really be a coincidence? Furthermore, we will witness in the chapters ahead how latter-day Americans, past and present, have clearly received these gifts as covenant blessings from God, even referring to their gifted land—most astonishingly—as the "New Israel." Such revelations will only further hinder our ability to write such connections off as coincidences.

Other latter-day evidence that the ancient prophecies have been fulfilled in modern America stems from leaders of the Restoration who have witnessed it. As we will see in the coming chapters, they recognized the profound American history of which they and their spiritual cause were a part. The Prophet Joseph, perhaps the most prominent latter-day Ephraimite, certainly made these connections after learning from the Lord Himself that the Founding Fathers were "wise men whom I raised up" (D&C 101:80). Furthermore, when asked to outline the most important tenants of the restored gospel, the Prophet even thought to include this particular point of doctrine. In the Tenth Article of Faith, the Prophet declared that "Zion (the New Jerusalem) will be built upon the American continent."[21] That the founding generations who built this land—upon which the New Jerusalem would find its foundation— were themselves of Israel is also reflected in a statement made by the Prophet Joseph: "[The] Holy Ghost...is more powerful in expanding the mind, enlightening the understanding, and storing the intellect with present knowledge of a man who is the literal seed of Abraham."[22] Such men and women are exactly the type God would need to "raise up" for the cause of America. Their task of creating a nation under God and for God would be next to impossible, especially given the circumstances of the time. The prophets have stated that "God has led away from time to time [his children] from the House of Israel, according to his will and pleasure. And...the Lord remembereth all them who have been broken off" (2 Nephi 10:22). The Lord certainly remembered these American founders.

They too were of Israel, and the privilege and authority was theirs to accomplish the purposes of God through the American Covenant.

★ ★ ★ ★

In summation and corroboration of all these arguments made above, we turn to Erastus Snow, an ordained Apostle of the Lord, who declared a direct connection between the promises of Ephraim and the Founding Fathers of America. Elder Snow's pronouncement —which he made as an Apostle, and which is recorded in the Church's *Journal of Discourses*—emphasizes both Ephraim's role in bringing forth the Restoration *and* Ephraim's responsibility in bringing forth the American Covenant:

> Now the same spirit of revelation that sought out the Prophet Joseph [Smith] from the loins of Joseph that was sold into Egypt...has also called the children of Abraham from among the kingdoms and countries of the earth to first hear and then embrace the everlasting Gospel; and the remnants of the seed of Ephraim who were scattered from Palestine and who colonized the shores of the Caspian Sea and thence made their way into the north of Europe, western Scandinavia and northern Germany, penetrating Scotland and England, and conquering those nations and reigning as monarchs of Great Britain, and mingling their seed with the Anglo-Saxon race, and spreading over the waters a fruitful vine, as predicted by Jacob, whose branches should run over the wall. Their blood has permeated European society, and it coursed in the veins of the early colonists of America. And when the books shall be opened and the lineage of all men known, it will be found that they have been first and foremost in everything noble among men in the various nations in breaking off the shackles of kingcraft and priestcraft and oppression of every kind, and the foremost among men in upholding and maintaining the principles of liberty and freedom upon this continent and establishing representative government,

and thus preparing the way for the coming forth of the fullness of the Gospel. And it is the foremost of those spirits whom the Lord has prepared to receive the Gospel when it was presented to them, and who did not wait for the Elders to hunt them from the hills and corners of the earth, but they were hunting for the Elders, impelled by a spirit which then they could not understand; and for this reason were they among the first Elders of the Church; they and the fathers having been watched over from the days that God promised those blessings upon Isaac and Jacob and Joseph and Ephraim.[23]

In the end, these many scriptural and prophetic evidences and connections can be summarized into the following conclusion: the latter-day American Covenant is real. It has roots that trace back to Abraham and Joseph. It was foreseen by many ancient prophets. It has been defined by the Tribe of Manasseh in the Book of Mormon. It has been delivered up and established by the Tribe of Ephraim (our American Founding Fathers) in the latter-days. And finally, with a newly established covenant nation "under God," modern-day generations of Ephraimites could at last begin to build upon this foundation and eventually fulfill Ephraim's most important mission. That mission is defined in the *Bible Dictionary*: "[I]n the last days it has been the tribe of Ephraim's privilege first to bear the message of the restoration of the gospel to the world and to gather scattered Israel (Deut.33:13-17; D&C 133:26-34; 64: 36)."[24] And thus is delivered, under the support of the American Covenant, God's work and glory: to supply the Abrahamic Covenant, complete with its promises of eternal life, to all who would come unto Christ.

The above-cited *Bible Dictionary* definition of Ephraim and his latter-day responsibilities sum up how we generally interpret the many scriptural references to Ephraim and America in the latter-days. That is, the focus of our interpretation is often almost exclusively on Ephraim's role in the gospel restoration, beginning from Joseph Smith's First Vision in 1820 until the present. To be sure, this is the most important part. However, with a greater understanding of our national covenant as offered by this study, we would do well to expand our comprehension of such scriptural references in order to see the American Covenant also represented therein. We need to recognize the prominent place of America's national covenant-makers, whose story actually began long before 1820. We need to recognize that the blessings of *liberty, protection,* and *prosperity*—as defined by scripture—necessarily arrived in America to pave the way for, and continue to provide support for, the restoration of the gospel. Yet none of these gospel-necessary national blessings would be ours without an American Covenant and American Covenant-makers. They crossed the sea to discover the New World. They administered a miraculous American war for independence that bought a more inspired and developed form of agency. They established an American constitution that secured this agency. And they have carried out a myriad of other efforts that have enhanced this agency unto the eternal salvation of God's children at home and abroad. And this they have done under the direction of the Almighty—under a covenant with the Almighty.

It is no wonder the First Presidency declared that early American settlers and founders were "the advance guard of the army of the Lord, to establish the God-given system of government under which we live...and prepare the way for the restoration of the Gospel of Christ."[25] And it is no wonder that Elder Bruce R. McConkie noted that these early American leaders "were all known and arranged for in advance...and those who are called and chosen to do the work receive their commission and ordination from [God], first in the pre-existence and then, if they remain true and faithful, again here in mortality."[26]

After connecting the dots from Abraham to America, our testimonies of the Restoration should be enhanced and our curiosity should be piqued with regard to how this covenant has functioned and is functioning in the world to accomplish God's work. The story of the American Covenant-makers truly is part and parcel of the scriptural prophecies dealing with the restoration of the gospel. And this book attempts to tell their story within this gospel context. It attempts to provide the fullest explanation of what Moroni saw when he declared that "after the waters had receded from off the face of this land it became a choice land above all other lands, a chosen land of the Lord" (Ether 13:2). Indeed, it attempts to demonstrate once and for all how America has always been reserved and ordained for a single purpose: to establish and reestablish a national covenant with the tools necessary to support and protect God's gospel, complete with its principles and ordinances unto eternal life.

★ ★ ★ ★

Skepticism and doubt may surface, even in the face of scriptural and prophetic evidence. Could individuals who did not have the priesthood really be covenant-makers on behalf of an entire nation? It is easy to imagine Jaredite prophets (like the brother of Jared) as being covenant-makers. Lehi easily fits the role as well. But George Washington? Thomas Jefferson? Benjamin Franklin? Not only did these men lack the priesthood and the fullness of the gospel, but they were famously fallible. Books have been written about their misconduct and mistakes. However, such sources—interested mostly in intrigue and profit—miss the evidence of who these covenant-makers really were. While the following chapters will surely dissipate such doubts and clarify the divinely appointed roles these covenant-makers played (in spite of their shortcomings), we will now turn our attention to one under-told miraculous event in the American narrative that immediately infuses some spiritual value among America's Founding Fathers.

Miracle at St. George

In August 1877, the American Founding Fathers appeared to the Apostle, Wilford Woodruff, in the St. George Temple. Shortly after the event, Elder Woodruff explained:

...[T]wo weeks before I left Saint George, the spirits of the dead gathered around me, wanting to know why we did not redeem them. Said they, "You have had the use of the Endowment House for a number of years, and yet nothing has ever been done for us. We laid the foundation of the government you now enjoy, and we never apostatized from it, but we remained true to it and were faithful to God." I straightway went into the baptismal font and called upon Brother McAllister to baptize me for the signers of the Declaration of Independence, and fifty other eminent men.[27]

On the same day these ordinances were performed...Sister Lucy Bigelow Young went forth into the font and was baptized for...seventy (70) of the eminent women of the world.[28]

One of Brigham Young's clerks, James G. Bleak, added the following:

I was also present in the St. George Temple and witnessed the appearance of the Spirits of the Signers....the spirits of the Presidents....And also others....who came to Wilford Woodruff and demanded that their baptism and endowment be done. Wilford Woodruff was baptized for all of them. While I and Brothers J.D.T McAllister and David H. Cannon (who were witnesses to the request) were endowed for them.[29]

In an effort to express that the above event was not some invention of mind, or a formalistic rite of passage, Elder Woodruff recorded that he spoke with these individuals (he uses the word "argued"), and that they "pled" to him that their ordinances be done "as a man pleading for his life." Later, upon performing the baptisms, Elder Woodruff noted that it seemed as if "the room was filled as with flaming fire."[30]

Hope of The World by Michael Bedard
Courtesy of BedardFineArt.com

Elder Woodruff recorded in his journal, as well as in the annals of the St. George Temple, the names of these choice people for whom the work was performed. As Elder Woodruff and others present with him at the time emphasized, beyond just the signers of the Declaration of Independence, the work was also done for many people who played an essential role in creating this and other nations of the world—people who laid the foundations that supported the eventual arrival of the gospel of Jesus Christ. Among them were fifty-four of the signers, fifteen of the presidents (with the exceptions of Buchanan and Van Buren), and over 140 other eminent men and women. Not surprisingly, most of these individuals play a fundamental role in the American Covenant story. They are people including Christopher Columbus, George and Martha Washington, John and Abigail Adams, Benjamin Franklin, Thomas and Martha Jefferson, James and Dolley Madison, Abraham Lincoln, and many others.[31]

These names will resurface throughout this book, as the case is continuously made that their thoughts and actions made them key American Covenant-makers. And when these names do reappear, this singular miracle at St. George should shed much light on what they *really* accomplished in mortality, particularly through the eyes of God.

Wilford Woodruff truly understood who they were in relation to God and covenant. As President of the Church, more than ten years after the miracle, he declared the following in an April 1898 General Conference address:

> I am going to bear my testimony to this assembly, if I never do it again in my life, that those men who laid the foundation of this American government and signed the Declaration of Independence were the best spirits the God of heaven could find on the face of the earth. They were choice spirits...General Washington and all the men that labored for the purpose were inspired of the Lord.
>
> Another thing I am going to say here, because I have the right to say it. Every one of those men that signed the Declaration of Independence, with General Washington, called upon me, as an Apostle of the Lord Jesus Christ, in the temple at Saint George, two consecutive nights, and demanded at my hands that I should go forth and attend to the ordinances of the House of God for them....I told these brethren that it was their duty to go into the temple and labor until they had got endowments for all of them. They did it. Would those spirits have called upon me, as an Elder of Israel, to perform that work if they had not been noble spirits before God? They would not.[32]

"We the People" of the Covenant

In light of the above story, we need not suppose that only ordained priesthood holders in mortality can fulfill God's purposes on the earth, or that in order to fulfill such divine objectives a higher knowledge must first be obtained. As Elder Orson F. Whitney explained in a conference address:

> [God] is using not only his covenant people, but other peoples as well, to consummate a work, stupendous, magnificent, and altogether too arduous for this little handful of Saints to accomplish by and of themselves…All down the ages men bearing the authority of the Holy Priesthood—patriarchs, prophets, apostles and others, have officiated in the name of the Lord, doing things that he required of them; and outside the pale of their activities other good and great men, not bearing the Priesthood, but possessing profundity of thought, great wisdom, and a desire to uplift their fellows, have been sent by the Almighty.[33]

It is true, but largely insignificant, that the founding generations of America probably did not fully comprehend what their nation building really meant for God's plan of salvation. If they did not know, however, they would be in good company. For, similarly, Nephi did not know why he was creating a second volume of records, even the small plates of Nephi.* Adam did not know exactly why he was building altars and offering sacrifices (Moses 5:6). Cyrus of Persia, though he was a non-Jew without an understanding of the gospel, was nevertheless "stirred up by the spirit" and thus conquered Babylon and restored religious freedom to the Jews, that they might rebuild their temple (2 Chronicles 36:22-23). And hundreds upon thousands of people on the earth have an overwhelming desire to work on their genealogy without comprehending that it is the Spirit of Elijah[34] that has compelled

---

* While we now understand that the small plates of Nephi were to replace the 116 lost pages of Book of Mormon manuscript, Nephi and Mormon did not. However, they created and included the small plates because they knew the Lord had inspired it for some "wise purpose" (1 Nephi 9:5; Words of Mormon 1:6-7).

them forward, that their work might assist in the great gospel plan of God. This principle surely applies to Americans, both past and present, who work towards the purposes of God through science, literature, politics, and countless other endeavors. Whether or not they fully understand the significance of their accomplishments now, as related to God's work, eventually they will. The important thing is that they were (and are) acting under the inspiration of God. Usually they have understood this point clearly—and usually that was all the Lord required.

As far as the earliest American founders are concerned, they had no choice but to act in some ignorance, as the gospel in its fullness did not exist. They were trapped in a *catch twenty-two* of sorts: They were needed to combat the effects of the Apostasy in order to prepare for the Restoration, yet their fight required them to live during the Apostasy, which made it impossible for them to enjoy the very gospel blessings they were ultimately fighting for.

But what about those who came after the Restoration? There still may be wisdom in the Lord withholding the full gospel from them in mortality, if only to allow them a larger sphere of influence for His purposes. For example, would Abraham Lincoln have been elected president if he had been a member of that strange and little understood sect called "Mormons"? And yet Lincoln was an indispensable man in the story of the American Covenant (as we shall see). The same can be said of hundreds of others, both past and present. Like the Founding Fathers at St. George, all of them will have (or have already had) their opportunity to make those most powerful priesthood covenants unto salvation. And when they do, whether in mortality or beyond, they will quickly understand the fuller meanings of the inspiration they received in their capacity as covenant-makers. They will more fully appreciate the wisdom of God. They will more fully enjoy the eternal fruits of their labor.

Thankfully it was (and continues to be) enough that inspired Americans past and present knew that their mission was divine and knew that their new nation was given to them by God through covenant. One of our first examples of one who possessed such knowledge without a full comprehension of the gospel was George Washington. He declared the following in his first inaugural address as the first president of the United States. His message not only reflects his own understanding of the American Covenant, but that of those who came before him in the discovering, settling, and founding of the new nation.

> [I]t would be peculiarly improper to omit in this first official Act, my fervent supplications to that Almighty Being who rules over the Universe, who presides in the Councils of Nations, and whose providential aids can supply every human defect, that his benediction may consecrate to the liberties and happiness of the people of the United States.

Washington then warns:

> We ought to be no less persuaded that the smiles of Heaven can never be expected on a nation that disregards the eternal rules of order and right, which Heaven itself has ordained.

And finally, he concludes:

> Having thus imparted to you my sentiments...I shall take my present leave; but not without resorting once more to the benign parent of the human race, in humble supplication that since has been pleased to favour the American people...for the security of their Union, and the advancement of their happiness; so his divine blessing may be equally conspicuous in the enlarged views, the temperate consultations, and the wise measures on which the success of this Government must depend.[35]

Can there be any doubt that Washington possessed an understanding of the American Covenant and his associated obligations to the people and to God? As he accepted the presidency, it seems as though he felt the weight of his responsibility within the context of that relationship.

Moments before this address, Washington was sworn in as the first president of the United States. This "swearing in" makes the inaugural address even more significant, as the ceremony truly portrays our first president in his role as American Covenant-maker. For example, consider the words of the oath of office, which are found in Article II, Section I of the Constitution of the United States: "I do solemnly swear that I will faithfully execute the office of the President of the United States, and will to the best of my ability, preserve, protect, and defend the Constitution of the United States."

The profundity of that promise is revealed as we examine the true nature of the Constitution as national scripture. The Constitution (as will be detailed later) does nothing less than prescribe the formula for securing those American Covenant blessings of *liberty, protection,* and *prosperity.* In swearing to uphold the Constitution, each president is committing himself and the nation to God and the American Covenant. Surely, these are covenant-making words; and just as sacred covenants are written in sacred scripture, so is this national covenant written in our national scripture.

In reflecting upon this singular event of our nation's first inaugural ceremony, we should not underestimate the manner in which this presidential oath or covenant is administered. The recipient raises his right arm to the square, placing his other hand upon the Bible, and repeats the words of the covenant. This should be a familiar pattern to many Latter-day Saints.

To further reflect how seriously this covenant is made, if the words are not said precisely as revealed in the Constitution, it will at times be re-done until correct—even to this day. In the presidential inauguration ceremony of 2009, there was question as to whether the president-elect repeated every word of the covenant correctly. And so, the chief justice was invited to the White House after the ceremony to repeat it again, just to be sure.[36] Again, the Latter-day Saint will recognize a familiar pattern.

In that first inauguration, Washington added two seemingly spontaneous actions to the ceremony, which suggest he had a spiritual understanding of what he was entering into. Upon completing his recital of the oath, Washington declared: "So help me God," then "bowed down reverently" and kissed the Bible.[37] Almost every president since followed this precedent.[38] It is an outward expression to demonstrate to whom the covenant was made. Fittingly, this first oath of office ushered in a new form of constitutional government, which many referred to (and still do) as the *federal* government; and the root word for *federal*—the Latin *foedus*—directly translates into the English word "covenant." Furthermore, the oath was taken in the nation's first capital city, New York, in a building called Federal Hall, or as we might interpret it, *Covenant Hall.* [39]

Perhaps the only thing that would convince us further of Washington's acknowledgment that he was entering into an American Covenant with God would be if he had taken this national oath with his hand over the pages of Lehi's American Covenant language in the Book of Mormon. Unfortunately, this book of scripture had not yet been made public. However, the Biblical equivalent of this national covenant language found in Genesis 49, even that American Covenant promise from Jacob to Joseph, did exist. And so Washington placed his hand over an opened Bible to take his oath. Historians assert that Washington's hand was placed on a random opened page within the Holy Bible. If it was random, then it was also amazingly coincidental. For, in a gesture almost too astonishing to believe, Washington placed his hand precisely on the pages that included Jacob's American Covenant promise to Joseph in Genesis 49, complete with its description of his posterity crossing "over the wall" to a new land of "everlasting hills," ringing with *liberty, protection,* and *prosperity.*[40] The reason historians have long commented on the randomness of the page selected by Washington has to do with the seemingly insignificant choice of verses on the page. After all, its meaning in reference to America only becomes clear through the light of the restored gospel. And yet, clearly something of eternal significance was revealed and comprehended on that historic day.

But Washington was certainly not alone in his role as American Covenant-maker. To be sure, every American from coast to coast and border to border is a participant in the covenant. Even though it was given to Ephraim to lead the administration of this early covenant, it would eventually be given to the entire citizenry of the United States to participate in its blessings and obligations. As it is with the gospel Restoration, though Ephraim was to lead it, members of other tribes have since joined in the effort and are beneficiaries of the blessings. Naturally, some understand it and/or live it better than others; but nevertheless, all have their place, regardless of race or creed. As President Hinckley noted: "Men and women of all denominations have helped settle this land—Catholics and Protestants, Jews and Greeks, Muslims and Hindus...those who helped establish this great country believed in and worshipped God."[41] These were and are all American Covenant-makers.

Not insignificantly, thousands of Americans take an almost identical oath to that of the president every year, raising their arms to the square and repeating the constitutional promise, as they are sworn in to positions of trust. As one who has participated in such an event on two occasions (once for the Central Intelligence Agency and once for the Department of Homeland Security), I can testify to the power and solemnity in which this oath is received. Furthermore, every year thousands more stand with their arms to the square and take a similar oath, as they are sworn in as citizens of the United States. They covenant to "support and defend the Constitution" and "to bear true faith and allegiance to the same;" and they publically promise to "bear arms on behalf of the United States when required by law." As one who has witnessed this solemn assembly, with its participants wiping tears from their eyes, I can attest to its spiritual power, as particularly manifested by the concluding phrase of the oath—"so help me God."[42] And countless others have made the ultimate sacrifice, signing their covenant with their own blood, in defense of those principles which ultimately provide the opportunity for freedom and thus for salvation.

Moreover, Americans far and wide make and renew this national covenant every time they take a stand on those God-inspired principles of the Constitution, every time they sacrifice for the good of others, every time they reflect upon our national motto— "In God we trust." Americans declare their participation in the covenant every time they plead to God through song to "stand beside her and guide her through the night with the light from above" (from *God Bless America*), or when they intone the words, "Long may our land be bright with freedom's holy light, protect us by thy might, Great God, our King" (from *My Country 'Tis of Thee*). And finally, Americans certainly covenant with God and country every time they put their hands over their hearts and "pledge allegiance" to "one nation under God." It is through making these sacramental gestures of our national covenant that *We the people of the United States* truly become *We the people of the American Covenant*.

Conclusion

Many prophets throughout the ages have recorded their visions and revelations, which oft times pertain to the people they lead and the issues of their day. There are a few events and experiences, however, that carry so much profundity in relation to God's plan that almost all ancient and modern prophets have seen them in vision and have recorded them in scripture. Examples include the coming of the Messiah and the latter-day restoration of the gospel. And another, as we have seen throughout this chapter, is the American Covenant! But more than just adding enormous credibility to the entire concept of the American Covenant, this study of ancient and modern scripture and history has led us to the powerful conclusion that, in the end, it is the modern-day citizens of the United States that have fulfilled the ancient prophecies—that have become the American Covenant-makers. Consequently, the story of the American Covenant—including the promised blessings and obligations given through Abraham to Joseph and on to Lehi and George Washington—becomes our story. As the torch has now been passed to us, if we adhere to the covenant as did our forefathers, the privilege will be ours as Americans to continue to assist God. And this we can do by living up to our obligations under the American Covenant, that His *liberty, protection,* and *prosperity* might thrive, thus enhancing agency in furtherance of His ultimate gospel plan.

Notwithstanding this interesting account and its intricate connections to heaven and history, the skeptic may still justifiably conclude that the arguments made in these first chapters are a matter of theory and conjecture. As such, in the chapters that follow, we will dive into the historical accounts that, together with additional scripture and other inspired sources, will expand the examination, develop the doctrine, corroborate the theory, and perhaps even satisfy the skeptic. And through it all, we will detail one of the greatest historical sagas ever told of God and country.

ENDNOTES

[1] Refer to the definition of "Abraham, Covenant of," Bible Dictionary, *Holy Bible, King James Version* (Salt Lake City: The Church of Jesus Christ of Latter-day Saints, 1986), 602.

[2] Ibid

[3] See also: Deuteronomy 33:13-17; D&C 133:26-34.

[4] The following includes scriptural backing for the claim that the Book of Mormon is the Stick of Ephraim: D&C 27:5; 2 Nephi. 3:12.

[5] See *Introduction* of the Book of Mormon (Salt Lake City: The Church of Jesus Christ of Latter-day Saints, 1986).

[6] Nephi also stated his knowledge that he was a descendant of Joseph in 2 Nephi 4:1-2.

[7] See Charles Mann, *1491-New Revelations of the Americas Before Columbus* (New York: Alfred A. Knopf, 2006); Chris and Ted Stewart, *Seven Miracles That Saved America* (Salt Lake: Shadow Mountain, 2009), 55.

[8] See Steven D. Greene, *The Tribe of Ephraim* (Springville: Horizon Publishers, 2007), xiii.

[9] See *Apocrypha*, 2 Esdras 13:39-47, full text available at www.sacred-texts.com.

[10] Elder George Reynolds, *We Are of Israel*, 27-28, as quoted in Bruce R. McConkie, *Mormon Doctrine* (Salt Lake City: Bookcraft, 1979), 455-457.

[11] *Utah Genealogical and Historical Magazine*, vol.11, July 1920, 107; *Journal of Discourses*, 7:290; *Journal of Discourses*, 2:269.

[12] Joseph's paternal ancestry stems from England and his maternal ancestry from Scotland, as discussed in *Church History in the Fullness of Times, Religion 341-43* (Salt Lake City: The Church of Jesus Christ of Latter-day Saints, 2000), 16-18.

[13] See Jeffrey R. Holland, "An Ensign to the Nations," General Conference, April 2011, available at http://lds.org/general-conference/2011/04/an-ensign-to-the-nations?lang=eng.

[14] See LeGrand Richards, *A Marvelous Work and a Wonder* (Salt Lake City: Deseret Book Co., 1976), 63.

[15] See the conclusion of Chapter 1 for a full analysis of these Book of Mormon verses and their connection to the American Covenant.

[16] See The Book of Mormon title page, Salt Lake City: The Church of Jesus Christ of Latter-day Saints, 1986.

[17] The following scriptures include Nephite prophecies concerning the ultimate destruction of their people: 1 Nephi 12:19; 2 Nephi 26:10; Alma 45:11.

[18] LeGrand Richards, *A Marvelous Work and a Wonder* (Salt Lake City: Deseret Book Co., 1976), 223-225. It should also be noted that in the LDS version of the King James Bible, the header synopsis for Jeremiah, Chapter 31, makes it clear that Jeremiah is prophesying over events administered by Ephraim in the latter-days.

[19] "The Bible Dictionary," *The Bible*, Authorized King James version (Salt Lake City: The Church of Jesus Christ of Latter-day Saints, 1986), 793.

[20] See *Old Testament Seminary Student Guide* (Salt Lake City: The Church of Jesus Christ of Latter-day Saints, 2002), 162.

[21] Article of Faith #10, *History of the Church*, Vol.4, 535-541; also quoted in *The Pearl of Great Price* (Salt Lake City: The Church of Jesus Christ of Latter-day Saints, 1986), 61.

[22] Joseph Smith, as quoted in Greene, *The Tribe of Ephraim*, 43.

[23] Erastus Snow, *Journal of Discourses* 23:186-187, May 6, 1882; also quoted in Howard H. Barron, *Judah, Past and Future* (Bountiful: Horizon Publishers, 1979), 49-50.

[24] "The Bible Dictionary," *The Bible*, Authorized King James version (Salt Lake City: The Church of Jesus Christ of Latter-day Saints, 1986), 666.

[25] First Presidency, as quoted by Tad Callister, *The Inevitable Apostasy* (Salt Lake: Deseret Book, 2006), 331.

[26] Bruce R. McConkie, as quoted by Tad Callister, *The Inevitable Apostasy* (Salt Lake: Deseret Book, 2006), 328.

[27] *Journal of Discourses*, 19:229, September 16, 1877.

²⁸ Wilford Woodruff Journal, 7:367-69, as quoted in Vicki Jo Anderson, *The Other Eminent Men of Wilford Woodruff* (Malta: Nelson Book, 1994), 420-1.

²⁹ Personal journal of James Godson Bleak, as quoted in Vicki Jo Anderson, *The Other Eminent Men of Wilford Woodruff* (Malta: Nelson Book, 1994), 420.

³⁰ Wilford Woodruff, as quoted by Truman G. Madsen, *The Presidents of the Church*, recorded lecture series (Salt Lake City, Bookcraft), tape/track 4, "Wilford Woodruff."

³¹ These are but a sample of the more than 190 men and woman recorded in church records, including Wilford Woodruff's personal journal at the BYU Special Collections library, to have received their temple baptisms and endowments pursuant to the visitation, as discussed in Anderson, *The Other Eminent Men of Wilford Woodruff*, Preface and Introduction, 1-2. See also Wilford Woodruff, *Wilford Woodruff's Journal, 1833-1898 Typescript,* ed. Scott G. Kenney (Midvale, Utah: 1985), 7:367-69.

But did *all* of these eminent spirits actually appear to Wilford Woodruff? Or was it more of a formalistic exercise in attempting to redeem the dead? Answering these questions definitively is somewhat complicated. As explained in the text of this book, Wilford Woodruff made it abundantly clear that at least the signers of the Declaration of Independence, along with George Washington, actually appeared to him in the spirit and spoke to him. I believe Elder Woodruff's testimony.

But what about the others whose temple work was done simultaneously? Did they also appear? It was a second witness, James Bleak, not Wilford Woodruff, who indicated that these other spirits, to include those of the presidents and others, also actually appeared. It should be noted, however, that whereas Elder Woodruff's accounts are contemporaneous with the actual temple event, Brother Bleak's account appears to have been recorded at the very end of his life. Notwithstanding when it was recorded, however, if Brother Bleak stated it, I believe it. Brother Bleak, after all, was in the temple with Elder Woodruff when the visitation occurred.

Gaining full clarity on the matter becomes somewhat complicated upon considering a book that seems to have played some role in the grand event. The book, written by Evert Duyckinck, and published in 1873, is titled *Portrait Gallery of Eminent Men and Women of Europe and America.* The book is a collection of biographies of important men and woman. It is significant in that it includes biographies of a very large percentage of those eminent men and women whose temple work was done pursuant to Elder Woodruff's vision. Furthermore, the names of many of the eminent spirits are listed in the temple baptismal record in the same general order (not alphabetical) as they are listed in Duyckinck's book. (I have personally viewed the book together with the temple records.)

So, should we conclude that the names of the eminent men and women from Duyckinck's book were not necessarily special, but instead represented what boils down to a formalistic temple exercise? Not necessarily. For one thing, there were many deceased persons in Duyckinck's book whose work was *not* done. In other words, even if the book—and not an actual visitation—was the primary reason these names were selected, it is significant that Elder Woodruff utilized discretion in selecting the names. At the very least, it appears that revelation played a role in the selection process. It is also possible that all the eminent men and woman actually appeared, and that Duyckinck's book was a divine tool to provide Elder Woodruff with biographical data, to include birth and death dates. Indeed, who can say that the Lord did not inspire Duyckinck to include biographies of these eminent people, knowing that the book would be utilized later by His apostle to assist in their miraculous temple appearance? After all, we do not know if Elder Woodruff had or utilized this book before or after the visitation.

Another element to consider, which (depending on who you talk to) adds either further clarity or further confusion to the matter, is the personal experience of historian and author Vicki-Jo Anderson. One can hardly speak of the vision of the Founders at St. George without mentioning Sister Anderson. Her book, *The Other Eminent Men of Wilford Woodruff*, has perhaps done more than any other written work, to date, to bring to light this St. George Temple miracle. In the Introduction of her book, Sister Anderson explains how she received a very special blessing as she was preparing to research and write her book about the other eminent spirits who were a part of the St. George Temple experience. The blessing came from her patriarch, who had recently retired from a research historian position at the Church Historical Department. As recorded in Sister Anderson's book, the patriarch was very clear in his blessing "that these men and women had appeared to Wilford Woodruff and to others" in the temple. Admittedly, the evidence of them actually appearing, in this case, stems from a personal blessing, not from any declaration made by Wilford Woodruff.

Unfortunately, the St. George Temple's first minute book, which would have likely shed more light and detail on what happened during this miraculous event, is missing.

And so, as no commentator or historian of today was there, all we can do is take what evidence we have and make our own conclusions. Whatever we conclude, however, we are probably safe to determine that, whatever actually happened, *all* the men and women whose work was done pursuant to the miraculous visitation were special people who had fulfilled special missions upon the earth to further God's plan. Also, in light of the above, it is my belief that all of these spirits had been prepared and accepted Elder Woodruff's offering of true temple ordinances and covenants.

The above commentary, to include evidences provided, can be verified and further studied in the following works: Jennifer Anne Mackley, "Wilford Woodruff: Pivotal Prophet," paper presented at the Mormon History Association Conference, May 27, 2011, used by permission of the author. Sister Mackley's research will also be available in her forthcoming book, *Wilford Woodruff's Vision of the Redemption of the Dead*. See also *Wilford Woodruff's Journal, 1833-1898*, Typscript, ed. Scott G. Kenney, 9 vols. (Midvale, Utah: Signature Books, 1983-1984); Vicki-Jo Anderson, *The Other Eminent Men of Wilford Woodruff* (Malta: Nelson Book, 2000); Evert A. Duyckinck, *Portrait Gallery of Eminent Men and Women of Europe and America*, 2 vols. (New York: Johnson, Wilson and Company, 1873).

[32] Wilford Woodruff, *Conference Report*, April 1898, 89-90, as quoted in Anderson, Appendix.

[33] Orson F. Whitney, as quoted by Howard W. Hunter, "The Gospel—A Global Faith," *Ensign*, Nov. 1991, 18.

[34] In 1836, Elijah the Prophet appeared to Joseph Smith and Oliver Cowdery, committing to them the priesthood keys that permit, among other things, ordinance work for the dead, thus fulfilling Malachi's prophecy that Elijah would turn "the heart of the children to their fathers" (see Malachi 4:5-6). Since that time, people of the earth have inexplicably turned to genealogical research as a hobby. As Elder LeGrand Richards explains: "The spirit of turning the hearts of the children to their fathers has swept the whole earth since Elijah came to accomplish his promised mission. While this spirit cannot be seen, the operation thereof has touched the hearts of men and women the world over. They do not know why they are compiling genealogical records, yet this work has made rapid strides—really it is a 'marvelous work and a wonder' in and of itself." See LeGrand Richards, *A Marvelous Work and a* Wonder (Salt Lake City: Deseret Book Co., 1976), 185.

[35] George Washington's First Inaugural Address, April 30, 1789, as quoted in William J. Bennett, *The Spirit of America* (New York: Touchstone, 1997), 381-382.

[36] See "Obama Retakes Oath of Office After Flub," available at http://www.msnbc.msn.com/id/28780417/

[37] Description by Washington Irving, as quoted in Bennett, 381.

[38] "Inaugural History," PBS Online News Hour (data online): available from www.pbs.org/newshour/inauguration/history.html

[39] Bruce Feiler, *America's Prophet* (New York: Harper Collins, 2009), 28, 78.

[40] That Washington had his Bible opened to Genesis 49 during his swearing-in ceremony is documented in H. Paul Jeffers, *The Freemasons in America* (New York: Kensington Publishing Corp., 2006), 28.

[41] Gordon B. Hinckley, *Standing for Something* (New York: Random House, Inc, 2000), xxiii.

[42] The Naturalization Oath of Allegiance can be found at www.cavanaughlegal.com/us-citizenship-naturalization/citizenship-ceremony.

Part II

★ ★ ★ ★

Living the American Covenant

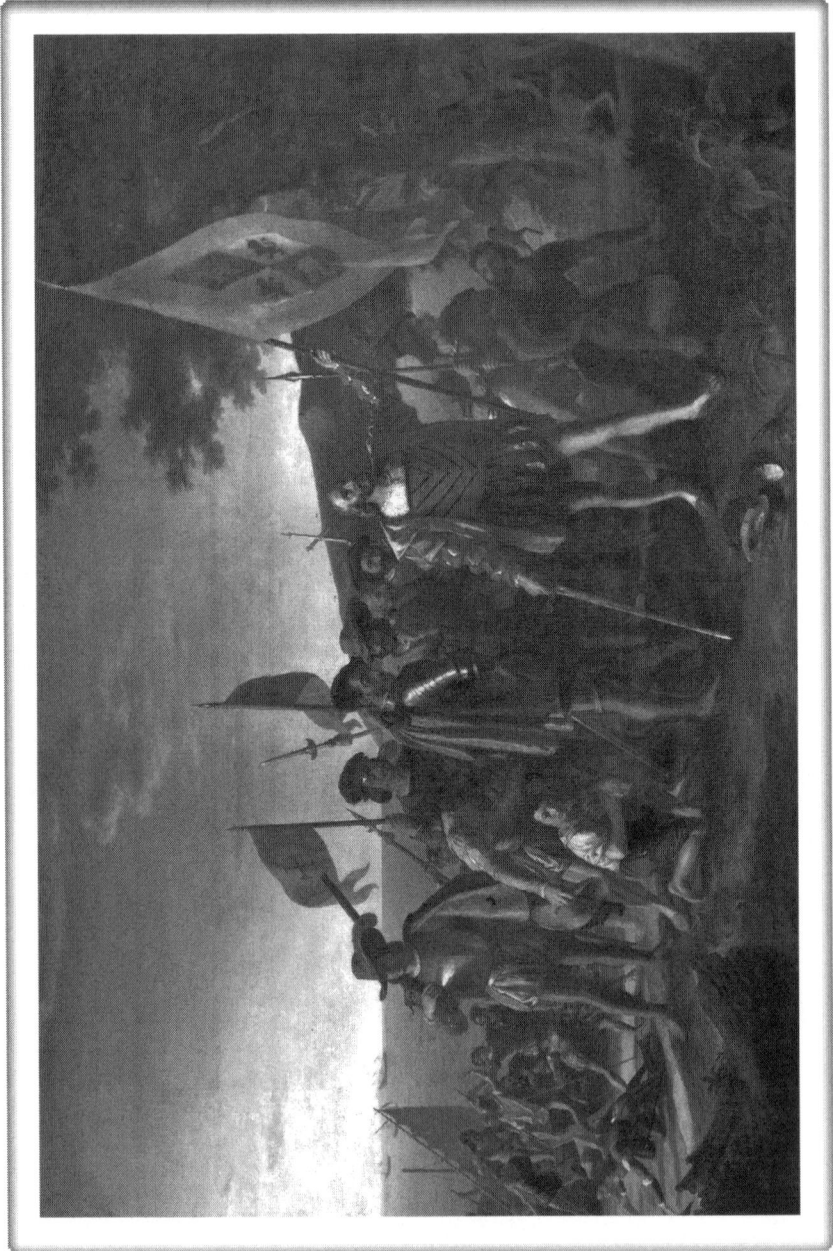

Landing of Columbus, by John Vanderlyn.
Courtesy of the Architect of the Capitol.

CHAPTER 3

DIVINE DISCOVERY

*Our Lord unlocked my mind, sent me upon the sea, and
gave me fire for the deed. Those who heard of my
enterprise called it foolish, mocked me, and laughed. But
who can doubt but that the Holy Ghost inspired me.*

—Christopher Columbus

T ragedy struck God's earth that dreadful day that Christ's chief apostle Peter, even he who was given the "keys of the Kingdom" (Matthew16:19), was nailed upside down on a cross, murdered in cold blood. According to tradition, this occurred during the Roman persecutions under Nero, around 65 AD, and it marked the beginning of the end of the gospel on the earth.[1] Other faithful disciples would share a similar fate, as the keys of the kingdom fell upon a slippery slope to oblivion. As President Joseph Fielding Smith explained, "Satan in his wrath drove the [Church] into the wilderness, or from the earth, then in his anger the serpent continued his war upon all who had faith and sought the testimony of Jesus, desiring to worship God according to the dictates of conscience. So successful did he become that his dominion extended over all the world."[2]

The long, dark night of apostasy had set in, just as ancient prophets had foretold. But, as President Smith indicated above, the adversary did not only attack the Church, but also attacked a fundamental foundation of (and prerequisite for) the Church: man's ability to worship according to "the dictates of conscience." The adversary had once again employed his age-old stratagem of striking God's children where he could best hamper their eternal progression; and so—as had occurred so many times before—"Satan rebelled...and sought to *destroy the agency of man*" (Moses 4:3-4, emphasis added). The adversary's success in this wicked endeavor is reflected in the fact that during the era of this great apostasy from the gospel fullness (or as some historians call it, the Dark Ages) virtually all governments took a page from Satan's war plan and wickedly oppressed, controlled, and/or limited their subjects, thus keeping the people from God and truth. Satan's influence over governments and men had caused such a withdrawal of light and inspiration, that he not only drove out the Church, but nearly drove out any possibility for God to establish a national covenant among His children. The adversary certainly knew the power of a national covenant in God's plan, and so he fought to subdue it.[3]

This dark era of world history was by no means Satan's first or last attempt to attack man's agency (again, Satan's efforts in this evil endeavor began in the pre-mortal existence, and continue still), but it was certainly one of his most successful ones. As such, the Lord would not stand idly by; for He had promised that His true gospel would be restored in the latter-days. And naturally, if the Lord was to commence His foretold latter-day restoration of the gospel, He would first have to restore a fullness of freedom and agency where that gospel might flourish. He would need to counter Satan's attack by establishing a national covenant. This new national covenant would require a new land, far from the poisonous environment of the Old World. This new land of the covenant was foreordained to be America.

With so much riding on America, its discovery and settlement would be no casual undertaking. As discussed earlier, the scriptures suggest this discovery and settlement would come about in a divine way. God would raise up a choice people and bring them "over the wall" to America, the land of their inheritance, where, under the American Covenant, *liberty, protection,* and *prosperity* would together support and enhance the agency necessary for mankind to progress and find access to the saving principles and ordinances of the gospel. But is there anything in the historical annals of America that support such scriptural claims? Did the discoverers and settlers of this land say or do anything that would corroborate the truthfulness of this scriptural and prophetic narrative? The answer to these questions is, most definitely, *yes!* And the next two chapters will prove it. We will see how the historical record is clear that these discoverers and settlers of America truly arrived under God and the American Covenant, settled their land under God and the American Covenant, and strived to live under God and the American Covenant. And this they did that God's work and glory might thrive.

The Raw Land

As America had always been a choice land, it is fitting that even a cursory review of America's raw, physical state—even the land itself before any latter-day heirs would arrive and develop it—demonstrates its inspired and preordained place under this national covenant. For example, the happy void of any obvious or credible oppressive force already on the American continent would enable God to influence and manipulate righteous political systems for His purposes, thus encouraging the reign of *liberty*. Furthermore, its abundant natural resources (from precious metals, to fertile ground, to rivers, to harbors, etc.) would allow for *prosperity* to flourish among its future inhabitants. And finally, its deep physical isolation, created by super-sized oceans on either side, would provide built-in *protection* against foreign evil-doers. In short—and not coincidently —the raw land itself would offer the beginnings of the three gospel-necessary blessings of the American Covenant: *liberty, prosperity,* and *protection*. This special land had certainly been set aside and reserved for a special purpose. Indeed, there was great wisdom in the Lord's keeping this promised land "from the knowledge of other nations" (2 Nephi 1:8) until He could bring His chosen ones to inhabit and inherit it according to His will (see 2 Nephi 1:5-6). This He did for both the ancient American Covenant-makers as well for the modern ones—and all for the same gospel purpose.

Additionally, the New World's vastness would provide God's restored Church, the Church of Jesus Christ of Latter-day Saints, with the ability to dodge (to some extent) the inevitable attacks and persecution promoted by the adversary; for there was always more land and territories to which the Saints could flee. And this vastness did more than provide limited safety from foes. It also provided an adequate venue whereby many cities consecrated to the Lord, even "stakes of Zion," could be developed. According to Joseph Smith's biographer, Richard Bushman, "only in the New World could such a scheme have been conceived, much less carried out."

> In the more tightly packed societies of the Old World, only kings and nobles dreamed of founding towns, while in the United States, spectators laid out hundreds of towns on the millions of acres stretching westward from the edges of settlement. The open landscape unleashed Joseph [Smith's] imagination. He became a developer, promoting the Church's land in Missouri...later Illinois [and by his influence, further west in the Rocky Mountains]. American conditions allowed him to move beyond the organization of a church toward the creation of a society. Rather than establishing beachheads in the form of church buildings all over the country, he took over a complete city, occupying all its space, consecrating every activity to God.[4]

Perhaps such a plan was necessary for the early Church, and perhaps at some point in the future, when the city Zion in Missouri is established, it will be necessary again. After all, Joseph envisioned

Zion as the capital, with sister cities throughout the land. "People could gather to any of these cities....where missionaries flowed out...and converts poured back in. The exchange would redeem the world in the last days."[5] Such prophetic vision gives further significance to the necessity of the discovery of new and vast territories, the likes of which America could provide.

As inspired as the raw, physical land of America was, however, it would remain in an embryonic state until the Lord brought His chosen ones to discover and settle it. Only then would the blessings of its national covenant come to fruition, allowing America to fill the measure of its creation.

The Renaissance

We scripturally established in the previous chapter how the Lord would bring to pass the discovery and settlement of the land America. After having selected and led His chosen ones to European lands, He would then lead them, in His due time, to the New World. But before they could attain the New World, two questions would need answering. First, how would the chosen discoverers journey the great distance from apostate Europe to the Promised Land? And second, how would the Lord identify and prepare these chosen, would-be American settlers and covenant-makers from among the European masses? God would provide answers and solutions to these questions and concerns through the inspired era of the European Renaissance.

It was during the fourteenth- and fifteenth-centuries that the dark clouds of apostasy began to part ever so slightly. The Lord began to open the heavens just enough to inspire a flourishing in the arts, sciences, and literature. Beautiful cathedrals were built, world famous artwork was created, advancements in medicine came forth, and printing by movable type was developed. People began to see outside the oppressive box that was the Dark Ages. It was a time of rebirth known today as the Renaissance. Among the many progressive happenings of the time, certain developments stand in the forefront as accomplishing the purposes of God. As Elder Bruce R. McConkie observed: "Beginning in the 14th century, the Lord began to prepare those social, educational, religious, economic, and governmental conditions under which he could more easily restore the gospel for the last time."[6]

One such development was the discovery of the compass. Though actually invented by the Chinese in around 1000 AD, it was rediscovered and further developed by the Europeans during the Renaissance period. Its usage launched both maritime trade and exploration to unprecedented levels.[7] The world's horizon began to extend a little further, and the Promised Land of God, even the New World, advanced to the brink of discovery.

While the compass would serve as a tool of deliverance to the Promised Land, the Lord would still need a way to develop a chosen people who would serve as the "delivered." The Lord, in large part, fulfilled this requirement through the inspired invention of the Gutenberg printing press in 1455. With the new and massive availability of literature, thanks to this brilliant development of the Renaissance, millions began to read the Bible and ask questions for the first time.[*] They began to seek out personal testimonies of God and establish relationships with Him. This led them to the realization of the true spiritual state of the world—that an apostasy from God's gospel had occurred. As these enlightened ones grew in both numbers and in their spiritual understanding, it would only be a matter of time before the Lord had enough of who He needed to begin the discovery and settlement of His new land and covenant.

Incidentally, as this spiritual growth of the would-be American Covenant-makers was born from the fruit of the Gutenberg press, it becomes ever significant that out of more than 130,000,000 items in the U.S. Library of Congress' collection, one of

---

[*] In the 1430's, Johann Gansfleisch zum Gutenberg developed a technique for mechanical printing. His invention "arrived in a world hungry for mental stimulation…. Within just fifty years of his first press, over twelve million books had been printed in more than one thousand print shops." From *Prelude to the Restoration, The 33rd Annual Sidney B. Sperry Symposium* (Salt Lake City: Deseret Book, 2004), 270-71.

the only two items on permanent display in the Library's Great Hall is a Gutenberg Bible (the other item is also a Bible).[8]

One person in particular who was inspired by the proliferation of the Bible, and who in turn inspired the would-be American-covenant-makers, was a German monk named Martin Luther. Luther longed for a purer Christianity, and so on October 31, 1517, he nailed to the door of the Wittenberg Church his Ninety-five Theses, which exposed and challenged certain false principles espoused by the Roman Catholic Church. The religious movement known as the Reformation had been born, as had a hero in the eyes of true Christian disciples.[9] It is of little wonder that Martin Luther was among those chosen spirits whose temple work was done as a result of Wilford Woodruff's vision in the St. George Temple.[10]

But Luther was not alone in his mission, as others would also help truth seekers discover some light in the darkness of the apostasy. This they did at great risk, knowing their actions would upset the authoritarian and oppressive religious order of the day. There was, for example, John Wycliffe, who produced the first English translation of the Bible in 1455, which ultimately inspired Luther's progression.[11] Another was the martyr William Tyndale, whose own translation of the Bible in 1526 had a direct influence both on the King James Version of the Bible and, sadly, on his own state-sponsored execution order for heresy in 1536. Before his life was taken, Tyndale publicly, and perhaps with a prophetic glimpse into the days of gospel restoration, justified his translation to his critics, saying, "I will cause a boy that driveth the plough shall know more of the scripture than thou dost."[12]

The list of persecuted reformers would continue on from John Zwingli, who convinced Zurich, Switzerland, that the Bible, not creeds and ceremony, was the only true religious standard, to John Calvin, who did the same in Geneva. And then there was John Knox, who helped spread these inspired ideas to the rest of Europe.[13] Speaking of these men, and the countless others like them, Joseph Fielding Smith declared:

In preparation for the restoration, the Lord...gave them power to break the shackles which bound the people and denied them the sacred right to worship God according to the dictates of conscience....Latter-day Saints pay honor to these great and fearless reformers, who shattered the fetters which bound the religious world. The Lord was their Protector in this mission, which was fraught with many perils. In that day, however, the time had not come for the restoration of the fullness of the gospel. The work of the reformers was of great importance... it was a preparatory work.[14]

We should thank our Heavenly Father for the mass printing of the Bible and for the reformers who encouraged its distribution. The fruits of these efforts inspired a reformed religious thought which, consequently, produced purer generations of Christians— even hundreds upon thousands of open-minded, God-fearing men and women, brave enough to ask questions and seek truth. It was, after all, from among these truth-seekers, inspired by the newly available Bible, that God would choose his first latter-day American Covenant-makers, leading them to the New World for the purposes of Heaven: to establish a new nation for the restoring of an old gospel.

Christopher Columbus

With the developments and progress surrounding both compass and printing press in Renaissance Europe, the Lord had set the stage for a major movement toward gospel restoration—the discovery and settlement of the Promised Land. Both the vehicle and the chosen ones it would carry were taking their places backstage. So significant were these events, that the Lord showed a part of them in vision to the Prophet Nephi over two-thousand years before they would commence. Immediately after describing the sickly state of the latter-day world in apostasy, as it had been shown him (see 1 Nephi 13:4-11), Nephi relates what was revealed to him as a pivotal moment of divine remedy. "And I looked and beheld a man among the Gentiles, who was separated from the seed of my brethren by the many waters; and I beheld the Spirit of God, that it came down and wrought upon the man; and he went forth upon the many waters, even unto the seed of my brethren, who were in the promised land" (1 Nephi 13: 12). Modern confirmation reveals that Christopher Columbus was in fact this appointed man sent on this divine mission.[15] (It should be noted that, as explained in the LDS *Bible Dictionary*, to be labeled a *Gentile*, particularly in the Book of Mormon, does not preclude one from being a literal descendant of the House of Israel.)[16]

Armed with the necessary tools and spirituality provided to him through the inspired era of the Renaissance, the chosen Columbus was prepared to fulfill Nephi's prophetic vision. He was prepared to be the instrument in God's hand who would find that New World which had been divinely set apart. And he was prepared to be the servant who would make known this discovery to Europe, even that land containing the remnants of scattered Israel. And with the news of this great discovery, these latter-day Israelites could then follow God's promptings and settle America, claim their blessings of the promised American Covenant, and thus serve God in ushering in the fullness of His gospel. Of such was the significance of Columbus and his discovery.

The following historical analysis of Columbus' life and writings serve as proof of his profoundly divine role in God's latter-day work and glory. We will see that Columbus, in his capacity as American Covenant-maker, did knowingly covenant with God in discovering the Promised Land. Furthermore, he even seemed to be blessed with at least a rudimentary knowledge of what great spiritual blessings his discovery would bring to the world. As we now explore these historical insights into this great discoverer, it will become obvious why he and his divine mission related to America are included in the Book of Mormon, even that book which is our greatest source of American Covenant literature.

★ ★ ★ ★

Born near Genoa, Italy, in the midst of the Renaissance, Columbus, from his earliest days, seemed connected with God and recognized heaven's influence in his life. Columbus wrote:

> When I was a young boy, I went to sea to sail and I
> continue to do it today....I have found our Lord very well
> disposed towards my desire, and I have from him the spirit
> of intelligence for carrying it out. He has bestowed the
> marine arts upon me in abundance and that which is
> necessary to me from astrology, geometry, and drawing
> spheres and situating upon them the towns, the rivers,
> mountains, islands and ports, each in its proper place.[17]

Columbus eventually married the daughter of the governor of a small Portuguese island in the western-most parts of the known Atlantic. Columbus and his wife moved to this island where Columbus became acquainted with maps and map-making. These maps excited him into a divine conviction of the existence of an untapped western route to the Indies.[18] He would solicit support from various governments for his exploration of this proposed route (ultimately convincing Spain to finance the enterprise), by emphasizing the economic benefits of more rapid and efficient trade, particularly the spice trade from the Indies. However, as the following historical references suggest, Columbus knew his desired mission meant more than this; he knew God had a wiser and more profound purpose for his western exploration.

This more profound purpose was perhaps revealed to Columbus through his consistent study of the Bible, which was made available to him through the above-referenced developments of the inspired Renaissance. According to one renowned Columbus scholar, he "was a careful student of the Bible."

> He studied it systematically together with the opinions of
> learned scholars and commentators who were held in the
> highest regard in his day. The focus of the discoverer's

interest was the prophesied latter-day enlargement of the Christian Church which would take place through the discovery and evangelization of all the world's nations and tribes, with the consequent renewal and enrichment of Christendom.[19]

Columbus perhaps sensed the advent of the Restoration. And he would stop at nothing to facilitate its coming.

But his vision of a gospel restoration ran deeper than his desire and intention to simply enlarge and enrich Christendom. He understood that something much bigger was at stake. Indeed, by embarking upon his journey, he was working towards a goal that would touch the very core of God's latter-day Restoration. Columbus' mind and heart was locked on the temple of God! As the renowned LDS scholar Hugh Nibley pointed out, "[Columbus] wished to discover the Indies to get enough money to rebuild the temple [at Jerusalem]," so that his fellow Christians might "go back to the temple to the Holy of Holies."[20] In her 2006 article, "Columbus's Goal: Jerusalem," Stanford scholar Carol Delaney laments the fact that, even today, too many intellectuals—blinded by preconceived notions—fail to see that "[Columbus'] ultimate goal, the purpose behind the enterprise, was Jerusalem!" She concludes that Columbus firmly believed that "what he accomplished was not so much a 'discovery' but a revelation—an important step in uncovering God's plan."[21] Delaney's colleague, Leonard Sweet, adds that Columbus' voyage was not a commercial venture as much as it was a "spiritual quest" and a "medium of redemption."[22]

The evidence of Columbus' inspired vision is clear and convincing. As he stated in his personal diary (from his initial 1492 voyage), he planned to take any monetary gain from his discovery and direct it to the "Holy Sepulchre."[23] Some ten years later, his life still dedicated to the development and further exploration of the New World, he maintained this vision. Columbus declared, "This enterprise was undertaken with the purpose of expending what was invested in aiding the holy temple and the holy Church."[24]

Furthermore, Columbus firmly believed, and testified, that Spain's financing of his voyage was a fulfillment of a certain prophecy. According to the Abbot Joachin, "Jerusalem and Mount Zion [were] to be rebuilt by the hand of a Christian" from Spain. Columbus recited this prophecy and declared himself to be that very Christian.[25] At one point during his voyage, one of his ships ran into serious trouble. And the record implies that, in that moment of doubt, the only thing that really concerned Columbus was whether his possible failure might hurt his ability to help rebuild Jerusalem and her temple.[26] Up until the day before his death, Columbus was still working on setting up a fund for the purpose of liberating and rebuilding Jerusalem.[27]

Remarkably, Columbus' mission and discovery would largely fulfill his intended goal. For after he found and publicized the New World, the Lord would carry His chosen ones to settle it, establish His national covenant therein, and finally, bring the fullness of His gospel, complete with temples, first to America, then to the rest of the world. This would include the establishment of a New Jerusalem in America. And this will, according to prophecies by Joseph Smith and others, eventually lead to the rebuilding of a temple in New Jerusalem (in America) and also in Old Jerusalem—just as Columbus had envisioned.[28]*

Columbus' vision of a rebuilt Jerusalem created a special place in his heart for the Jewish people. In light of the generally negative attitudes towards Jews in Columbus' day, particularly in Spain, Columbus' feelings of attachment to them is remarkable. He often spoke of his admiration for the Hebrew nation and his desire to be one with them. Perhaps this had to do with Columbus' inspired notion (if only an inclination) about who he really was.

---

* In light of Columbus' vision of what his discovery would bring, we might find something of the prophetic in the United States' role in assisting and allying itself with the modern nation-state of Israel. As the covenant blessings flow out of America and into Israel, the future and prophesied of temple in Israel will have a firmer foundation upon which to be built and maintained.

Columbus' son wrote about his father, stating, "[His] progenitors were of the Royal Blood of Jerusalem."[29]

With knowledge of Columbus' deep conviction of true gospel principles, and with an understanding of his belief that these principles were related to his western exploration, we are now prepared to understand the richness of his story. We are now prepared to comprehend profound aspects of his western exploration that would otherwise fall by the wayside.

And so, as the story goes, Columbus secured three ships for his journey—the *Nina*, *Pinta*, and *Santa Maria*—all of which embarked on August 2, 1492. As could be expected, considering the nature of this particular voyage, the crew was apprehensive and restless from the beginning. As the weeks passed without success, and with rations diminished to threatening levels, murmurings of mutiny began resounding through the decks of the ships. Eventually the captains of the other vessels informed Columbus that the men could no longer be restrained. Columbus asked for three days. Though there is no record of what Columbus did next, one might assume he dedicated himself to much prayer. There is at least one indication that perhaps some spiritual confirmation was received. For on the night he spoke to his captains, Columbus wrote in his journal that the root meaning of his own name was *Christo-feren*, or "Christ-bearer."[30] The discoverer was so overcome by this self-recognition, that he even changed his official signature to represent this new title.[31]

Before the three days had expired, signs of land appeared, and on October 12, 1492, the ships landed on the shore of a Caribbean island. With Native Americans watching in awe, Columbus disembarked triumphantly, then, with tears streaming down his face, gave thanks to the Almighty, in Whose honor he named the land San Salvador ("Holy Savior").[32]

That Columbus would praise God for this discovery was only natural; for he knew it was the power of God that made his discovery possible. He was not shy about expressing this fact. For example, on a particularly difficult occasion during one of his New

World explorations, Columbus received a revelation, which he himself later described in the following words:

> Exhausted, I fell asleep, groaning. I heard a very compassionate voice, saying: "O fool and slow to believe and to serve thy God, the God of all!...Thou criest for help, doubting. Answer, who has afflicted thee so greatly and so often, God or the world?...Not one jot of His word fails; all that He promises, He performs with interest; is this the manner of men? I have said that which thy creator has done for thee and does for all men. Now in part He shows thee the reward for the anguish and danger which thou hast endured in the service of others." I heard all of this as if I were in a trance, but I had no answer to give to words so true, but could only weep for my errors. He, whoever he was, who spoke to me, ended saying: "Fear not; have trust; all these tribulations are written upon marble and are not without cause."[33]

Further proof of Columbus' understanding of the covenant nature of his journey is represented in the events surrounding his return voyage to Spain. Knowing that the news of the great discovery would begin a chain of events leading to a gospel restoration, the adversary seemed intent on doing all possible to deny Columbus' return; for the storms against them raged so violently that the crew believed they would not make it. The adversary certainly knew that if Columbus and his crew were to perish, so would news of the discovery perish with them.

Columbus responded by leading his crew in much prayer. This, of course, was not unusual for Columbus. He was known for holding regular church services on deck.[34] However, this particular set of prayers was perhaps more pronounced than the others. As days passed with no reprieve from the storm, the crew decided to make an offering to God. They promised that if their lives were spared, they would make a pilgrimage to a chapel back home and hold a special meeting and worship service. Lots were drawn on at least three occasions in the midst of the storm to determine who would lead the pilgrimage. All three times it fell on Columbus himself. The crew believed it a sign from God (the odds against Columbus picking the winner all three times were 60,880 to 1). When the ship finally arrived off the shores of Portugal, with hardly a sail having remained intact, the crew knew who it was that had brought them safely to harbor. The covenant was in force.[35]

But perhaps the greatest proof of Columbus' knowledge of God's hand in these historic events is found in his personal testimony, as written by his own hand: "Our Lord unlocked my mind, sent me upon the sea, and gave me fire for the deed. Those who heard of my enterprise called it foolish, mocked me, and laughed. But who can doubt but that the Holy Ghost inspired me?"[36]

In a similar spirit, Columbus wrote the following to the king and queen of Spain concerning his discovery of America. The following is recorded in a little-known collection of Columbus' writings, known as his *Libro de las profecias*, or his *Book of Prophecies*:

> With a hand that could be felt, the Lord opened my mind to the fact that it would be possible to sail from here to the Indies, and He opened my will to desire to accomplish the project. This was the fire that burned within me when I came to visit Your Highnesses. All who found out about my project denounced it with laughter and ridiculed me....Only Your Majesties had faith and perseverance. Who can doubt that this fire was not merely mine, but also of the Holy Spirit who encouraged me with a radiance of marvelous illumination from his sacred Holy Scriptures, by a most clear and powerful testimony from the forty-four books of the Old Testament, from the four Gospels, from the twenty-three Epistles of the blessed Apostles—urging me to press forward? Continually, without a moment's hesitation, The Scriptures urge me to press forward with great haste.

I spent six years here at your royal court, disputing the case with so many people of great authority, learned in all the arts. Finally they concluded that it was in vain, and they lost interest. In spite of that, [the voyage west] later came to pass as Jesus Christ our Savior had predicted and as He had previously announced through the mouths of His holy prophets. [37]

The fact that the Lord had, actually, "predicted" Columbus' discovery through the Prophet Nephi (over two-thousand years earlier) makes this statement by Columbus especially astonishing. Also astonishing is the fact that Columbus—though he did not have access to the Book of Mormon—recognized Biblical passages that reflected the sacred work God had accomplished through him. In support of his claim that the Lord "predicted" his discovery through His prophets, Columbus included within his *Book of Prophecies*, a number of Biblical references. Among these references are certain noteworthy prophecies: Isaiah 14:1-2, Isaiah 66:19 and John 10:16. [38]

Isaiah 14:1-2 reads: "For the Lord will have mercy on Jacob, and will yet choose Israel, and set them in their own land: and the strangers shall be joined with them, and they shall cleave to the house of Jacob. And the people shall take them...and the house of Israel shall possess them in the land of the Lord." This scripture ties into Columbus' discovery in that it appears to make reference to the promises of the American Covenant, as detailed in Chapter 2 of this study. For it references heaven's gift of a new land given to the descendants of Jacob and Israel, which gift would be a blessing also to other groups of God's children who would join Israel.

Isaiah 66:19 similarly prophesies the following: "And I will set a sign among them...to the islands afar off, to them that have not heard my fame, neither have seen my glory; and they shall declare my glory among the Gentiles."

John 10:16 reads: "And other sheep I have, which are not of this fold: them also I must bring, and they shall hear my voice; and there shall be one fold and one shepherd." This scripture, familiar in LDS theology, refers to Christ's glorious visit to the ancient inhabitants of America, as recorded in the Book of Mormon (3 Nephi 15:21). But what connection is to be made between this scripture and Columbus' discovery? One connection is the fact that the ancient Book of Mormon inhabitants that received Christ's visit were, quite possibly, the ancestors of those Native Americans who witnessed Columbus' arrival. But more than that, Columbus' arrival meant that a renewed advent of Christ to these more modern Native American inhabitants was on the horizon, as his discovery would pave the way for Ephraim to enter the Americas and eventually provide them the restored gospel, the Book of Mormon, and (in essence) Jesus Christ Himself. Indeed, Columbus' discovery began a series of events that might cause us to believe that the more modern Native Americans were also the "other sheep" who would at last be able to "hear my voice; and there shall be one fold and one Shepard" (3 Nephi 15:21). Perhaps this New Testament prophecy was meant also to include—in addition to the ancient American inhabitants—a more modern remnant of Lehi's descendants. After all, Christ promised Lehi's people (the Native Americans) that he would "remember my covenant" and return to them in the last days (3 Nephi 16:11-12).

Amazingly, Columbus' scriptural references, which he clearly implied were related to his voyage and discovery, have direct connections to the gospel restoration in the last days, particularly America's place in it. Yet few, if any, understood these ancient prophecies to possess such meaning until the scriptures of the restoration (the Book of Mormon, Doctrine and Covenants, etc.) arrived hundreds of years later to clarify these points. Again, one is compelled to consider how much revealed knowledge Columbus really possessed concerning the significance of what he had accomplished.

In light of the above, it seems likely that, at some point, Columbus truly understood that his discovery of the New World meant a renewed opportunity for the Lord to restore His gospel to the earth. This might explain the following words he wrote to his friend Amerigo Vespucci: "I feel persuaded, by the many and wonderful manifestations of Divine Providence, that I am the chosen instrument of God in bringing to pass a great event—no less than the conversion of millions who are now existing in the darkness...."[39] He would similarly inform the king and queen of Spain that, with his discovery now completed, "[t]he Gospel must now be proclaimed to so many lands in such a short time."[40] Columbus was especially desirous and anxious for this spiritual endeavor concerning the New World to develop sooner rather than later. For he voiced his opinion often that the end of times was fast approaching, and that his mission in the New World was key to preparing the way for the Second Coming.[41] The very first sentence Columbus placed in his sacred *Book of Prophecies* perhaps sums it up best: "Here begins the book, or handbook, of sources, statements, opinions and prophecies on the subject of the recovery of God's Holy City and Mount Zion, and on the discovery and evangelization of the isles of the Indies and of all other peoples and nations."[42]

In a symbolic gesture of Columbus' divine missionary intentions and profound understanding about his voyages, he insisted on erecting a large cross upon every island he landed upon.[43] Considering what his discovery would eventually mean in a land which had forgotten the Christ, his symbolic gesture was profound.

Apart from his obvious interactions with the Spirit, Columbus' deeper gospel comprehension might also have been inspired by another special visitor from heaven. According to the latter-day apostle Orson Hyde, the Angel Moroni, who he called the "Prince of America," influenced Columbus on his journey. According to Elder Hyde, Moroni gave Columbus "deep impressions, by dreams and by visions, respecting the New World." He said Moroni "was with him on the stormy deep, calmed the troubled elements, and guided his frail vessel to the desired haven."[44]

But whatever his knowledge might have been, one thing is certain: considering all the aforementioned historical evidence, a second look at Nephi's vision of Columbus leaves us with an added sense of the discoverer's divine mission. To again quote Nephi: "And I beheld the Spirit of God, that it came down and wrought upon the man; and he went forth upon the many waters, even unto the seed of my brethren, who were in the promised land" (1 Nephi 13:12). Columbus heard the call of the American Covenant and bravely adhered. And the world took one giant step closer to the glorious restoration of the gospel. Fittingly, this Book of Mormon chapter, wherein we find this Columbus prophecy, affirms the idea that the gospel restoration was the ultimate purpose of this American discovery; for, after outlining Columbus' divine mission, (and after outlining the similarly divine missions of other early Americans to be discussed later), this chapter concludes by indicating that all such inspired historical events culminate into one final fruit—the great gospel restoration (see 1 Nephi 13: 34-41).

Columbus' dying words were: "In mansus tuas, Domine, commendo spiritum meum" (into thy hands Lord I commend my spirit).[45] It is of little wonder that Christopher Columbus was among those choice spirits whose work was performed pursuant to Wilford Woodruff's grand vision in the St. George Temple. His gospel covenants were at last administered.[46] The temple he had sought to claim his entire life had at last fully enveloped him. It would appear that he finally came to know how the promptings and revelations he had received in mortality were correct—that his discovery had, in fact, led to the restoration of temple worship. Remarkably, in St. George he became a direct beneficiary of the ultimate fruits of his mortal accomplishment.

★ ★ ★ ★

In addition to the historical evidences above, there exists another account, though anecdotal in nature, worth mentioning regarding Columbus' discovery of America and its connection to the restored gospel. In his work entitled *The Life and Voyages of Christopher Columbus*, the renowned American historian and author, Washington Irving, spends much time discussing the spiritual inspiration of

Columbus, and how he seemed to be "selected by Heaven as an agent" in carrying out his western explorations.[47] Irving then recounts a report he discovered—while poring over documents in Spain—which describes an event that allegedly occurred during Columbus' exploration of the Caribbean. According to the report, one member of Columbus' crew, an archer, while hunting for wild game on the island known today as Cuba, encountered three strange looking men. These men "were of as fair complexions as Europeans" and were wearing long "white tunics reaching to their knees." The strangers were described as being "so like a friar of the order of St. Mary of Mercy." The three were interacting with a tribe of Natives. Frightened at the scene, the archer ran back to the ship and told his commander what he had witnessed. Columbus then sent at least two separate expeditions to search for the three men, but to no avail.[48]

Irving then apologizes for including the account in his book, as no corroborating evidence existed that such light skinned people wearing such clothing resided in the New World at the time of the discovery and exploration. Though Irving concluded that the story was most likely born of error, he did feel so inclined to include it in his book.

Responding to Irving's account years later, Brigham Young University scholar E.D. Partridge wrote the following for the *Improvement Era*:

> No apology is needed...by the Latter-day Saints. The account given by the archer portrays conditions just as they would naturally be with the "Three [Nephite] Disciples." They lived among the people when the vision recorded in 1st Nephi was taught [Nephi's vision of Columbus]. They were, of course, looking forward to its fulfillment. They were to bring souls to Christ till he should come again, and had probably been busy gathering bands of followers all over the country....Columbus and his sailors were looked upon by the natives as visitors from heaven, and their appearance was heralded all over the country. Their movements were watched closely from the

shores, since whenever they landed they found themselves not unexpected. It does not take much imagination to see the "disciples" and one of their bands following the movements of the ships from the trees or mountains, awaiting a favorable opportunity to make themselves known. In fact, there is nothing in the report of the archer which is in the least at variance with what might be expected from our knowledge of the Book of Mormon.[49]

Perhaps Irving's find and publication of the archer's story was divinely inspired. If so, it may be relevant to note that Irving, who also wrote volumes on the founding era (himself being a witness to much of it), was also counted among the "other eminent men," along with Columbus, who's temple work was done pursuant to Wilford Woodruff's St. George Temple miracle.[50]

There is possible corroboration of the idea that the Three Nephites were present for the discovery. The evidence stems from an event recorded by the historian, Bartolome de Las Casas, who was a personal friend of Columbus. During the crucial moments at sea, as described above, when Columbus agreed, on threat of mutiny, to find land within three days or turn around, he would spend time fretting and watching for signs of land late into the night. On the final night, Columbus and one of his crew members spotted a small light due west, shining from the direction they were traveling. According to Las Casas, Columbus said the light "was like a small wax candle being raised and lowered." Columbus believed it was a heavenly sign (perhaps someone holding a candle, awaiting them?), and it gave him encouragement to press forward at a more rapid pace. Shortly thereafter, a cliff was spotted in the moonlight; the Americas had been discovered.[51]

Were the Three Nephites (3 Nephi 28:29) truly present and involved during this historic occasion? If so, it only adds to the miraculous and God-driven event that was the discovery of the modern-day Promised Land.

★ ★ ★ ★

Notwithstanding the greatness of Columbus' work under God, as recently explained, there has been a growing sentiment in the world to degrade him and his accomplishments. His detractors regularly offer up two criticisms: first is the allegation that Columbus forced the Natives into an oppressive socio-political state, and second is the allegation that Columbus really did not discover anything, as people were already inhabiting the land upon his arrival.

Admittedly, Columbus did support a policy of forced servitude upon certain segments of the Native American population, and at times even commanded violent death raids upon them. Before the critics condemn him all at once, however, certain contextual explanations should be noted. For one thing, though Columbus came in peace, and initially thought he had secured peace with the Natives, there were many violent Native uprisings against him and his crew, which resulted in bloodshed on both sides.[52] While this does not justify the tragedies that fell upon the Native Americans at the hands of the discoverers, it at least explains the fear and paranoia which led to Columbus' controversial actions. Furthermore, Columbus did, at one point, come to recognize the immoral conditions being forced upon the Natives. He argued that the Natives should be converted to Christ "by love and friendship rather than force."[53] Additionally, in a letter dated from 1496 to the king and queen of Spain, he wrote: "Procure for the Indians, that are coming under our rule, the same protections as those we have been speaking of [in Spain]...I want them to have the same protection like I have as if they were my own flesh."[54] Columbus wrote a similar plea the following year, but his letters did little to curve the terrifying fate that was to fall upon the Natives, as seen in vision by Nephi (see 1 Nephi 13:14).

There is no question that Columbus made mistakes in his dealings with the Natives, making him susceptible to a vast array of criticism and scrutiny. But Columbus surely recognized these failings better than any critic and openly confessed, "I am a most unworthy sinner, but I have cried out to the Lord for grace and mercy, and they have covered me completely."[55] Fortunately for us all, perfection is not a requirement to be an instrument in the hands of God.

The second prominent critique of Columbus—that too much credit is given him, as America had in fact already been "discovered" centuries before him— is reflected in cries from around the nation demanding that Columbus be downgraded in our history books and educational curriculum. I remember walking on the campus of Brigham Young University one Columbus Day and witnessing a group of BYU students and Native American protestors wearing T-shirts with an image of a Native American (Indian) Chief, complete with headdress, along with the words, "Columbus Who?". Perhaps without the gospel insight into Columbus and his work, as laid out above, such behavior might be understood; but more should be expected from those blessed with the restored gospel.

No believing Latter-day Saint would suggest that Columbus' discovery somehow trumps those earlier discoveries of the Natives and their forbearers. After all, the Book of Mormon flatly contradicts such a notion, and instead honors and reveres the inspired discoveries of the earliest Native Americans. Furthermore, Columbus was not even the first *latter-day* explorer to touch down on the New World.* But these arguments are irrelevant to Columbus' greatness. For in spite of the fact that Columbus was not the first to discover the land (as it *had* indeed already been found many times before), he was the one who, in the last days, did it with the backing of the Lord and with the inspiration of the Spirit. He was also the one who, under this same inspiration, publicized his discovery at the right time and to the right people, thus commencing the great migration of those chosen ones who would come to the New World.

---

* It is recorded that hundreds of years before Columbus discovered America, explorers from Scandinavia and other parts of the world visited its shores, but they did not publicize their voyage as inspired of God and did not share their discovery in a way to inspire any mass migration. (See Greene, *The Tribe of Ephraim*, 127-128.)

And who were these chosen ones that would settle the New World? Again, these were, for the most part, the European descendants of Joseph, even the Ephraimites, whose responsibility it would be to establish a national covenant in America, and then, building upon this covenant, usher in the gospel restoration. And as we know, this restoration is the key to salvation for the dead, living, and yet unborn. As President George Q. Cannon noted: "Columbus was inspired to penetrate the ocean and discover this Western Continent, for the set time of its discovery had come.... This Church and Kingdom could not have been established on the earth if [Columbus'] work had not been performed."[56]

Perhaps the simple beauty of Columbus' accomplishment has become so obvious to some that it is taken for granted, forgotten, or even scoffed at. Though modern-day critics may never fully comprehend what his discovery really meant to the world, the restored gospel certainly informs us why Columbus should be celebrated and honored as an inspired man and a key American Covenant-maker.

Amerigo Vespucci

Columbus was not alone in his role as inspired explorer. One who would share his spotlight was the Italian explorer, Amerigo Vespucci. Vespucci was born in Florence, Italy, in 1454 to a prominent and respected family. His early education converted him into one of the rare scholars of his day, particularly in math and science. Weightier, perhaps, was his religious upbringing, which instilled in him, according to one historian, a "profound sense of dependence upon the protection of God."[57]

By 1492, when Columbus made his discovery, Vespucci was residing in Spain attending to family business. He became so enthusiastic about the discovery that he developed a long lasting friendship with Columbus. While he revered what Columbus had done, he was not shy about respectfully disagreeing with Columbus on one point: Vespucci believed that the new land was not an extension of the Eastern continents, as Columbus taught, but that it was an independent continent. He wanted to prove it and told Columbus: "I am strongly moved to tempt the ocean myself."[58]

By 1497, Vespucci had convinced the king of Spain to sponsor his voyage in order to "assist in the discovery." Shortly thereafter, Vespucci landed on the American mainland. With his skills using the astrolobe and quadrant, Vespucci was able to confirm that this land was in fact a completely separate continent, even a "New World."[59]

But what real significance does such a discovery bear on the development of America, her national covenant, and the Restoration? America and her covenant—and by extension, the restoration of the gospel—were developed out of a sense of new hope, new life, and an independent culture, completely cut off from the Old World. Without Vespucci's find, those chosen Ephraimites might not have viewed their new land in such a light, and might not have ventured out on their many journeys in the first place. They might not have known or felt that America was in fact a "new world," even a land far from the reach of oppressive rulers, where new ideas could be explored and any question could be asked; a land where a fourteen-year-old boy could pray confidently in a grove of trees, and where the Lord could reveal and grow His work and His glory. And so we should thank Vespucci for his courageous discovery.

Vespucci, like Columbus, indicated an understanding of covenant principles with God and strived to adhere to what he considered his calling. In a letter to a friend, Vespucci explained the dangerous, even life-threatening, storms that had plagued his small fleet throughout its initial voyage. He then stated that "during these tempests of sea and sky, so numerous and violent, the Most High was pleased to display before us a continent, new lands, and an unknown world....To Him be honor, glory, and thanksgiving."[60]

After his return home, the king appointed Vespucci to train every Spanish naval captain. By carrying out this particular mandate, Vespucci did much for the then future exploration and settlement of the newly discovered continent. It was during this time that the "New World," as Vespucci regularly described it, would begin to take on his first name, as scholars began referring to it as the "Land of Amerigo" (or Land of Americus). The name stuck and later evolved into *America*.[61]

As great an honor it was for Vespucci to be the namesake of the New World, it was surpassed by yet another honor, which occurred hundreds of years after his mortal existence. For in death, Vespucci was apparently granted the opportunity to receive his temple covenants, along with his old friend Columbus, in the St. George Temple. According to the records of Wilford Woodruff, Vespucci was counted among the eminent men whose work was done pursuant to the grand vision of the American nation builders.[62]

Conclusion

Upon exploring the historic facts leading up to and through the discovery of America, there is no doubt that the Lord took a very active role. He most certainly had a plan for the New World. Admittedly, His plan was still in its early phases of accomplishment, and therefore the American Covenant, while obviously present, was only just beginning to take form. But the discovery was nonetheless an essential part of God's work and glory in the latter-days; for it set the stage for the settlement of a divine land where God could at last bring forth the principles and ordinances that would lead His children to salvation.

As President Joseph Fielding Smith declared in powerful simplicity: "The discovery [of America] was one of the most important factors in bringing to pass the purpose of the Almighty in the restoration of his gospel in its fullness for the salvation of men."[63]

ENDNOTES

[1] *Church History in the Fulness of Times* (Salt Lake City: Church of Jesus Christ of Latter-day Saints, 2000), 4.

[2] Joseph Fielding Smith, *The Progress of Man* (Salt Lake City: Deseret News Press, 1952), 166.

[3] For a thorough analysis, including historical corroboration, of how the adversary executed this great apostasy on governments and gospel, see James Talmage, *The Great Apostasy* (Salt Lake City: Deseret Book Company, 1978); and Tad Callister, *The Inevitable Apostasy and the Promised Restoration* (Salt Lake City: Deseret Book, 2006).

[4] Richard L. Bushman, *Joseph Smith Rough Stone Rolling* (New York: Alfred A. Knopf, 2005), 221.

[5] Ibid, 220-221.

[6] McConkie, *Mormon Doctrine*, 717.

[7] "The Compass," available from www.neo-tech.com/businessmen/part5.html; *Church History in the Fullness of Times,* 6.

[8] Newt Gingrich, *Rediscovering God in America* (Nashville: Integrity House, 2006), 96-97.

[9] *Church History in the Fulness of Times*, 6-7.

[10] Recorded in Wilford Woodruff's journal and temple records, as quoted in Vicki Jo Anderson, *The Other Eminent Men of Wilford Woodruff,* (Malta: Nelson Book, 2000), Preface.

[11] Andrew C. Skinner, "Forerunners and Foundation Stones of the Restoration," *Prelude to the Restoration* (Salt Lake City, Deseret Book Company, 2004), 13-14.

[12] David Rolph Seely, "Words 'Fitly Spoken,' Tyndale's English Translation of the Bible," *Prelude to the Restoration* (Salt Lake City, Deseret Book Company, 2004), 212- 214.

[13] *Church History in the Fulness of Times*, 8.

[14] Joseph Fielding Smith, *Doctrines of Salvation*, comp. Bruce R. McConkie, 3 vols. (Salt Lake City: Bookcraft, 1954-56), 1:174-75.

[15] *Church History in the Fulness of Times*, 9. Some of the latter-day prophets and apostles who recognized the Lord's hand in inspiring Columbus' discovery, and who implied or declared that Nephi's vision (1 Nephi 13:12) was in fact a vision of Columbus, included Brigham Young, George Q. Cannon, Mark E. Petersen, Spencer W. Kimball and Ezra Taft Benson. These are quoted in J. Michael Hunter, *Mormon Myth-ellaneous* (American Fork: Covenant Communications, 2008), 101-102.

[16] According to the Bible Dictionary, the term *Gentile,* "as used throughout the scriptures... has a dual meaning, sometimes to designate peoples of non-Israelite lineage, and other times to designate nations that are without the gospel, even though there may be some Israelite blood therein. This latter usage is especially characteristic of the word as used in the Book of Mormon." Definition is from the "Bible Dictionary," *The Holy Bible, King James Version* (Salt Lake City: LDS Church, 1986), 679.

[17] Pauline Moffat Watts, "Prophecy and Discovery: On Spiritual Origins of Christopher Columbus' Enterprise to the Indies," *American Historical Review* (Feb.1985): 95; alternate translation of the same offered by Jacob Wasserman, *Columbus, Don Quixote of the Seas,* translated by Delno C. West, and August Kling (Gainesville, FL: 1991), as quoted in Greene, *The Tribe of Ephraim,* 117.

[18] Anderson, 115.

[19] Delano West and August Kling, in their introduction to Christopher Columbus, *Libro de las profecias,* trans. Delano C. West and August Kling (Gainesville: University of Florida Press, 1991), 3.

[20] Hugh Nibley, *Temple and Cosmos* (Salt Lake City: Deseret Book Company, 1992), 31.

[21] Carol Delaney (2006), "Columbus's Ultimate Goal: Jerusalem." *Comparative Studies in Society and History,*48, pp. 261-287.

[22] Leonard Sweet, "Christopher Columbus and the Millennial Vision of the New World," *The Catholic Historical Review* 72, 3 (1986), 383.

[23] Delaney, 261.

[24] Delaney, 266.

[25] Ferdinand Columbus, *The Life of Admiral Christopher Columbus by His Son Ferdinand Columbus* (New Brunswick: Rutgers University Press, 1959), 8; Chris and Ted Stewart, *Seven Miracles That Saved America,* 43- 44; Delaney, 266.

[26] Delaney, 275.

[27] Delaney, 266.

[28] In General Conference, April 1843, Joseph Smith prophesied that before the coming of the Lord, the temple at Jerusalem would be restored, as quoted in Gerald N. Lund, *The Coming of the Lord* (Salt Lake City: Deseret Book, 1971), 185. That a temple will be built in the New Jerusalem in America is prophesied, among other places, in D&C 84:4-5).

[29] David Hatcher Childress, *The Lost Cities of North and Central America* (Kempton: Adventures Unlimited Press, 1998), 414; See also Francesco Tarducci, *The Life of Christopher Columbus,* Volume 12 (H.F. Brownson Publishing, 1891), 2.

[30] Peter Marshal, *The Light and the Glory* (New Jersey: Fleming H. Revell Co.: 1940), 39. See also Anderson, 118.

[31] Delaney, 263.

[32] Columbus (Ferdinand), 59.

[33] Columbus, as quoted by De Lamar Jensen, "Columbus and the Hand of God," *Ensign*, October 1992, 6-13; also quoted in J. Michael Hunter, *Mormon Myth-ellaneous* (American Fork: Covenant Communications, 2008), 102-103.

[34] Delaney, 262.

[35] These events surrounding Columbus' first return to Europe are more particularly described in Marshall and Manuel, *The Light and the Glory*, 49-53.

[36] Columbus, as quoted by Jacob Wasserman, *Columbus, Don Quixote of the Seas,* translated by Delno C. West, and August Kling (Gainesville, FL: 1991); and as quoted in Greene, *The Tribe of Ephraim*, 117.

[37] Anderson, *The Other Eminent Men*, 113, 121; Also quoted in *Book of Prophecies*, translated by Delno C. West and August Kling (Gainesville: 1991); Also quoted in Greene, *Tribe of Ephraim,* 116-117.

[38] Anderson, *The Other Eminent Men*, 113; Delaney, 270-2

[39] Lester Edwards, *The Life and Voyages of Vespucci* (New York: New Amsterdam Books, 1903), 79.

[40] Christopher Columbus, as quoted by Steven Waldman, *Founding Faith: Providence, Politics and the Birth of Religious Freedom in America* (New York: Random House, 2008), 4.

[41] Delaney, 261, 263, 268-9.

[42] As quoted in Delaney, 268.

[43] Peter Marshal and David Manuel, *The Light and the Glory* (Grand Rapids: Revell, 2009), 45.

[44] Orson Hyde, "Celebration of the Fourth of July," *Journal of Discourses,* 6:368; also cited in John Lund, *Mesoamerica and the Book of Mormon* (Salt Lake: The Communications Company, 2007), 38.

[45] Columbus (Ferdinand), 284.

[46] Discourse by Wilford Woodruff, as recorded in *Journal of Discourses* (Salt Lake City: LDS Church, 1877), 19:229; Also recorded in Wilford Woodruff's journal and temple records, as quoted in Vicki Jo Anderson, *The Other Eminent Men of Wilford Woodruff*, Preface.

[47] Delaney, 274.

[48] Washington Irving, *The Life and Voyages of Christopher Columbus*, Vol. 6 (New York: Peter Fenelon Collier, 1897), 329-332.

[49] E.D. Partridge, "An Experience of One of Columbus' Sailors," *The Improvement Era* Vol. 12 (June 1909): 621-624, as quoted in R. Clayton Brough, *They Who Tarry* (Bountiful: Horizon Publishers, 1976), 60-63.

[50] Recorded in Wilford Woodruff's journal and temple records, as quoted in Vicki Jo Anderson, *The Other Eminent Men of Wilford Woodruff*, Preface

[51] Marshall and Manuel, *The Light and the Glory*, 42.

[52] Marshall and Manuel, *The Light and the Glory*, 62.

[53] Christopher Columbus, as quoted by Steven Waldman, *Founding Faith: Providence, Politics and the Birth of Religious Freedom in America* (New York: Random House, 2008), 4.

[54] Christopher Columbus, *Letters to King Ferdinand and Queen Isabel 1496 Raccolta Collection* (Roma: Raccolta di Documenti e Studi Publicati dalla R. Commissione Colombiana, pel Quarto Cenetenario dalla Scoperta dell' America, 1894), 270; as quoted in Anderson, 119.

[55] Christopher Columbus, as quoted in *God Bless America: Prayers & Reflections For Our Country* (Grand Rapids: Zondervan, 1999), 111.

[56] George Q. Cannon, as quoted by Tad Callister, *The Inevitable Apostasy and the Promised Restoration* (Salt Lake City: Deseret Book, 2006), 330.

[57] Edward Lester, *The Life and Voyages of Americus Vespucius* (New York: New Amsterdam Book Company, 1903), 62; Anderson, 366.

[58] As quoted by Anderson, 368.

[59] Anderson, 369.

[60] Amerigo Vespucci, *Mundus Novus*, translated by George Tyler Northrup (New Jersey: Princeton University Press, 1916), 17.

[61] Anderson, 370.

[62] Recorded in Wilford Woodruff's journal and temple records, as quoted in Anderson, Preface.

[63] Joseph Fielding Smith, *The Progress of Man* (Salt lake City: Deseret News Press, 1952), 166.

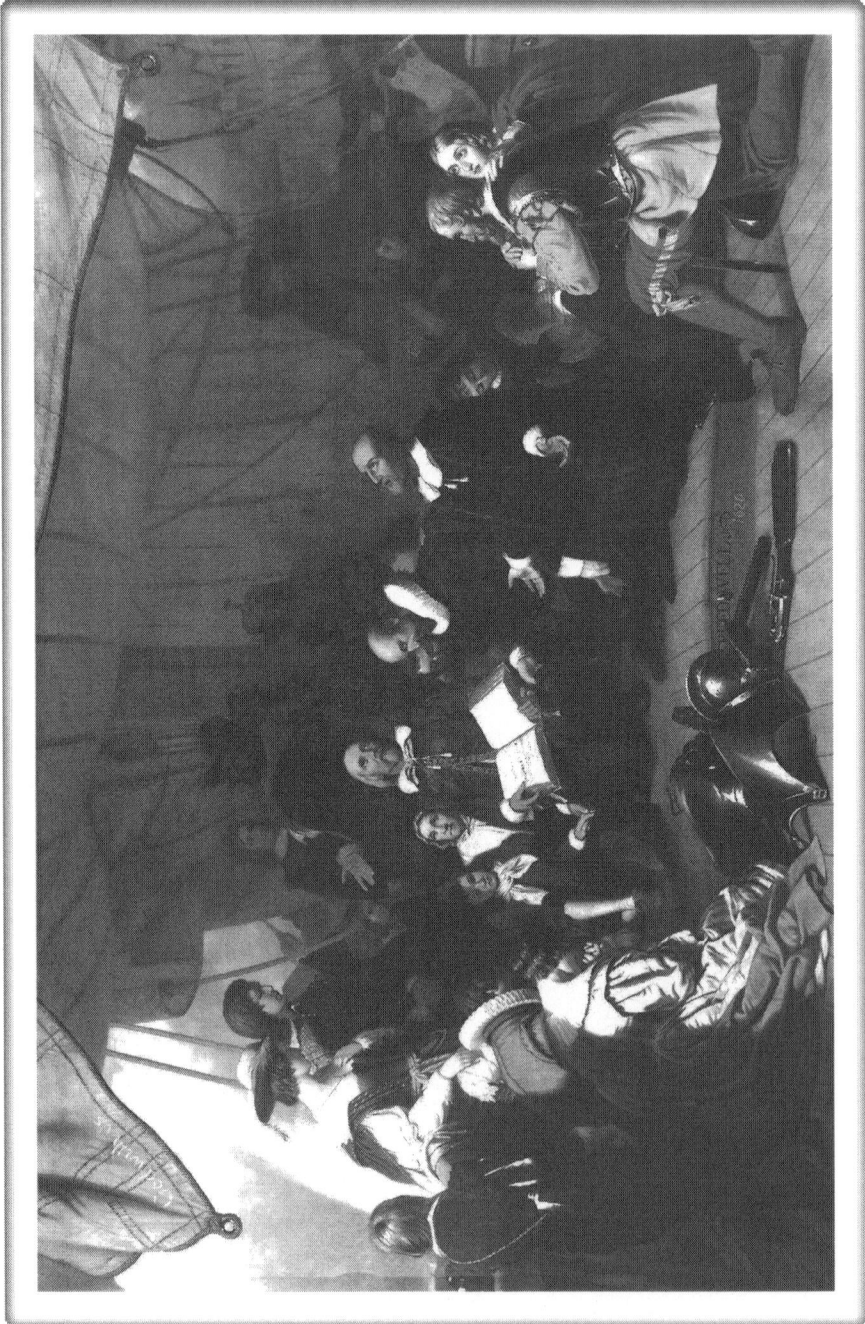

Embarkation of the Pilgrims, by Robert W. Weir.

Courtesy of the Architect of the Capitol.

CHAPTER 4

SACRED SETTLEMENT

*Now as the people of God in old time were called out
of Babylon civil, the place of their bodily bondage, and
were to come to Jerusalem, and there to build the
Lord's temple...so are the people of God now to go out
of Babylon spiritual to Jerusalem (America)...and to
build themselves as lively stones into a spiritual
house, or temple, for the Lord to dwell in....for we are
the sons and daughters of Abraham by faith.*

—Pilgrim Leader, John Robinson

With the discovery accomplished, the next phase in God's plan for America could commence: the settlement of the Promised Land by his chosen ones of the covenant. That these early migrants and settlers of America were, in fact, led and inspired by God is evidenced not only by scriptural suggestion, but also by the testimonies they themselves bore. As we will see below, the settlers understood that they were settling the land under a national covenant with God and that this covenant was connected to the ancient covenants of Israel. They further comprehended that this covenant, if adhered to through righteousness, offered the blessings of *liberty*, *protection*, and *prosperity*, and that it would ultimately take them out of the apostate world and lead them and their posterity to truth, light, and eternal salvation. And though these first American settlers would not witness the ultimate gospel fruits of their divine mission, it was their deep understanding of, and commitment to, the national covenant which provided future generations with a foundation to build upon—a foundation which would bring the fullness of the American Covenant and, in turn, bring the fullness of the gospel of Jesus Christ.

Scriptural Foundations

Immediately following his vision of Columbus, Nephi expounds on the significance of what Columbus ushered in to America: "And it came to pass that I beheld the Spirit of God, that it wrought upon other Gentiles; and they went forth out of captivity, upon the many waters. And it came to pass that I beheld many multitudes of the Gentiles upon the land of promise" (1 Nephi 13:13-14). Perhaps no other scripture describes better the images Jacob left us in his American Covenant blessing to Joseph, as recorded in Genesis 49 and as detailed in Chapter 2 of this book. Indeed, Nephi opens our eyes to see these chosen American Covenant-makers being brought "over the wall" to the land of their inheritance for the grand purposes of God. This imagery brought to light by Nephi's vision similarly ties in to the many other Old Testament and Book of Mormon references cited in Chapter 2, which testify of Israel's/ Ephraim's latter-day migration and inheritance of the New World under the new American Covenant.* (It should be noted that the term *Gentile* in Nephi's account of the vision is not used to deny these latter-day immigrants and settlers a connection to Israel, but to demonstrate how they hailed from apostate lands lacking in gospel light. As the Bible Dictionary states, the term *Gentile* in the Book of

---

* A short list of these previously cited scriptures include Genesis 49, Zechariah 10, Jeremiah 31, 2 Nephi 10, Jacob 5, 3 Nephi 21, and Ether 13.

Mormon is often used "to designate nations that are without the gospel, even though there may be some Israelite blood therein.")[1]

Apart from the imagery Nephi's vision offers us of latter-day Israel's exodus from apostate lands to the new promised land of their inheritance, there is more in this vision that reflects its tight connection to the latter-day American Covenant. For example, Nephi explicitly states that these early latter-day Americans "went forth *out of captivity*, upon the many waters" (1 Nephi 13:13, emphasis added), implying that the American Covenant blessing of *liberty* would to be granted them. Furthermore, Nephi beheld that, once ashore, they "did prosper in the land" (1 Nephi 13:15; 20), implying that the American Covenant blessing of *prosperity* would also be granted them. There is little doubt that Nephi understood the connection between this vision and the promised American Covenant blessings he studied in the Biblical prophecies and promises (which his father held in the Brass Plates) that his great ancestor, even Jacob, offered to the seed of Joseph.

It is also worth noting that the inspired Gentiles in this vision most definitely include those early Americans who predated the restoration of the gospel. In fact, due to the placement of the verses that describe these early settlers within Nephi's prophetic narrative, it is clear that he was foreseeing generations of covenant-makers that predated even the American Revolution (see 1 Nephi 13:13-18). This is significant in that it places the burden, responsibility, and divine mandate of the American Covenant on our earliest forbearers, thus corroborating the arguments made in the previous chapters concerning who these earliest covenant-makers really were.

Nephi further connects his vision to the American Covenant by describing the fact that these latter-day settlers brought the words of this covenant—even the Holy Bible—with them: "And I beheld a book, and it was carried forth among them....The book...is the record of the Jews which contains the covenants of the Lord, which he hath made with the House of Israel" (1 Nephi 13:20-23). Nephi, who clearly understood the American Covenant (having lived it himself), indicates here how important it would be that these early latter-day settlers possessed and understood the ancient covenants with Israel. The covenants he refers to, however, were not limited to priesthood covenants like baptism and confirmation (such covenants and ordinances in their fullness were, after all, not even available to these earliest immigrants). The covenant Nephi *did* foresee in the book (the Bible) brought by these early settlers, which covenant these early settlers *did* need to understand, was that precursor and national covenant. Nephi knew that they would need to at least gain a minimal comprehension of the concept that they were the chosen ones to re-establish Israel's national covenant, even the American Covenant, as it is explained in the Bible. Such an understanding would be necessary so that they might apply these covenant principles to their new land, that the Restoration would have a solid foundation upon which to flourish.

Nephi's above vision, along with the additional Biblical and Book of Mormon references detailed in the previous chapters, truly lay a scriptural foundation for the chosen and foreordained place these early latter-day settlers of America would have in the eternal plan of God.

Comprehending the Covenant

But does the historical record of these early settlers vindicate such powerful prophecy? Did they say or do anything that would lead us to believe that they understood the American Covenant, as their counterparts Lehi and Nephi did anciently, or as the previously cited scriptural references imply that they might have? The answer to such questions is most definitely affirmative.

According to one historian, "Particularly noteworthy was the ever-present religiously oriented sense of mission which guided people of all ranks to the New World early during the period between 1607-1820....A favoring Providence was seen as directing the destiny of His 'chosen people' in the abundant wilderness called America."[2] The renowned nineteenth century French author Alexis de Tocqueville would describe this exodus to America as "the scattering of the seed of a great people which God with His own hands is planting on a predestined shore."[3] These founding generations of Americans even referred to their land as the "New Israel,"[4] as if they understood the prophecies surrounding Joseph of old and his son Ephraim, even long before the scriptures of the Restoration arrived to confirm this point of doctrine.[5]

These early Americans understood and worked to keep the American Covenant. They understood early on that if they were to receive *liberty, protection,* and *prosperity,* it would only be through obeying God and adhering to this national covenant. For example, in 1620, the Pilgrims' pastor, John Robinson, after leading his people in fasting and prayer, sent them off to America with profound instructions for living the covenant. "We are daily to renew our repentance with our God," stated Robinson, "especially for our sins known...[For] sin being taken away by earnest repentance and pardon thereof from the Lord...great shall be [your] security and peace."[6]

Upon arriving to America in 1620, after a treacherous journey at sea, the Bible-carrying Pilgrims aboard the *Mayflower,* according to their leader William Bradford, "fell upon their knees and blessed the God of Heaven who had brought them over the vast and furious ocean."[7] It is no coincidence that the earlier Jaredite arrival to ancient America is described in the Book of Mormon in almost identical fashion: "And when they had set their feet upon the shores of the promised land they bowed themselves down upon the face of the land, and did humble themselves before the Lord, and did shed tears of joy before the Lord, because of the multitude of his tender mercies over them" (Ether 6:12). The Pilgrims and the Jaredites (and also the Nephites) were, after all, brought to the Promised Land for the same purposes under God. As the Pilgrims shared a similar experience as their ancient counterparts, they too could testify to the Book of Mormon statement that "there shall be none come into this land [America] save they shall be brought by the hand of the Lord" (2 Nephi 1:6).

The Pilgrims' connection to the American Covenant—and to their ancient Book of Mormon counterparts—is further developed as we witness their continued actions towards God. Bradford stated that just when they thought they would perish in the wilderness, "they cried unto the Lord, and he heard their voice."[8] Bradford described how his people's intensified relationship with God took on a covenant nature: "So," stated Bradford, "they committed themselves to the will of God and resolved to proceed."[9] And, notwithstanding severe hardships, blessings were poured out upon them. For example, upon their arrival to the Promised Land, the Pilgrims had little to eat. A search party went ashore and miraculously found a large cache of Indian corn that had been placed in a large iron pot and left abandoned.[10] Like manna from heaven, this miracle saved them.

Similar miracles came in the form of unlikely alliances formed with the local Native American population. One Native American, Squanto, showed up one day at the Pilgrims' camp. Not only did he speak English, but he stayed with the Pilgrims during their first year in the wilderness and taught them how to plant corn, hunt, and fish. This "special instrument sent of God," as Bradford described him, literally saved their lives.[11] And then there was the Indian Chief, Massasoit, who commanded his braves to resist the temptation to show violent resistance to the European settlers, and instead helped and supported them. According to one historian, "Massasoit was a remarkable example of God's providential care for the Pilgrims. He was probably the only chief on the northeast coast of America who would have welcomed the Europeans as friends."[12]

Not only do these examples of friendly alliances give insight into the fulfillment of the national covenant, but they might also represent a very profound connection; for perhaps we see in this interaction a miraculous relationship between Manasseh and his brother Ephraim. Indeed, we see the remnants of ancient Israel by way of Manasseh (the Native American posterity of Lehi) assisting and passing the covenant "torch" to modern Israel, represented by Ephraim (the Pilgrims).

Even in the Pilgrims' first written charter, which may be modern America's earliest form of a written constitution, the national covenant is made clear. Consider the following introductory words of this document, known as the Mayflower Compact of 1620:

> In the name of God, Amen...Having undertaken for the glory of God, and Advancement of the Christian faith...a Voyage to plant the first colony...do by these Presents, solemnly and mutually in the Presence of God and of one another, covenant and combine ourselves together into a civil Body Politick for our better Ordering and Preservation, and Furtherance of the Ends aforesaid.[13]

A similar comprehension of the American Covenant was expressed by a second group of migrants known as the Puritans, who also settled in New England—not far from the Pilgrims' Plymouth Plantation—and established the Massachusetts Bay Company. In the spring of 1630, John Winthrop, the newly elected governor of the Bay Company, offered one of the most famous speeches ever given concerning the American Promised Land. This speech, given as the Puritans were en route to America, has been deemed by scholars the "Ur-text of American literature;"[14] and for the purposes of this study, it could also be deemed one of the most significant American Covenant texts as well. In explaining to his fellow American Covenant-makers how they had "taken out a Commission" under the Lord in crossing the great waters to the Promised Land, Winthrop declared: "Thus stands the cause between God and us, we are entered into Covenant with him for this work.... Now if the Lord shall please to hear us, and bring us peace to the place we desire, then hath he verified this Covenant and sealed our Commission."[15] Winthrop reminded his early American migrants and covenant-makers what happened to ancient Israel when they failed to live their end of their national covenant: "it lost [them] the Kingdom." And that his people would not fall into the same tragic state, he implored them to live the covenant correctly, lest the Lord "make us know the price of the breach of such a Covenant."[16]

Winthrop then famously prophesied that God "shall make us a praise and glory,"

> that men shall say of succeeding plantations: the Lord make it like that of New England for we must consider we shall be as a City upon a Hill, the eyes of all people are upon us; so that if we shall deal falsely with our God in this work we have undertaken and so cause Him to withdraw his present help from us, we shall be made a story and a byword through the world. [17]

Upon internalizing Winthrop's words, we can almost hear echoed exhortations from an earlier American Covenant-maker, even the Prophet Lehi, who declared: "[S]erve him according to the commandments [and] it shall be a land of liberty....Inasmuch as ye shall keep [God's] commandment ye shall prosper in the land...but inasmuch as ye will not...ye shall be cut off..." (1 Nephi 1:7, 20).

Winthrop further tempts us to believe that he somehow had accessed a copy of the Book of Mormon, even some two hundred years before its publication, when, in this speech, he detailed the covenant obligations. Winthrop explained that his people must, under their covenant, "delight in each other, make each others' Conditions our own, rejoice together, mourn together, labor, and suffer together, always having before our eyes our Commission and Community in the work..." [18] (compare to Mosiah 18:9). As one Puritan wrote of his early American countrymen, "they joined together in a holy Covenant with the Lord and with one another, promising by the Lord's assistance to walk together...and to cleave to the Lord." [19]

Winthrop went on to list the promised blessings of the covenant. Fittingly, the promised blessings he revealed to his people were identical to those blessings promised by Jacob to Joseph, as detailed in the Old Testament and Book of Mormon scriptures cited earlier—even the blessings of *liberty*, *protection*, and *prosperity*. Indeed, the blessings, according to Winthrop, for living this covenant, included God's "wisdom, power, goodness and truth," along with the promise that the "God of Israel is among us, when ten of us shall be able to resist a thousand of our enemies." And finally, Winthrop reminded his people that by "obeying [God's] voice and cleaving to him" they secure "our life, and our prosperity."[20]

Winthrop's colleague in the cause, Pastor John Cotton, also weighed in on the power and importance of the American Covenant. Using 2 Samuel as the basis for his sermon, he applied Old Testament principles to his American Puritans. Quoting the Bible, Pastor Cotton declared: "Moreover I will appoint a place for my people Israel, and will plant them, that they may dwell in a place of their own, and move no more; neither shall the children of wickedness afflict them any more, as before time." Cotton went on to explain that such would be their covenant blessing if they "with a public spirit" lived in righteousness, "that they do not degenerate as the Israelites did." Only then would the covenant take force and only then, as Cotton concluded, would the Puritans "prosper and flourish....[For] when He promiseth peace and safety, what enemies shall be able to make the promise of God of none effect?"[21]

Further evidence that the Puritans knew their national covenant was somehow an extension of the ancient covenants with Israel, is found in the fact that they named their city Salem. The Hebrew word "salem" is a root of the word Jerusalem. Furthermore, the meaning of this word (translated from Hebrew) means "peace," even that prominent fruit of the national covenant. Their self-proclaimed connection to Israel perpetuated into later Puritan generations, which oft referred to their founder Winthrop as *Nehemias Americanus*, thus comparing him to the ancient Israelite leader Nehemiah. The Bible records that Nehemiah led his people out of Babylon back into the Promised Land, rebuilt the walls of Jerusalem, and inspired his people to return to their national covenant.[22]

The American Covenant perhaps reached a climax among the Puritans when Winthrop's good friend and colleague, Thomas Hooker, had a most inspired revelation. Hooker thought to take these national covenant principles and apply them to a more democratic system of government. Hooker was concerned that a theocracy, however well intended, could stifle the liberty necessary for true progression.

Declared Hooker: "There must of necessity be a mutual engagement, each of the other, by their free consent, before by any rule of God they have any right or power, or can exercise either, each towards the other." Hooker felt so strongly about it that, after gaining the blessing of Winthrop, he left the Bay Colony and established his own colony under the *Fundamental Orders of Connecticut*.[23] The first type and model of a free and democratic government under God in America had been set. And though it was far from what the Lord would need as a political foundation for His Restoration, America had, under its covenant, taken one step closer.

And it would only be a matter of time before these covenant principles reached that chosen American generation, which God would raise up to first declare and achieve independence from Britain and then to build His American nation as we know it today. Though the early Puritans struggled on and off to live their covenant, they persevered enough to keep it alive for those chosen ones. As late as 1676, Puritan leaders fought hard to remind their country to renew their covenant. One such Puritan, Peter Folger, was especially concerned about the national covenant. Folger insisted that his people must "turn to God," then added poetically: "Let us then search what is the sin that God doth punish for; And when found out, cast it away, and ever it abhor." Folger's name stands out as one covenant-maker who served as a bridge to that chosen revolutionary generation of Americans, for his grandson was none other than Benjamin Franklin.[24] And just what miracles and progress Franklin's generation witnessed under the American Covenant, even that covenant which their forbearers delivered to them, will be detailed in later chapters.

The American Covenant legacy of these early settlers would continue even beyond Franklin and his revolutionary generation. On December 22, 1820, during the bicentennial celebration of the founding of the Mayflower Compact, renowned statesman Daniel Webster gave a speech in which he famously invoked the American Covenant. He emphasized the American Covenant's promised blessings, even "those principles of civil and religious liberty," which he concluded had only come to America through the early settlers' great sacrifice and endurance. He then exhorted his fellow Americans "to transmit the great inheritance unimpaired" that all in the future might enjoy these same blessings.[25] And finally, he acknowledged that this national covenant was brought to us by and though Jesus Christ (even He who Latter-day Saints recognize had been crowned long before by Heaven as the "God of the land [America]" [Ether 2:12]). Webster concluded:

> Finally, let us not forget the religious character of our origin. Our fathers were brought hither by their high veneration for the Christian religion. They journeyed by its light, and labored in its hope. They sought to incorporate its principles with the elements of their society, and to diffuse its influence through all their institutions, civil, political, or literary. Let us cherish these sentiments, and extend this influence still more widely; in the full conviction, that this is the happiest society which partakes in the highest degree of the mild and peaceful spirit of Christianity.[26]

That this statement was made only months after the Lord commenced His gospel restoration with Joseph Smith's First Vision only seems fitting; for it was this concept of a national covenant under God, so eloquently expressed by Webster, that would provide this great gospel restoration the support it needed to survive. As long as the nation would adhere to their obligations, the gospel foundations would be secure. John Adams later said of the speech that "if there be any American who can read it without tears, I am not that American. It ought to be read at the end of every year, forever and forever."[27] Appropriately, Daniel Webster was also named as one of the eminent men who, at the St. George Temple, was given the opportunity to receive his priesthood covenants at the hands of Wilford Woodruff.[28]

The spiritual and political covenant foundations that supported the Restoration indeed had their beginnings in America's first sacred settlements. As we imagine these great migrants and settlers, it is difficult not to compare them to the Jaredite and Nephite migrants and settlers. Furthermore, it is difficult not to see the fulfillment of Jacob's previously cited promises to latter-day Israel and Nephi's previously cited description of how it would all play out: that they would *go forth out of captivity, upon the many waters* crossing *over the wall*, to Joseph's promised land of *the everlasting hills*, carrying with them *the record of the Jews which contains the covenants of the Lord*. And this they did that they might receive for themselves and their posterity those covenant blessings of *liberty, protection,* and *prosperity* in furtherance of God's latter-day work. Surely these sacred settlements represent a significant element of the American Covenant.

★ ★ ★ ★

In spite of these wonderful connections between history, heaven, and the American Covenant, many might find it ironic to credit these early American settlers for helping to develop the promised land of liberty. For their religious heritage, particularly their Puritan heritage, is often recognized as being intolerant and even cruel toward dissenting viewpoints—something not conducive to the American Covenant purposes of offering religious freedom unto eternal salvation. And though they felt they needed strict codes in order to maintain unity, and thus strength, in confronting the challenges of cultivating a wild and dangerous land, no amount of reasoning can easily justify the banishments, beatings, and even executions carried out at times against congregants for not agreeing with and/or obeying their church leaders.[29] Though there is plenty of evidence that the Lord was attempting to counter this evil culture, even early on,* there is no question that the adversary was using and influencing these extreme elements in early America to counter God's gospel plan for America.

---

* During this period of early settlement in the seventeenth century, certain inspired colonies, such as the one established by the aforementioned Puritan, Thomas Hooker, attempted a more liberal society. Pennsylvania and New York at times employed (though not always successfully) a policy of religious freedom. During this early period, Rhode Island, under the inspired guidance of Roger Williams, and Maryland, under the inspired guidance of Lord Baltimore, also fought the adversary's attack on America by enforcing religious tolerance. See Steven Waldman, *Founding Faith: Politics, Providence and the Birth of Religious Freedom in America* (New York: Random House, 2008), 14-16.

(How would Joseph Smith and the restored gospel have been treated by these early religious societies?) Fortunately for us all—and as we will see through the continuing story of the American Covenant—the Lord would eradicate these wicked cultural and political elements from the land in furtherance of his gospel purposes.

But notwithstanding the early presence of such wickedness, we must recognize that at this point of migration and settlement, the American Covenant was merely in its embryonic state in the New World. Therefore, a degree of tolerance must be offered to these early American Covenant-makers. After all, and in spite of their imperfections, they had, in fact, entered into the American Covenant with God, which set the spiritual precedent for America. Thanks to this spiritual precedent, as the nation developed and formed its Constitution (thus ridding itself of much of the wicked intolerance), it made sure to keep the national covenant intact. And this would allow God to bless the government with what it needed to ensure the safety of the Restoration. In reflecting upon these early American societies, we must take care not to throw the proverbial baby out with the bath water.

Historian Steven Waldman, one of the fiercest modern-day critics of the cruelty and intolerance of these earliest Americans, even conceded—after launching into a detailed analysis of the wickedness described above—that "[c]ountless settlers created families, grew communities, and survived against great odds in large part because of their faith in Jesus Christ."

> These stories do not generally make the history books because they deal with the mundane, and awesome, power of God in people's lives. It's quite possible none of us would be here today if their religious beliefs and practices hadn't enabled...[them] to persevere against gruesome odds. They were not for the most part hypocrites or sadists. In most cases, they tried to create a world that would bring them closer to God, following his commandments as best they knew how.[30]

A Deeper Understanding

Now that we have justified the divine existence and accomplishments of the early American settlers, there is one remaining inquiry into their history that we have yet to explore. For if it is true that the works of these earliest settlers and American Covenant-makers were in furtherance of the Restoration, we naturally wonder if these chosen ones ever said or did anything to validate such claims. Though it is clear they comprehended elements of the new *national* covenant, did they ever indicate a deeper gospel comprehension of what their mission in relation to America was *really* all about? Did they know that what they were working on was something that transcended a national covenant and entered into something infinitely more powerful—even God's restoration of the fullness of His gospel? If the Lord had revealed such things to them, it would certainly make sense. For if these early settlers believed and taught their posterity that such a restoration was possible, and possibly on the horizon in America, then the later generations would be open to the restored gospel when it at last arrived.

Though it is impossible to fully comprehend what deeper understanding these settlers possessed, the historical record implies that they did have something of a more profound gospel understanding. And though this study is focused on America's national covenant, it would be incomplete without analyzing what they knew concerning their divine role in building upon this national covenant in preparation for the establishment of God's true church and gospel on the earth.

One of the earliest expressions of this deeper comprehension came from the aforementioned Pastor John Robinson who, in speaking to the Pilgrims just before they set sail for the New World, encouraged these brave Christian settlers to seek out further light and knowledge in their new land, as greater gospel progress was yet to come:

> Here also he put us in mind of our church covenant, at least that part of it whereby we promise and covenant with God and one another to receive whatsoever light or truth shall be made known to us from His written Word...For saith he, it is not possible the Christian world should come so lately out of so thick anti-Christian darkness, and that perfection of knowledge break forth at once.[31]

Robinson provided a similarly powerful allusion to gospel restoration when he stated:

> Now as the people of God in old time were called out of Babylon civil, the place of their bodily bondage, and were to come to Jerusalem, and there to build the Lord's temple...so are the people of God now to go out of Babylon spiritual to Jerusalem (America)...and to build themselves as lively stones into a spiritual house, or temple, for the Lord to dwell in....for we are the sons and daughters of Abraham by faith.[32]

Robinson's message would not be lost on his most prominent congregant, and leader of the Pilgrim migration, William Bradford, who also knew why his people were called to America. Bradford recognized long before what Satan had done to the Old World. "... [W]hat wars and oppositions ever since [the true gospel was on the earth], Satan hath raised, maintained and continued against the saints," explained Bradford. Bradford went on to explain that Satan did this so as to prevent the "truth [from] prevail[ing] and the churches of God [from] revert[ing] to their ancient purity and recover their primitive order, liberty and beauty."[33] Bradford recognized the Great Apostasy and, like his brethren, naturally had his mind on restoration.

The Pilgrims at Plymouth were not the only ones to receive this deeper comprehension; for their Puritan neighbors in Salem also knew something more profound concerning their own divine mission under the covenant. Winthrop, for example, was very clear on why he had led the migration to, and the settlement of, the Promised Land. He explained that he did so "to carry the Gospel into those parts of the world…[away from] all other Churches of Europe [which] are brought to desolation…and who knows but that God hath provided this place [America] to be a refuge for many whom he means to save out of general calamity."[34] He may not have known all the detailed plans of God, but Winthrop no doubt recognized the Apostasy and had his mind on a restoration of truth. He knew why he was there. "I have assurance that my charge is of the Lord," he declared, "and that he hath called me to this work."[35]

Another early American Puritan of New England, who shared this vision, was the minister Jonathan Edwards. A major participant in developing a God-centered nation during early eighteenth century America, Edwards declared: "God presently goes about doing some great thing in order to make way for the introduction of the church's latter-day glory—which is to have its first seat in, and is to rise from [this] new world."[36]

Edwards' colleague, Judge Samuel Sewall,* took it a step further. He declared that America was to be the host-nation of the "New Jerusalem."[37] He believed God had revealed this to him. He stated that his New England colony was but a preface to the future millennial city. This, according to Sewall, is why the New England settlers had named the colony Salem.[38] He believed the actual New Jerusalem would be built somewhere on the new continent, perhaps south of the Puritan colony.[39] If this is not enough to prove his inspired nature, Sewall also pled with his brethren to include the Native Americans in their plans to build the spiritual America. The Natives were, according to Sewall, "Israelites unawares" who deserved a place in building the New Jerusalem and the kingdom of God on earth.[40]

---

* Samuel Sewall's inspired nature was revealed when he stood before his congregation and humbly confessed before man and God that the Salem Witch Trials, which he had participated in, were an abomination and that he and his brethren had been wrong to pursue this course of action. See Richard Francis, *Judge Sewall's Apology*, xiii.

The historian Perry William summed it up succinctly:

> Winthrop and his colleagues believed...that their errand
> was not a mere scouting expedition: it was an essential
> maneuver in the drama of Christendom. The Bay
> Company was not a battered remnant of suffering
> Separatists thrown upon a rocky shore; it was an organized
> task force of Christians, executing a flank attack on the
> corruptions of Christendom. These Puritans did not flee to
> America; they went in order to work out that complete
> reformation which was not yet accomplished in England
> and Europe.[41]

Let us not take for granted the divine purpose and calling felt
by these Pilgrim and Puritan American Covenant-makers. They
were more correct in their vision than even they could have possibly
known at the time. For they had not only been establishing the
spiritually infused political foundations that would set the nation on
its proper course, but they also brought to America a culture,
mission, and appetite, for further gospel truth. They foresaw the
Restoration. They knew it was bound for America. And they knew
they were to help initiate it. But only at that then future date, when
the Restoration would at last take hold in America, would the
fullness of what they had done come to light. Only then do we begin
to see what they so clearly and prophetically felt.

This inspired vision was emphasized in the prominent
colonist and Puritan leader Roger Williams. Arriving in America in
1631, Williams, in the spirit of Robinson, Bradford, Winthrop, and
others, believed in and taught of a future gospel restoration. Many,
however, believed Williams took his belief too far, and he was
subsequently banished from his Massachusetts Bay Colony. He then
founded his own colony he called Providence, in what is now Rhode
Island. Once secure in his new colony, he eventually left his new
church, the First Baptist Church in America, of which he was a
founder. He left due to his persisting belief and testimony that true
religion "had died and would remain dead until God restored the

spark of the early church through the love and authority of the apostles he would raise up at some point in the future." Williams ultimately made the following conclusive statement: "There is no regularly constituted church on earth, nor any person qualified to administer any church ordinances; nor can there be until new apostles are sent by the Great Head of the Church for whose coming I am seeking."[42] Williams considered himself a "waiter" and saw "no alternative but to wait patiently until that restoration."[43] (Incidentally, apart from being an inspired "waiter," Williams was also among the few aforementioned American visionaries who, even early on, fought against the adversary for religious tolerance in colonial America).[44]

Perhaps such "waiters" were inspired by Biblical references to the Restoration,[45] or perhaps they were privy to personal revelation on the matter. Either way, when God at last began His "marvelous work and a wonder" (Isaiah 29:14) in nineteenth century America, it was from among this truth-seeking culture, developed through generations of such inspired Christians, that He found His first Latter-day Saints. Such an argument is supported by the story of yet another pre-restoration "waiter" named John Lathrop.

Lathrop was a reverend and the vicar of the Egerton Church in Kent, England. Like Williams, Lathrop recognized that the keys to administer the gospel, as set forth in the Bible, were nowhere to be found on earth. As such, in 1623 he resigned his position in the church and began voicing his concerns and alternative viewpoints regarding the gospel of Christ. For this he was arrested and imprisoned. While in prison his wife died, leaving his children orphaned. Feeling sympathy for the children, the bishop released Lathrop on the condition that he would leave the country, never to return. Lathrop, along with his children and thirty-two members of his following, then migrated to America where he could worship freely. Lathrop no doubt passed his testimony and desire for truth on to his own descendants.

Fittingly, in climactic resolution to this story, the Prophet Joseph Smith and the many faithful from that chosen family were among these Lathrop descendants.[46] Furthermore, in a letter dating from the 1850's, Elder Orson Pratt reminded his brother, Elder Parley P. Pratt, of a vision the Prophet Joseph had received. In the vision, Joseph learned that the Smith family and Pratt family had a common ancestor just a few generations back. Nobody seemed to know who this ancestor was in the Prophet's vision until the Pratt letter was discovered sometime around 1930. It was only then that genealogist Archibald F. Bennett found the common ancestor; it was John Lathrop. It is estimated that up to one fourth of the early Church members in America, to include Wilford Woodruff and Oliver Cowdery, came from Lathrop's line.[47]

And yet another example is that of a little known lay preacher named Robert Mason, who lived in Sainsbury, Connecticut, through the beginning of the nineteenth century. Known to the community as "Father Mason," his insights into the Bible and the miracles he performed through faith in Christ, caused many to refer to him as a prophet. One day, towards the end of his life, Father Mason took a certain young man aside and told him that he had received a revelation and "felt impelled by the Spirit of the Lord to relate it to [the young man]." In recounting the vision—which shared several characteristics with Lehi's Tree of Life vision—Father Mason told the young man that he had seen out of a dead land, the rising of great trees, whose fruit "was the most beautiful to look upon of anything my eyes had ever beheld...but when I was about to eat of it the vision closed." Father Mason then explained to the young man:

> At the close of the vision I bowed in humble prayer and asked the Lord to show me the meaning of the vision. Then the voice of the Lord came to me saying: "Son of man, thou hast sought me diligently to know the truth concerning my Church and Kingdom among men. This is to show you that my Church is not organized among men in the generation to which you belong; but in the days of your children the Church and Kingdom of God shall be made manifest with all the gifts and the blessings enjoyed by the Saints in past

ages. You shall...not partake of its blessings before you depart this life. You will be blest of the Lord after death because you followed the dictation of my Spirit in this life."[48]

When Father Mason had finished relating the above account of his vision and its interpretation, he turned to the young man and said, "I shall never partake of this fruit in the flesh, but you will and you will become a conspicuous actor in the new Kingdom."[49]

The young man in the story, by whom the above account was recorded, was the future prophet, Wilford Woodruff. Wilford would find the true and restored gospel and be baptized a few years after learning of this vision. And though Father Mason did, in fact, die before joining himself, Wilford recorded that "the first opportunity I had after the truth of baptism for the dead was revealed, I went forth and was baptized for him in the temple font at Nauvoo."[50]

Certainly hundreds upon thousands of early settlers and forerunners of the Restoration like Williams, Lathrop, and Mason were scattered throughout early America—the fruits of the aforementioned sacred settlements of the New World. It should be noted that by 1628, the great Puritan migration to America had occurred, which would, over the following sixteen years, see the arrival to America of over 20,000 Puritans.[51] As one author put it, this placed into America an overwhelming influx of "people who had entered into a deep covenant relationship with God, through the person of His Son, Jesus Christ."[52] These chosen ones who rode this later wave of the great migration had just as clear a vision of what they were doing as their predecessors had. As one second generation American Puritan, John Higginson, so prophetically explained:

It hath been deservedly esteemed one of the great and wonderful works of God in this last age, that the Lord stirred up the spirits of so many thousands of his servants...to transport themselves...into a desert land in America...in the way of seeking first the kingdom of God...for the purpose of "a fuller and better reformation of the Church of God, than it hath yet appeared in the world."[53]

Again, their vision could not have been truer. Earlier in this chapter, we saw how the settlers' understanding of the national covenant had set the appropriate foundations required to give support to the Restoration. But more than that, we now see how these early settlers' deeper gospel understanding also planted in America an awareness of greater things to come. These early settlers, after all, were the remnants of scattered Israel, and as such possessed that *believing blood*. According to Apostle Bruce R. McConkie, "The more of the blood of Israel that an individual has, the easier it is for him to believe the message of salvation as taught by authorized agents of the Lord. This principle is the one our Lord had in mind when he said...'My sheep hear my voice, and I know them, and they follow me' (John 10:14, 26-27)."[54] American historians have commented on this unique religious characteristic in early America, often referring to these early Americans as "seekers" who broke with the authoritative religious structures of the Old Word and sought things like "personal revelation" and "witnesses of the Spirit."[55] That these early settlers possessed such *believing blood*—passing it on from generation to generation—was no accident. For it was their children—also infused with this blood and culture—who would become God's first latter-day prophets, apostles, and converts.

Pulitzer Prize-winning historian Gordon Wood attributes much of this liberal and democratic approach to religion as stemming from the revolutionary spirit that pervaded America, particularity after it won its independence from Great Britain. In his work, *Evangelical America and Early Mormonism,* this renowned, non-LDS, historian argued that for first time on a very large scale, people took "responsibility for their salvation like never before." This, according to Wood, created in America an increase in "visions, dreams [and] prophesyings" which ultimately spawned the spirituality that attracted people to Mormonism.[56] And so, the

American Covenant is connected to the restoration of the gospel in a powerful way—for it was this American Covenant that ultimately provided liberty and democracy, which in turn created the spirit and environment that facilitated the opening of hearts and minds to eternal truth. In short, the American Covenant helped activate the *believing blood* of Israel.

Examples of those chosen Americans that were positively affected by this religious phenomenon were Newel K. and Elizabeth Whitney, who immediately recognized the restored gospel as "the fulfillment of the vision we had seen of a cloud as of glory resting upon our house." Another such convert prepared early on by the Lord was Jonathon Crosby, who claimed to have foreseen the Restoration through a dream in which "some new preachers came with a book containing new doctrine, and which threw new light on the Bible, and their preaching was different from all others, and I rejoiced in it." And yet another, Edward Tullidge, an early British convert, stated that "at about the same time Joseph Smith was receiving the administration of angels, thousands both in America and Great Britain were favored with corresponding visions and intuitions."[57]

And so we see how the *believing blood* of Israel, supported by the American Covenant, and delivered by the earliest settlers of the land, contributed immensely to God's work and glory. President Spencer W. Kimball stated that "the Lord led the Pilgrims and the Puritans across the ocean...so that when they came to the American shores with their righteous blood and their high ideals and standards, they would form the basis of a nation which would make possible the restoration of the gospel."[58]

So important was the settlers' role as forerunners to the Restoration that the ancient prophet, Nephi, saw it and spoke of it in his above-mentioned America Covenant vision. At the conclusion of the very Book of Mormon chapter that provides the vision of Nephi's "other Gentiles" which were to inherit the land America (1 Nephi 13: 13-14), the final outcome and ultimate fruit of this discovery and settlement is also detailed. And the Lord declared: "I will be merciful unto the Gentiles in that day...that I will bring forth unto them, in mine own power, much of my gospel....And in them shall be written my gospel, saith the Lamb, and my rock and my salvation (1 Nephi 13: 34, 36)." Nephi expounds on the prophecy, declaring that these other Gentiles would offer the world "other books, which came forth by the power of the Lamb, from the Gentiles..."

> Which [books] shall make known the plain and precious things which have been taken away...and shall make known to all kindreds, tongues, and people, that the Lamb of God is the Son of the Eternal Father, and the Savior of the World; and that all men must come unto him, or they cannot be saved" (1 Nephi 13:39-40).

This scripture seems to indicate that God's actions, inspiration, and guidance pertaining to Nephi's "other Gentiles" were nothing if not in furtherance of His work to restore His gospel to the earth. And so we see how Nephi's prophetic American Covenant vision of the discovery and settlement of the New World (as detailed throughout 1 Nephi Chapter 13), and the similarly powerful prophecies of the same, as expressed in other scriptural references (cited in Part I of this book), become ever more validated by the thoughts and actions of these early American covenant-makers. For they made this vision and those prophecies a reality. And they made this vision and those prophecies a reality not only by adhering to God's call to discover and settle a land and thus usher in His *national* covenant, but also by adhering to the greater inspiration that would usher in His *priesthood* covenant.

Let us then respond to Edward Johnson, a first generation American Puritan and contemporary of Winthrop, who opened his book *Wonder Working Providences of Sion's Saviour in New England*, with the following declaration: "Then judge, all you, (whom the Lord hath given a discerning spirit), whether these poor New England people be not forerunners of Christ's army, and the marvelous providences which you shall now hear, be not the very finger of God."[59]

Dark Stirrings

In spite of the spiritually glorious sentiments connected with this latter-day American discovery and settlement, there was also evil lurking therein. The adversary certainly understood the powerful tool America and her covenant would be in God's great war against evil and oppression. As such, Satan would deploy his armies early to America in an effort to preempt and stomp out this national covenant before it became operational in the advancement of righteousness.

The results of these evil tactics would find themselves represented in at least two obvious attacks on America and her purposes under God. First, and as already mentioned above, certain American settlements, colonies, and states would allow their local governments to influence, support, and even sponsor specific religious denominations, while at the same time discriminate against others. In some instances these state-run religions would go so far as to apply corporal punishment, banishment, and even executions upon those who refused to adhere to certain religious obligations, such as church attendance and other subjective religious standards.[60] And second, the importation and practice of slavery would introduce to America not only the absolute oppression of a race, but also a sense of justified intolerance of any given set of minorities— racial or religious. So pervasive were such wicked sentiments, that they found themselves codified and legislated in the land.

These two cancers in America were planted early and, if left unchecked, would grow and stifle the hope of Christ and His gospel restoration. They represented Satan's plan as set forth from the beginning of time. Whether it was forced obedience (which can never lead to true conversion unto true salvation) or flat denial of the freedom necessary to access saving principles and ordinances, the *modus operandi* was that same old ploy: control and limit man's agency to thwart his eternal progression.

America's ability to counter these attacks would only be as good as its ability to live the American Covenant; for if the people adhered to the covenant successfully, the Lord would provide America with the tools necessary to defeat Satan, thus securing a fullness of agency and thus providing a strong and happy venue for the restored gospel to flourish. As the story of the American Covenant continues to develop in the chapters ahead, we will see how this eternal struggle over liberty and salvation plays out in the hands of God, as He leads His American Covenant-makers through heaven-backed wars and through inspired constitutions until America sufficiently rejects wickedness and congeals into that nation God requires it to be. As we witness this inspired transformation, we will come to understand why President Ezra Taft Benson called America the "Lord's base of operations,"[61] whose ultimate purpose it has always been to provide the blessed support and enhancement of agency, that the restoration of the fullness of Christ's gospel—even His "marvelous work and a wonder" (Isaiah 29:14), prophesied of through the ages—might go forth and bless God's children.

Conclusion

Throughout the past two chapters we have seen how the historical record corroborates what the scriptural-based theory put forth in Part I of this book proposed. That is, we have achieved validation of the notion that God indeed set up a latter-day American Covenant and inspired its recognition in the hearts and minds of the chosen discoverers and settlers of the chosen land. These first explorers, voyagers, immigrants, and settlers were an integral part of the American Covenant, as would be the millions that would follow them. It was through the obedience and adherence to God displayed by Columbus, Vespucci, Nephi's "other Gentiles," and the generations they would breed, that God would provide the *liberty*, *protection,* and *prosperity* promised through the American Covenant, just as we saw prophesied in the previous chapters by father Jacob to the heirs of Joseph (Genesis 49:22-26) and as foretold by father Lehi and his posterity (2 Nephi 1:5-7, 20; 10:7-17).

To be sure, in these last two chapters of the American Covenant story, we have witnessed the partial fulfillment of the promised *protection*, as given to Columbus, Vespucci, and others as they successfully braved vast and unknown waters and forged through vast and unknown lands. We have seen the partial fulfillment of the promised *liberty*, as given to the Pilgrims, Puritans, and other settlers who, at last, could worship God according to their conscience. And we know of the fulfillment of the promised *prosperity* that these early Americans would eventually create for the future heirs of the covenant.*

And though the American Covenant and its ultimate gospel fruits would not fully manifest themselves in the early settlements of America, we have certainly seen how the early settlers did understand the covenant and did foresee greater things to come. They were forerunners of the American-Covenant called to set the precedent and spirit in the land, so that later generations might take this precedent and spirit and improve upon it, all in preparation for God's future work and glory. The First Presidency of the Church of Jesus Christ of Latter-day Saints declared: "It was not by chance that the Puritans left their native land and sailed away to the shores of New England, and that others followed later."

> They were the advance guard of the army of the Lord, predestined to establish the God-given system of government under which we live, and to make of America, which is the land of Joseph, the gathering place of Ephraim, an asylum for the oppressed of all nations, and prepare the way for the restoration of the gospel of Christ and the reestablishment of his church upon the earth.[62]

---

* In spite of great hardships, we know that by the mid-1750's, America had grown to maintain the highest per capita wealth in the world. See Joseph J. Ellis, *Patriots, Brotherhood of the American Revolution*, (lectures recorded by Recorded Books, Inc, and Barnes and Noble Publishing, 2004), Study Guide, p. 10. And America has since only grown stronger and stronger until eventually becoming, as it is today, the world's superpower.

In an astonishing and inspiring (albeit an under-appreciated) gesture, the oversized oil-on-canvas paintings that decorate the interior of the great rotunda of the U.S. Capitol Building outline the very American Covenant story we have witnessed in these last two chapters. Within this impressive display are three paintings placed in chronological order, which express three deeply symbolic events pertaining to the American Covenant. First, the painting *Landing of Columbus* depicts the miraculous arrival on the shores of the Promised Land. Second, the painting *Embarkation of the Pilgrims* depicts the chosen Ephraimites observing a day of fasting and prayer on the decks of a ship preparing to lead them *over the wall* to America. Depicted in the work is a rainbow, which "symbolizes hope and divine protection"[63]—even those hallmarks of the American Covenant. Finally, the painting *Baptism of Pocahontas* depicts a native American girl who, after the long night of gospel apostasy, at last finds access to spiritual light, reminding us of those sacred principles and ordinances soon to be delivered to the world as a result of this divine discovery and sacred settlement.

ENDNOTES

[1] Consider the following definition of *Gentile* in the "Bible Dictionary," *The Holy Bible, King James Version* (Salt Lake City: LDS Church, 1986), 679: "As used throughout the scriptures it has a dual meaning, sometimes to designate peoples of non-Israelite lineage, and other times to designate nations that are without the gospel, even though there may be some Israelite blood therein. This latter usage is especially characteristic of the word as used in the Book of Mormon." See also Bruce R. McConkie, *Mormon Doctrine* (Salt Lake City: Bookcraft, 1966), 31 and D&C 45:28-30.

[2] R. Mathisen, *The Role of Religion in American Life* (Washington D.C.: University Press of America, 1982), 1.

[3] William J. Bennett, *The Spirit of America* (New York: Touchstone, 1997), 365-366.

[4] William J. Bennett, *The Spirit of America*, 366.

[5] See chapter 2 of this book: *The Covenant-Makers*; also refer to 3 Nephi 21 and Ether 13.

[6] John Robinson, as quoted by Marshall and Manuel, 145, 148.

[7] William Bradford, as quoted in Jon Meacham, *American Gospel: God, the Founding Fathers, and the Making of a Nation* (New York: Random House, 2006), 38.

[8] Meacham, *American Gospel: God, the Founding Fathers, and the Making of a Nation*, 38.

[9] Meacham, *American Gospel: God, the Founding Fathers, and the Making of a Nation*, 39.

[10] Marshall and Manuel, 157.

[11] Marshall and Manuel, 165, 168-9.

[12] Marshall and Manuel, 168.

[13] "The Mayflower Compact, 1620," quoted in *Let Freedom Ring, The Words That Shaped Our America* (New York: Sterling Publishing Co., Inc, 2001), 11.

[14] Matthew S. Holland, *Bonds of Affection* (Washington D.C.: Georgetown University Press, 2007), 1.

[15] H. Sheldon Smith et al, *American Christianity, An Historical Interpretation with Representative Documents*, Vol.1: 1607-1820 (New York: Charles Scribner's Sons, 1960), 102; Also quoted in Holland, 273-4.

[16] Winthrop, as quoted in Matthew S. Holland, *Bonds of Affection* (Washington D.C.: Georgetown University Press, 2007), 273-274.

[17] John Winthrop, "A Model of Christian Charity," *Winthrop Papers, 1498-1649,* Vol. 2 (Boston: The Massachusetts Historical Society), 282-95.

[18] Winthrop, as quoted in Holland, 274.

[19] Edward Johnson, as quoted in Marshall and Manuel, 204.

[20] Holland, 274-275.

[21] John Cotton, as quoted by Marshall and Manuel, 197.

[22] Marshall and Manuel, 207-8.

[23] Marshall and Manuel, 251-2.

[24] Marshall and Manuel, 279.

[25] Daniel Webster, as quoted in Toby Mac and Michael Tait, *Under God* (Minneapolis: Bethany House, 2004), 144.

[26] Verna M. Hall, *The Christian History of the Constitution of the United States of America* (San Francisco: Foundation for American Christian Education, 1975), 248.

[27] John Adams, as quoted in Mac and Tait, 144.

[28] Recorded in Wilford Woodruff's journal and temple records, as quoted in Vicki Jo Anderson, *The Other Eminent Men of Wilford Woodruff* (Malta: Nelson Book, 2000), Preface.

[29] For a full account of the abuses inflicted upon dissenters, see Steven Waldman, *Founding Faith: Politics, Providence and the Birth of Religious Freedom in America* (New York: Random House, 2008), 6-13.

[30] Waldman, *Founding Faith: Politics, Providence and the Birth of Religious Freedom in America* (New York: Random House, 2008), 17.

[31] Timothy L. Hall, *Separating Church and State* (Chicago: University of Illinois Press, 1998), 184.

[32] John Robinson, as quoted by Marshall and Manuel, 142-3.

[33] William Bradford, as quoted by Marshall and Manuel, 139.

[34] John Winthrop, as quoted by Marshall and Manuel, 195.

[35] Marshall and Manuel, 196.

[36] Edwards, quoted from Cleon Skousen, *The Majesty of God's Law* (Salt Lake City: Ensign Publishing, 1996), 19.

[37] Richard Francis, *Judge Sewall's Apology* (New York: Harper Collins Publishers, 2005), 37, 201.

[38] Richard Francis, *Judge Sewall's Apology*, 201.

[39] Richard Francis, *Judge Sewall's Apology*, 355.

[40] Richard Francis, *Judge Sewall's Apology*, 37, 201.

[41] Marshall and Manuel, 196.

[42] Roger Williams, as cited in *The Great Prologue: A Prophetic History and Destiny of America* (Salt Lake City: The Church of Jesus Christ of Latter-day Saints, 1976), 4.

[43] Timothy L. Hall, *Separating Church and State* (Chicago: University of Illinois Press, 1998), 25; Roger Williams, *Bloody Tenant of Persecution for Cause of Conscience* (1644), 139; quoted in "Roger Williams: Father of Religious Freedom in America," *Twelve Tribes, The Commonwealth of Israel*, available at www.twelvetribes.com/publicatitons/roger-williams-religious-freedom.

[44] Waldman, *Founding Faith: Politics, Providence and the Birth of Religious Freedom in America* (New York: Random House, 2008), 14.

[45] Some Biblical prophecies of the restoration: Acts 3:19-21, Malachi 4:5-6, Isaiah 29, Micah 4:1-4, Revelation 14:6-7.

[46] James E. Faust, "The Restoration of All Things," 176th General Conference of the Church of Jesus Christ of Latter-day Saints, as recorded in *Ensign*, May 2006, Vol.5, No.5, 62.

[47] Truman Madsen, *Joseph Smith, The Prophet* (Salt Lake City: Deseret Book, 2008), 107-108.

[48] Father Mason's account is retold by Wilford Woodruff, as quoted by Mathias F. Cowley, *Wilford Woodruff, History of his Life and Labors* (Salt Lake City: Bookcraft, 1964), 16-18.

[49] Cowley, *Wilford Woodruff, History of his Life and Labors*, 17.

[50] Cowley, *Wilford Woodruff, History of his Life and Labors*, 18.

[51] Marshall and Manuel, 185.

[52] Marshall and Manuel, 186.

[53] John Higginson, as quoted by Marshall and Manuel, 21.

[54] Bruce R. McConkie, *Mormon Doctrine* (Salt Lake: Bookcraft, 1979), 81.

[55] Author Terryl Givens quotes several historians who made these claims, to include Ronald Walker, Timothy Smith and Dan Vogel, in his book, *By the Hand of Mormon* (Oxford: Oxford University Press, 2002), 230.

[56] Gordon S. Wood, "Evangelical America and Early Mormonism," *New York History* 61 (October 1980): 364, 367, and 361, as quoted in Terryl Givens, *By the Hand of Mormon*, 230.

[57] Richard Bushman, *Joseph Smith, Rough Stone Rolling* (New York: Alfred A. Knopf, 2005), 147-48.

[58] Spencer W. Kimball, as quoted in Bruce Porter and Rod Meldrum, *Prophecies and Promises* (Mendon: Digital Legend, 2009), 68-69.

[59] Edward Johnson, as quoted in Marshall and Manuel, 199.

[60] Jon Meacham, *American Gospel: God, the Founding Fathers, and the Making of a Nation* (New York: Random House, 2006), 43; and Steven Waldman, 5.

[61] Ezra Taft Benson, "The Lord's Base of Operations." Talk given at the 132nd Annual General Conference of the Church of Jesus Christ of Latter-Day-Saints, 8 April. *The Improvement Era* 65, no.6 (1962): 454-56.

[62] First Presidency Message, as quoted by Porter and Meldrum, *Prophecies and Promises*, 68.

[63] Newt Gingrich, *Rediscovering God in America*, 79.

Washington Crossing the Delaware, by Emanuel Leutze.
The Metropolitan Museum of Art.

CHAPTER 5

A HEAVEN-SENT REVOLUTION

*And I beheld that their mother Gentiles were
gathered together upon the waters, and upon the
land also, to battle against them. And I beheld
that the power of God was with them...*

—1 Nephi 13:17-18

*We have it in our power to begin the world over
again. A situation, similar to the present, hath not
happened since the days of Noah until now.*

—Thomas Paine, 1776

With the discovery and settlement of America complete, the Lord would elevate His choice land to the next level by making it completely free and independent from the Old World proprietors, whose Old World influence in America continued to threaten the liberty required for man's eternal progression. The Lord would call for a clean political slate in America that He might more effectively influence the making of a new government to serve as His vehicle for the Restoration. Unfortunately, such a new and independent system would only come through a bloody revolution. And so God would inspire His new American settlers to turn to their American Covenant, that He might pour upon them the covenant blessings of *liberty, protection,* and *prosperity,* even those blessings required to ultimately secure independence against all odds. Indeed, the American Revolution represents one of the clearest examples of the American Covenant in action; for through it we can see how, as the Founders worked to live according to their obligations, the Lord continued providing the covenant blessings that ultimately created an independent nation whose hallmark would be an abundance of agency unto a fullness of salvation.

The next wave of chapters will reveal how America worked under God and this national covenant in achieving, through the Revolution, such freedom unto gospel salvation. This chapter, as a sort of introduction, will outline the scriptural foundations and eternal purposes under God related to the American Revolution. After having established the Revolution's preeminent place and purpose in the designs of the Almighty, the chapters that follow will review the historical account. This historical account will corroborate the scriptural and gospel-based idea put forth in this book, and particularly in this chapter, that God was wholly behind the American Revolution—and that He backed His actions by the American Covenant. All together, the following narrative will not only further prove the reality and power of this national covenant, but will show how this covenant clearly advanced, through these historic times, the work and glory of God.

A Scriptural Revolution

As the American Revolution is so tightly woven with God and His gospel, an introduction to these next chapters would be incomplete without considering what the scriptures declare concerning the matter. As detailed in the Book of Mormon, and as discussed in the previous chapter, the Prophet Nephi beheld a vision, even an American Covenant vision, of how God would utilize latter-day America in bringing the world out of the darkness of apostasy and into the light of the gospel (see 1 Nephi, Chapter 13). We have already discussed how this vision included scenes of God's influence over the discovery and settlement of this choice land. As part of this vision, and as part of

God's divine plan for America and the Restoration, Nephi describes another event to follow this discovery and settlement of America:

> And it came to pass that I, Nephi, beheld that the Gentiles who had gone forth out of captivity did humble themselves before the Lord; and the power of the Lord was with them. And I beheld that their mother Gentiles were gathered together upon the waters, and upon the land also, to battle against them. And I beheld that the power of God was with them, and also that the wrath of God was upon all those that were gathered together against them to battle. And I, Nephi, beheld that the Gentiles that had gone out of captivity were delivered by the power of God out of the hands of all other nations (1 Nephi 13: 16-19).

Nephi clearly beheld that the latter-day American settlers and covenant-makers, after having "humbl[ed] themselves before the Lord" in obedience to the American Covenant, would, under God's power and American Covenant promises, fight and win a great war against their mother Gentiles (Great Britain) and thus gain their independence. The proof of this war's great significance in God's plan is not only reflected in the fact that a prophet beheld it thousands of years before its occurrence, but also in the idea that Nephi described this scene—along with the other aforementioned American Covenant scenes—as being part of a divine solution to carry the world out of apostasy. Again, after describing the world in its darkened and gospel-deprived state (1 Nephi 13:1-11), Nephi launches into a narrative of prophetic solutions, beginning with the discovery and settlement of America (verses 12-15), followed by the victorious war for independence (verses 16-19); and finally, after a description of the benefits, yet incomplete nature, of the Bible within this new nation (verses 20-30), Nephi sees what will be the culminating effects of these great American events: the restoration of the gospel of Jesus Christ (verses 32-42).

We also read in the Book of Mormon how the Lord Himself, while visiting the Nephites in America, prophesied of this American

Covenant and its application to latter-day America's fight for independence. He declared that latter-day Americans "should be established in this land, and be set up as a free people by the power of the Father, that the covenant of the Father may be fulfilled which he hath covenanted with his people, O house of Israel" (3 Nephi 21:4).

Later revelations also confirm the notion that God did in fact back the war for independence. After revealing that He Himself was behind the making of the new American government, the Lord also added that it was He who had "redeemed the land by the shedding of blood" (D&C 101:80). And many latter-day prophets have added their testimony of the same, to include President Gordon B. Hinckley, who, in making reference to the American revolutionary army, asserted that "the God of Heaven fought its battles."[1]

Additional scriptural support for such claims is revealed through analyzing the significance of the American Covenant scriptures and promises, as discussed earlier. For, as detailed in Chapter 2, it was promised to these Americans that through their national covenant, declared by Jacob through Joseph, their "bow [would] ab[i]de in strength, and the arms of [their] hands [would be] made strong by the hands of the mighty God of Jacob" (Genesis 49:24). They were further promised by Book of Mormon prophets that they "shall be free from bondage" (Ether 2:12) and that "they shall never be brought down into captivity" (2 Nephi 1:7). (And, of course, these are but a few of the many afore-cited scriptural references which testify of the same.) The American Revolution was clearly a direct fulfillment of scriptural prophecy.

A Gospel-Necessary Revolution

The scriptures make it clear that God inspired and supported the American Revolution, and they imply that this Revolution would somehow lead to the latter-day restoration of the gospel. However, we are largely left alone to flesh out the details concerning how exactly the Revolution would help deliver the Restoration. It is only through resolving this issue that we might fully comprehend *why* God so powerfully intervened in America and its war for independence. While it will take the following several chapters to fully explain His actions, we will now open up the discussion by reviewing three eternally enduring reasons God brought the American Revolution.

Reason 1: A Needed Separation from Britain

 T he most obvious gospel purpose of the American Revolution can be explained through reviewing the socio-political developments that were occurring at the time of America's beginning. After the discovery of America, a series of conflicts ensued among the European powers over who would control the new continent. Great Britain emerged victorious as the principle proprietor of the most developed parts of North America. Though the British government initially respected and supported the early American colonists, its political structure would not support God's purposes for America. Britain's power structure consisted of a parliament and a monarchy, which meant that while it practiced a form of representative democracy, such representation was limited, as the king still controlled many aspects of government. For the Americans, who had no representation in parliament, the king's power seemed even more overbearing. Furthermore, the king controlled a state religion, which was capable of making things difficult for new and non-traditional religious thought.[2]

In short, Britain's monarchical system (however partially democratic it might have been) placed a disproportionate amount of power in the hands of a few. Accordingly, under such a system, Satan would need only influence the hearts of these few to successfully implement wicked politics against the Lord's work. And, as the Book of Mormon prophet/governor Mosiah suggests, such a task may prove easy, as "it is common for the lesser part of the people to desire that which is not right" (Mosiah 29:26). A democracy, however, would counter such dangers, as Satan would have to influence a majority, and, as Mosiah assures us, it is "not common that the voice of the people desireth anything contrary to that which is right" (Mosiah 29:26). Considering Satan's relative success in persecuting the early restored church, even under such an American democratic-type system of government, how much more effective and successful would he have been if Joseph Smith had begun his work under the British system, where "the lesser part" ruled? Certainly the Cunning One would have employed every tactic to ensure that the few in charge, already susceptible to the selfish corruption of royalty, stomped out the young prophet and his cause of truth. As such, Britain had to be routed out by the Almighty's American faithful so that democracy's protection could be ushered into America and that the Lord's kingdom and fullness of salvation might safely follow.

The revolutionaries recognized this unsafe political environment stemming from Britain, which explains their oft quoted revolutionary refrains, to include "No taxation without representation," "Don't tread on me," and "All men are created equal." However, they did not (for the most part) fully comprehend that the break with Britain was ultimately about creating religious freedom in America in preparation for God's Restoration. In fact, they did not even necessarily comprehend or emphasize the notion that that they were fighting for religious freedom at all. After all, most of the colonists worshipped God as they desired without major obstruction from the British.

Furthermore, America would never have justified its revolution on religious persecution from Britain because America was not overwhelmingly concerned with this issue at the time. To be sure, the American colonial system allowed its own home grown religious sects (such as those in New England) to dominate certain colonial and local governments, which often led to persecution of minority religious sects. Such practices occurred independently of any British meddling and continued long after independence from Britain was secured.

And finally, the Declaration of Independence, which lists the many American grievances against the British, thereby justifying the Revolution, does not even hint at religious intolerance or religious persecution by the British as one of America's justifications for independence. As will be shown later, the principle justifications had more to do with political rights and property rights than with religious rights.

In short, without being able to witness what horrible things the adversary could do to God's true and restored church under a monarchical system—as the Lord did not permit this scenario to occur —the revolutionaries would find it difficult to emphasize a threat of British religious persecution. They would find it difficult to see God's ultimate designs for the Revolution. However, just because the revolutionaries did not see the end from the beginning does not mean that God could not inspire them to work on His behalf for His ultimate purposes. It was enough that they knew they were on God's errand and that they knew this errand included a separation from British rule and a new form of independence and liberty. The Lord's Latter-day prophets would, with the light of the restored gospel, fill in the details of God's purposes for the Revolution in due time. One such prophet was President Joseph Fielding Smith, who stated the following:

> This great American nation the Almighty raised up by the power of his omnipotent hand, that it might be possible in the latter-days for the Kingdom of God to be established in the earth. If the Lord had not prepared the way by laying the foundation of this glorious nation, it would have been impossible (under the stringent laws and bigotry of the monarchical governments of the world) to have laid the foundations for the coming of his great kingdom. *The Lord has done this.*[3]

Reason 2: A Needed Expansion of Religious Freedom at Home

Another reason the Lord would have inspired the Revolution was to secure greater religious freedom in the land of His future Restoration, not only from monarchical threats, but also from American-based, domestic threats. As recently noted, in addition to monarchical threats to freedom, colonial America was also plagued by religious intolerance stemming from its own American-based religions, which had taken too much control over colonial governments and thus made it difficult for minority religions. Even with the British gone, the restored gospel still might have struggled much under such an American environment. Fortunately, as we will see in the forthcoming chapters, the Revolution not only pushed back a foreign monarchy, but also initiated a process that would shore up religious protections at home against domestic religious persecution. This occurred in part because the Revolution made it difficult for Americans, on a moral level, to fight to the death to eradicate Great Britain's domineering influence over America, while at the same time tolerate its own domestic-based persecution over its own religious minorities. Consequently, through the experience of the Revolution, a new era of religious tolerance and liberation of thought had been born at home.

We recognize this new and positive influence through statements born out of the Revolution, such as the following declaration made by Thomas Jefferson in 1777, at the height of the Revolution: "Almighty God hath created the mind free...All attempts to influence it by temporal punishments or burthens...are a departure from the plan of the Holy Author of our religion...all men shall be free to profess and by argument to maintain, their opinions in matters of religion." Jefferson made this statement in support of "A Bill for Establishing Religious Freedom in Virginia"; but as the issue of increased religious freedom was still only budding and congealing as a byproduct of the Revolution, it would remain but a bill until 1786, some three years after the war, when it at last became state law.[4] But it was the Revolution which stirred men's hearts toward that positive end.

As outlined last chapter, the Pulitzer Prize-winning historian Gordon Wood described how the Revolution brought this new American perspective on religious liberation, and even stated that the birth of "Mormonism" was due to such positive changes in America.[5] He was correct. And not only did this revolutionary fever cause Americans to feel free enough to look for God outside of their traditional framework, but it also inspired them to apply this new feeling of freedom to their new government. When they at last developed their new Constitution, they naturally included those religious protections that would defend minority religions— religions like the restored gospel of Jesus Christ.

In short, though the Revolution's initial purpose was to push back a foreign threat, it also shook up oppressive establishments at home, thus creating the political foundations of religious freedom that the restored gospel would one day utilize. The Founders did not enter the Revolution to cause such a shake-up at home (their target was most certainly a foreign one and not domestic-based religious oppressors), but we can be assured that the Lord knew the end from the beginning, and inspired His founding American generation accordingly.

Reason 3: A Needed Influence for the World

Another reason the Lord would have inspired the American Revolution has to do with how positively the nations of the earth responded to it. The Great Apostasy had turned the lights off on inspired governments throughout the world. At the time of the Revolution, even the most "progressive" and supposedly "enlightened" governments in the world—to include England, France, and their European cousins—were dominated by corrupt and oppressive monarchies and aristocracies. But the American Revolution would challenge all this; for it was the American Revolution that provided the world the opportunity to see, witness, and feel the powerful flame of liberty produced by that spirit generated through righteous revolutions. This American example and influence would ultimately awaken God's chosen, would-be revolutionaries in these oppressed lands near and far, thus providing them with the confidence to contract that infectious spirit of independence and successfully fight to be free from their own oppressive governmental regimes. It was this world-wide awakening stemming from America that would ultimately compel those chosen revolutionaries in the world, from South America to Europe and beyond, to bring liberty and agency—and by extension, the opportunity to access restored gospel truths—to God's children everywhere. But without the spark and flame of an American Revolution, liberty's fire might not have extended the world over in preparation for God's latter-day work.

One example of a national movement commencing under the influence of this American spark and flame was the French Revolution which began in 1789 and which brought the masses to the realization of their self-worth in relation to something greater than kings and queens, thus instilling in them a sense of their God-given right of agency. Occurring directly on the heals of the American Revolution, this French movement had adopted this American spirit and then proceeded to spread it on to all the peoples of Europe longing to be free.* Within two decades of the American Revolution, the world saw democratic uprisings, revolutions, and constitutional reforms in places like Sweden, Poland, Belgium, the Dutch Provinces, Naples, Russia, Spain, and Portugal.[6] It was a miracle. As historian Richard Bushman observed, "As late as 1860, the United States occupied a singular position in the world. The democratic spirit of the American Revolution had inspired European reformers for eighty-five years, and the impulse was not yet extinguished."[7] These movements, inspired by America, marked the beginning of the end of European totalitarian and monarchical powers, and thus set the stage for the democracy, the religious tolerance, and, ultimately, the fullness of the gospel we see there today.

And it was not just in Europe. Within approximately eighty years from the time America declared its independence in 1776, over eighteen countries in the Western Hemisphere alone, also drawing on the American example, had fought and gained their independence from their respective monarchical oppressors.[8] This,

---

* It should be noted that some of these revolutions, including the French Revolution, had initially ended tragically with thousands executed by revolutionaries turned tyrants. But even in these tragedies, the political situations eventually stabilized under constitutional principles of civil and religious freedom, thus achieving the inspired result in the end.

of course, led to even more open governments and societies where the gospel could be accepted.

The American Revolution has even influenced modern-day movements in both China (students at Tiananmen Square) and in the nations of the Former Soviet Union, whose peoples, struggling to be free of Communism, would incessantly quote Thomas Jefferson and his American revolutionary companions. They found in these American patriots their inspiration for freedom.[9]

Furthermore, the newly-born free nations stemming from these revolutionary movements would oft times emulate the U.S. Constitution in drafting and forming their new governments. This also clues us in on where their inspiration for independence and civil and religious liberty truly was derived. But again, had America remained revolution-less, such an infectious spirit which brought so much good to the world might never have been born and spread. The political barriers to religious freedom might not have fallen so swiftly in the world in preparation for the Restoration.

Also, it has been suggested above that it was the American revolutionary spirit of independence which—beyond encouraging religious freedom on a political level—also generated in American hearts a feeling of personal and spiritual liberation, which allowed many to feel confident and inspired to seek for God outside traditional frameworks. This openness and freedom allowed such individuals in America to find and accept the fullness of the gospel. That being the case, the same can be said for other nations of the world, whose own revolutions similarly created open, enlightened, and searching spirits among their citizenry. This eventually led many to the true gospel light, once that gospel light was made available to them. And so, more than just removing political barriers to religious freedom, these revolutions also removed personal barriers to God's gospel truth. As these spiritual feelings sprung from revolutions, and as these revolutions sprung from that first revolution, even the American Revolution, we see why God brought on the American Revolution in the first place.

The spiritual impulses, which carried these eternal purposes of the Revolution, were so powerful that even the earliest of the Founding Fathers—without the luxury of historical hindsight, but with the light of God's inspiration—could articulate the magnificent blessings their successful revolution would offer to all the world. Though the Founders could not fully comprehend how their revolution would inspire other revolutions, thus facilitating the delivery of the restored gospel to the world, they knew enough to catch glimpses of the eternal plan. For example, the American sage, Benjamin Franklin, declared:

> Tyranny is so generally established in the rest of the world that the prospect of an asylum in America for those who love liberty gives general joy, and our cause is esteemed the cause of all mankind....It is a common observation here that our cause is the cause of all mankind, and that we are fighting for their liberty in defending our own.[10]

Furthermore, in a 1776 letter published by the *New England Chronicle*, signed simply by "A Freeman," the following was declared to all America: "[W]e expect soon to break off all kind of connection with Britain, and form into a Grand Republic of the American United Colonies, which will, *by the blessing of heaven, soon work out our salvation....*"

> Never was a cause more important or glorious than that which you are engaged in; not only your wives, your children, and distant posterity, but humanity at large, the world of mankind, are interested in it; for if tyranny should prevail in this great country, we may expect liberty will expire throughout the world. Therefore, more human *glory and happiness* may depend upon your exertions than ever yet depended upon any of the sons of men.[11]

It was this same spirit that inspired the founder Thomas Paine to eloquently and prophetically proclaim the following in his 1776 work, *Common Sense* (which, very fittingly, was responsible for much revolutionary spirit in colonial America): "We have it in our power to begin *the world* over again. A situation, similar to the present, hath not happened since the days of Noah until now."[12]

And finally, Abraham Lincoln (who had the added insight of historical perspective, having served some eighty years after the Revolution), inspiringly declared the following about what American independence meant for the world:

> It was not the mere matter of separation of the colonies from the motherland, but that sentiment in the Declaration of Independence which gave liberty not alone to the people of this country, but hope to all the world, for all future time. It was that which gave promise that in due time the weights would be lifted from the shoulders of all men, and that all should have an equal chance. This is the sentiment embodied in the Declaration of Independence.[13]

It is no wonder that Lincoln called the United States the "last best hope on earth."[14]

Such commentaries by such inspired founders as Franklin, the "Freeman," Paine, and Lincoln lend credibility to the idea that the Revolution truly was bigger than just America. The Revolution's influence would eventually be so far reaching in the world that even those early Americans in the trenches, quite amazingly, felt it from the beginning. The fact that history has vindicated their prophetic suggestions should cause us to pause and reflect upon the truly inspired nature of our founding generations.

But regardless of what they knew or did not know, it is clear the Lord understood these world-wide gospel benefits that would be born of the American Revolution. This adds yet another explanation for His intervention in revolutionary America.

Conclusion

 The Revolution was clearly a powerful movement brought to America by Heaven. Not only do the scriptures testify of this truth, but the eternal fruits of the Revolution reveal why the Lord would inspire and guide it through to its victorious end. Whether we are discussing the needed break with Britain's dangerous system of government, the needed spark for religious freedom at home, or the need for freedom's influence to spread abroad, all justifications for the Revolution lead to the same eternal purpose. In every case it is about freedom and liberty trumping various forms of tyranny and oppression, so that man might progress under a fullness of agency and that the gospel of Jesus Christ might flourish at home and abroad. Seen in this light, the Revolution was nothing less than an extended version of the War in Heaven, which was clearly fought over these same principles surrounding man's agency and salvation. Perhaps this helps us understand why the Lord declared that He created America in order to protect and support "moral agency," and not for America alone, but for "all flesh" (D&C 101:77-78). And perhaps this further explains why the Lord intervened in the American Revolution utilizing one of His most powerful tools: a covenant with His children.

 While the revolutionaries could not fully understand these purposes, even though they sometimes caught glimpses, God knew what He was doing. Like Lincoln said of the Civil War, so it can be said of the Revolutionary War: "[T]he Almighty has his own purposes."[15] As long as God was on their side, the revolutionaries did not need a full explanation. It was enough that they knew they were fighting for liberty under God, and that they knew victory would come only to the extent that they righteously adhered to the American Covenant. This, as we shall see, they most definitely understood.

★ ★ ★ ★

W hile the scriptures and arguments presented above lend ample credibility to the notion that the American Revolution is inseparably connected to God's Plan of Salvation, the details concerning exactly *how* God worked through the American Covenant in blessing this American revolutionary cause are less known. As such, the next several chapters will utilize the historical record to expound not only on *why,* but *how,* the Lord executed the miracle that was the American Revolution and War for Independence. As we explore this fascinating era of American history, we will identify the fingerprints of God everywhere upon it. Along the way, we will corroborate the scriptural and gospel-based claims put forth in this book, and particularly in this chapter, regarding God's hand and covenant in America and her revolution. And in the end, we will have no doubt about the power and reality of this covenant and its grand purposes under Heaven.

END NOTES

[1] Gordon B. Hinckley, *Standing for Something* (New York: Times Books/ Random House Incorporated, 2000), xv-xvi.

[2] William J. Bennett, *America, The Last Best Hope* (Nashville, Nelson Current, 2006), 40.

[3] Joseph Fielding Smith, as quoted in Bruce R. McConkie, *Gospel Doctrine* (Salt Lake City: Deseret Book, 1986), 409, emphasis in original.

[4] Thomas Jefferson (1777), as quoted by Newt Gingrich (Nashville: Integrity House, 2006), 45.

[5] Gordon S. Wood, "Evangelical America and Early Mormonism," *New York History* 61 (October 1980): 364, 367, and 361, as quoted in Terryl Givens, *By the Hand of Mormon,* 230.
[6] Richard Bushman, "1830: Pivotal Year in the Fulness of Times," *Ensign.* September 1978, 9.

[7] Richard Bushman, "1830: Pivotal Year in the Fulness of Times," *Ensign.* September 1978, 9.

[8] For a complete list of these nations and the dates of their independence, see Kenneth W. Thompson, *The U.S. Constitution and the Constitutions of Latin America* (New York: University Press of America, 1991), 87-94.

[9] Stephen Ambrose, *To America, Personal Reflections of an Historian* (New York: Simon and Schuster, 2002), 7.

[10] Benjamin Franklin, as quoted by Walter Isaacson, *Benjamin Franklin, An American Life* (New York: Simon and Schuster, 2003), 339.

[11] McCullough, *1776,* 63, emphasis added.

[12] From Thomas Paine's *Common Sense*, as quoted by John Ferling, *Adams vs. Jefferson, The Tumultuous Election of 1800* (New York: Oxford University Press, 2004), 25, emphasis added. The full text of Paine's *Common Sense* is available at www.earlyamerica.com/earlyamerica/milestone/commonsense/text.html.

[13] Abraham Lincoln, as quoted in Gordon Leidner, *Lincoln on God and Country* (Shippensburg: White Mane Books, 2000), 44.

[14] Lincoln, as quoted by Bushman, "1830: Pivotal Year in the Fulness of Times," *Ensign.* September 1978, 9.

[15] Leidner, *Lincoln on God and Country*, 113.

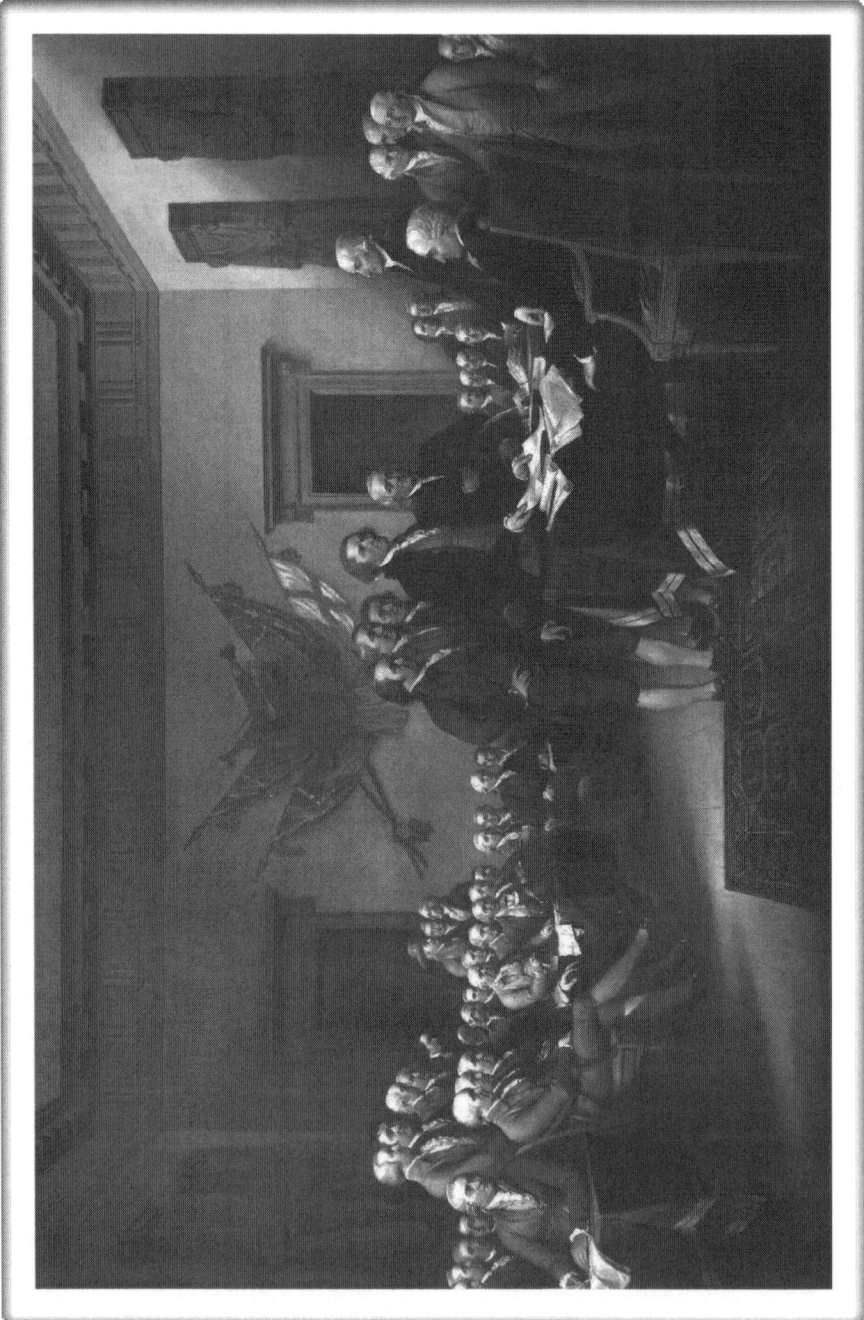

Declaration of Independence, by John Trumbull.
Courtesy of the Architect of the Capitol.

CHAPTER 6

THE SPIRIT OF INDEPENDENCE

*The men in the revolution were inspired by the
Almighty, to throw off the shackles of the mother
government....For this cause were Adams,
Jefferson, Franklin, Washington, and a host of
others inspired to deeds of resistance to the acts of
the King of Great Britain...to bring to pass the
purposes of God....It was the voice of the Lord
inspiring all those worthy men who bore influence
in those trying times.*

—Brigham Young

In the previous chapter we asserted that the American Revolution holds a preeminent place in the plan of the Almighty. We will now corroborate this powerful assertion through exploring the historical account. In so doing, we will witness powerful and heavenly manifestations, both on and off the battlefields of war; we will see tokens and signs of the gospel, which are astonishingly laced throughout the Revolution's history; and we will identify the American Covenant, which was always at the core of this heavenly movement and is thus reflected in God's actions toward the American revolutionaries and, in turn, is reflected in the

167

revolutionaries' actions toward God. Ultimately, we will see that it was through this covenant that America received the blessings of *liberty, protection,* and *prosperity,* even those blessings necessary to defeat its enemies and eventually create the foundation for the Restoration.

We will begin our analysis of this historical narrative by discussing God's spiritual and physical interventions into revolutionary America. While the next chapter will focus on God's miraculous and *physical* interventions on the battlefields of the American War for Independence, it is the purpose of this chapter to reveal how His powerful and *spiritual* influence touched the hearts and souls of the Founders, and thus called them, directed them, and upheld them in the cause of revolution. In exploring this spiritual influence over the Founders, we will validate Nephi's prophetic claim that "the power of God was with them" (see 1 Nephi 13:16-19). The gospel informs us that such spiritual influences are the fruits of the Holy Ghost or perhaps even the Light of Christ. But without a full understanding of such gospel terminology, yet with a desire to label this powerful influence from above that was so prevalent during the Revolution, patriots both past and present have referred to this heavenly power as the *The Spirit of Independence* or *The Spirit of '76.* As the Founders listened and adhered to this Spirit, they were in essence fulfilling their end of the covenant, thus allowing God to bless their righteous cause.

Though the presence of this revolutionary American spirit, and the nomenclature we have assigned it, are well known, the actual details concerning how it was delivered and received during this historic time are perhaps less known. As such, in an effort to further prove God's hand in America and thus further validate His national covenant with America, we will attempt here to make such details known by exploring and developing five evidentiary concepts found within the historical record. These concepts show how the Lord hurled His power and influence, even this *Spirit of Independence,* down upon colonial America. They are, in no particular order, 1) The Spiritual Preparation of George Washington;

2) The Otherwise Inexplicable Decision of the Revolutionaries; 3) The Testimonials of the Rebels; 4) the Great Awakening; and 5) The Conversion of the Founders.

The Spiritual Preparation of George Washington

President Spencer W. Kimball once declared that "God does notice us, and He watches over us. But it is usually through another person that He meets our needs."[1] In light of this truth, if God was to impart the blessings of the covenant to the American people, then we might expect that He would do it, to at least some degree, "through another person." History certainly supports the notion that George Washington was one such person. It seems clear that the unseen hand of the Lord intervened early and often in the life of Washington, thus preparing him for the preeminent role he would play in the creation of America and the establishment of the national covenant.

Washington was born in Westmorland County, Virginia, in 1732 (the same year as Joseph Smith's maternal grandfather, Solomon Mack, who would serve two tours of duty under Washington in the Revolutionary War).[2] Washington's forbearers first immigrated to America in 1658, in large part to be free of the Old World's religious persecution[3]—an appropriate heritage for Washington. Though precious little is known about his childhood, we do know that his father, Augustine, was a relatively successful planter, businessman, and civil servant, and that his mother, Mary Bell, was both attentive and strict with her children. Both were devout parents to George and instilled in him the important values that would serve him later in his divine calling. Such values included strict obedience, deep humility, and an enduring love of God.

One of the few stories we know of his childhood demonstrates the parental teaching of such obedience and humility. When George was four-years-old, he decided to surprise his mother one morning by bringing her a bunch of her award-winning peonies from the family garden. As young George warmly and enthusiastically presented his offering, he was met by a stern reproach and a vigorous paddling. Such tough love may seem inappropriate for a four-year-old, but his father explained to him that the peonies were intended to stay where they were. The deeper lesson, as Augustine lovingly taught, is that every action made, even if done with good intention, is accompanied by consequences. Young George had to learn to develop the foresight to see such consequences and act responsibly.[4]

Another story told of young Washington was when his father helped him plant cabbage seeds in a pattern that spelled out the name G-E-O-R-G-E. When the cabbage grew out enough to make visible the boy's name, he was astonished. According to one source, upon seeing the boy's reaction, Washington's father pointed to the cabbage and then told him, "This is a great thing, an important thing, a vital thing...I want you to understand, my son, that I am introducing you to your *true* Father, the source and sustenance of all life."[5]

In addition to such lessons, Augustine taught George the more profound meaning of life based in obedience, humility, and love towards God. "The Ten Commandments," he would repeatedly tell his children, "cover the major issues of life; there is nothing that equals them...in application to our general problems."[6] Furthermore, young George was instructed to write, repeat, and apply several maxims, one of which stated, "Labour to keep alive in your breast that little spark of celestial fire called conscience"[7]— something we know today, through the restored gospel, as the Light of Christ.

These lessons would be invaluable to Washington when confronted with the great challenge that was the American Revolution and nation building. One might even draw direct correlations between these childhood lessons and Washington's poised and wise decisions on the battlefield, as will be seen throughout the following chapters. We will see these attributes reflected, for example, in his constant submission to the Congress during the conflict, his impressive concession of power back to the people at war's end, and most importantly, his ever-enduring appeals to, reliance upon, and constant recognition of the Almighty's hand in the affairs of America.

Though his upbringing helped form the exceptional man he would become, his youth was spent largely in the usual pursuits of the Virginia gentry: riding, fishing, hunting, planting, and dancing. He eventually made a prosperous career for himself as a land surveyor, spending much time exploring the uncharted territories in the western parts of Virginia. At the age of twenty-one, due in part to his exceptional knowledge of these uncharted lands, Washington became a major in the Virginia militia, which would serve under the British during the American land claim battles known as the French and Indian War. Though he fought and led courageously—making a name for himself within Virginia—his short military career was less than successful, as he lost most of his engagements with the French, including his embarrassing surrender of the British Fort Necessity. After not receiving the promotion he desired, Washington abandoned the military for what he thought would be forever.

With his military service completed at age twenty-seven, he returned to private life, married the wealthy widow Martha Custis, and eventually inherited, and developed, the plantation known as Mount Vernon. Apart from his responsibilities of running a successful plantation operation, Washington was active in church and community affairs. He also served in the Virginia House of Burgesses, but consistently maintained a low profile, introducing no legislation and making few speeches. He would maintain this same quiet demeanor as a Virginia delegate to the Continental Congress in 1774, when the whispers of revolution were evolving into a solidified voice. Though he expressed disdain for British tyranny, he failed to make any speeches or earn any appointment to a congressional committee.[8]

As such, it may have come as a surprise to some when—at the Second Continental Congress in June 1775—the delegate from Massachusetts, John Adams, perhaps the loudest and most influential voice for American independence, nominated Washington to be Commander-in-Chief of the Continental Army.[9] And perhaps more surprising was the ease with which his nomination was accepted by the Congress. After all, though Washington's appointment would bring much needed support from the southern states (particularly the powerhouse that was Virginia), and though he had indeed been a military man at one time in his life, critics would have had good reason to balk at the decision.

First, with so little formal education, which ended for him at age fifteen, Washington's academic training paled in comparison to the many highly-educated and accomplished delegates that surrounded him, namely, Thomas Jefferson, John Adams, Richard Henry Lee, Benjamin Rush, James Wilson, and many others. Second, Washington had been retired from any military service for *fifteen* years. As the Pulitzer Prize-winning scholar David McCullough pointed out, "he was by no means an experienced commander. He had never led an army in battle, never commanded anything larger than a regiment. And never had he directed a siege."[10] In fact, the only military experience he possessed, as already noted, had yielded less than impressive results.

Washington himself recognized his inadequacies before Congress. In his acceptance speech, he stated:

> I am truly sensible of the high honor done to me in this appointment, yet I feel great distress from a consciousness that my abilities and military experience may not be equal to the extensive and important trust....I beg it may be remembered by every gentlemen in the room that I this day declare with utmost sincerity, I do not think myself equal to the command I [am] honored with.[11]

And it wasn't as though the Congress had no other choices for their commander-in-chief. On the contrary, there were several whose military experience far surpassed that of Washington. For example, Washington's original second-in–command, Charles Lee, had traveled the world fighting as a British officer and had even served as a military advisor to the King of Poland; Lee was most definitely "a professional soldier."[12] Another long standing professional soldier was Horatio Gates, who at one point during the war almost managed to oust Washington as commander. Gates was many years older than Washington and displayed a far greater familiarity with military affairs. Having served at length as a British officer, he possessed without question "greater professional experience than Washington." And still there were others such as Thomas Conway and Thomas Mifflin, both of whom, as military executives and chief administrators, had more military experience than Washington (which may explain why they both would aspire underhandedly to unseat Washington as commander).[13] Even the famous and highly competent John Hancock, who presided over Congress, desired the position for himself and thought it might be his.[14]

Yet, notwithstanding, reason alone seemed overshadowed by something bigger than any of the delegates could fully comprehend. It was perhaps only in the wisdom and influence of the Lord that Washington could have been so readily selected. Adams, as will be shown later, was unarguably a spiritually connected man, which lends credibility to the idea that his supporting and propping up of the general was perhaps wholly inspired. It seems as though Washington agreed with this sentiment when, as the newly appointed commander, he wrote to his wife that "far from seeking this appointment, I have used every endeavor in my power to avoid it, not only from my unwillingness to part with you and the family, but from a consciousness of its being a trust too great for my capacity....it has been a kind of destiny that has thrown me upon this service...."[15]

Perhaps it was "destiny," or better yet, *divine intervention*, which prompted and encouraged Adams and Congress to select Washington. The Lord needed someone who was sufficiently humble and obedient—someone worthy to responsibly manage the vast power that was to be handed to America's first commander-in-chief. Incidentally, Charles Lee and Horatio Gates would—like thousands of others—betray and / or cower from the American cause by war's end, seeking the selfish above all else.* Washington, on the other hand, would stay faithful, always respecting his position as servant to the people, always conceding power to Congress, whom he consistently acknowledged as the rightful representatives of the people, and always seeking the guidance of God. Even his harshest critics agreed that "he could not be bribed, corrupted, or compromised."[16]

Indeed, Washington was the Lord's choice. Like other religious and political leaders raised up by God for divine purposes, Washington's humility and obedience compelled him to look so often to God, which in turn, allowed God to influence and direct the affairs of His people.[17] Such qualities in Washington are what ultimately built this nation and its covenant. For, as cited earlier, the Book of Mormon makes clear that the Lord would only rescue and support the latter-day, colonial Americans through the national covenant if they first "humbled themselves before the Lord" (See 1 Nephi 13: 16). As Washington applied this principle, he made himself and the nation compliant with the covenant obligations, thus calling down the needed covenant blessings. It is no wonder

---

* Lee was captured by the British in 1776, and then almost immediately volunteered information to the British command on how to defeat the struggling Continental Army. See David McCullough, *1776*, 266. Lee was later suspended by Congress for betraying Washington. See Willard Sterne Randall, *Alexander Hamilton, A Life* (New York: Harper Collins, 2003), 176.

In an effort to gain Washington's seat as commander, Gates became a "cunning egoist" who conspired against Washington when Washington most needed his generals' support. Then, perhaps worse, in 1780, Gates led a counter-attack in the south which resulted in his defeat at Camden. When defeat was imminent, Gates jumped on the "fastest horse he could find, [and] did not stop retreating until he was 160 miles from the battlefield." Plunged into deep disgrace, he was replaced by Nathaniel Greene and did not return to the army for two years. An investigation into his conduct was subsequently ordered. See Thomas Fleming, "Unlikely Victory," *What If? The World's Foremost Military Historians Imagine What Might Have Been* (New York: Penguin Putnam Inc, 1999), 173; See also "Horatio Gates," *Columbia Encyclopedia, Sixth Edition. 2001-2005*, available online at www.bartleby.com/65/ga/Gates.

that a man of Washington's humility and obedience would be the chosen American revolutionary head.

Notwithstanding the above analysis of Washington's divine ascension to power, prominent historian Joseph Ellis would reject the idea that God had anything to do with it, arguing instead that John Adams' role in the affair was exaggerated and that Washington's place as commander was a logical, secular-minded, "forgone conclusion." As proof, Ellis offers up the valid point that perhaps Washington was the most obvious Virginian, and Virginia's support was a necessity. Ellis' other argument was that Washington's physical appearance and his use of military fatigues in Congress swayed the judgment of the delegates in favor of him.[18] He was, after all, a man continuously described by his peers as "noble and majestic," a "commanding figure" with abundant "martial dignity...strength and sagacity," and with a "softness in his eyes that people remembered," which produced "joy on every countenance."[19] That his physical attributes swayed the masses is one thing, but that they caused the delegates to appoint Washington is much less convincing, as it would require us to believe that the very intelligent and deliberate-minded congressional delegates could be taken by such physical trivialities.

However, there is one way in which these apparent "physical trivialities" could be seen as something far from trivial. Indeed, there is one explanation that validates and sheds light on Ellis' argument that Washington's physique played a role in his selection. However, this explanation is most readily understood in a spiritual context— not a secular one as offered by Ellis. This spiritual context is based in the notion that the Lord has oft times manifested His Spirit through the physicality of His mortal leaders as a testimony to the people of these chosen leaders. Consider, for example, the many early Latter-day Saints who described their attraction to the Prophet Joseph in terms of his physical stature, often commenting upon—in the very words that had been used to describe Washington—his "commanding presence."[20] Early leaders like Wilford Woodruff, David Whitmer, Orson Pratt, and many others testified of a radiance, illumination, and even transfiguration revealed at certain times in Joseph's physical appearance, which swayed them to follow him.[21] During a church gathering soon after Joseph's death, the Lord again used this tactic to testify to the disoriented Saints that Brigham Young was the rightful successor, though others were making opposing claims. While Brigham was addressing the Saints, the Lord transformed his physical appearance to reflect the power and majesty of Joseph's, thus calming doubts about who to follow.[22]

Perhaps the Lord utilized such manifestations, even if to a lesser degree, to reveal to the Congress that Washington was the chosen man. After all, such divinely manifested power is the only convincing argument to explain how the collective intellectual and rational force of the Congress could be swayed by something as seemingly insignificant as physical appearance. Perhaps the only thing capable of trumping the delegates' secular reasoning was an overriding sense of a God-fearing, miracle-accepting Christianity, which seemed to dictate their consciences.

But regardless of what role, if any, Washington's physical appearance played, the real issue underlying his unlikely ascension to power was his indisputable lack of military experience. Ellis himself admits, in the same language as McCullough, the military inadequacies of Washington, adding that the desperate general even turned to military textbooks to teach himself how to organize an army.[23] Could such a man, so lacking in a comprehensive knowledge of the task at hand, be deemed an "obvious choice" or "forgone conclusion"? Only by God's influence upon the hearts of his fellow countrymen could such a notion be conceived.

The highly-educated, over-opinionated delegates of the Congress, who seemed to bicker and debate about anything and everything, were risking, as they put it, "our lives, our fortunes, and our sacred honor"* in this cause of independence. They were willingly and knowingly placing their lives, fortunes, and sacred honor in the hands of Washington, yet there was little, if any, real

---

* As quoted from the Declaration of Independence

debate surrounding his appointment when, as evidenced above, there was much to be debated. The truth is, while Washington was not void of obvious qualities that lent themselves to positive judgments by purely secular minds, it was largely divine intervention that led to his rapid approval and ascension as commander of the Continental Army.

Beyond the events surrounding his inspired appointment by Congress, the evidence is clear that, from an even earlier time, a divine mantle accompanied Washington to his national calling. One oft-told account, once found in American history textbooks (when it was still acceptable to speak of God in school) reflected this very sentiment. On July 9, 1755, in the battle of Monongahela, during the French and Indian War, a young Washington would miraculously survive an onslaught of enemy firepower that killed or wounded over half of the participants. With "death leveling my companions on every side of me," Washington would later explain, "by the miraculous care of Providence, that protected me beyond human expectations; I had four bullets through my coat, and two horses shot from under me, and yet escaped unhurt."[24] God's preserving hand was upon him. Washington's work had not yet been accomplished.

An epilogue to this story occurred some fifteen years later when a certain Indian chief named Grand Sachem, who had been at the battle of Monongahela, sat in a meeting with a group of Virginians, one of which was an older and more mature Washington. The meeting, which occurred in 1770, was recorded by Washington's adopted grandson, George Washington Parke Custis, in his 1827 work entitled "Recollections of Washington." During the meeting, the chief, recognizing Washington—still years before Washington would become famous—stood and said:

> I am a chief and ruler over many tribes. The hunting grounds of my people extend from the thunder of the Onigara and the Great Lakes to the far blue mountains. I have traveled the long and weary path of the wilderness

road that I might once again look upon the young warrior [Washington] of the great battle. By the waters of the Monongahela, we met the soldiers of the King beyond the Seas, who came to drive from the land my French Brothers. They came into the forest with much beating of drums and many flags flying in the breeze. Like a blind wolf they walked into our trap, and the faces of these red-clad warriors turned pale at the sound of our war-whoop. It was a day when the white man's blood mixed with the streams and forests, and 'twas then I first beheld this Chief. [Points to Washington.] I called my young men and said: "Mark you tall and daring warrior! He is not of the red-coat tribe, he is of the Long knives. He has an Indian's wisdom. His warriors fight as we do—himself alone is exposed to our fire. Quick! Let your aim be certain and he dies. Our muskets were leveled—muskets that, for all but him, knew not how to miss. I, who can bring the leaping squirrel from the top of the highest tree with a single shot, fired at this warrior more times than I have fingers. Our bullets killed his horse, knocked the war bonnet from his head, pierced his clothes, but 'twas in vain; a Power mightier far than we shielded him from harm. He cannot be killed in battle. I am old and soon shall be gathered to the great council fire of the Land of the Shades, but ere I go, there is something bids me speak in the voice of prophecy. Listen! Give ear to my words ye that are gathered here. The Great Spirit protects that man and guides his footsteps through the trails of life. He will become the chief of many nations, and when the sun is setting on the remaining few of my people and the game has departed from our forests and streams, a people yet unborn will hail him as the founder of a mighty empire. I have spoken.

Washington reportedly responded after a long pause:

Our destinies are shaped by a mighty Power, and we can but strive to be worthy of what the Great Spirit holds in store for us. If I must needs have such lot in life as our Red Brother presages, then I pray that the Great Spirit give unto me those qualities of fortitude, courage, and wisdom possessed by our Red Brother. I, the friend of the Indian, have spoken.[25]

The prophetic nature of this dialogue is emphasized by the fact that it occurred some five years before Washington was called to lead the Continental Army.

Also prophesying about a young Washington, years before he would become a household name, was the Reverend Samuel Davies, who proclaimed: "I cannot but hope Providence has hitherto preserved [him] in so signal a Manner for some important Service to his Country."[26] In a similar spirit, Washington's mother, upon her deathbed, reportedly told her son, "Go, George, fulfill the high destinies which Heaven appears to have intended for you."[27]

That Washington had been prepared by God for his calling under the covenant is evident enough. But the most convincing evidence will be detailed in later chapters, as we see the General in action under God. We will see him powerfully represented in his role as the revolutionary leader of the covenant, as he turns so often to both the Almighty and to the principles of that sacred text which details America's covenant obligations. As Washington himself explained, "It is impossible to rightly govern the world without God and the Bible."[28] It is no wonder historians have called Washington the "Moses of the New World" and portrayed "the war [for Independence] as another exodus from Egypt."[29] Washington is surely worthy of this honor and distinction. There is a reason that the very spiritually and politically involved Abigail Adams (John Adams' wife) described Washington using the following words: "Mark his majestic fabric. He's a temple sacred from his birth and built by hands divine."[30]

★ ★ ★ ★

Before entering the following chapters, which vindicate such powerful descriptions of Washington, we will first address certain false, exaggerated, or misunderstood claims about him which have recently taken aim at his life and legacy. First, in a 2004 best-selling biography, Washington is accused of being overly self-absorbed and ambitious—the "most ambitious" of all the congressional delegates. Ironically, according to the critic, this deep pride manifests itself in Washington's seemingly humble demeanor, actions, and words (as reflected in Washington's aforementioned letters to his loved ones). As proof for such a claim, the critic points out that Washington displayed the same self-doubt and reticence in response to all three of his great promotions: as commander of the army, as chairman of the Constitutional Convention, and as President of the United States. Apparently, nobody could *really* be that humble. "After all, Washington had been talked about as the leading candidate [for commander] for several weeks [before his appointment] and did nothing to discourage such talk, and had been wearing his uniform" in posturing for the position. Therefore, concludes the critic, Washington must have "fabricated" his humble acceptance of authority in an effort to hide his selfish motivation—hence, his obvious "pattern of postured reticence" in response to the honors given him.[31]

While not denying that, like any great leader, Washington possessed the necessary ambition to accomplish his goals, this critique hurled upon him must overcome the following questions: Would not a pattern of humility be more easily attributed to one's *actual* humility than to a "fabrication"? Does one's failure to actively discourage his own promotion by others really constitute an act of pride and ambition? Do we really know Washington's true motive for dressing in his old military fatigues from time to time? Would the most ambitious, power-seeking delegate of Congress return his great power to the people as Washington did at war's end—though thousands of years of military tradition would have justified him keeping it—just to maintain his fabricated show of humility? Would he have returned to Mount Vernon after only two presidential terms, when no law at the time compelled it and when the people would have elected him for life? And how do we explain David McCullough's comment that by age twenty-seven, "if he [had] seemed at times flagrantly, unattractively ambitious, he had long since overcome that"?[32] Finally, how do we explain the opinions of Washington's close friends and peers who called him "amiable" and "modest," "void of austerity" and with "no hint of arrogance"?[33]

The second critique, also advanced by modern-day scholars, puts into question Washington's relationship with God. One award-winning author recently described Washington's personal religion as follows: "A lukewarm Episcopalian, he never took Communion, tended to talk about 'Providence' or 'Destiny' rather than God, and —was this a statement?—preferred to stand rather than kneel when praying."[34]

This author's suggestion—which is a popular one among modern critics—is problematic on several levels. For example, if Washington was not overly active as an Episcopalian, this says nothing of his feelings toward God. Like Adams and Jefferson (as will be discussed), and in the spirit of Roger Williams before them, and Joseph Smith Sr. after them, perhaps Washington tacitly acknowledged the religious apostasy he lived under, finding only limited benefit in a particular denomination. Notwithstanding this rationale, however, several eyewitnesses testified that Washington did, in fact, take communion regularly.[35]

Furthermore, the notion that Washington was less than a true believer because he used a variety of titles for God (other than "God") is weak and misleading for at least two reasons. First, it is documented that Washington used the title "God" on more than one hundred occasions. Second, it was customary for Anglicans in eighteenth-century Virginia to refrain from using the title of "God." As one historian pointed out, "The avoidance [of using the title "God"] was not out of unbelief, but from a reverence for the sacred names and a desire to keep them from being profaned."[36] And so Washington often used alternate titles for God, such as *Providence* and *Almighty*.

The argument that Washington's alleged weak religion is somehow represented by the notion that he refrained from kneeling when praying is equally problematic and misleading. For how many praying people kneel in public? Indeed, such a practice is generally confined to private moments, far from the eye of reporters and historians. Perhaps this critique was aimed at the idea that Washington stood during formal church religious devotionals, while others knelt. If such is the case, we should defer to Washington's adopted granddaughter, Nelly Custis, who explained that her grandfather did in fact stand, "as was the custom" for Virginia gentlemen at that time.[37]

Perhaps the most frustrating element concerning these many attempts to belittle Washington's religion is that these critics make their analysis and simply omit the rich and abundant historical evidence which disproves their arguments. That is, they ignore the evidence that clearly shows how important God was to Washington. We have already outlined many examples that show the Lord was Washington's absolute strength and inspiration. And there are many more examples. Indeed, there are at least 270 documented references in which Washington recognizes the activity and interest of God in his life and in the life of America.[38]

In addition to ignoring such references, critics also have a tendency to omit the testimonies of his family and friends who declared unequivocally that Washington was a profoundly religious man. His family remembered seeing him "upon his knees at a small table, with a candle and open Bible thereon."[39] His secretary, Tobias Lear, confirmed the regular occurrence of these religious devotionals.[40] Colonel B. Temple, an aide to Washington, stated that in the absence of a chaplain, Washington himself would read the Bible to his troops. Temple further noted that, on more than one occasion, he walked into Washington's quarters and "found him on his knees at his devotions." Another of Washington's aides commented that "whenever the General could be spared from camp, on the Sabbath, he never failed riding out to some neighboring church, to join those who were publicly worshipping the Great Creator."[41] And these testimonies only scratch the surface of Washington's deep relationship with God and covenant, as we will see in the forthcoming chapters.

Indeed, Washington was deeply religious. He was also very private about his personal testimony, thus making himself vulnerable to critics who want so badly for him to be a purely secular character. Using the weak arguments discussed above, these critics often suggest that Washington was a Deist—one who believes in a God, but also believes that this God is not actively involved or interested in the affairs of man. However, based on the facts thus far presented concerning Washington and his relationship with God, any attempts to cast doubt on his personal religion, or to classify him as a Deist, seem futile—and by the end of the next few chapters will seem absolutely absurd.

The third and final popular critique of Washington relates to the unfortunate and very real fact that he participated in the evil practice of slavery. Though born into this culture, which taught him of slavery's benign normalcy, Washington struggled with it internally, particularly during the war years. On several occasions, Washington recognized the great immoral irony of his American generation: that it would enslave others while pursuing independence for itself. In an effort to resolve his internal struggle, Washington would endorse plans to emancipate slavery by war's end, but support for such schemes would be unattainable due to—in Washington's words—the "selfish passion" which reigned in the South.[42] By 1779, Washington himself had decided to sell his own slaves in exchange for hired labor (which made sense to him on an economic level as well), but later realized he could not, as most of his slaves belonged to his wife's family. Furthermore, selling his slaves would have resulted in the reprehensible separation of his slave families, which on a moral level he refused to permit—even when such refusal brought a decline in profits and transformed Mount Vernon into a "retirement home and child-care center for many of his slave residents."[43]

Unfortunately, Washington's own weakness perhaps barred him from the simple act of freeing the slaves he could (over one hundred of the Mount Vernon slaves belonged exclusively to him). Such an act of mercy would have partially solved his moral dilemma. In his defense, however, Washington was one of the precious few of the founding generation that did free his slaves upon his death. Not only did he free them, but, as instructed in his Last Will and Testament, each was to be provided for and educated through a trust fund he established "to help them in their freedom." Washington's trust fund "continued to support his former slaves and their descendants well into the nineteenth century."[44]

Other evidence of Washington's more progressive feelings regarding blacks in America stem from accounts of his unusual willingness to work side by side with them, his constant instructions to his foremen to treat them well and not overwork them, and his acceptance of their enlistment into his Continental Army (up to fifteen percent of the Continental regulars were black).[45] We gain further insight on the issue through a letter Washington wrote to the black slave and poet, Phyllis Wheatley, in which he thanked her for her kind words, graciously praised her prose, and invited her to visit him at his headquarters.[46] We also witness his softened heart towards blacks through a note in his will, in which he describes an "attachment" to his personal man-servant Billy Lee, whose "faithful service" to Washington earned him his freedom, along with his own annuity and free room and board for the rest of his life.[47]

Finally, in the years just following the creation of the United States, and with the South already threatening secession over the slave question, Washington's own thoughts, influenced by his understanding of America and her covenant with God, were nothing less than prophetic: "I clearly foresee," he declared, "that nothing but the rooting out of slavery can perpetuate the existence of our union." According to his attorney general, Edmund Randolph, if a civil war over the issue ensued, Washington—though a proud Southerner—"had made up his mind to move and be of the northern."[48]

Admittedly, these actions and sentiments towards his slaves, and blacks in general, seem inconsequential and petty within a twenty-first century viewpoint. However, in light of the times in which he lived, Washington certainly rose higher than could be expected from a Southern plantation owner.

But regardless of what one gleans from any of the above insights into his complexities and controversies, Washington's preeminent place in history is anchored to something far more significant, even his principal role in creating one nation under God for the eternal purposes of God. The biographical sketches offered above certainly demonstrate the Lord's influence in his early preparation and character. And this spiritual influence would only continue to grow in Washington, as the *Spirit of Independence* drove him to understand and regularly invoke the principles of the American Covenant. The following pages and chapters will continue to detail this history, allowing all to judge for themselves this man and the cause that he and his fellow Americans gave themselves to.

The Otherwise Inexplicable Decision of the Revolutionaries

The textbook reasons for why the American colonists went to war against Britain are simply not strong enough or compelling enough alone to explain the passion, dedication, and sacrifice displayed in revolutionary America. This is not to say that these textbook reasons do not justify a decision to enter the war; on the contrary, even the most rudimentary explanations for why the colonists went forward with their rebellion justify their actions. However, upon considering the full historical landscape in which the American colonists lived, their decision to proceed with the Revolutionary War, and thus endure what they did, compels even the patriots among us to ask, *Why did they do it? How did they think it was worth it in their time and space?* We shall see that there were overwhelming reasons *not* to fight for independence, which explains the perhaps surprising fact that only about one-third of the colonial American population remained consistently in favor of the war.[49] So what kept this one-third focused and determined at any cost? What rounded out their reasoning and justification, giving them that extra push to endure unspeakable pains to separate themselves from Britain? It was the

Spirit of Independence, even that divine, unseen hand that influenced, inspired, and supported this chosen American minority. Without the variable of this divine power and influence, the equation for why the American colonists did what they did simply does not add up. With it, however, it all makes perfect sense. As we now discuss the full scope of how the colonists ended up in full-blown rebellion and revolution, we will see this *Spirit of Independence* manifest itself, thus offering further proof of God's hand in America and validating, once again, our American Covenant with Him.

In an attempt to prove this unconventional argument, let us first consider some key historical facts surrounding the decision to declare independence from, and commence war with, Great Britain. It is through analyzing this ultimate decision to go to war that we see how the *Spirit of Independence* must have played a key role. The events leading to this decision grew out of a series of political events beginning in 1763. Prior to 1763, the British refrained from over-engaging in the affairs of her American subjects, thus sustaining relative peace between the two nations. The following events, however, changed that relationship forever:

1763:   *The Proclamation*: After pushing back the French, as a result of the French and Indian War, King George feels obliged to secure his American interests by reigning in all his American subjects, prohibiting their migration west of the Allegheny Mountains. This move is seen by many as an attempt to virtually confiscate much of the western land claims held by some of the colonists, now to be used by the British to repay the debt for the recent war with the French.

1765:   *The Stamp Act*: The British impose a light tax on all paper goods (everything from stamps and legal documents to playing cards) for the purpose of offsetting some of the costs incurred by Britain to provide for the physical and economic security of the colonists. In response, some colonists form the secret organization, Sons of Liberty, which persecutes those agents responsible for enforcing the Stamp Act, forcing them to resign or face destruction to their persons and/or property.

1767: *The Townshend Act*: After repealing the very controversial Stamp Act (after major protest and pressure from the colonists), Britain imposes a new set of indirect taxes on commodities as diverse as glass, paint, and tea.

1768: Britain sends soldiers to enforce its royal acts.

1770: *The Boston Massacre*: A handful of British soldiers open fire on a group of sixty American colonists who are physically harassing them. Five colonists are killed. The soldiers are ironically defended by the great American revolutionary, John Adams, who argues successfully that the soldiers acted in self-defense. They were acquitted in an American court.

1773: *The British Tea Act:* After the Townshend Act is repealed (again, after much American protest), the British determine to maintain a standing tax on one commodity: tea.

1773: *Boston Tea Party*: In response to the tea tax, colonial rebels, dressed as Mohawk Indians, board British vessels docked in Boston harbor and dump 23,000 pounds of tea into the waters below.

1774: *The British Coercive Acts:* In response to the "Boston Tea Party," Britain enacts and enforces a policy which virtually takes over Boston and closes its ports.

1775: *Lexington and Concord*: In an effort to make preparations to counter the Coercive Acts, some colonists begin stockpiling arms in towns outside of Boston. British forces confront Massachusetts militiamen guarding their small strongholds and weapons caches in the towns of Lexington and Concord. (It was on this occasion that Paul Revere made his famous ride alerting the "Minutemen" that the "Redcoats" were coming.) The armed conflict that ensued went down in history as "the shot heard round the world," and opened the curtains to the American War for Independence.

We will pause at this point in our chronology to examine *why* the Americans decided to push back at every effort Britain made to assert her influence, even when such rebellious action meant armed conflict with the world's leading superpower. The short answer, and the one taught to us in school textbooks, can be summed up through a series of speeches and writings by people like John Adams, Thomas Jefferson, Tom Paine, and Patrick Henry. These men authored or recited the famous phrases that incited the *Spirit of Independence*: phrases such as "No taxation without representation," "Unite or die," "Don't tread on me," "All men are created equal," "Give me liberty or give me death," "natural rights," and the novel, even radical, argument for their day, that there is "no natural or religious reason [for] the distinction of men into kings and subjects."[50]

Without a doubt, the colonists were feeling the heavy hand of a monarchical system. They were being taxed without even indirect consent (no representation), their local laws were scrutinized by the king and abolished and adjusted from time to time, and they were forced to house and care for the British soldiers within the borders of America. But did these offenses in and of themselves really warrant a rebellion which would cause an unprecedented amount of blood to fall upon American soil? Perhaps so. Perhaps the revolutionaries were correct to fear they were headed down a road of oppression. Americans were certainly justified to fight for their inherent right of self-governance.

However, the American cause was not the popular campaign we might have imagined. To be sure, its critics, especially those from America, had reason to believe the revolutionaries were overreacting —that they were being paranoid. According to the great American revolutionary leader, John Adams, and as confirmed by a modern-day Pulitzer Prize-winning historian of the American Revolution, over fifty percent of Americans (perhaps as many as sixty-five percent of Americans) at various times during the Revolution, believed the American sacrifice for independence was *not* worth it.[51] (These percentages fluctuated month to month depending on how

America was doing in the war.) Why would so many Americans oppose war with Britain? Because of the following unromantic facts that have been void from so many of our historical textbooks.

First, King George was not the crazy, power-hungry, inflexible tyrant—unwilling to make any concessions—that many interpretations of the American Revolution have painted him to be. Evidence suggests he was very modest for a king, close to his many young children (he had fifteen children) and faithful to his wife (which says a lot for one living in the adulterous royal culture that he did).[52] Most importantly, he was not unsympathetic to the complaints of the colonists. As noted above, he did repeal many of his taxes and policies in response to the protests of the Americans.[53] His goal was not to have unhappy American subjects. Just after the war had ended, the king expressed the following to the first American ambassador to Britain: "I wish you, sir, to believe, and that it be understood in America, that I have done nothing in the late contest but what I thought myself indispensably bound to do by the duty which I owed my people."[54] Perhaps extended patience by the colonists, along with more peaceful protests and dialogue with the Crown, would have borne fruit. Instead, the colonists turned to destruction and violence early on, mostly through groups like the Sons of Liberty, which—though again, was perhaps justified— promptly forced the British hand.

Second, the taxes that were laid on the Americans did not even exceed five percent of their individual incomes—and even less if the colonists refrained from consuming taxable commodities (the British levied a sales tax, not an income tax). Based on revolutionary rhetoric, modern Americans should have long ago overthrown their own government, which today demands upwards of twenty percent to forty percent of its citizens' income (and this modern tax is not only a sales tax, as it was for the colonists, but also a direct tax on actual *income*). Furthermore, was five percent (or less) too much to ask for the protection and infrastructure provided to the colonists? Similarly, was it too much to ask the colonists to provide for the wellbeing of the British soldiers who had protected them against foreign aggression? After all, not many years had passed since the king had repelled France's efforts to overtake their continent.

Third, apart from the British offenses listed above, additional complaints, as expressed in the Declaration of Independence, are vague and largely unsupported. Accusatory statements against the king, such as "he has excited domestic insurrections among us," "he has plundered our seas," "[he has] destroyed the lives of our people" and "[he has] declared us out of his protection and wag[es] war against us," seemed exaggerated to many critics of colonial America, who rightfully asked, *What proof do you have of this?* Indeed, few specific examples are given in the Declaration to support these claims.

Of course, these critics of colonial America would readily admit to the British "offenses," such as the levying of taxes, the Boston Massacre, the Coercive Acts (Siege of Boston harbor), and the attack on Lexington and Concord. But they could also make compelling arguments as to why these British actions could be seen as reasonable, defensive, and reactionary to colonial aggression. Again, the taxes were being levied mostly in order to pay for services rendered to the colonists. Furthermore, the British soldiers in the Boston Massacre were defended by John Adams and acquitted in a colonial court from any wrongdoing, as they were acting in self-defense against colonial rioting. Even Benjamin Franklin tacitly expressed understanding of British frustrations at colonial aggression, such as the Boston Tea Party, which he called an "an act of violent injustice on our part."[55] And finally, when the British sent soldiers to the scene of what they reasonably viewed as an insurrection, and when they learned that the colonists were stockpiling weapons against them in nearby towns, they were only acting reasonably to attack these colonial strongholds at Lexington and Concord.

Indeed, many of the colonial complaints were not unlike the one-sided, political, partisan rhetoric we hear daily, that only sounds fully justified when key facts are withheld. That spewing such propaganda was Jefferson's intent (to at least some degree) when drafting this section of the Declaration of Independence can be seen in an earlier draft of the Declaration, in which he goes so far as to accuse King George himself for the very evil practice of the slave trade in America—though slavery existed in the New World hundreds of years before King George's birth. (The reason it was rejected by the delegates was that it was offensive to Southern slave owners who quite liked the practice in America.)[56] The point is this: without detracting from the very inspired and true principles of freedom laced throughout the Declaration, and notwithstanding the very legitimate complaints such as lack of political representation, there is reason to believe the revolutionaries painted a gloomier picture than the truth. With the situation perhaps not as bad as we have imagined, we can see why so many Americans were opposed to war with Britain. Such reasoning to oppose this war is even more emphasized when considering the fourth and final argument many made against the need for revolution.

Fourth, as early as the 1750's, it was British policies and protections provided to the colonists that had caused America to possess the *highest per capita wealth in the world*.[57] Indeed, things were good in America, in that jobs and opportunities flourished. It was, after all, British America that welcomed an illegitimate child to its shores—a child who would arrive alone from a foreign land and shortly thereafter become the successful attorney and statesmen called Alexander Hamilton. It was British America that provided the system whereby a teenage runaway could arrive at Philadelphia without a penny in his pocket and become the wealthy, world-renowned inventor, businessman, and statesman called Benjamin Franklin. And the success stories go on and on.

Even the Book of Mormon explains that—even though the American Gentiles had to be free from their motherland for the gospel cause, and even though the Lord would ensure this freedom —the kings and queens of the Gentiles were "great in carrying them forth to the lands of their inheritance" and in being "nursing fathers" and "nursing mothers" to the young modern-day American nation (see 2 Nephi 10:8-16). Did such great and beneficial political and economic infrastructure offered by the British not overshadow any other complaint held by the colonists? Did it not justifiably warrant the relatively light taxes and other obligations placed on them?

King George certainly thought it did and understandably marveled at how the colonists could bite the hand that had fed them. He wondered out loud to his parliament how the Americans could forget that "to be a subject of Great Britain, with all its consequences, is to be the freest member of any civil society in the known world." And though the king claimed to be "anxious to prevent...the effusion of blood" and would "receive the misled [revolutionaries] with tenderness and mercy," he expressed his duty to not let America go:

> The object is too important, the spirit of the British nation too high, the resources with which God hath blessed her too numerous, to give up so many colonies which she has planted with great industry, nursed with great tenderness, encouraged with many commercial advantages, and protected and defended at much expense and treasure.[58]

The king was making the very compelling argument that the American cause of independence was not a war of necessity for the colonists, but of choice. And, as witnessed by the many Americans (usually the vast majority) who thought war with Britain was foolish, the king's message was not ill-received. The American delegate to the Continental Congress, Edward Rutledge, declared that the "sensible part of the house opposed the motion" for independence, then dramatically added, "No reason could be assigned for pressing into the measure [of declaring independence], but the reason of every madman."[59] Yet, by some miracle it seemed, there still existed throughout the colonies a group of men and women, consisting of roughly one-third of America's populace, who *never* wavered and were willing to sacrifice all for independence. And what's more, and further miraculous, these few, these chosen, found themselves at the proverbial helm of the American political ship.

Notwithstanding the powerful words of liberty and true principles of good government proclaimed by these revolutionary few, the questions still lingered then, as they do today: *Why* sacrifice all when things were pretty good at home? Though admittedly there were problems, how intolerable could they have been when prosperity abounded and America was one of the freest nations in the world at that time? Were members of the Continental Congress (who got America into the war) hungry, impoverished, suffering? To the contrary, there was very little these colonial elites did without. Were they being forced into a religion or limited in their ability to worship freely? In actuality, they participated in various religious denominations and, for the most part, enjoyed religious freedom. Then *why* throw themselves and the rest of America into a war of choice (not necessity) that would last eight years and result in the second most costly war—second only to the Civil War—in terms of casualties proportionate to population in all of American history? In today's numbers, the Revolutionary War would be akin to losing three-million American lives.[60]

Even the Pulitzer Prize-winning historian, David McCullough, in apparent awe at America's decided course, reminds us that "the Americans of 1776 enjoyed a higher standard of living than any people in the world...How people with so much, living on their own land, would ever choose to rebel against the ruler God had put over them and thereby bring down such devastation on themselves was...incomprehensible."[61] Another Pulitzer Prize-winning historian, Joseph Ellis, expressed a similar sense of bewilderment, when, upon explaining how he understood why the faithful began the war (they indeed were justified), "I'll be darned if I know why [they] stayed" (the justification seemed unworthy of the sacrifice).[62]

But no historian, even searching high and low for historical evidences, could ever tell us *why*, as only God—the same which guided our Founders—can fully explain it. The Lord did, after all, reveal that He "raised [them] up unto this very purpose, and redeemed the land by the shedding of blood" (D&C 101: 80), which is but one of several references He made to His hand in the Revolution (as cited in the previous chapter). It is this spiritual foundation, not secular knowledge alone, that allows us to understand the actions of the Founders. No secular-based historian can explain why the Founders did what they did any more than they can explain why Moses put everything on the line and did what he did, challenging the Pharaoh; or why Joseph Smith sacrificed all in doing what he did, challenging the religious establishment of the world. In each of these cases, God's chosen ones were acting on inspiration, having been "raised up unto this very purpose." And though admittedly the Founders were not prophets in the mold of Moses or Joseph, they were perhaps the closest thing God had to prophets in that time. They were His American Covenant-makers, and their inspired actions, though not fully understood by the world in which they lived, laid the groundwork for the Restoration.

As explained in the previous chapter, America needed to be free from a monarchical system (however relatively benign some felt it was at the time), as it could have too easily come down upon God's restored church when it at last arrived. America also needed a rebirth of liberty at home in order to root out its own domestic-based religious intolerance against minorities. Though this was a byproduct of the Revolution, and not a colonial justification for war, it was nonetheless God's intention; for this would also clear the way for the Restoration. And finally, America needed to ignite the flame of righteous rebellions in the world, that this freedom unto gospel salvation might spread to all mankind. The Revolution would provide all these prerequisites for the Restoration, that mankind might access eternal life. Had this been common knowledge among the colonists, any and all sacrifices pursuant to the Revolution would be fully comprehended today. However, as these godly justifications were generally unknown to the colonists, we see why the Lord needed to send the influential power of the *Spirit of Independence*. And, notwithstanding the logical reasons not to fight—and despite severe consequences and sacrifices—the Founders felt this spirit and obeyed.

★ ★ ★ ★

We have only scratched the surface on the mountain of evidence proving the powerful existence of God's *Spirit of Independence*, which worked unceasingly upon the hearts and souls of those inspired Founders. While we have outlined the abundant reasons why the mere decision to go to war was, on a secular level, void of perfect sense—though perfectly understood on a spiritual level—we have yet to examine the unbearable sacrifices this decision required. We will now examine some of these specific sacrifices made by the American faithful. In doing so, we will further comprehend how only God could influence good human beings to voluntarily endure what these revolutionary faithful endured, and we will, therefore, better appreciate the divine power and significance of the *Spirit of Independence* He sent as part of the covenant.

So, as the story goes, to the astonishment of Europe and Americans loyal to the Crown, these chosen few rebels, these recipients of the *Spirit of Independence*, these American Covenant-makers, would sacrifice everything. Consider, for example, the concluding words of the Declaration of Independence: "And for the support of this Declaration...we pledge our Lives, Fortunes and Sacred Honor." And they fully understood the meaning of these words and the consequences that would come to them for signing their names should their cause fail. Thomas Jefferson would love to recount how, on the heels of the Declaration, Benjamin Harrison, the very fat delegate from Virginia, nervously joked with the thin delegate Elbridge Gerry, saying, "Gerry, when the hanging comes, I shall have the advantage; you'll kick in the air half an hour after it is all over with me!"[63]

By war's end, out of the fifty-six signers, nine had been killed, five had been captured and suffered great pains at hands of the British, twelve had seen their homes burned, looted, or otherwise destroyed, and others literally went bankrupt investing all they possessed into the cause. Thomas Nelson, Jr., for example, a one-time governor of Virginia, borrowed almost two-million dollars using his own property as collateral, and handed it over to the American war machine. In the end, he was unable to make good on his debt and lost all he possessed. At one point in the war, Nelson even directed the cannons to destroy his Yorktown home, which had been captured, and was being utilized by British forces.[64]

Another signer, Samuel Adams, repeatedly turned down handsome bribes from the British to cease and desist from spewing his revolutionary rhetoric, even though he and his family were oft times on the brink of poverty and badly needed the money. And though he was reminded that his rebellious attitude toward the British might just find him on the end of a hangman's rope, Adams simply replied: "I have long since made my peace with the King of Kings! No personal consideration shall induce me to abandon the righteous cause of my country."[65] It was his stalwart position under God that inspired him in the early days of the Revolution to organize much of the initial rebellious activity against the British in New England, which led many to refer to him thereafter as the *Father of the Revolution*.

Then there was Robert Morris, known as the "financier of the American revolution," who personally raised war funds when the Congress was unable to act for itself. He was responsible for funding at least two of the most crucial events of the war. First was the 1776 campaign in which Washington crossed the Delaware and took Trenton and Princeton (America's first real victory that turned the tide of war), and second was the Battle of Yorktown, which secured American independence. This he did without the slightest guarantee of ever seeing a penny of it returned to his coffers.[66]*

And of course there were the greats—Adams, Jefferson, Franklin, and others of whom much will be said later in this book.

It should again be noted that every one of these signers was present in the spirit at the St. George Temple to receive temple covenants at the hands of Wilford Woodruff.

The signers were not the only ones compelled by the Spirit to sacrifice everything. There was, after all, the equally amazing group of inexperienced soldiers, referred to by the enemy as the "ramble in arms," but officially known as the Continental Army. As one prominent historian explained:

> It was the first American army and an army of everyone, men of every shape and size and makeup, different colors, different nationalities, different ways of talking, and all degrees of physical condition. Many were missing teeth or fingers, pitted by smallpox or scarred by past wars or the all-too-common hazards of life and toil in the eighteenth century. Some were not even men, but smooth-faced boys of fifteen or less.[67]

These were the unsung heroes that kept the Revolution alive. The British could conquer every major American city (which they did), but as long as these dedicated soldiers remained together and on the move, striking where they could at the inspired direction of their beloved General Washington, the British could never stomp

---

* Perhaps Morris' most important ally in his efforts to finance the war was the Jew, Haym Solomon. Solomon immigrated to America in 1775, precisely as the Revolution began, and he threw himself into the American cause immediately and whole-heartedly. First working as a spy for General Washington (for which the British tried to hang him), Solomon later helped Morris raise funds for the colonial army. Adding his significant personal savings to the cause, Solomon died a penniless man. Passing away in 1785, just on the heels of the Revolution, this Hebrew-American patriot disappeared from the scene as quickly and mysteriously as he had arrived upon it. He came and fulfilled his divine mission.

them out. Thus lived on the *Spirit of Independence*! It was this endurance that convinced Washington that he did not need to win the war as much as he simply needed to *not lose* it. And at the end of the day, it was the perseverance of these citizen soldiers that wearied the British into surrendering their lost cause.

The *Spirit of Independence* was manifested in soldiers like Nathan Hale, who upon being captured by the British as the first American spy would say, while being led to his execution by hanging, "I regret I have but one life to give for my country." [68] It was further manifested in those like the twenty-five-year-old Boston bookstore keeper Henry Knox and the thirty-year-old Rhode Island Quaker and metal worker Nathaniel Greene. Both these men possessed military knowledge only to the extent of what they had read in books, and yet both would become Washington's most trusted and successful field commanders, enduring the entire eight years of war. [69]

What's more, these chosen soldiers would endure without the prospect of a GI Bill or an extended peacetime military career waiting for them upon their return. In fact, they would often sacrifice all without even the prospect of food, blankets, shoes, or even payment! The only guarantee they really had was that death or serious casualty would threaten them at every turn. Naturally, many deserted the group. But that a sufficient number for eventual triumph would endure is something beyond the reach of mortal comprehension. It was a miracle.

Another unlikely champion for the American cause was British statesman Edmund Burke, who incessantly stood up to the king and parliament in defense of America's right to exist independently. He was instrumental, for example, in influencing his country to repeal the Stamp Act. But such opposing opinions were offered at great risk of offending the majority of parliament and, more dangerously, the king himself. Yet in spite of the possible consequences in speaking out against the Crown, the *Spirit of Independence* seemed to work on Burke, who would champion the causes of freedom, justice, and religious tolerance (not only in

America, but wherever else in the world his British nation maintained an influence). That he was on the Lord's errand is perhaps evidenced by the fact that he, along with his wife Jane, also were counted among those choice spirits whose temple ordinances were performed by Wilford Woodruff, pursuant to his grand vision.[70]

But of all those who displayed this incomprehensible dedication to the cause, none could top him who they say embodied the revolutionary generation—George Washington. His indomitable spirit can most readily be seen during what would perhaps be the most crucial period of the war. It was mid-November 1776, and Washington and his men had recently seen their first real battle with the British on and around Long Island, New York. America failed miserably in this battle. It was an absolute disaster. As the world's superpower landed on the beaches of New York and attacked, all the Americans could do was turn around and run for their lives (and, as will be detailed later, they only managed this escape through divine intervention). Nathanial Greene called it "the dark part of the night," Thomas Paine called it "the times that try men's souls," and over sixteen-thousand of the approximately twenty-thousand American troops that began with Washington at New York called it "quits," mostly by way of blatant desertion.[71]

And there stood the humiliated Washington in the middle of it all, leading the retreat out of New York, southward through New Jersey. All Washington had was his remaining, and meager, band of three-thousand men—scarcely fifteen percent of what he possessed just weeks prior. And most of those were due to be honorably discharged in less than fourteen days. With well over thirty thousand British troops possibly on his trail, it was no wonder he blurted out, while stroking his throat, "my neck does not feel as though it was made for a halter."[72] Washington commented about his feelings at this time, saying that "if I were to wish the bitterest curse to an enemy on this side of the grave, I should put him in my stead with my feelings....In confidence I tell you that I never was in such an unhappy, divided state since I was born."[73]

Just when things could not possibly get worse, they did. During the retreat southward, Washington received word that the colonial governments, after learning of the New York debacle, had lost interest in pursuing war and were refusing to send backup troops. According to the dispatch, his would-be comrades in arms were "divided and lethargic, slumbering under the shade of peace and in the full enjoyment of the sweets of commerce."[74] As pointed out earlier, why fight a hopeless fight when things were, after all, pretty good at home?

Also during the retreat, the already heart-broken Washington mistakenly opened a letter from one of his trusted officers and friends (the letter was intended for another officer) in which he blamed and criticized Washington for the military failure.[75] Even members of Congress, in whom he had trusted and depended upon for direction, had themselves blamed Washington and began fleeing Philadelphia for fear of being captured. [76] A few congressmen even betrayed the cause, offering their services to the enemy.[77] As one-time patriots began switching over to the British side by the thousands, the enemy was well aware of America's hopeless state. "The fact is" reported one British captain in the field, "their army is broken all to pieces, and the spirit of their leaders and their abettors is all broken....I think one may venture to pronounce that it is well nigh over with them."[78] He was correct. By all accounts the war was over. America had lost.

And, again, there stood Washington in the midst of the turmoil—all alone. For a moment all he could think about was how to escape, where to hide. Should they flee to the mountains of Augusta County, West Virginia? Or should they attempt to cross the Allegheny Mountains?[79] There was, however, an alternative solution that, at the moment, seemed too good to be true. Britain had offered a "free and general pardon" to all American rebels, including a guarantee of the "preservation of their property, the restoration of their commerce, and the security of their most valuable rights," if they would but denounce the rebellion and swear a simple oath of "peaceable obedience" to the king, as they had done so often before the conflict.[80] Furthermore, if Washington and the leaders in the Congress would swear to the same, the British even promised to capitulate and concede to give them what they had asked for before the conflict, even to be "treated as a separate country within the framework of the empire" with "control over their own legislation and taxes."[81] In response to this offer, thousands more would immediately betray the American cause, lining up to take their oaths.[82]

The voice of reason spoke loud and clear to Washington and his men. *George, officers, enlisted men: Stop the madness! Accept the pardon! Go back to your plantations and farms. Go back to your families. Go back to the comforts of being the wealthiest nation per capita in the world. Go back to the pleasure of being counted amongst the freest people on earth. Britain's generous offer provides you with what you have asked for. Give the proposal a chance. Everyone else seems to see this and has surrendered. Nobody will blame you. It is over! Give it up!*

And yet, inexplicably, Washington and his inadequate band of patriots would not give it up. The General would excuse his betrayers, as he often would, saying that "we must bear up against them, and make the best of mankind as they are, since we cannot have them as we wish."[83] Then, as if total madness had set in, he would prepare for a counterattack at Trenton and Princeton, New Jersey. The *Spirit of Independence* was clearly working on Washington in these crucial moments of decision. Only the power of divine impulse could compel such illogical perseverance in such a great man.

By turning down the royal pardon and continuing the fight, Washington was sealing his fate if captured. And by all estimations at the time, he would most likely be captured. He had been given his chance, and Britain would not forgive him for rejecting it. As best-selling author and historian Stephen Ambrose pointed out, had Washington been captured, "[h]e would have been brought to London, tried, found guilty of treason, ordered executed, and then drawn and quartered."

Do you know what that means? He would have had one
arm tied to one horse, the other arm to another horse, one
leg to yet another, and the other leg to a fourth. Then the
four horses would have been simultaneously whipped and
started off at a gallop, one going north, another south,
another east and the fourth to the west. That is what
Washington was risking to establish your freedom and
mine.[84]

And it was not only during this crucial moment that
Washington would show such unimaginable dedication, even at the
great risk of losing everything he held dear. To be sure, Washington
would push every human limit, both physical and emotional,
throughout the entirety of the conflict. He would, for example,
regularly rally his men by dangerously, even insanely, riding out
beyond the front lines, coming within one hundred yards of the
enemy, while aids would rush out to grab the bridle of his horse,
forcing him to safety.[85] At one point, while British ships made plans
to extort the plantations lining the Potomac River for supplies,
including Washington's dear Mount Vernon, Washington expressed
to his caretaker that it would be "less painful...that they burnt my
house and laid the plantation in ruins" than to comply with their
demands for supplies.[86] What's more, Washington would make all
these sacrifices while refusing any and all payment due to him for
his service, even though his long absence was forcing him to neglect
his business, thus pushing him further and deeper into debt. [87]

Furthermore, there is no convincing evidence to explain any
alternative intention for his sacrifices. By all accounts, what
Washington desired more than anything else was a private life at his
beloved Mount Vernon. "By God," Washington would say, "I had
rather be on my farm."[88] As General of the Continental Army,
Chairman of the Constitutional Convention, and as President of the
United States, Washington openly and continuously expressed his
overriding reluctance to accept, and temptation to abandon, such
callings due to his overwhelming desire to return to his neglected
family, work, and peace at home.[89] But Mount Vernon was *always* his

to return to, from the time before his appointments (he could have declined), to the British offer of general pardon (he could have accepted), and on through his entire service to his country after the war (he could have retired). Yet he denied himself, just as his faithful contemporaries denied themselves of their own "Mount Vernons," and instead risked death for the sake of God and country. Only a heavenly influence could compel the sane to so freely and willingly act in a manner so contrary to both logic and to such strong personal desires. God had "raised [them] up unto this very purpose" (D&C 101: 80); Indeed, "the power of the Lord was with them" (1 Nephi 13: 16).

The Testimonials of the Rebels

If it is true that the Spirit of God was especially active in the minds and actions of the American revolutionaries, then certainly those present in revolutionary America would have had something to say about it. Shamefully, far too many modern-day historical accounts of the Revolution minimize or simply omit any references to God and His influence over the whole affair. However, minimizing or slighting the spiritual testimonials of those who participated in the Revolution is most certainly disingenuous. For the leaders and followers of revolutionary America spoke loud and spoke frequently about the hand of God in America's struggle for independence. And they were, after all, *there*, which makes them infinitely more qualified to opine on the issue than any modern critic.

The long list of Founders who declared God's presence and influence during the Revolution is far too exhaustive to detail here. However, their voices will be documented throughout this narrative in the pages and chapters ahead. As you, the reader, come across them, you will see the overwhelming evidence of the existence of God's *Spirit of Independence*.

But in order to offer, here and now, a representative sample of this deeper understanding that existed in revolutionary America, let us briefly consider the words of certain colonial Americans who testified of God's hand. The following sample of those who bore this testimony is composed mostly of lesser known colonial Americans who do not play as prominent a role in the historical narrative represented in this book and therefore will be overlooked in later chapters. However, their testimonies are no less important and certainly represent how far reaching the Spirit was. The samples below are also limited to comments made during the height of the Revolution—even in the years leading up to and during the war itself—as post-war statements related to God and America will be discussed later.

One powerful testimony came from the Reverend Abraham Keteltas who, in the middle of the conflict, declared: "It is the cause of Justice…and the cause of heaven and against hell—of the kind Parent of the universe against the prince of darkness, and the destroyer of the human race."[90] The Connecticut minister Ebenezer Baldwin, referring to the Lord and His Second Coming, prophesied (correctly!) that the Revolution was "preparing the way for this glorious event."[91]

The great statesman Patrick Henry declared, in his famous *Give Me liberty or Give Me Death* speech in 1775, that "[w]e shall not fight our battles alone. There is a just God who presides over the destinies of nations, and who will raise up friends and fight our battles for us."[92] And Elbridge Gerry, a signer of the Declaration of Independence, recognized as early as 1775 that when it came to the Revolution, "the hand of Heaven seems to have directed every occurrence."[93]

Others who understood God's power in the Revolution—and appeared to even understand the national covenant and from where this covenant originated—were the New England colonials of Marlborough. In 1773, they collectively proclaimed that they had "implore[d] the Ruler above the skies, that he would make bare his arm in defense of His Church and people, and let Israel go."[94] In a similar spirit, the leader of the men of Pepperrell, Massachusetts, wrote to his New England countrymen—who were then suffering the wrath of Britain—in order to offer assistance. "Let us all be of one heart," declared the 1774 letter, "and stand fast in the liberty wherewith Christ has made us free. And may He, in His infinite mercy, grant us deliverance out of all our troubles."[95]

Also in 1774, the prominent John Hancock—president of Congress and signer of the Declaration of Independence—reminded his countrymen that they should "humbly commit our righteous cause to the great Lord of the Universe...let us joyfully leave our concerns in the hands of Him who raises up and puts down empires and kingdoms."[96]

Similarly, in March 1776, Chaplain William Linn made what appears to be an astonishing connection between the war, the restoration of the gospel, and the Second Coming—astonishing because such insight at this early point could only have come through the Spirit. Chaplain Linn, upon invoking the blessings of God in battle, prayed the following: "Above all, may the peaceful reign of King Jesus soon commence, when the earth shall be filled with the knowledge of the Lord."[97]

Others with apparent insight included the Third Connecticut Regiment, whose motto during the war was, "An Appeal to Heaven." And Pennsylvania troops carried a flag with words that seemed thematic of the War in Heaven and seemed to reflect the very purpose of the American Covenant: "Resistance to Tyrants Is Obedience to God."[98]

One participant at the First Continental Congress, William Livingston, prophesied the following in 1768: "The finger of God points out a mighty empire....The land we possess is the gift of heaven to our fathers, and Divine Providence seems to have decreed it to our latest posterity....The day dawns in which the foundation of this mighty empire is to be laid, by the establishment of a regular American Constitution...before seven years roll over our heads, the first stone must be laid." This prophecy, which was published in the New York *Gazette* in April 1768, occurred exactly seven years before the first shots rang out at Lexington, Massachusetts.[99]

Apart from the Founders' obvious recognition of God's influence in the Revolution, there is further proof to hush the inevitable critic, who will claim that all of the above was mere rhetoric. Such proof appears when we realize that the Founders not only spoke of God's influence around them, but actually acted, as a nation, in order to live worthy of His blessings. In doing so, they grew to understand and live the American Covenant. Such action is represented in the many declarations put forth by the first representatives of the people of the United States, even the Continental Congress, to encourage righteous living among their countrymen. One of the earliest of such declarations was announced in 1774, even at the threshold of the Revolution. It was a national plea to Americans, asking them to refrain from "every species of extravagance and dissipation," and specifically pointed out the dangers to the nation of sinful behavior, to include gaming, cockfighting, and exhibition of shows.[100] As one historian put it, "the colonials believed that they needed to prove themselves worthy of God's help."[101]

This was just the beginning of such congressional calls to national repentance—or, in other words, calls to the American Covenant. A study done by historian Derek Davies concluded that during the American Revolution, the Continental Congress invoked God so many times that—perhaps in order to break the monotony—they felt compelled to begin officially referring to Him with various titles, to include God, Nature's God, Lord of Hosts, His Goodness, Providence, Creator of All, Greater Governor of the World, Supreme Judge of the Universe, Supreme Disposer of All Events, Jesus Christ, Holy Ghost, and others. Concluded Davies: "So powerful were the religious influences on the independence movement that it becomes possible to say that those in the Continental Congress who made the political decision to separate from Great Britain did so only because they fully believed... [it to be] their religious duty."[102]

Whether or not these founders and revolutionaries knew the more profound reasons God was on their side—that it was all about creating a political foundation of freedom for the restoration of true religion—does not really matter. For they knew what they needed to know: that they were fighting for a new and better system of government based in liberty, that God was behind them, and that they would only be successful as they recognized Him and adhered to His commandments.

The Great Awakening

One largely overlooked experience which touched almost all of colonial America, and which supports the claim that God's Spirit was influencing the revolutionary cause, was the Great Awakening —that tremendous wave of spirituality which inundated the country in the years leading up to the Revolution. Led in large part by the inspired preacher, George Whitefield—who preached over eighteen thousands sermons throughout colonial America between 1736 and 1770—the Great Awakening marked a return to God and, hence, a return to the covenant.

According to one non-LDS historian,

> Through the universal, simultaneous experience of the Great Awakening, Americans began to become aware of themselves as a nation. They began to see themselves as God saw them: as a people chosen by Him for a specific purpose...Now through the shared experience of coming together as a group to hear the Gospel of Jesus Christ, Americans were rediscovering God's plan to join them together by His Spirit in the common cause of advancing His Kingdom. Furthermore, they were returning to another aspect of his plan—they were not to operate as lone individualists but in covenanted groups. [103]

One prominent American who lived during the Great Awakening and caught this vision was Ezra Stiles, president of Yale. As early as 1760, he taught that God "is now giving this land to us who in virtue of the ancient covenant are the Seed of Abraham." He further taught that Israel's past is America's history: "The Lord freed us from Egypt by a mighty hand, by an outstretched arm and awesome power, and by signs and portents. He brought us to this place and gave us this land, a land flowing with milk and honey."[104]

Not only did this recommitment to God help colonial Americans understand their national covenant, but naturally encouraged them to live this covenant through obedience to the commandments. As the Pulitzer Prize-winning American historian, Gordon Wood, commented:

> In the eyes of the Whigs, the two or three years before the Declaration of Independence always appears to be the great period of the Revolution, the time of greatest denial and cohesion, when men ceased to extort and abuse one another, when families and communities seemed particularly united, when the courts were wonderfully free of that constant bickering over land and credit that had dominated their colonial life.[105]

According to historian Steven Waldman, the Great Awakening not only led people back to God and covenant, but consequently encouraged them to seek Him out more freely and openly, thus inspiring a desire and movement for more religious freedom in America.[106] We have already pointed out that God's purpose in the Revolution was to encourage such religious freedom. We have also pointed out that most colonists did not initially see religious freedom as the cause for the Revolution, and therefore they did not fully recognize or comprehend that God was planning an enhancement of religious freedom as the principal purpose of their revolutionary movement. However, the fact that the Great Awakening was stirring hearts to this inspired end is a witness to God's hand in directing this era of American history. God certainly knew what we can only see in hindsight—that with American victory in independence, religious freedom would emerge as a powerful byproduct and then serve as a foundation for the Restoration. That the Lord infused these sentiments in America through the Great Awakening is evidence of His hand in preparing America for what would be the ultimate purpose of the Revolution.

Considering how the Great Awakening played right into the American Covenant and God's gospel purposes for America, and considering that it occurred and climaxed precisely during those crucial years leading up to the Revolution, it is difficult to deny the hand of the Lord. He had inspired this movement in order to improve His revolutionary generations and thus prepare them to humbly implore Him and to adhere to His covenant with them. For only then might He, in return, bless them with the gifts of the covenant. Only then might His plan for America be fully realized. In all this, we surely see the *Spirit of Independence*.

The Conversion of the Founders

That the *Spirit of Independence* existed and played an indispensable role should now be clear. What has not been made clear, however, is *how* the conversions to the American cause, as influenced by this Spirit, took place. And so, in an effort to understand the miracle by which the Spirit converted its adherents, and to add further proof of the existence of this Spirit, we will now briefly explore how such inspiration took hold of the Founders.

As is the case with most spiritual experiences, the Founders' individual conversions to the American cause for independence seemed to vary as to time, place, and circumstance. For those like Adams and Jefferson (respectively the *Voice* and the *Pen* of independence), they seemed to be born with it, long awaiting the opportunity to shower the world with principles pertaining to God and His blessings of liberty. Others, like Washington, seemed to gain their powerful testimonies upon receiving a specific call to duty.

But the one common thread in almost all such conversions was, very fittingly, a connection to the Christian churches of the day. It was from the pulpits that independence was preached and where hearts were changed and convinced to support the Revolution. As a witness to these miraculous conversions, Adams commented in 1775 that the ministers would "thunder and lighten every Sabbath" in the cause for American independence. Jefferson would likewise state that the passion for this independence grew out of a "pulpit oratory [that] ran like a shock of electricity through the whole colony."[107]

As one American scholar proposed: "No other institution in America was so responsible for inspiring and motivating the War for Independence as the Protestant churches—and the few thousand Jews and Catholics of the land along with them."[108] There is even one account of a Virginia pastor, Peter Muhlenbery, who one Sunday morning in 1775 told his congregation (in the middle of a sermon) that the time had come to fight. He then threw off his robe to reveal his combat uniform. He forthrightly recruited three hundred men, and marched off to war that very day.[109] That the zeal for independence was bred and spread through the churches of America certainly adds validity to the notion that God was behind the great conversions to the cause.

The *Spirit of Independence* not only filled the churches, but also made its way into the state legislative houses, where the decisions relating to American independence and revolution were being hotly debated. If the few converts to the cause were to convince their colleagues to join them (especially in light of the many logical reasons not to) the Spirit would certainly need to be among these legislative bodies. And God did send it there in abundance. Patrick Henry was one chosen to disseminate this Spirit. One historical commentator noted—after analyzing his public life— that Henry "had grown to understand how God moved through him and how to yield to the Holy Spirit to say what God wanted him to say."[110] Not coincidentally, Henry dedicated himself to daily personal prayer and Sunday evening family nights dedicated to the Lord.[111] And it was his famous *Give Me Liberty or Give Me Death* speech of 1775—packed with references to God and His will for America—that was largely responsible for moving his fellow Virginians to join the cause of independence. According to one witness, as Henry spoke there appeared an "unearthly fire burning in his eyes...Men leaned forward in their seats with their heads strained forward, their faces pale and their eyes glaring like the speaker."[112] "To Arms! To Arms!" was the response of his countrymen. Shortly thereafter, they voted, as a state, to support independence from Britain.[113]*

Similar impressions and conversions took place among the delegates at the Continental Congress in the most crucial moments. One of the most prominent examples of this took place on July 1, 1776, as the delegates convened one last time to debate and vote on whether the Declaration of Independence should be signed and executed. The highly respected delegate John Dickinson stood and made one final plea, with plenty of reason on his side, to stop the madness of declaring independence. To go forward with the declaration, he warned, would be "to brave the storm in a skiff made of paper." Aware of his logic, the delegates sat in silence as Dickinson took his seat. John Adams, whose spiritual character was no doubt inspiring his actions, then stood and countered Dickinson. In so doing, Adams delivered what David McCullough called, "the greatest speech of [his] life."[114]

Strangely, little is known about the precise content of this improvised speech, as nobody recorded it. Yet it was called his greatest based on the reaction it produced. Jefferson stated that though the speech was neither "graceful nor elegant," Adams delivered it "with a power of thought and expression that moved us from our seats." Adams himself testified that he had been "'carried out in spirit' as enthusiastic preachers sometimes express themselves." So powerful was the speech that, upon finishing, he was—most unusually—asked to stand and give it again. He set the tone of the day and converts to the cause were made. Joseph Hewes of North Carolina, who up until this point had opposed independence, was one of many that were overcome. As Adams later recorded, Hewes "started suddenly upright, and lifting up both his hands to Heaven, as if he had been in a trance, cried out, 'It is done! And I will abide by it.'"[115] The following day, July 2, 1776, the delegates voted to

---

* Among the statesmen in the room that heard these spiritually compelling words were George Washington and Thomas Jefferson. See O'Reilly and Dugard, 38.

declare independence. There is no doubt that the *Spirit of Independence* had been converting souls to the cause.

But what about those chosen few who, for whatever reason, might have been initially unfeeling to this "electricity" from the pulpits of the churches and from the legislative houses throughout the country? The Lord would certainly need them as well. He would have to recruit them. The epitome of such recruits was none other than America's First Citizen, Benjamin Franklin. His almost emotionless and scientific rationale would give him much pause at America's sudden cries for independence. Furthermore, his tendency towards Deism would require more work on the Lord's part. But as Franklin—with his uncanny skills in everything from science to diplomacy—would further the cause in ways others could not, the Lord would most certainly prompt him off the sidelines.

To illustrate Franklin's significant conversion, consider his initial and very open opinion against American claims of overbearing British persecution, which implied to many that Franklin had taken a firm stance against the need for any talk of independence. As late as January 1775, he would comment that "the two countries really have no clashing interests," and that it was merely an issue that "reasonable people might settle in half an hour."[116] Even after the dreaded Stamp Act and the colonial outrage that followed—and though he was no proponent of the act—he would write to a friend: "A firm Loyalty to the Crown and faithful Adherence to the Government of this Nation… will always be the wisest course for you and I to take, whatever may be the madness of the [American] populace or their blind leaders."[117]

In addition to such comments, which clearly undermined the American cause, as a delegate to Congress in the spring of 1775, the usually opinionated Franklin remained silent and passionless, even after the British had sacked Boston in response to the colonists' Tea Party. (As pointed out earlier, Franklin had sided with Britain in expressing disgust at America's destruction of the tea in the first place.) [118] Such behavior was alarming to his fellow delegates. One observer reported to James Madison that the delegates "beg[a]n to entertain a great suspicion that Dr. Franklin came rather as a spy than as a friend, and that he means to discover our weak side and make his peace with the ministers."[119] Even after the Battle of Bunker Hill and the burning of Charleston, both in June 1775, Franklin still supported a policy of unification with Britain by signing the Olive Branch Petition (written by delegate John Dickinson—the same delegate who would refuse to ever sign the Declaration of Independence).[120]

Furthermore, and on a personal level, why should he desire to revolt over the very system that had permitted him to become one of the wealthiest men in America, and perhaps the most famous individual in the world? Indeed, by risking an unlikely revolution, which seemed doomed to failure, both his wealth and fame might be pulled out from under him. Or worse, his life might be taken by the hangman's noose.

In spite of all this, by the end of July (seemingly overnight) Franklin had become "one of the most ardent opponents of Britain in the Continental Congress." This he would remain even after the British accepted the basic terms of his Olive Branch Petition (this British offer was part of the same rejected by Washington, as outlined above). "He does not hesitate at our boldest measures," wrote John Adams, "but rather seems to think us too irresolute."[121]

Almost immediately, Franklin volunteered to replace the British-run postal service and serve as America's first postmaster general. He designed and oversaw construction of a secret system of underwater obstructions to prevent enemy naval invasions. And he rushed to the scene of war—a Boston recently seized by the British. He went there that he might consult the newly appointed Commander-in-Chief, General Washington, on everything from warfare and troop discipline to ration allocation. At age seventy, he could have been expected to remain in Philadelphia and consult from the comforts of his home. Instead, he insisted, not merely on traveling to Boston, but on taking a life-threatening diplomatic journey to Canada (during which he almost died).Then he traveled to New York in a final (and unsuccessful) attempt at independence through diplomacy with the recently landed British invaders. After returning to Philadelphia and acting as editor of the Declaration of Independence, he most poignantly relocated to France (in yet another death-defying voyage), where he would spend the balance of the war seeking and, through masterful diplomacy, securing France's support—an act that was largely responsible for the American victory. Finally, he would lead negotiations with Britain in the treaty officially ending the war, wherein Britain recognized the United States "to be free, sovereign and independent."[122] In an almost humorous understatement, a follow-up report to James Madison, delivered shortly after Franklin's sudden and passionate conversion, included the reassurance that "[t]he suspicions against Dr. Franklin have died away...I believe he has now chosen his side and favors our cause."[123]

But what caused the sudden and almost overwhelming change in Franklin that not only led to the dramatic string of events mentioned above, but also cost him his relationship with his only son, the British loyalist William (a relationship never to be recovered)? What prompted the change within, which he knew would place him squarely onto the death list of the British? Upon signing the Declaration of Independence he would declare, "We must indeed all hang together, or most assuredly we shall all hang separately."[124] While scholars theorize over his largely inexplicable change of heart, a gospel perspective perhaps fills in the missing pieces. Knowing what we do about what American independence meant to God's purposes, and knowing the indispensable role played by this elder American, can there be any doubt the Lord influenced his heart with His Spirit? Such an idea is even supported by Franklin himself, who declared while serving in France: "Glorious it is for the Americans to be called by Providence to this post of honor....it is a miracle in human affairs...the greatest revolution the world ever saw."[125]

The insightful Abigail Adams, herself devoutly dedicated to the Lord, even saw or felt this spiritual conversion in Franklin. Upon meeting Franklin shortly after his public commitment to independence, she wrote to her husband, stating, "I thought I could read into his countenance the virtues of his heart; among which patriotism shone in its full luster, and with that is blended every virtue of a Christian: for a true patriot must be a religious man."[126]

Of course, critics will argue that his sudden change of mind came about by what was expected of him politically as an American delegate to Congress, and that God had nothing to do with it. Franklin was—so the theory goes—simply playing to the American crowd. As historian Gordon Wood points out, Franklin's actions for independence came about as a result of him having to "overcome suspicions that many of his countryman had of him." Wood further explains, as mentioned earlier, that "some thought his position in the 1760s and 1770s had been sufficiently ambiguous that he might not be a true patriot after all."[127]

However, there are problems with this interpretation. Firstly, Franklin had just as many, if not more, friends and supporters in Britain and other European countries as he did in America. After all, he had spent over two decades in celebrity status (as scientist and philosopher) in Europe. Furthermore, he was void of any family ties that would sway his allegiance to America rather than Great Britain. His wife had already died, and his only surviving son was a British loyalist. In other words, he had just as many people to disappoint—just as much political pressure on him—whether he voted for or against independence. If the only reason he could find for supporting American independence was the pressure he felt from his American colleagues, then it would have made much more sense for him to shun what appeared to be an ill-conceived revolution and simply return to Europe with the celebrity status that would be awaiting him there.*

Secondly, if Franklin had been unconvinced of the wisdom behind a revolution, but did not want to shun his country and hazard a trip back to Europe, there was a much easier solution for him. He could have simply voiced his support for independence then floated off into retirement, even casually consulting from the comforts of his home just to keep up the act. He was already in his

---

* Though some contend that Franklin would not have returned to Great Britain because he had been snubbed by certain officials, it is important to remember that he was a celebrity in *all* of Western Europe, particularly in France, where he was adored by all and would have been more than welcome to return for good.

seventies and suffering from chronic gout and kidney stones; nobody would have batted an eye.

Yet his actions, as outlined above, reflect an unnaturally passionate, even overactive, approach to the American cause. Indeed, Franklin's conversion and subsequent actions are overwhelmingly inconsistent with the allegation that he acted on pressures stemming from colonial political correctness, especially in light of the alternatives available to him. The truth of the matter is that no other solid, secular explanation for Franklin's actions has ever been offered. Even Wood, putting his own analysis into question, ultimately concedes to this fact, stating that "[Franklin] had everything to lose and seemingly nothing to gain by participating in a revolution."[128] Only by placing God and His powerful inspiration into the equation are Franklin's actions comprehensible.

Unfortunately, many scholars would rather have *no* explanation than give credit to God, and thus they attempt to secularize Franklin as much as possible. However, such scholars have to contend with the fact—as they do when attacking Washington's conversion—that Franklin himself explained on several occasions that his conversion to the cause was indeed based in divine intervention. Admittedly, critics may claim that the few quotes utilized above regarding what was said by and of Franklin during the actual conflict represented nothing but quintessential politicking—even the disingenuous act of invoking God's name only to stir an audience. However, a glimpse into his post-war life confirms that when Franklin declared during the war that he had been "called by Providence,"[129] he meant it.

Consider, for example, the following statement he made near the end of his life while reflecting upon the War for Independence and his conversion to it: "If I had ever before been an atheist, I should now have been convinced of the Being and government of a Deity...If it had not been...for the interposition of Providence, in which we had faith, we must have been ruined."[130] That he had felt this during and after the war is supported by his obvious change of focus from scientist and rational philosopher (pre-war) to servant of the Almighty (post-war).

Whereas before the war he tended to find limited use for God and religion, his post-war activities included the following: penning defenses against early American secularist attacks on religion;[131] proposing that the nation utilize as its official seal a depiction of Moses freeing Israel by the power of God;[132] proposing to the Congress that it open sessions with prayer;[133] promoting the general need for religion and virtue in order to stabilize the Republic;[134] and, as his final project in this life, publicly invoking the Almighty and exerting much energy in an effort to eradicate the evil practice of slavery.[135]

Furthermore, it was this change of heart that led to his other inspired commentaries on God and man's obligation (our covenant) to Him. The following includes a sample of such statements he made in the sunset of his life:

- "I have lived, Sir, a long time, and the longer I live, the more convincing proofs I see of this truth— that God governs in the affairs of men."[136]

- "Doing good to men is the only service of God in our power; and to imitate his beneficence is to glorify him."[137]

- "I believe in one God, Creator of the Universe. That he governs it by his Providence. That he ought to be worshipped. That the most acceptable service we render to him is doing good to his other children."[138]

Franklin's conversion to God and the American Covenant would not only prepare him to fulfill his earthly mission of being a tool and light for American independence, but would also prepare him in a personal way to participate in the ultimate opportunity provided by American independence. For his conversion would help him to accept and live higher priesthood covenants.

That Franklin perhaps had an idea that such eternal blessings in the afterlife could or would be his is indicated by a comment he made in his very last days concerning his testimony of the truthfulness and divinity of Christ's gospel. Writing to a friend, Franklin confessed that "I apprehend it [referring to the Christian religion] has received various corrupt changes...though it is a question I do not dogmatize upon, having never studied it, and think needless to busy myself with it now, when *I expect soon an opportunity of knowing the truth....*"[139] Perhaps feeling the effects of the apostasy (that too much truth was missing at the time to be overly preoccupied with such questions), and knowing his days in mortality were drawing to an end, Franklin seemed to feel his chance at ultimate truth would be coming shortly. He had, after all, been convinced, at least later in life, that death and afterlife would be a joyful experience. "If [God] loves me," he declared, "can I doubt that he will go on to take care of me, not only here but hereafter?"[140] In light of what has since been revealed, we now know that both the gospel truth and the joy he hoped for, most certainly were awaiting him in the Spirit World.

Franklin entered the Spirit World on April 17, 1790. Near his deathbed, he had placed a picture of the Day of Judgment.[141] As further expression of his hope for eternity, he had originally penned the following epitaph for his tombstone:

> The body of B. Franklin (Like the cover of an old book, its contents worn out, stripped of its lettering and gilding) Lies here, food for worms. But the work is not lost: for it will (as he believed) appear once more, In a new and more elegant edition, Revised and corrected By the Author.[142]

Upon entering immortality, it appears that Franklin's faith and works during his life were acceptable to the Lord. According to both temple records and the testimony of Wilford Woodruff, Benjamin Franklin accepted the gospel, as administered by the Church of Jesus Christ of Latter-day Saints, and presented himself in the spirit, along with Washington and the others, at the St. George Temple. His work was done and he received those most sacred covenants.

A fascinating epilogue to this story took place over fifteen years later, on the night of March 19, 1894. Benjamin Franklin, who had been one of the few along with Washington and Columbus to receive the High Priesthood in 1877, appeared once again to President Woodruff, this time in a dream. President Woodruff wrote the following concerning this event:

> I spent some time with him [Benjamin Franklin] and we talked over our Temple ordinances which had been administered for Franklin and others. He wanted more work done for him than had already been done. I promised him it should be done. I awoke and then made up my mind to receive further blessings for Benjamin Franklin and George Washington.[143]

As in life, his relentless passion for progress kept him in constant pursuit of the greater gifts.

How fulfilling such an experience must have been for Franklin, knowing that his work in mortality had helped tear down the political and social barriers in America and (eventually) in the world, so that gospel truths and priesthood keys might be restored in safety. It was Franklin who prophetically declared that the Revolution would eventually be responsible for destroying tyranny the world over, and that "our cause is the cause of all mankind, and that we are fighting for their liberty in defending our own."[144] He was right. As detailed in the previous chapter, it was because of his and his colleagues' actions pursuant to the Revolution, and under the American Covenant, that there was a proliferation of freedom in America and the world. This freedom would one day permit temples to dot the globe—temples offering promises of eternal life. He was now a recipient of such promises given to him in one of these sacred temples. Franklin's story certainly emphasizes the significance of the American Covenant, not only by providing evidence of its veracity, but by expressing its universal and eternal benefit.

Returning to the focus of this chapter, it was indeed that *Spirit of Independence* which was ultimately responsible for commencing the chain of events leading to gospel restoration and salvation. Clearly, Franklin's conversion by this Spirit is like unto the conversions of thousands of others who, through their efforts and the grace of God, also helped offer the world such eternal blessings. The inspired Founders even officially recognized the importance of such conversions to the cause in what was entitled the Congressional Decree of 1781. In this national decree, "Almighty God" is officially and formally thanked specifically for "heightening the number and zeal of the friends of liberty."[145] In other words, they were thanking God for the *Spirit of Independence* which ultimately converted enough people to the cause to bring victory to the righteous. It was a spiritual conversion inspired by God that was at the heart of the American Revolution. As John Adams—even he who was at the center of the entire revolutionary experience—explained: "What do we mean by the American Revolution? The war? That was no part of the Revolution; it was only an effect and consequence of it. The Revolution was in the minds of the people...a change in their *religious* sentiment."[146]

Conclusion

When reflecting upon the ultimate fruit of America's independence, which included a free government, even the "Lord's base of operations" in these latter-days, where His truths could be restored, the idea that God was behind it is a foregone conclusion. Too much was at stake, in terms of His ultimate work and glory, to leave to chance. America's fate was most certainly His design and foreordained plan. This chapter has offered corroborating evidence of this notion. Through analyzing Washington's preparation, the unlikely decision by the colonists to go to war, the testimonies of the revolutionaries themselves, the Great Awakening, and the powerful conversions of the Founders, it is clear that the compelling factor driving American freedom was the Spirit of God. While working under the American Covenant in his day, the righteous Nephite governor, Pahoran, recognized this same spirit working on the souls of his own freedom fighters. Turning to the covenant, Pahoran invoked this Spirit when, in an epistle to Captain Moroni, he declared: "give unto them power to conduct the war...according to the Spirit of God, which is also the spirit of freedom which is in them" (Alma 61:15). Thus it was for the American revolutionaries who were working under this same covenant and under this same spirit—and all for the same gospel purpose.

The evidence clearly suggests that the Founders were acting, enduring, and sacrificing under this powerful Spirit. It was a Spirit only God could provide them. It was a Spirit that many of them openly recognized. And for those who did not recognize it, it was a Spirit that worked on them just as the Spirit of Elijah works on hundreds of thousands of non-LDS genealogists*—compelling its recipients to act in a way and for a reason they cannot fully rationalize. Indeed, it was a Spirit that hit the founders hard, and which provides for us, today, the only fully convincing explanation for why these few and chosen Americans endured what they did to create an America under God. It was, in fact, the *Spirit of Independence*. As the Founders adhered to this Spirit, so did the nation become all the more worthy of the covenant blessings. And as these blessings flowed in greater measure, America received what it needed to become that covenant land and country capable of hosting God's true Church on the earth.

In concluding this chapter, we will turn to one of our most powerful latter-day prophets, who clearly understood the purposes

---

* In 1836, Elijah the Prophet appeared to Joseph Smith and Oliver Cowdery, committing to them the priesthood keys that permit, among other things, ordinance work for the dead, thus fulfilling Malachi's prophecy that Elijah would turn "the heart of the children to their fathers" (see Malachi 4:5-6). Since that time, people of the earth have inexplicably turned to genealogical research as a hobby. As Elder LeGrand Richards explains: "The spirit of turning the hearts of the children to their fathers has swept the whole earth since Elijah came to accomplish his promised mission. While this spirit cannot be seen, the operation thereof has touched the hearts of men and women the world over. They do not know why they are compiling genealogical records, yet this work has made rapid strides—really it is a 'marvelous work and a wonder' in and of itself." See LeGrand Richards, *A Marvelous Work and a Wonder* (Salt Lake City: Deseret Book Co., 1976), 185.

of the Revolution and the *Spirit of Independence*. Brigham Young declared:

> [T]he men in the revolution were inspired by the Almighty, to throw off the shackles of the mother government...For this cause were Adams, Jefferson, Franklin, Washington, and a host of others inspired to deeds of resistance to the acts of the King of Great Britain, who might also have been led to those aggressive acts, for aught we know, to bring to pass the purposes of God, in thus establishing a new government upon a principle of greater freedom, a basis of self-government allowing the free exercise of religious worship. *It was the voice of the Lord* inspiring all those worthy men who bore influence in those trying times, not only to go forth in battle but to exercise wisdom in council, fortitude, courage, and endurance in the tented field.[147]

ENDNOTES

[1] Spencer W. Kimball, as quoted in *Teachings of President's of the Church, Spencer W. Kimball* (Salt Lake: The Church of Jesus Christ of Latter-day Saints, 2006), 82.

[2] *Church History in the Fulness of Times, Religion 341-343* (Salt Lake City: The Church of Jesus Christ of Latter-Day Saints, 2000), 15, 18.

[3] Janice T. Connell, *The Spiritual Journey of George Washington* (New York: Hatherleigh Press, 2007), 3.

[4] William H Wilbur, *The Making of George Washington* (DeLand: Patriotic Education, Inc, 1970), 47-50.

[5] Quoting Mason Locke Weems, *A History of the Life, Death, Virtues and Exploits of George Washington* (Philadelphia: Lippencott, 1918). See also Novak and Novak, *Washington's God, op cited* Note 11, Chapter 1; see also Connell, 6.

[6] Wilbur, 42.

[7] Michael Novak and Jana Novak, *Washington's God* (New York, Basic Books, 2006), 8.

[8] John Bowman, *The History of the American Presidency* (North Dighton: World Publication Group, Inc), 12-13.

[9] David McCullough, *1776* (New York: Simon and Schuster, 2005), 43.

[10] McCullough, *1776*, 49.

[11] McCullough, *1776*, 49.

[12] McCullough, *1776*, 51.

[13] Joseph J. Ellis, *His Excellency* (New York: Alford A. Knopf, 2004), 80-81.

[14] McCullough, *John Adams*, 28.

[15] McCullough, *1776*, 49.
[16] Ellis, *His Excellency,* 74.

[17] It is interesting to note that the Lord often raises leaders unto Himself who lack an abundance of knowledge on their mission at hand. Like Washington, this compels such servants to humbly seek out the assistance of heaven, allowing the Lord to manipulate the affairs of His children. Obvious examples would be two of the Lord's most important prophets: Joseph Smith, the young inexperienced farm boy, and Peter, the unassuming fisherman. Some less obvious examples, which directly apply to the American Covenant, would be U.S. presidents such as Abraham Lincoln, Ronald Reagan, or George W. Bush. All three of these came to the White House with almost no military or foreign policy experience, yet their leadership in these particular areas have (and are having) a tremendous effect on expanding the God-given rights of freedom and democracy to God's children at home and abroad, which freedom is always necessary to usher in the gospel of Christ. Not surprisingly, all three of these U.S. presidents are praying men who have acknowledged God's hands in their presidential decision-making.

[18] Ellis, *His Excellency,* 68-69.

[19] McCullough, *1776*, 33-34, 43; Ellis, *His Excellency*, 69, 243.

[20] Richard Bushman, *Joseph Smith, Rough Stone Rolling* (New York: Alford A. Knopf, 2005), 4-5.

[21] Matthew B. Brown, *All Things Restored* (American Fork: Covenant Communications, 2000), 47-53.

[22] *Church History in the Fullness of Times* (Salt Lake City: The Church of Jesus Christ of Latter-day Saints, 2000), 291-292.

[23] Ellis, *His Excellency,* 71.
[24] Ellis, *His Excellency,* 22-23; Michael D. Evans, *American Prophecies* (New York: Warner Faith, 2004), 42-43.

[25] Robert Hieronimus, *Founding Fathers, Secret Societies* (Rochester: Destiny Books, 2006), 51-52.

[26] Ellis, *His Excellency*, 23.

[27] Steven Waldman, *Founding Faith* (New York: Random House, 2008), 57.

[28] George Washington, as quoted in H.L. Richardson, "A Most Uncivil War," *California Political Review*, Jan/Feb 2006, Vol. 17, No. 1.

[29] Lynn D. Wardle, "The Constitution as Covenant," *BYU Studies* 27, no. 3 (1987): 9.

[30] Abigail Adams, borrowing the words of John Dryden to describe Washington, as quoted in Stephen Ambrose, *To America* (New York: Simon and Schuster, 2002), 10-11.

[31] Ellis, *His Excellency* 70-71.

[32] McCullough, *1776,* 45.

[33] McCullough, *1776,* 42.

[34] Ellis, *His Excellency,* 45.

[35] Some of the eye witness accounts of Washington having taken Communion came from General Robert Porterfield, family members of Rev. Timothy Johnes, and family members of Alexander Hamilton, refer to Marshall and Manuel, 461.

[36] Marshall and Manuel, 358.

[37] Nelly Custis, as quoted in Marshall and Manuel, 460.

[38] Marshall and Manuel, 357.

[39] Testimony of Washington's private religious devotionals, as documented by his adopted daughter Nelly, can be found quoted in Novak and Novak, *Washington's God,* 136; and testimony of the same, as documented by his adopted son George and others can be found quoted in Connell, *The Spiritual Journey of George Washington*, 83, 95.

[40] Marshall and Manuel, 459-60.

[41] Marshall and Manuel, 457-459.

[42] Ellis, *His Excellency,* 162-163.

[43] Ellis, *His Excellency*, 164-167.

[44] Bennett, *Spirit of America*, 359-360.

[45] McCullough, *1776,* 37; Ellis, *His Excellency*, 46; Joseph J. Ellis, *Patriots, Brotherhood of the American Revolution*, Lectures recorded by Recorded Books, Inc, and Barnes and Noble Publishing: 2004, Lecture 7, Track 6, 00:06 min.

[46] McCullough, 1776, 77; a more detailed account of the incident can be found in the audio version of *1776* produced by Simon and Schuster Audioworks, New York, New York (2005); details of the account are also found in Mac and Tait, *Under God*, 39-42.

[47] Ellis, *His Excellency,* 263.

[48] Bennett, *America, The Last Best Hope*, 147.

[49] Joseph J. Ellis, *Patriots, Brotherhood of the American Revolution*, Lectures recorded by Recorded Books, Inc, and Barnes and Noble Publishing: 2004, Lecture 7, 3:40 min; John Adams also documented these same basic ratios between those who supported the war and those who did not, as quoted in McCullough, *John Adams*, 78.

[50] Walter Isaacson, *Benjamin Franklin, An American Life* (New York: Simon and Schuster, 2003), 307.

[51] Joseph Ellis, *Patriots*, lecture 7, 3:40min; John Adams, as quoted by McCullough, *John Adams*, 78.

[52] McCullough, *John Adams*, 333.

[53] McCullough, *1776,* 5, 11-12.

[54] King George, as quoted by McCullough, *John Adams*, 336.

[55] Walter Isaacson, *Benjamin Franklin* (New York: Simon and Schuster, 2003), 275.

[56] David McCullough, *John Adams* (New York: Simon and Schuster, 2001), 131.

[57] Joseph J. Ellis, *Patriots, Brotherhood of the American Revolution*. Lectures recorded by Recorded Books, Inc, and Barnes and Noble Publishing: 2004. Study Guide, 10.

[58] McCullough, *1776,* 11.

[59] Edward Rutledge, as quoted by McCullough, *John Adams*, 118.

[60] David McCullough, "The Glorious Cause of America," *BYU Magazine* , Winter 2006, 48-49.

[61] McCullough, *1776*, 158.

[62] Joseph J. Ellis, *Patriots, Brotherhood of the American Revolution*, Lectures recorded by Recorded Books, Inc, and Barnes and Noble Publishing: 2004, Lecture 7, Tr.6, 2:00 min.

[63] Jon Meacham, *American Gospel* (New York: Random House, 2006), 76.

[64] Marshal Foster and Mary Elaine Swanson, *The American Covenant, The Untold Story* (Thousand Oaks: The Mayflower Institute, 1981), 118-119.

[65] Sam Adams, as quoted by Marshall and Manuel, 330.

[66] Marshal Foster and Mary Elaine Swanson, *The American Covenant, The Untold Story,* 119; see also Benjamin Lossing, *Signers of the Declaration* (New York: J.C. Derby Publisher, 1856).

[67] McCullough, *1776,* 34.

[68] Nathan Hale, as quoted in *Let Freedom Ring, The Words that Shaped Our America* (New York: Sterling Publishing Co., 2001), 34.

[69] McCullough, *1776,* 20-21, 58.

[70] Vicki Jo Anderson, *The Other Eminent Men of Wilford Woodruff* (Malta: Nelson Book, 1994), 45-50.

[71] McCullough, *1776,* 168, 247, 249, 251.

[72] McCullough, *1776,* 249.

[73] McCullough, *1776,* 227.

[74] McCullough, *1776,* 250.

[75] McCullough, *1776,* 254-255.

[76] McCullough, *1776,* 255-256.

[77] McCullough, *1776,* 270.

[78] McCullough, *1776,* 251.

[79] McCullough, *1776,* 249.

[80] McCullough, *1776,* 258.

[81] Isaacson, 318-319.

[82] McCullough, *1776,* 258.

[83] McCullough, *1776,* 256.

[84] Stephen Ambrose, *To America, Personal Reflections of an Historian* (New York: Simon and Schuster, 2002), 12.

[85] Ellis, *Patriots, Brotherhood of the American Revolution,* lecture series; McCullough, *1776,* 213. In an effort to rally his men, Washington was seen exposing himself dangerously close to the enemy at the Battles of Kips Bay, Trenton/Princeton and Yorktown.

[86] Ellis, *His Excellency,* 74-75.

[87] McCullough, *1776,* 48.

[88] Bennett, *America,* 163.

[89] Ellis, *His Excellency,* 191.

[90] Abraham Keteltas (1777), as quoted by Steven Waldman, *Founding Faith: Providence, Politics, and the Birth of Religious Freedom in America* (New York: Random House, 2008), 41.

[91] Waldman, *Founding Faith,* 41.

[92] Waldman, *Founding Faith*, 42.

[93] Waldman, *Founding Faith,* 42.

[94] Marshall and Manuel, 324.

[95] Marshall and Manuel, 329.

[96] John Hancock, as quoted in Marshall and Manuel, 330.

[97] Waldman, 70.

[98] Waldman, 69.

[99] Marshall and Manuel, 331 and 323.

[100] Waldman, 43.

[101] Waldman, 43.

[102] Waldman, 43.

[103] Marshall and Manuel, 306-307.

[104] Bruce Feiler, *America's Prophet: Moses and the American Story* (New York: HarperCollins, 2009), 59-60.

[105] Gordon Wood, *The Creation of the American Republic: 1776-1787* (Chapel Hill: The University of North Carolina Press, 1969), 102; as quoted in W. Cleon Skousen, *The Five Thousand Year Leap Forward* (Washington D.C.: The National Center for Constitutional Studies, 1981), 52.

[106] See Waldman, 27-32.

[107] Jon Butler, *Awash a Sea of Faith: Christianizing the American People* (Cambridge: Harvard University Press, 1992), 201-202.

[108] Novak, *On Two Wings*, 34.

[109] Marshall and Manuel, 367.

[110] Mac and Tait, *Under God*, 158.

[111] Mac and Tait, *Under God*, 157.

[112] Report of Henry Speech by a Witness, "An Old Baptist Clergyman," reprinted in Patrick Henry: Life Correspondence and Speeches, Vol. 1, 267-268.

[113] Available at http://en.wikipedia.org/wiki/Patrick_Henry; and Mac and Tait, *Under God*, 157-159.

[114] McCullough, *John Adams*, 126-7.

[115] The details and background of this great speech of Adams, to include the quotes used in this book to describe it, can be found in McCullough, *John Adams*, 126-129.

[116] Isaacson, 285.

[117] Gordon S. Wood, *Revolutionary Characters* (New York: Penguin Press, 2006), 80.

[118] Walter Isaacson, *Benjamin Franklin* (New York: Simon and Schuster, 2003), 275.

[119] Isaacson, 292.

[120] Isaacson, 296.

[121] Isaacson, 298.

[122] Isaacson, 415.

[123] Isaacson, 298.

[124] Isaacson, 313.

[125] Isaacson, 339, 332.

[126] Isaacson, 304.

[127] Wood, *Revolutionary Characters*, 84.
[128] Wood, *Revolutionary Characters*, 70.

[129] Isaacson, 339.

[130] Isaacson, 467.

[131] Isaacson, 468.

[132] Waldman, *Founding Faith*, 107.

[133] William J. Bennett, *The Spirit of America* (New York: Simon and Schuster, 1997), 383-385.

[134] Isaacson, 468.

[135] Isaacson, 465.

[136] Benjamin Franklin, as quoted in Bennett, 385.

[137] Benjamin Franklin, as quoted by Bennett, 366.

[138] Benjamin Franklin, as quoted by Isaacson, 468.

[139] Benjamin Franklin, as quoted by Novak, *On Two Wings,* 156; and Isaacson, 469.

[140] Waldman, 24.

[141] Isaacson, 469.

[142] Isaacson, 470.

[143] Wilford Woodruff, as quoted in Mathias F. Cowley, *Wilford Woodruff—His Life and Labors* (Salt Lake City, Bookcraft, 1964), 586.

[144] Benjamin Franklin, as quoted by Isaacson, 339.

[145] Novak, *On Two Wings*, 21.

[146] John Adams, as quoted by Dinesh D'Souza, "Created Equal: How Christianity Shaped the West," *Imprimis*, November 2008, Volume 37, Number 11, 4, emphasis added.

[147] Brigham Young, as quoted in John A. Widtsoe, *Discourses of Brigham Young* (Salt Lake City: Deseret Book Co., 1954), 359-60, emphasis added.

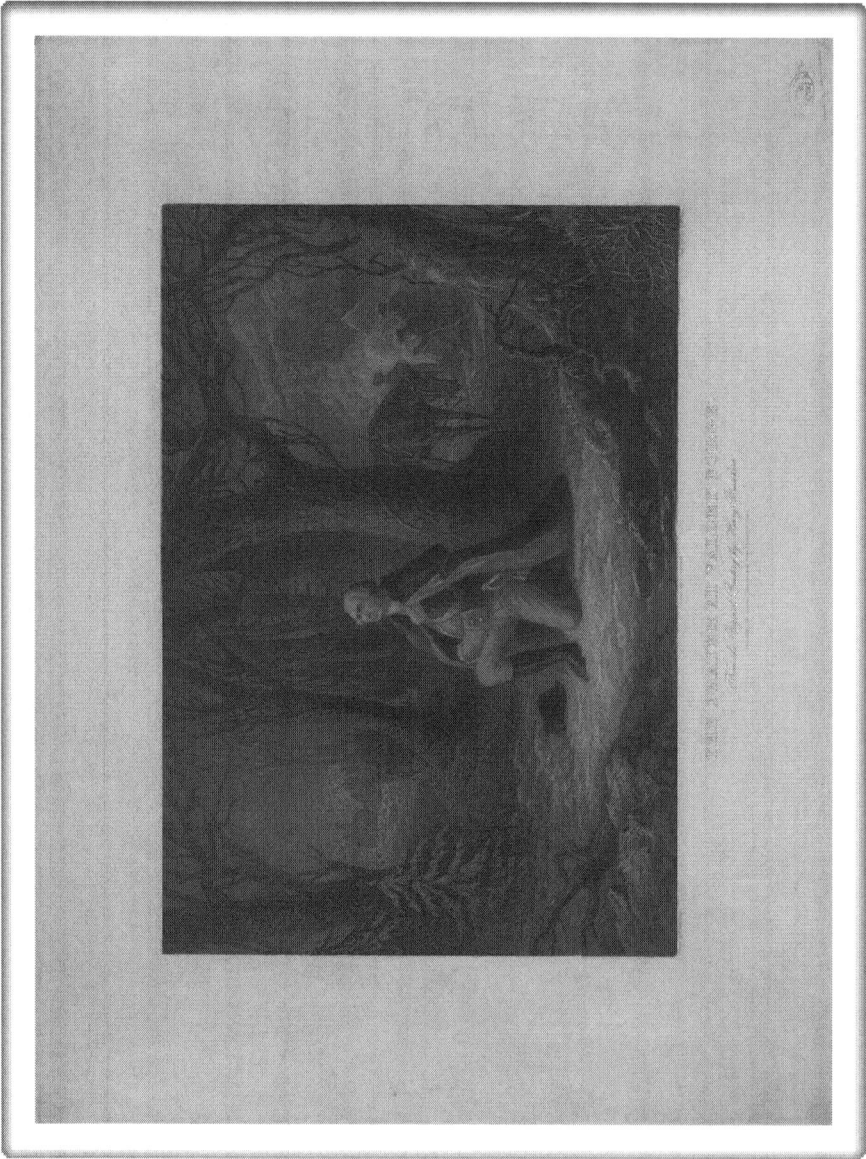

The Prayer at Valley Forge, by H. Brueckner.
Courtesy of The Library of Congress.

CHAPTER 7

MIRACLES AT WAR

[America has] without arms, ammunition, discipline, revenue, government or ally, with "staff and sling" only, dared, "in the name of the Lord of Hosts," to engage a gigantic adversary.

—Continental Congress, 1779

Providence has heretofore saved us in remarkable manner and on this we must principally rely.

—George Washington, 1777

Our discussion of the Revolutionary War has thus far been focused on the divine inspiration that governed the individual actions of those chosen American revolutionary leaders. However, in spite of their greatness, these American colonists were, in fact, a group of imperfect, under-prepared human beings challenging the world's superpower. As such, if they were to defeat Britain on the battlefields of war, they would have to rely on their covenant with the Lord, pleading often for further assistance from above. And in light of what gospel significance hung in the balance, such prayers would be answered time and time again. Particularly in crucial moments of the conflict, God would unveil His hand and deliver some of the greatest miracles recorded in battlefield history.

The Revolution's first armed conflict occurred in April 1775, near Boston, at Lexington and Concord, Massachusetts. In response to colonial resistance, and in an effort to arrest rebel leaders and seize stockpiled weapons, the British attacked America at these sleepy New England villages. These initial skirmishes would fittingly be called the "shot heard round the world." Beginning from this point in the Revolution's chronology, we will see how the colonists tried to remember God and keep His commandments. As they did, He would bless them with miracles to *protect* them, *prosper* them, and ultimately, provide them the *liberty* they sought—and this He did to advance His gospel purposes for His children. These miracles at war were nothing less than the American Covenant in action.

Miracle at Boston

The events at Lexington and Concord were the result of a build-up of British forces in Boston, which had come to America to quash the rebellion. Emboldened by Britain's aggressive movements, the faithful New Englanders, though largely unorganized, began preparing militias to fight back. By June 1775, these American militias had taken a stand against the British at Boston, but were attacked and driven further back and away from Boston at the Battle of Bunker Hill (a battle which actually took place mostly on neighboring Breed's Hill). With the loss of this high ground, the American militias lost their only real tactical advantage over the enemy. As Britain's complete control of Boston and its harbor congealed, Washington had only barely received his congressional commission as commander-in-chief. By July 1775, Washington had arrived to meet his largely scattered and disoriented citizen soldiers who were camped just outside of Boston, across the Charles River, near and around Cambridge. Notwithstanding his troops' weakened and unprepared state, Washington had come in eager anticipation to fight back, retake Boston, and end the British occupation of America.

Boston and its surrounding areas were indeed shaping up to be the location of the first large-scale battle of the war; for if the British did not attack first, Washington most certainly would. However, within hours of an intended attack (from one or both sides), the British picked up and left. This decision by the British to abandon Boston possibly saved the American cause. For had there been an armed conflict, Washington's Continental Army would most likely have been crushed. To be sure, the Americans had already lost their strategic advantage at Bunker and Breed's Hills. Furthermore, upon entering and studying Boston several days after the British evacuation, it became stunningly clear to Washington and his men that the British position there had been far too powerful for the Americans to overcome. This was in addition to numerous other disadvantages plaguing Washington's enfant army. In retrospect, it seems Washington's plan to attack the British in their Boston stronghold would have proved suicidal to America and her cause.

The British commander, General William Howe, knowing he had possessed such advantages while still controlling Boston, had himself already begun a full scale assault against the rebels. Shortly after calling for the attack, however, he called off the attack and pulled his troops completely out of Boston.

So *why* did the British decide to forsake their Boston stronghold, from whence they might have ended the conflict? The easy answer has to do with the suspicion that the British had always intended to leave Boston in order to instead launch an attack at New York. However, the details behind how the British evacuation actually played out leave little doubt that it was *the Lord* who made sure the British left, thus ensuring the survival of the Revolution. It is within the details of this story that we witness the first battlefield miracles of the war.

In an effort to explain how this miracle took effect, we return to the newly appointed Washington. For months after his arrival outside of Boston, he had been frantically preparing for his ill-conceived attack, while the British waited patiently to see if he dared walk into their trap. Washington had decided that the loss of Bunker and Breed's Hills required that he find another favorable position from whence to stage his assault. The location he chose was the unoccupied high ground south of Boston. This sought-after land was called Dorchester Heights, and was separated from Boston only by the harbor. Not only would Dorchester give Washington excellent battlefield position, but it would also, he hoped, compel the British, under threat of an imminent American attack, to launch a preemptive strike against the Americans at this new position. This would draw the British out of Boston and allow Washington to use his advantageous high ground to engage and defeat them in battle. Once this began, Washington planned on sending other troops across the water by boat, where they would attack the British stronghold at Boston and take the city back.[1]

Washington's long-shot plan clearly hung on his ability to gain the high ground at Dorchester. However, considering the close proximity of Dorchester to Boston, in clear sight of the ever-vigilant British eye, the American officers could only wonder how Washington could possibly move on such a position without causing an immediate and devastating British response. Furthermore, even if by some miracle he could take this high ground, American troops, having sensed the hopeless situation, were beginning to walk off the scene with the already scarce supply of weapons and powder, leaving Washington with fewer and fewer resources with which to man the proposed position.[2] Washington commented on his difficult situation, stating that, rather than commanding the army during this siege on Boston, he would have "retired to the backcountry and lived in a wigwam."[3]

So secure was General Howe of Washington's predicament, that he confidently declared: "We are not under the least apprehension of an attack on this place from the rebels." Even upon considering the prospect that Washington might move on Dorchester, Howe remained unconcerned. For if Washington attempted something so foolish, Howe made it clear that, "We must go at it with our whole force."[4] The British could not afford to allow the Americans to gain the high ground, and Howe knew that if the Americans made an attempt for it, he would see it and immediately and powerfully prevent it. Washington understood this, which is why he had to configure some way to take the Heights in complete secrecy.

The necessity to work in secrecy had already been in the forefront of Washington's mind. Since he arrived outside of Boston, he knew his ability to conceal knowledge from the British would be paramount. He knew, for example, that if Howe, at any point, had learned how extensively disadvantaged the Americans were, he would have commanded a British attack immediately upon the Americans and ended the conflict. If the Americans survived, said Washington, it would only be because "the finger of Providence is in it, to blind the eyes of our enemies...from knowing the disadvantages we labor under."[5] But if there was ever to be a *specific* moment during the Boston conflict when Washington would *especially* need this finger of Providence to blind his enemies, it would be upon his orders to advance on Dorchester.

A glimmer of hope entered in for the Americans when, after over two months and three-hundred miles of "rough forest roads, freezing lakes, blizzards, thaws, mountain wilderness, and repeated mishaps that would have broken lesser spirits several times over," Henry Knox, the twenty-five-year-old Boston bookseller had accomplished the impossible. He transported, by horse and sled, over 120,000 pounds of mortars and cannons from Fort Ticonderoga to an anxious Washington outside of Boston.[6] Though Washington had sent Knox on this difficult errand, the probability of a positive outcome had never been great. But Knox had accomplished it. And the timing of his return with the desired cannons could not have been better, for Washington was on the eve of advancing on Dorchester.

Notwithstanding this miracle, however, Washington knew he was in immediate need of another. He still had to accomplish the impossible task of moving these guns and his troops to the heights of Dorchester without the British first discovering and then thwarting his designs. He needed Providence to blind the British eye. And it seems Washington believed God would in fact intervene in this venture. For, despite every reason to think it would not work, the General would faithfully (if not a bit naively) persevere with his plan.

At midnight on March 2, 1776, the Americans launched a series of cannon and mortar fire from their position outside of Boston upon the British inside of Boston. The British immediately returned the gesture. The exchange continued on and off through March 4, but did little damage. Washington's intention, after all, was not to destroy, but to cause a loud distraction while his men, armed with Knox's cannon, advanced on the unoccupied heights of Dorchester. This they attempted on the night of March 4. With some four thousand troops and hundreds of wagons carrying thousands of pounds of weaponry, taking this high ground in secret, and directly in front of the British position, seemed an impossible feat. Even with the distraction of cannon fire and the scattered hay bales stretching across the landscape, which had been placed there earlier for concealment, it seemed doubtful. Then out of nowhere, heavenly cloud-cover dropped down to provide concealment for the Americans. As one witness to the event, Reverend William Gordon, observed, "A finer [night] for working could not have been taken out of the whole 365. It was hazy below [the Heights] so that our people could not be seen, though it was a bright moonlight night above on the hills." Even the Pulitzer Prize-winning historian David McCullough had to admit that it was "as if the hand of the Almighty were directing things."[7]

By the next morning, at least twenty cannon and thousands of troops were in position to make a move. When daylight appeared, the shock was overwhelming to the British. "My God," exclaimed General Howe, "these fellows have done more work in one night than I could make my army do in three nights." One British officer reported back to London: "This morning at day break we discovered two redoubts on the hills of Dorchester…They were all raised with an expedition equal to that of the genie belonging to Aladdin's wonderful lamp."[8]

Though shocked and less confident, Howe decided that his soldiers and his Boston stronghold were still enough to defeat Washington. Just as Washington had anticipated, Howe would prepare for a preemptive strike against the Americans. Howe ordered his men to ready themselves for the attack, which would commence on March 5. Washington had recently given similar orders to his own men to prepare for his pre-conceived amphibious assault on Boston. As the British troops pushed off into Boston Harbor in their advance toward the Americans, God once again intervened, in what one of Washington's officers called the "hurrycane."[9] As McCullough explains:

> What had been an abnormally warm, pleasant day had changed dramatically…By nightfall, a storm raged, with hail mixed with snow and sleet…windows were smashed, fences blew over. Two of the [British transports]…were blown ashore. The American lieutenant Isaac Bangs, who was among those freezing at their posts on the high ground of Dorchester, called it the worst storm 'that ever I was exposed to.' Clearly there would be no British assault that night.[10]

The British had been temporarily stopped. Howe was then forced to reconsider his options. Whereas before he was full of confidence that victory would be his, suddenly much had changed. With the Americans standing strong on Dorchester, and with the recent humbling blow caused by the great storm, Howe and his men were losing their will to fight. "I could promise myself little success," wrote Howe, "by attacking them under all the disadvantages I had to encounter; wherefore I judged it most advisable to prepare for the evacuation of the town."[11] And so they left.

As stated before, however, if there had been a battle at any point during the standoff (whether that battle commenced from the British side or from the under-experienced and over-zealous American side) it seems the colonists would have been defeated, perhaps even putting an end to the American cause. After all—and notwithstanding the American's new position and the recent storm —the British maintained a superior stronghold. Upon entering Boston several days after the British evacuation, a stunned Washington determined it to be "amazingly strong. 20,000 men could not have carried it against one thousand...The town of Boston was almost impregnable, every avenue fortified."[12] Washington added that the British position had been "the strongest by nature on this Continent, and strengthened and fortified in the best manner and at an enormous expense."[13] Additionally (and this goes without saying), the British possessed far more professional and seasoned troops. The colonial troops were merely citizens and farmers who had not had adequate time to train. As McCullough points out, Washington had "insufficient arms and ammunition, insufficient shelter, sickness, inexperienced officers, lack of discipline, clothing and money."[14]

Washington's plan to send troops into Boston, then, would have ultimately been suicide for America. Washington "had been repeatedly saved," according to McCullough, "from his headlong determination to attack, and thus from almost certain catastrophe."[15] To make matters even worse, and unbeknownst to anyone at the time, an overwhelming British naval fleet was already on its way to support Howe.[16]

But God's actions (first, bringing Knox and his artillery just in time; second, delivering Washington to Dorchester Heights; and third, thrusting down the devastating storm on the advancing British) had influenced Howe to throw up his hands and retreat. It was a triple miracle too hot for the British to handle. In the wisdom of God, and through His power, the British withdrew and Washington's well-intended, but ill-conceived plan to move on Boston, would not be carried out. The Americans had been preserved, that they might further prepare and fight again another day. McCullough called it "The 'miracle' of Dorchester Heights."[17]

That the Lord had wrought a miracle was not lost on Washington, especially as he entered Boston and became awakened to the superior position Howe had possessed. Though Washington had had his own intentions for seizing and arming Dorchester (to instigate battle), it seems that he now realized why the Lord had delivered his men and artillery to Dorchester—to deter the British so as to prevent a battle America would have lost. Similarly, though Washington was initially disappointed that the storm had quashed his plan of attack, he now seemed to understand why it had happened. He began to accept the storm as God's protection for America. Washington confessed as much to his secretary, Joseph Reed, declaring that he did not ultimately "lament or repine at any act of Providence," for, "whatever is, is right."[18] Additionally, in a letter to his brother, Washington explained that he now realized that "much blood was saved and a very important blow...prevented." Washington called it a "remarkable interposition of Providence" and admitted that it was carried out by Heaven for a "wise purpose."[19]

Abigail Adams, who as a resident of a Boston suburb witnessed these events from afar, shared these same sentiments. Declared Abigail: "Surely it is the Lord's doings and it is marvelous in our eyes."[20] Others agreed that the Lord had been in Boston. More than just saving the Continental Army, it seems God's intervention had also served as an opportunity for Americans to feel the power of their national covenant.

Reflecting upon this first miracle of war, Americans would graciously remember that it was not long before that the First Continental Congress had passed its very first act—an official and heartfelt prayer to God, which included the words from Psalm 35: "Plead my cause, O Lord, with them that strive with me: fight against them that fight against me." John Adams would later comment that the prayer was one that "heaven had ordained" and that it brought tears to eyes of the delegates. "It was," he said, "enough to melt a heart of stone."[21] Washington himself had participated in this prayer. Shortly thereafter, this prayer had been codified into a national covenant of sorts, when Congress officially called upon the nation to forsake sin and turn to the Lord for His blessings.[22]

By the time Washington had arrived outside the British occupied Boston in July 1775, the Congress had again covenanted with the Lord in its official Declaration of the Causes and Necessity of Taking Up Arms, which stated: "With a humble confidence in the mercies of the Supreme and impartial God and ruler of the universe, we most devoutly implore His divine goodness to protect us happily through this great conflict."[23] Days later, Congress backed this covenant with the announcement of a national day of prayer, which again called on Americans to "unfeignedly confess and deplore our many sins."[24] John Adams declared, during this month of national covenant awareness, that "[m]illions will be upon their knees at once before their great Creator, imploring His forgiveness and blessing; his smiles on American Councils and arms."[25]

In addition to actions of Congress, Washington himself put forth great efforts to secure the blessings of the American Covenant prior to the siege of Boston. He called for government-sponsored chaplains for his troops, instructed his soldiers to attend Sunday service "to implore the blessings of heaven upon the means used for our safety and defense," and encouraged his men to "shew their gratitude to Providence, for thus favouring the Cause of Freedom and America" that they might "deserve his future blessings."[26]

But perhaps most importantly, on March 6, 1776, almost immediately after having secured Dorchester Heights, and days before the British evacuation—indeed, right when the miraculous intervention would be needed—Washington issued the following General Order. It was a direct call to the American Covenant.

> Thursday...being set apart by...this Province as a day of fasting, prayer and humiliation, to 'implore the Lord and Giver of victory to pardon our manifold sins and wickedness, and that it would please Him to bless the

Continental army with His divine favor and protection,' all officers and soldiers are strictly enjoined to pay all due reverence, and attention on that day to the sacred duties of the Lord of hosts, for his mercies already received, and for those blessings, which our Holiness and Uprightness of life can alone encourage us to hope through his mercy to obtain.[27]

America had clearly called on God, and God had clearly answered.

As such, the scene in the newly-liberated Boston could not have been more joyous for the American beneficiaries of this divine answer and intervention. With the British at last evacuated and with the Americans high in spirits, a triumphant Washington was preparing to leave the now safeguarded New Englanders. But first he would pause on the Sabbath to hear a sermon by the Reverend Abiel Leonard, who fittingly chose for his text, Exodus 14:25: "The Egyptians said, Let us flee from the face of Israel; for the Lord fighteth for them."[28] The colonists were indeed a branch of modern-day Israel, fully equipped with that same national covenant the reverend was now sermonizing over. Perhaps many of them remembered that, not long before the events at Boston, the preacher William Stearns had exhorted them, declaring, "[L]et America's valorous sons put on the harness, nor take it off till peace shall be to Israel."[29] They seemed to know the covenant was real and that it was now theirs. And they would rely upon it again in the very near future.

Miracle at Long Island

Nobody was naïve enough to believe the British evacuation of Boston meant an end to hostilities. In fact, as the British fleet headed southward down the eastern coastline, it became clear to everyone that Howe would begin preparations for a military strike against the commercial and cultural hub of America—New York City. New York would make an ideal headquarters for Howe, as it was crawling with loyalists in support of Britain. New York was also surrounded by rivers and harbors, making it an easy target for the world's most powerful navy. In anticipation, Washington immediately sent his forces to defend New York. By April 1776, the Continental Army had arrived in New York and began making its preparations for battle.

If Washington had been at all disadvantaged in Boston, he was next to hopeless in New York. In addition to the large amount of loyalists in New York, and the many bays, rivers, and waterways conducive to a British naval attack there, a fresh and enormous British fleet had recently arrived and joined with Howe's already powerful forces. By the end of June, this reinforced British fleet began its impressive advent into New York Harbor. With some four hundred ships, at least seventy of which were state-of-the-art war ships with fifty guns or more, it was—at that time—the largest naval force ever sent forth by any one nation against another. One of Washington's men recorded, "I do declare that I thought all London was afloat."[30] Furthermore, upon the decks of these ships were close to thirty-thousand armed troops—more soldiers than the entire civilian population of New York or Philadelphia. With New York completely surrounded by water, the British could advance on land with these troops wherever and whenever they desired.

Washington, on the other hand—himself never having commanded a significant battle—led only a rag-tag group of civilian soldiers, who counted well under half the number of British troops; and most of these American volunteers had never even seen a battle, let alone fought in one. Worse yet, Washington did not have even a single warship at his disposal.[31] But what he *did* have was a promise from the Lord, bound by the American Covenant, on which he would rely.

This one advantage, however, would require a certain adherence by the Americans. Its benefits were, after all, contingent upon their worthiness. This was especially worrisome as, with the increase of sinful opportunity in New York City, immorality among the troops was on the rise. Washington recognized it. And so, in addition to leading the physical preparations for battle, Washington also led the spiritual ones. On May 15, shortly after the Continental Army's arrival at New York, Washington issued a General Order to all under his command, which read:

> Instant to be observed [on Friday the 17th] as a day of fasting, humiliation and prayer, humbly to supplicate the mercy of Almighty God, that it would please him to pardon all our manifold sins and transgressions, and to prosper the Arms of the United Colonies, and finally establish the peace and freedom of America, upon a solid and lasting foundation.[32]

Then again on July 2, Washington in another General Order would remind his men that "the fate of unborn Millions will now depend, under God, on the courage and conduct of this army...Let us therefore rely upon the goodness of the Cause, and the aid of the Supreme Being, in whose hands Victory is."[33] Two days later, in Philadelphia, these same sentiments would be immortalized by the Congress in the Declaration of Independence, which concludes, "And for support of this Declaration, *with firm reliance on the protection of divine Providence*, we mutually pledge to each other our Lives, our Fortunes, and our sacred Honor."

So convinced was Washington of his utter dependence upon the covenant, and the need to fulfill its obligations, that he would extend further reminders and calls to repentance. On July 9, Washington issued another General Order in which he called for chaplains in each regiment to ensure that the soldiers "attend carefully upon religious exercises." The order concluded with the following: "The blessing and protection of Heaven are at all times necessary but especially so in times of public distress and danger— the General hopes and trusts, that every officer and man, will endeavor so to live, and act, as becomes a good Christian soldier defending the dearest Rights and Liberties of his country."[34] Just days before battle would commence, Washington issued yet another General Order in which he recommended the keeping of the Sabbath and pleaded with his men to shun the immoral temptations that abounded in the city, exhorting them to "endeavor to check [such behavior] and ...reflect, that we can have little hopes of the blessing of Heaven on our Arms, if we insult it by our impiety and folly."[35] Such orders and encouragements from Washington are reminiscent of the actions of Captain Moroni, who fought in a different time but under the same American Covenant. He declared to his own soldiers, "Surely God should not suffer that we [who] take upon the name of Christ, shall be trodden down and destroyed until we bring it upon us by our own transgressions" (Alma 46:18).

That Washington was assured the Lord would again provide in the upcoming battle was evidenced by the army's positive response to their commander-in-chief's spiritual encouragements. One observant New Yorker, unaccustomed to seeing a pious group of soldiers, wrote of his surprise to see how Washington's men attended prayers "evening and morning regularly." "On the Lord's day," commented the observer, "they attend public worship twice, and their deportment in the house of God is such as becomes the place." Washington's trusted officer, Henry Knox, wrote to his wife that he would daily "rise with or a little before the sun and immediately, with part of the regiment attend prayers, sing a psalm or read a chapter [from the Bible]."[36] They were trying to keep their end of the American Covenant.

The faith and influence of Washington was extended through other revolutionary leaders who caught his vision and acted upon it. One such leader, Connecticut Governor Jonathon Trumbull, upon learning of Washington's impending battle, called for nine fresh regiments to march in support of Washington (and this was in addition to the five regiments he had already sent). In line with Washington's vision, Trumbull's call to arms sounded much like a call to the American Covenant: "Be roused and alarmed," declared Trumbull, "to stand forth in our just and glorious cause. Join...march on; this shall be your warrant: play the man for God, and for the cities of our God! May the Lord of Hosts, the God of the armies of Israel, be your leader."[37]

On July 2, 1776, the same day the Congress had officially voted for the Declaration of Independence, the British landed on the southern shores of Long Island, New York. Long Island is located to the east of Manhattan Island (home of New York City and Washington's headquarters), separated by the mile-wide East River. Having anticipated such advancements, Washington had already begun sending his troops from Manhattan over the East River to the western shores of Long Island at Brooklyn. Over the next several weeks, the two forces inched their way toward each other—the first great battle of the war was upon them.

On August 27, several miles inland from Brooklyn's shores, the Battle of Long Island commenced. The Americans were devastatingly defeated. Almost immediately, Washington lost over one thousand men, while Howe lost less than one hundred.[38] All the Americans could do was run back toward the western shores of Brooklyn, Long Island, in hopes of escaping over the East River back into New York City before the advancing enemy could catch up to them. The British responded by sending its fastest ships up the East River to cut off Washington's escape route with the intention of surrounding the rebels from all sides. Howe knew that such action would compel an American surrender, as Washington's entire Continental Army would be trapped. This would be the end of America's hope for independence. As one prominent historian stated, "If Washington and his army had been trapped in Brooklyn...the war would have ended quickly."[39] After giving their all, the Americans were now in a devastatingly hopeless state, which is often when the Lord enters the scene—and enter He did!

As the British fleet raced northward and entered the mouth of the East River in order to block Washington's retreat and crush his rebel army, a ferocious wind from the north began pushing the British back down. A total of five ships carrying over seventy-two guns attempted—but failed—to advance up the river to cut off the Americans.[40] Washington would have a small window of opportunity to evacuate his troops from this would-be British trap.

On the night of August 29, under the cover of darkness, Washington began gathering every boat that could be acquired, and prepared to secretly ferry his men back across the East River and back into New York City. Knowing that the British would respond to such an evacuation with a swift land assault, Washington ordered his men to continue firing long-range guns through the night at the British land troops. He further ordered a few soldiers to maintain the noise and campfires indicative of a busy campsite, thus making the British believe the Americans were anything but on the move.

In the meantime, these British land forces would wait until the advancing British fleet made its way up the river, thus enabling them to surround Washington from all ends. Until this happened, the British land troops, convinced that the rebels were in fact bedding down for the night, would wait patiently. (Fortunately for the Americans, there was no telecommunication system for the British naval troops to alert the British land troops that the ships could not get up the river.)

Convinced that his ruse was working on the British land troops, and with the blessed storm holding back the British navy, Washington would attempt the impossible—to secretly ferry over nine thousand troops, along with their baggage, guns, horses, etc., across the mile-wide river, and all before the light of day exposed his scheme. If the British land troops were to discover what was happening, it would be over for the Americans.

As the evacuation began, the Americans again fell into despair, as the same wind that kept Howe from advancing up the river, was also making it impossible for them to manage their over-crowded rowboats and advance their army westward to safety. Then, a little after nine, the wind miraculously shifted and blew due west, facilitating the exodus with most favorable conditions.[41]

But even with the favorable wind, the night was dying fast. The rising sun would soon expose Washington's scheme. Another miracle was needed. David McCullough explains:

> Troops in substantial number had still to be evacuated and at the rate things were going, it appeared day would dawn before everyone was safely removed. But again the "elements" interceded, this time in the form of pea-soup fog. It was called "a peculiar providential occurrence," "manifestly providential," "very favorable to the design," "an unusual fog," "a friendly

fog," "an American fog." "So very dense was the atmosphere," remembers Benjamin Tallmadge, "that I could scarcely discern a man at six yards' distance." And as daylight came, the fog held, covering the entire operation no less than had the night...while over on the New York side of the river there was no fog at all.[42]

Washington waited until the last man evacuated Long Island, then he himself boarded a ferry boat. The escape was a success, and without a single casualty. Washington and his men would, yet again, live to fight another day.

Alexander Graydon, an eyewitness to the event, commented that "in less than an hour after [the complete evacuation], the fog having dispersed, the enemy was visible on the shore we had left." The British were as bewildered as they had been when they awoke to see the American guns pointing down at them from Dorchester Heights. "That the rebel army had silently vanished in the night right under their very noses," according to McCullough, "was almost inconceivable." British Major Stephen Kemble wrote in his diary that "[i]n the morning, to our great astonishment, [we] found they had evacuated...and the whole escaped to...New York." British General James Grant wrote, "We cannot yet account for their precipitate retreat."[43]

McCullough summed up the entire event:

But what a close call it had been. How readily it could have gone all wrong—had there been no northeast wind to hold the British fleet in check through the day the Battle of Long Island was fought, not to say the days immediately afterward. Or had the wind not turned southwest the night of August 29. Or had there been no fortuitous fog as a final safeguard when day broke....Incredibly, yet again—fate, luck, Providence, the hand of God, as would be said so often —intervened. [44]

This miracle at Long Island would cause many to think twice about the seemingly prophetic words spoken three months earlier by the very influential Reverend John Witherspoon, who presided over the College of New Jersey (what is now Princeton University) and thus was mentor to one vice president, over fifteen delegates to the Continental Congress and Constitutional Convention, forty-nine members of the House of Representatives, twenty-eight senators, three Supreme Court Justices, and scores of other government officers and patriots. Himself a signer of the Declaration of Independence, Witherspoon would prophetically describe, on May 17, 1776, how God would secure America's victory: "The armies of the enemy...are rendered irresolute when...rains make the terrain of the final charge impossible; [and] an unforeseen fog brings operations to a halt. Nature affords countless chinks in its regular workings through which the Divine Artist...can govern events."[45]

Washington himself made an independent yet concurring prophetic statement in January 1776, also many months before Long Island (and Boston for that matter), when he expressed that victory could only come if "the finger of Providence is in it, to blind the eyes of our enemies."[46]

God heard America's plea and honored the American Covenant. In His wisdom, He allowed Washington and his band of inexperienced men to engage the enemy at Long Island, thus acquiring the much needed taste of battle that would serve them in the future, while at the same time miraculously pulling them out from the grips of destruction. The Revolution would live on.

Miracle at Trenton and Princeton

Though the Lord certainly worked His miracle at Long Island, Washington's situation in the aftermath remained bleak. The overwhelming defeat at New York had convinced some fifteen thousand American troops to immediately abandon the cause, leaving Washington with a meager three-thousand men. And the only thing these faithful soldiers could do in that moment was run away as fast as possible from the thirty-thousand British troops on their tails. Thus began Washington's famous retreat southward through New Jersey.

Yet despite the overwhelming reason to lose all hope, Washington and his band of faithful would not. As discussed in the previous chapter, the Spirit was with them. Furthermore, they knew that God had not worked the aforementioned miracles only to have His soldiers quit. And so, Washington would again appeal to the American Covenant, which was perhaps made a bit easier considering Congress had codified the covenant at least twice between the events at New York and the southward retreat: first, through the Declaration of Independence, and second, through the declaration for a Day of Fasting and Repentance (December 11, 1776), whose purpose was to officially "implore of Almighty God the forgiveness of the many sins prevailing among all ranks, and to beg the countenance as assistance of his Providence in the prosecution of the present just and necessary war."[47]

Armed with this tried and true covenant, Washington would go forward with faith—not only in courageously leading a dangerous retreat, but in preparing a counter-strike at the British-held town of Trenton, New Jersey, located just east of the Delaware River. On Christmas night, 1776, Washington's men, whose retreat had led them down the west side of the Delaware River, would divide into three parties and cross at separate locations over the Delaware River, then attack the enemy at dawn. The operation got off to a bad start when Washington's party was the only one able to break through the ice and successfully land on the shores near Trenton. His main concern at the time was to land without alerting the enemy. Once again, the Lord would intervene by helping to make this mission stealth. McCullough stated, "as during the escape from Brooklyn, Washington's other daring river-crossing by night, a northeaster [wind/storm] was again, decisively, a blessing...."[48] The enemy could not see or hear them coming.

As Washington's party was the only one that made it across, thus diminishing greatly his expected resources, the element of surprise would be all the more essential. As such, the Lord's storm would remain healthy, thus covering the Americans (both the sound and sight of them) until the early morning attack. Washington's specific target was the fifteen-hundred professional Hessian soldiers (mercenaries hired by the British) guarding Trenton. The Hessians would certainly not expect an ailing citizen army on the run to attack them the day after Christmas, especially in such awful weather. Even if the Americans did attempt such a thing, the Hessians had every reason to believe that their defensive posts just outside the town would surely detect any such American advance. Unfortunately for the Hessians, nobody had informed them about the American Covenant.

At just after eight o'clock on the morning of December 26, 1776, Nathanial Greene led the charge into Trenton. The Lord's cover had worked, and He literally had their backs. "The storm continued with great violence," wrote Henry Knox, "but was in our backs, and consequently in the faces of the enemy."[49] The Hessians were completely caught off guard. Knox noted that "[t]he hurry, fright and confusion of the enemy was not unlike that which will be when the last trump will sound."[50]

After what resulted in a violent display of house to house fighting, which lasted about forty-five minutes, the Hessians laid down their weapons and surrendered. With over twenty Hessians killed and over ninety others wounded, the Americans stood victorious without a single death in battle and with only four wounded men. Knox concluded that "Providence seemed to have smiled upon every part of this enterprise."[51] Among the brave American soldiers standing proud at battle's end were several future greats: Alexander Hamilton (first U.S. Secretary of the Treasury), John Marshall (second U.S. Chief Justice of the Supreme Court), and James Monroe (fifth U.S. president).[52]

Hope for America had returned. However, on January 1, 1777, all enlistments would expire. The entirety of the Continental Army, at least what was left of it, would be free to go home. Washington knew this would cripple the Revolution; and so he gathered his troops. The drum roll began and the General asked all those willing to extend their tours to step forward. Not a soul budged. A depressed Washington turned his horse and began riding away. Then suddenly he stopped, returned to his men, and according to a credible witness, stated the following:

> My brave fellows, you have done all I asked you to do, and more than could be reasonably expected, but your country is at stake, your wives, your houses, and all that you hold dear. You have worn yourselves out with fatigues and hardships, but we know not how to spare you. If you will continue to stay one month longer, you will render that service to the cause of liberty, and to your country, which you can probably never do under any other circumstance. [53]

If ever there was a Captain Moroni / Title of Liberty moment during the American Revolutionary War, this was it. Washington's message was remarkably similar to that given by Moroni: "And he took a piece [of cloth] and wrote upon it—In memory of our God, our religion, and freedom, and our peace, our wives, and our children...and he called it the Title of Liberty and he bowed himself to the earth, and he prayed mightily unto his God for the blessings of liberty to rest upon his brethren" (Alma 46:12-13). Washington, like Moroni, had expressed such a sentiment, not only in this crucial moment, but throughout the war, as described above.

Needless to say, as the drums began to sound again, the men, this time, stepped forward. According to Nathanial Greene, "God Almighty inclined their hearts to listen to the proposal and they engaged anew." [54] Washington would capitalize on the spirit accompanying this renewal of covenant and attack the enemy forthwith, this time up the road from Trenton at another British stronghold—the town of Princeton, New Jersey.

The British, aware of such a possibility, employed one of their brightest field commanders, Lord Charles Cornwallis, to protect Princeton. Upon arriving at Princeton on January 1, 1777, an anxious Cornwallis left a portion of his troops to guard the town, and then led over five-thousand troops down the ten mile road to Trenton to squash the rebellion once and for all. With the temperature above freezing, the muddy roads made it very difficult for the British to mobilize troops and cannons. Fatigued, Cornwallis' troops camped just outside of view from Washington, who was nestled in at Trenton. Cornwallis claimed he would "bag him" in the morning. But when the British arose and launched their attack at dawn, not an American was to be found. Like at Long Island, Washington had managed to fool the British by keeping a few soldiers behind to stoke the fires, giving the perception that they had camped down for the night, when in reality the Americans had mobilized.

But this time, they were not on retreat. In an almost insanely risky move, Washington, in the dead of night, led thousands of troops with horses, baggage, and cannons through obscure back roads that twisted right around Cornwallis' position. Though the Americans were traveling over the same muddy roads which had slowed Cornwallis only hours earlier, a providential drop in the temperature had frozen the roads, making it possible for the Americans to move their carriages and cannon rapidly.[55] By morning, when Cornwallis realized he had been duped, Washington was already hitting the British stronghold at Princeton. "I believe," declared Knox, "they [the British at Princeton] were as astonished as if an army had dropped perpendicularly upon them."[56] And why wouldn't they be astonished? With Cornwallis having just left in the direction of the American rebels, the prospect of Washington getting through him to Princeton would have been nothing short of miraculous. Yet it had happened.

The battle of Princeton was more violent and furious than that at Trenton. Sensing his troops' need of spirit and courage, Washington would lead the charge himself on horseback. This was something he would often do, much to the chagrin of his aides, who would run to his side and attempt to reign him back in to safety. "I shall never forget," wrote one young officer present, "what I felt...when I saw him brave all the dangers of the field and his important life hanging as it were by a single hair with a thousand deaths flying around him. Believe me, I thought not of myself."[57] As other troops entered in from strategic points around the town, the British surrendered.

The fall of Trenton and Princeton, though minor battles in and of themselves, had an enormous effect throughout the colonies. The author Mercy Warren, who personally witnessed the Revolution, wrote that Washington's victories created a "change instantaneously wrought in the minds of men." Warren continued, "[There are] no people on earth in whom a spirit of enthusiastic zeal is so readily kindled, and burns so remarkably, as among Americans."[58] This spirit, even the *Spirit of Independence*, was not only alive and well, but was at last proliferating throughout all of America. It would seem the Lord knew such a spirit was necessary for the years ahead. As such, He inspired the miraculous events surrounding the Trenton and Princeton experience.

McCullough concluded that even though it had only been weeks earlier that America was bogged down in "as dark a time as any in the history of the country...suddenly, miraculously it seemed, that had changed because of a small band of determined men and their leader."[59] Though McCullough was most likely, and rightly, referring to Washington as this leader, the true leader of the victories was He who sat in a higher realm. Washington himself understood and believed this. Days after his victory at Princeton, he declared: "Providence has heretofore saved us in remarkable manner and on this we must principally rely."[60] Convinced more than ever that his success on the battlefield was fully contingent on the binding power of America's national covenant with the Almighty, Washington would "principally rely" on it again and again.

Miracles of 1777: Saratoga and Valley Forge

As great as those initial victories had been, the war would require over five more years of heartache, pain, and bloodshed before the Americans would achieve their independence. Fully aware of what lay ahead, Washington would again turn to God. Not long after Trenton and Princeton, Washington declared to his men that he, the commander-in-chief, "has the full confidence that in another Appeal to Heaven (with the blessing of providence, which it becomes every officer and soldier humbly to supplicate), we shall prove successful."[61]

It would not take long for Washington to be proven correct once again. In the fall of 1777, just weeks after Washington's above-quoted invocation and "appeal to heaven," the national covenant would bless the American cause at the very significant Battle of Saratoga. In September 1777, British General John Burgoyne invaded the Mohawk Valley near the town of Saratoga where an American regiment was detached. After an unsuccessful attempt at the Americans, Burgoyne decided to wait for reinforcements before attempting a second strike. By all accounts, Burgoyne's principal weakness was his inability to mobilize due to the large amount of material goods he had selfishly seized for his personal gain, including the fine china he and his men refused to part with. Furthermore, while the British waited, they entertained themselves with their large entourage of prostitutes that Burgoyne permitted to follow along.[62] In the meantime, Washington repeatedly rebuked such behavior in his own men. He was issuing official pleas to the Almighty, and demanding strict moral behavior of his soldiers. That the Americans were fighting under a covenant with the Lord, and that the British were not, is clearly reflected in their very different perspectives on moral behavior.

It was perhaps this difference that explains why the Americans were able to defeat Burgoyne and the British at Saratoga in October 1777. Washington understood that it was God and covenant that provided the victory. Upon learning of the triumph, he promptly ordered services of thanksgiving and stated, "Let every face brighten, and every heart expand with grateful joy and praise to the supreme disposer of all events, who has granted us this signal success."[63] This American victory was not only significant in that it demonstrated the power of adhering to the national covenant, but also in that it provided the proof required by would-be American allies that the American cause was winnable. As a direct result of Saratoga, both France and Spain began their indispensable support of the American Revolution.

Following this victory, Congress would reemphasize the true source of America's strength and success—its national covenant with God. On November 1, 1777, Congress once again officially invoked this covenant in its Thanksgiving Proclamation, in which Congress called on Americans to perform acts to "please God through merits of Jesus Christ" and to support "the means of religion, for the promotion and enlargement of that Kingdom, which consisteth 'in righteousness, peace and joy in the Holy Ghost.'" The proclamation further instructed Americans to "join the penitent confession of their manifold sins, whereby they had forfeited every favor, and their humble and earnest supplication that it may please God, through the merits of Jesus Christ, mercifully to forgive and blot them out of remembrance."[64]

This public invocation to Heaven could not have been timelier, for the Lord and His blessings would be needed almost immediately thereafter. Within weeks of Saratoga (and after earlier American defeats at the Battle of Brandywine Creek and then at the Battle of Germantown), Washington and his very spent colonial army were compelled to hunker down for the winter of 1777 in Valley Forge, near Philadelphia. Without proper supplies (some went without shoes or shirts) and without adequate food (some were forced to eat a soup of burnt leaves and dirt), the army's suffering was acute. Yet notwithstanding, Washington and some of his officers seemed to hint at something divine even in this situation. For while the British grew fat and happy in New York and Philadelphia, Washington's men were forced to learn humility, resilience, and other needful lessons for eventual victory. Wrote Washington, "To see Men without Cloathes to cover their nakedness, without Blankets to lay on, without Shoes, by which their Marches might be traced by the Blood from their feet, is a mark of Patience and obedience which in my opinion can scarce be paralel'd."[65] One of Washington's most faithful commanders, Nathaniel Greene, would concur, adding that "we bear beatings very well...the more we are beat, the better we grow."[66]

Such lessons would be taught again in the not too distant future to a different generation of the Lord's faithful. When the Prophet Joseph Smith pleaded with the Lord for an understanding of the unbearable burdens he and his Saints were required to suffer, the Lord calmed his anxiety, saying, "know thou, my son that all these things shall give thee experience, and shall be for thy good" (D&C 122:7). These words would have resonated with Washington and his men at Valley Forge. In both cases, the Lord needed to strengthen His faithful servants through the "refiner's fire," that His ultimate purposes might come to pass.

Washington, who stayed close to his men in Valley Forge (when he certainly could have justified relocating to more comfortable quarters), would also experience the spiritual growth of such a humbling experience. Two legendary stories of Washington at Valley Forge, both of which are apocryphal, tell the tale. First is the well-known account of his mighty prayer. According to the story, a local resident and Quaker named Isaac Potts, whose religion had initially compelled him to stand against the Revolution, happened upon the spiritually powerful scene. The fullest account of what he saw was written by the Rev. Nathanial Snowden (1770-1851) in his "Diary of Remembrances." Rev. Snowden, an ordained minister and graduate of Princeton, related the following experience:

> I was riding with him [Mr. Potts] in Montgomery County, Penn, near to the Valley Forge, where the army lay during the war of ye Revolution. Mr. Potts was a Senator in our

State & a Whig. I told him I was agreeably surprised to find him a friend to his country, as the Quakers were mostly Tories. He said, "It was so and I was a rank Tory once, for I never believed that America could proceed against Great Britain whose fleets and armies covered the land and ocean, but something very extraordinary converted me to the Good Faith!"

"What was that?," I inquired. "Do you see that woods, & that plain?" It was about a quarter of a mile off from the place we were riding, as it happened. "There," said he, "laid the army of Washington. It was a most distressing time of ye war, and all were for giving up the ship except for that great and good man. In that woods pointing to a point in view, I heard a plaintive sound as, of a man at prayer. I tied my horse to a sapling & went quietly into the woods & to my astonishment I saw the great George Washington on his knees alone, with his sword on one side and his cocked hat on the other. He was at Prayer to the God of the Armies, beseeching to interpose with his divine aid, as it was ye Crises, & the cause of the country, of humanity & of the world.

Such a prayer I never heard from the lips of man. I left him alone praying. I went home & told my wife. I saw a sight and heard today what I never saw or heard before, and just related to her what I had seen & heard & observed. We never thought a man could be a soldier and a Christian, but if there is one in the world, it is Washington. She also was astonished. We thought it was the cause of God, & America could prevail.[67]

Critics—mostly secularists—have attempted to discredit this story due to another account of a praying Washington at Valley Forge. In this second account, as printed in the *Aldine Press*, Washington was seen by one of his soldiers praying in a barn, which critics claim is a discrepancy of the original story. Critics therefore discredit any claim that Washington was ever seen praying at all in Valley Forge. Of course, the more reasonable explanation, perhaps beyond the reach of such secularists, is that a God-fearing man like Washington prayed many times at Valley Forge and, therefore, many accounts were witnessed and recorded. One of Washington's generals at Valley Forge, Robert Porterfield, told of how he once entered Washington's private quarters to report an emergency. Porterfield found Washington on his knees in prayer. He reported the incident to Washington's aide, Alexander Hamilton, who replied that "such was his constant habit."[68]

Furthermore, in light of the claims by close friends and family members that Washington consistently "maintained daily intercourse with Heaven by prayer," that he "observed stated seasons of retirement for secret devotion,"[69] and that he was constantly encouraging/ordering his men to pray often (he was, after all, never known to be a hypocrite), Potts' story becomes all the more believable.

The second story has to do with the account of Anthony Sherman, one of Washington's aides at Valley Forge, who reportedly recalled the following experience, later to be recorded and published by his friend, Wesley Bradshaw. The account appeared in an 1880 edition of the *National Tribune*:

> The darkest period we had I think, was when Washington, after several reverses, retreated to Valley Forge, where he resolved to pass the winter of 1777. Ah! I have often seen the tears coursing down our dear commander's careworn cheeks, as he would be conversing with a confidential officer about the condition of his poor soldiers. You have doubtless heard the story of Washington's going to the thicket to pray. Well, it was not only true, but he used often to pray in secret for aid and comfort from God. The interposition of whose Divine Providence brought us safely through the darkest days of tribulation.

One day, I remember it well [in Valley Forge], the chilly winds whistled through the leafless trees, though the sky was cloudless and the sun shone brightly, [Washington] remained in his quarters nearly all afternoon alone. When he came out I noticed that his face was a shade paler than usual, and there seemed to be something on his mind of more than ordinary importance. Returning just after dusk, he dispatched an orderly to the quarters of the officer I mentioned who was presently in attendance. After a preliminary conversation of about half an hour, Washington, gazing upon his companion with that strange look of dignity which he alone could command, said to the latter:

"I do not know whether it is owing to the anxiety of my mind, or what, but this afternoon, as I was sitting at this table engaged in preparing a dispatch, something seemed to disturb me. Looking up, I beheld standing opposite me a singularly beautiful female. So astonished was I, for I had given strict orders not to be disturbed, that it was some moments before I found language to inquire the cause of her presence. A second, a third, and even a fourth time did I repeat my question, but received no answer from my mysterious visitor...By this time I felt strange sensations spreading through me. I would have risen but the riveted gaze of the being before me rendered volition impossible."

"Presently I heard a voice saying 'Son of the Republic, Look and Learn' while at the same time my visitor extended her arm eastwardly. I now beheld a heavy white vapor at some distance rising fold upon fold. This gradually dissipated, and I looked upon a strange scene. Before me laid spread out in one vast plain all the countries of the world—Europe, Asia, Africa and America.... 'Son of the Republic,' said the same mysterious voice as before, 'look and learn.' At that

moment I beheld… [another] angel, standing or rather
floating in mid-air, between Europe and America.
Dipping water out of the ocean in the hollow of each
hand he sprinkled some upon America….A second time
the angel dipped water from the ocean, and sprinkled it
as before…"

"A third time I heard the mysterious voice saying, 'Son of
the Republic, look and learn.' I cast my eyes upon
America and beheld villages and towns and cities
springing up one after another until the whole land from
the Atlantic to the Pacific was dotted with them. Again, I
heard the mysterious voice say, 'Son of the Republic, the
end of the century cometh, look and learn.'*And the
bright angel planted the standard upon them [in America]
crying out, 'While the stars remain, and the heavens send
down dew upon the earth, so long shall the Union last.'"[70]

Washington's reported encounter at Valley Forge with angels
becomes all the more interesting when we consider the words of an
ordained latter-day Apostle, Orson Hyde, who declared in a July 4,
1854 talk in the Tabernacle that the Angel Moroni, even that
"Prince of America" who "presides over the destinies of America…
was in the camp of Washington."[71] Admittedly, Elder Hyde does
not connect his statements to the above account, nor does the
above account necessarily describe the angel Moroni (though the
angel that dipped water onto America *was* described as male).
Either way, and in light of what we know concerning America's
divine place, it does seem significant that, in this reported vision,
Washington seemed to sense that Heaven was endowing him with
knowledge that America had most certainly been anointed for

---

* It is interesting to note the parallel in language used by the angel in this vision
and the angel that visited the Prophet Nephi, as recorded in First Nephi, Chapter
11. As in Washington's vision, the angel would open Nephi's spiritual eyes by
continually and repetitively commanding him to "Look!"

some great purpose, and that, in spite of his current difficulties, he should go forward with faith in God.*

Washington did just that. On December 18, 1777, Washington again asked his men "to observe a day of prayer and fasting, to give thanks to God for blessings already received, and to implore the continuing favor of Providence upon the American cause." After Washington read a sermon by one of his chaplains, which had been given to accompany and support the General's day of fast and prayer at Valley Forge, Washington wrote to thank him for "the force of reasoning that you have displayed." He then added that "it will ever be the wish of my heart to aid your pious endeavors to inculcate a due sense of the dependence we ought to place in that all wise and powerful Being on whom alone our success depends."[72]

Months later, Washington further instructed on the American Covenant in issuing the following General Orders:

> While we are zealously performing the duties of good Citizens and soldiers we certainly ought not to be inattentive to the higher duties of Religion. To the distinguished Character of Patriot, it should be our highest Glory to add the more

---

* In yet another anecdotal account (this one reported by Time Magazine), while at Valley Forge, George Washington requested that Chaplain John Gano baptize him by immersion. "I have been investigating the Scripture," declared Washington, "and I believe immersion to be the baptism taught in the Word of God, and I demand it at your hands. I do not wish any parade made or the army called out, but simply a quiet demonstration of the ordinance." The ordinance was reportedly carried out in secret because Washington did not desire to make himself a member of Gano's Baptist congregation. Gano therefore had to break his church's policy by baptizing one who had no intention of joining the congregation. In 1889, Gano's grandchild and another relative swore in an affidavit that Gano's daughter had told them that the baptism had taken place. Historians have been unable to confirm or deny the veracity of the account. In Gano Chapel, at William Jewell College in Missouri, there is a painting of Gano baptizing Washington by immersion. See www.time.com/time/magazine/article/0,9171,744297,00.html, and http://en.wikipedia.org/wiki/John_Gano#Alleged_baptism_of_George_Washington, and http://www.sluiceboxadventures.com/learn_history/JohnGano_02.htm

distinguished Character of Christian. The signal Instances of providential Goodness which we have experienced and which have now almost crowned our labours with complete Success, demand from us in a peculiar manner the warmest returns of Gratitude and Piety to the Supreme Author of all Good.[73]

It was also during this time that Washington would again encourage his fellow countrymen to give thanks and credit to God, this time for France's decision to enter the war on America's side. "It having pleased the Almighty Ruler of the Universe propitiously to defend the cause of the United States," declared Washington, "by raising us up a powerful friend." This single act was, according to Washington, brought forth through God's "benign interposition."[74]

This was followed by yet another Washington reference to the importance of the American Covenant and America's obligation to it. On August 20, 1778, Washington wrote the following to one of his generals: "The Hand of Providence has been so conspicuous in all this [Revolutionary War], that he must be worse than an infidel that lacks faith, and more than wicked, that has not gratitude enough to acknowledge his obligations."[75]

Congress would also follow-up shortly thereafter with yet another reminder to Americans of their national covenant at this crucial point in the war. This time they appropriately connected America and her covenant with that ancient national covenant God had maintained with Israel. In a 1779 letter to the nation, Congress declared that America had "without arms, ammunition, discipline, revenue, government or ally, with 'staff and sling' only, dared, 'in the name of the Lord of Hosts,' to engage a gigantic adversary."[76] America was as disadvantaged against the British as David had been against Goliath. However, armed with a divine covenant, neither would lose.

Miracle at Yorktown

By 1781, the war had entered a stalemate of sorts, with the exception of the skirmishes in the South, brought on in large part by

American guerilla-style attacks. In response, in January of 1781, General Lord Charles Cornwallis, commander of the British troops in the South, sent Colonel Tarleton to attack the American's under George Morgan at Cowpens, South Carolina. Tarleton's British forces were unexpectedly defeated. In response, on March 15, an embarrassed and aggravated Cornwallis moved on the American troops under Washington's southern commander, Nathanial Greene, at Guilford Court House in North Carolina. Though Greene was defeated there, he was not subdued, and forthwith decided to preserve his remaining troops by fleeing northward together with Morgan's troops. Still desirous to finish off Greene completely, Cornwallis would regroup and follow him northward. The chase was on.

In an attempt to cut off the fleeing Americans, Cornwallis ordered his soldiers to shed their heavy baggage, which helped them to rapidly gain ground. Cornwallis reached the Catawba River just hours after the Americans had crossed. Confident that victory would be his in the morning, Cornwallis decided to cross the river at dawn the following day. But during the night a storm flooded the river making a morning crossing impossible and allowing the Americans a head start.[77]

Cornwallis would again almost catch the Americans, first at the Yadkin River in North Carolina on February 3, and then at the Dan River, at the Virginia border, on February 13. In both cases, the Americans would safely cross just in time for a storm to flood the river, thus blocking a British attack. The British commander, Sir Henry Clinton, to whom Cornwallis answered, had to admit that God seemed to have intervened on America's behalf. Wrote Clinton, "...here the royal army was again stopped by a sudden rise of the waters, which had only just fallen [miraculously] to let the enemy over, who could not else have eluded Lord Cornwallis' grasp, so close was he upon their rear."[78]

After Cornwallis' failed chase left him in Virginia with nothing left to do, Clinton directed him to move his army, consisting of some 7,500 Redcoats, to secure the tobacco port at the peninsula of Yorktown, Virginia. From there, reasoned Clinton, Cornwallis' troops could be easily mobilized via the Chesapeake Bay by the superior British navy. As Cornwallis waited, Washington considered his options. Both sides immediately began plotting and scheming, believing that—as both armies were on the verge of collapse— whoever laid the next blow would secure ultimate victory. Times were tense.

Washington, who at the time was directing the northern campaign, thought to launch an attack on the British in the north, believing an attack on Yorktown would be fruitless; for who could stop a Cornwallis retreat by sea? Perhaps he remembered that the Lord surely could. So, he changed his plans and went forward with faith, ordering his soldiers to begin congregating around the Yorktown peninsula in an attempt to box in Cornwallis. As the best-selling author and historian Thomas Fleming put it, "Instead, Washington marched south [to Yorktown] and a series of miracles occurred." [79]

The first of these miracles was witnessed as the British fleet out of New York set sail for Yorktown in order to rescue Cornwallis and his troops. However, the British fleet did not expect to run into a French fleet, which had barely arrived at the Chesapeake Bay, off the coast of Yorktown, in support of the American effort to trap Cornwallis. On September 5, 1781, the French ships turned on the incoming British and defeated them in what became known as the Battle of the Capes. The French fleet then proceeded to rejoin their American allies at Yorktown, while the British fleet was forced to return to New York to refit its ships, all the while leaving Cornwallis trapped and in an even more precarious situation. As William Bennett explained in his book, *America, The Last Best Hope*, between the years 1588–1941, the British "ruled the waves...with one important local exception...in the waters off Yorktown, Virginia, in 1781." [80] This one exception in over 350 years of British naval warfare history would directly contribute to the final battlefield victory that sealed American independence. This was no coincidence.

On October 10, having gathered many troops from around the country, Washington directed a young Alexander Hamilton to lead an eastward charge on Cornwallis' position on the Yorktown peninsula. Hamilton obeyed the orders and subsequently pushed the British right up against the Atlantic coast, and succeeded in capturing British fortifications along the way. This put the Americans in an ideal position.[81]

Even as he watched his men fall by the hundreds, a humiliated and panic-ridden Cornwallis was asking the same perplexing question that Washington (and every other man on the battlefield) was asking—*Where is that promised, superior British navy to rescue its soldiers?* The answer, as perplexing as the question, is the result of yet another divine intervention.

Having regrouped after their unlikely naval defeat at the hands of the French, the British at last prepared once again to move out of New York to rescue the ailing Cornwallis. With plenty of time still to save Cornwallis' troops at Yorktown, the British fleet confidently made their preparation. Then the Lord stepped in once again. As Fleming explains:

> In New York, a frantic Sir Henry Clinton proposed…a rescue plan that called for putting most of the army on navy ships and fighting their way into the Chesapeake to join Cornwallis….On October 13, the fleet was supposed to sail—when a tremendous thunderstorm swept over New York harbor. Terrific gusts of wind snapped the anchor cable on one of the ships of the line, smashing her into another ship and damaging both of them….[The British] could not leave until the damage was repaired.[82]

By October 15, Washington and his French allies had begun launching a highly successful bombardment upon an ever-more trapped Cornwallis. As he had done before, and at great peril to his own life, Washington rallied his men by directing the attack from a forward deployed position, causing his aides, once again, to pull him back and away.[83]

Under severe fire, and with a tragic recognition that the British navy would not be coming to his rescue after all, Cornwallis immediately resorted to his desperate contingency plan—evacuate the Yorktown peninsula by ferrying his men northward over the York River and then march toward the British friendly New York. In a plan which resembled that of Washington's at Long Island years earlier, Cornwallis would attempt the crossing on October 16, by the cover of night. The only discrepancy of course was that when Washington attempted such an escape, he had been acting under a covenant with God. Unfortunately for Cornwallis, it was this single factor that would make all the difference. Fleming explains:

> About ten minutes [after midnight]...a tremendous storm broke over the river. Within five minutes, there was a full gale blowing, as violent, from the descriptions in various diaries, as the storm that had damaged the British fleet in New York. Shivering in the bitter wind, soaked to the skin, the exhausted soldiers and sailors returned to the Yorktown shore. Not until two A.M. did the wind moderate. It was much too late to get the rest of the army across the river. Glumly, Cornwallis ordered the guards and the light infantry to return. [84]

With no other option available, Cornwallis was forced to surrender to Washington on October 19, 1781. This final blow was enough to convince the British to terminate their war efforts (though the peace treaty signed at Paris—which officially ended the war— would not be realized until 1783). America was at last free.

As British soldiers approached the Americans to surrender Cornwallis' sword, the depressed British band began to play, very fittingly, the popular tune, "The World Turned Upside Down."[85] Indeed, the world was turning upside down, just as the Lord had planned it, in preparation for His latter-day work.

In emphasizing the significance of the details of the Battle at Yorktown, as outlined above, Fleming offers the following insight:

A Cornwallis getaway would have left the French and Americans frustrated and hopeless, facing a stalemated war they no longer had the money or will to fight. American independence—or a large chunk of it—might have been traded away in the peace conference. A Clinton invasion...would have triggered a stupendous naval and land battle that might well have ended in British victory—enabling them to impose the harshest imaginable peace on the exhausted Americans and shattered the French. Instead the Allies had landed the knockout blow.[86]

Though Fleming's above analysis is no doubt a sound one, Washington might take issue with one point from his conclusion. The "knockout blow" was first and foremost landed, not by the Allies, but by the Lord. "I take particular pleasure," Washington would explain in reference to his Yorktown victory, "in acknowledging that the interposing hand of Heaven, in various instances of our preparations for this operation, has been most conspicuous and remarkable."[87]

★ ★ ★ ★

We pause here briefly to insert an interesting note concerning the many miraculous and dramatic changes in weather that proved indispensable to the Americans. It should be recalled that, just as Washington and his faithful followers recognized God behind the strange, yet timely, weather changes related to the Battle at Yorktown, they also acknowledged the similar heavenly tactics used at Boston, Long Island, and Trenton. Critics would write off these weather patterns as "chance" or "luck." However, these events seem more like divine intervention than mere coincidences when we consider that the Lord used these same tactics to save His early Latter-day Saints.

One example of such an occurrence took place during the 1834 Zion's Camp march, led by the Prophet Joseph, which had departed Ohio in an effort to assist the persecuted saints in Missouri.

At one point during the march, the LDS group had camped down for the night on a small piece of land nestled in-between two branches of the Fishing River. Unbeknownst to the camp, some four hundred enemies of the Church waited on the opposite side of the river to raise havoc with the Saints. With a plan to "utterly destroy the Mormons," the mob had promised that Zion's Camp would "see hell by morning." Then suddenly, a dark cloud dropped over the scene, after which Joseph exclaimed, "Boys, there is meaning to this, God is in this storm." What followed was a torment so ferocious that it forced the schemers to scatter for shelter. Whereas the evening before, the river was ankle-deep, within an hour it was flowing forty-feet deep. Trees and vegetation were torn to shreds. One of the mobbers was struck by lighting and killed. Another had his hand torn off. The storm formed a protective circle around Zion's Camp but left the Camp itself largely unaffected. The Mormons were not harmed and felt little of the storm's devastating power.[88]

As the storm "soaked and made the mobbers' ammunition useless...and raised the level of the Fishing River," an attack would be impossible.[89] Joseph later commented that "the wind, rain, hail and thunder met [the enemy] in great wrath...and frustrated their plans to 'kill Jo Smith and his army'....when Jehovah fights, they would rather be absent."[90*] Like Washington before him, Joseph received protective blessings by a covenant, which his camp and army were required to live (See D&C 105).

A similar miracle occurred in 1857 when U.S. General A.S. Johnston led a 2,500-man march on Salt Lake City, under the false assumption that Brigham Young was stirring up a rebellion against the Union. An unusually early snowstorm over western Wyoming stopped the advancing army in its tracks, giving the Church time to clear its name with the truth, and thus resolve the issue peacefully.[91]

---

* In a related miracle, a separate group of mobbers were stopped as they sought to attack Zion's Camp and kill the Prophet. Led by James Campbell, eleven mobbers attempted to cross the Missouri River to get at the Mormons. Campbell, along with seven others in his party, drowned. See Brandon G. Kinney, *The Mormon War*, 54.

The point of this digression is to show how God works in patterns. These patterns, such as we have recently established, validate the individual instances. In the case of the Revolutionary War, identifying these patterns certainly lends additional credibility to the notion that God was behind the seemingly mysterious events which shaped the Revolution. For He would use the same tactics again and again, and always for the same purpose—to protect and preserve his covenant-makers. Whether these were national covenant-makers or gospel covenant-makers, they were preserved in their crucial hour of need, that His work and glory might go forth. As cited earlier, in Nephi's prophetic vision of the Revolutionary War, he stated clearly that American independence would come through the "power of the Lord" and that the "wrath of God was upon all those that were gathered against them to battle" (see 1 Nephi 13: 16-19).

★ ★ ★ ★

Returning to our narrative of the Revolution, we emphasize once more that Washington knew from whence his victory had come. On October 20, 1781, only one day after Cornwallis surrendered, Washington directed yet another General Order to "recommend that the troops not on duty should universally attend with that seriousness of Deportment and gratitude of Heart which the recognition of such reiterated and astonishing interpositions of Providence demands of us."[92] Though the war was over, Washington would waste no time at all (not even one day) in encouraging compliance to that American Covenant which he had learned so convincingly to trust in and love. Somehow he knew that its power would be needed in the near future, even in the building-up of the newly independent nation.

Conclusion

Thus far in this book, we have seen many examples of the American Covenant in action. But, as seen above, there is perhaps no better representation of this covenant in action than the events surrounding the battles of the American Revolution. Consider again the prophecies, provided in Part I of this book, which speak of God and righteous war within the context of the American Covenant. There is that earliest recorded version of the American Covenant in the Book of Genesis, which states that Joseph and his posterity (American colonists) will thwart their enemies, even "the archers" that "shot at him and hated him;" and that he would defeat them, as his "bow abode in strength." And all of this was made possible through the strength provided "by the hands of the mighty God of Jacob" (see Genesis 49: 1, 22-26 and Chapter 2 of this book).

We may also reflect again upon the Lord's revelation to the Prophet Joseph when He declared, while speaking of America and her inspired modern-day founding, that He had "redeemed the land [America] by the shedding of blood" (D&C 101:80). As the word "redeem" is defined as "to buy back; to recover; and/or to restore,"[93] we understand what the Lord is saying: That through the miracles of war, as described above, He has taken (bought back, recovered, and restored) America unto Himself for His own divine and glorious purposes. Such was the spirit of President Hinckley's affirmation concerning the Revolution, that "the God of Heaven fought [America's] battles."[94] As also outlined earlier, the Lord promised that as colonial America humbled itself before God, He would bless the nation and deliver them (see 1 Nephi 13:16-19), and that America would never "be brought down into captivity" (2 Nephi 1:7).

Have we not seen in this chapter the literal fulfillment of these promises and prophecies of the American Covenant? How many times did Congress, Washington, and others turn to the Lord, invoking the covenant, asking for national forgiveness, and pleading for national blessings? How often did these founding leaders invoke this covenant by pleading with the people to live worthy of its blessings? The Americans had indeed adhered to the covenant; and the blessings had, in turn, arrived in powerful measure.

This same covenant was as present and active during the time of the Revolutionary War as it was in the ancient American, Book of Mormon wars—and for the same gospel purposes. Consider what we have learned above about Washington and his colleagues, and let us compare their actions to the ancient American Covenant-makers, who also fought "for a better cause" including "their rites of worship" (Alma 43:45). These revolutionary heroes, like Captain Moroni, exhorted their people to obey the commandments of God and "cry with one voice unto the Lord their God for their liberty," even in the midst of armed conflict with the enemy (see Alma 43: 45-54). And thus we see how history repeats itself. It is no wonder that Brigham Young declared that God inspired Washington to fulfill his calling "in the same way He moved upon ancient and modern prophets" to fulfill their own.[95]

Furthermore, we have seen in this chapter how the Lord accomplished what he did during this American movement through applying one of the great Book of Mormon principles, "that it is by grace we are saved after all we can do" (2 Nephi 25:23). Washington and his faithful Founders clearly did all that they could, and where they fell short, the Lord provided the balance of what was required.* Who could say this was not the case at Boston, Long Island, Trenton, Princeton, Yorktown, and other major events during the Revolution? Such a divine plan ensured American success, but also allowed the revolutionaries to work, toil, bleed, and sacrifice, thus producing an American example and legacy that others could follow. The eternal law, after all, teaches that it is *sacrifice* that brings forth the blessings of heaven.

---

* We see examples of this pattern laced throughout the Book of Mormon. Captain Moroni, for example, fought for his national freedom under these rules of Heaven. The Brother of Jared did the same when the Lord commanded him to devise and work out a plan whereby the Jaredite vessels would be lit. Only after he did all in his power to create the receptacles did the Lord provide what was needed to light them.

These blessings have been developed and carried on to the present. For, the Revolution's ultimate fruit to the world is enjoyed today. And what is this fruit? It is the expansion and development of freedom, even that freedom necessary to access, accept, and live the gospel of eternal salvation. Such is the significance of this story.

ENDNOTES

[1] Thomas Fleming, "Unlikely Victory," *What If? The World's Foremost Military Historians Imagine What Might Have Been,* James Cowley, ed (New York, Penguin Putnam Inc,1999), 162-163.

[2] McCullough, *1776*, 79.

[3] McCullough, *1776,* 79.

[4] McCullough, *1776*, 72.

[5] McCullough, *1776*, 79.

[6] McCullough, *1776*, 82.

[7] McCullough, *1776*, 92.

[8] McCullough, *1776*, 93.

[9] Fleming, 162-163.

[10] McCullough, *1776,* 96.

[11] McCullough, *1776*, 97.

[12] McCullough, *1776*, 107; full quote available from *The Papers of George Washington: Revolutionaries War Series, Series 3*, 493-494, available at www.consource.org.

[13] Letter from Washington to his brother John Augustine Washington, March 31, 1776, as quoted in *The Writings of George Washington, Volume 4, Electronic Text Center, University of Virginia,* available from http://etext.virginia.edu/toc/modeng/public/WasFi04.html.

[14] McCullough, *1776*, 111.

[15] McCullough, *1776*, 111.

[16] Fleming, 163.

[17] McCullough, *1776*, 111.

[18] McCullough, *1776,* 110.

[19] Letter from Washington to his brother John Augustine Washington, March 31, 1776, as quoted in *The Writings of George Washington, Volume 4, Electronic Text Center, University of Virginia,* available from http://etext.virginia.edu/toc/modeng/public/WasFi04.html; also quoted in part in McCullough, *1776*, 110.

[20] McCullough, *1776,* 105.

[21] Novak, *On Two Wings,* 13-14 (prayer delivered on September 7, 1774).

[22] Waldman, *Founding Faith*, 43 (This congressional declaration was issued on October 20, 1774). Details of this congressional act were provided in Chapter 6 of this book, under the subheading *Testimonials of the Rebels.*

[23] Foster, *The American Covenant*, 33. (This congressional act was issued on July 6, 1775)

[24] Waldman, *Founding Faith*, 70 (This congressional act was issued on July 20, 1775).

[25] John Adams, as quoted by Waldman, *Founding Faith,* 108

[26] Michael Novak and Jana Novak, *Washington's God* (New York: Basic Books, 2006)*,* 65.

[27] General Orders from George Washington, March 6, 1776, as quoted in *The Writings of George Washington, Volume 4, Electronic Text Center, University of Virginia,* available from http://etext.virginia.edu/toc/modeng/public/WasFi04.html.

[28] McCullough, *1776*, 106.

[29] William Stearns, as quoted by Marshall and Manuel, 366-7.

[30] McCullough, *1776*, 134, 148.

[31] McCullough, *1776*, 131-132, 163.

[32] Bennett, *The Spirit of America,* 393.

[33] Novak, *Washington's God*, 71.

[34] Bennett, *The Spirit of America*, 390.

[35] Novak, *Washington's God,* 89.

[36] McCullough, *1776,* 123, 147.

[37] Jonathon Trumbull, as quoted in Marshall and Manuel, 394.

[38] McCullough, *1776*, 179-180.

[39] Fleming, 165.

[40] McCullough, *1776*, 184.

[41] David McCullough, "What the Fog Wrought," *What If? The World's Foremost Military Authorities Imagine What Might Have Been,* James Cowley, ed (New York, Penguin Putnam, Inc, 1999), 197.

[42] McCullough, "What the Fog Wrought," 198; McCullough, *1776*, 191.

[43] McCullough, *1776*, 191-192.

[44] McCullough, "What the Fog Wrought," 199; McCullough, *1776,* 191.

[45] John Witherspoon, as quoted in Novak, *On Two Wings*, 15.

[46] Washington, as quoted in Novak, *On Two Wings*, 79.

[47] "Fast Day Proclamation of the Continental Congress, December 11, 1776," Worthington C. Ford, Gaillard Hunt, et al., eds., *The Journals of the Continental Congress, 1774-1789* (Washington, D.C.: Government Printing Office, 1904-37), vol. 6. p. 1022; also quoted in Novak, *On Two Wings*, 18.

[48] McCullough, *1776*, 275.

[49] McCullough, *1776*, 280.

[50] Henry Knox, as quoted in Marshall and Manuel, 400.

[51] Marshall and Manuel, 401.

[52] Bennett, *America, The Last Best Hope*, 89.

[53] Sergeant R------, "Battle of Princeton," *Pennsylvania Magazine of History and Biography*, vol. 20 (1896), 515-16. Also quoted in *BYU Magazine*, Winter 2006, 51.

[54] Nathanial Greene to Nicolas Cooke, Jan. 10, 1777, in *The Papers of General Nathanial Greene,* ed. Richard K. Showman and Dennis Conrad (Chapel Hill: University of North Carolina Press, 1980), vol.2, 4. Also quoted in *BYU Magazine*, Winter 2006, 51.

[55] Green, *The Tribe of Ephraim*, 151.

[56] McCullough, *1776*, 288.

[57] McCullough, *1776*, 289.

[58] McCullough, *1776*, 291.

[59] McCullough, *1776*, 291.

[60] George Washington (January 22, 1777), as quoted by Waldman, *Founding Faith*, 70.

[61] George Washington, "General Orders" September 1777, as quoted in Novak, *Washington's God*, 65-66.

[62] Larry Schweikart and Michael Allen, *A Patriot's History* (New York: Sentinel, 2004), 81-83.

[63] George Washington (October 18, 1777, in response to victory at Saratoga), as quoted by Waldman, *Founding Faith*, 69.

[64] Thanksgiving Proclamation November 1, 1777, as quoted by Waldman, *Founding Faith*, 71, 87.

[65] Ellis, *His Excellency*,112.

[66] Nathanial Greene, as quoted in Schweikart and Allen, *A Patriot's History*, 86.

[67] Quoted in "A Prayer at Valley Forge," *National Review*, December 5, 2005; variation of the story recorded by Bennett, *The Spirit of America*, 372-373.

[68] Marshall and Manuel, 457.

[69] Novak, *Washington's God,* 221.

[70] Wesley Bradshaw, *National Tribune* 4 (12) (December 1880), as quoted in Robert Hieronimus, *Founding Fathers, Secret Societies*, 49-50.

[71] Orson Hyde (July 4, 1854), as quoted in *Journal of Discourses* 6:368 (Liverpool, England: F.D. and S.W. Richards, 1854-1866); also quoted in J. Michael Hunter, *Mormon Mythellaneous*, 99-100.

[72] Novak, *Washington's God*, 129-130.

[73] George Washington (May 2, 1778) as quoted in Novak, *Washington's God,* 90.

[74] George Washington (Spring 1778), as quoted in J. Michael Hunter, *Mormon Mythellaneous*, 104.

[75] George Washington (August 20, 1778), as quoted by Janice Connell, *The Spiritual Journey of George Washington* (New York: Hatherleigh Press, 2007), 96.

[76] Waldman, *Founding Faith*, 70.

[77] Foster and Swanson, *The American Covenant*, 161-162.

[78] Henry Clinton, as quoted in William Hosmer, "Remember Our Bicentennial—1781," Foundation for Christian Self-Government *Newsletter*, June 1981, 5; the account is also recorded in Foster and Swanson, *The American Covenant: The Untold Story*, 162; and is also recounted in Marshall and Manuel, 416-418.

[79] Fleming, 179.

[80] William J. Bennett, *America, The Last Best Hope* (Nashville, Nelson Current, 2006), 29, 101.

[81] Joseph J. Ellis, *Patriots, Brotherhood of the American Revolution*, Lectures recorded by Recorded Books, Inc, and Barnes and Noble Publishing: 2004, Lecture 7, Tr.6, 2:15 min; also recounted in Fleming, 180-1.

[82] Fleming, 180.

[83] Ellis, *Patriots, Brotherhood of the American Revolution*, Lecture 7, Tr.6, 2:15 min; also recounted in Fleming, 180-1.

[84] Fleming, 181.

[85] Marshall and Manuel, 420; Bennett, *America, The Last Best Hope*, 102.

[86] Fleming, 182.

[87] George Washington, as quoted in Foster and Swanson, 163.

[88] *History of the Church*, 1834-1837, Vol. II (Salt Lake City: Deseret Book Co., 1978), 104-105; *Church History in the Fulness of Times*, 148-149.

[89] *Church History in the Fulness of Times*, 148-149.

[90] Bushman, *Rough Stone Rolling*, 243-244.

[91] *Church History in the Fulness of Times*, 374-375.

[92] George Washington, as quoted in Novak, *Washington's God*, 66.

[93] Definition of the word "redeem" from *Random House, Webster's College Dictionary* (New York: Random House, 2000).

[94] Hinckley, *Standing for Something*, xv-xvi.

[95] Brigham Young, as quoted by J. Michael Hunter, *Mormon Myth-ellaneous*, 103

George Washington, by Horatio Greenough, on display at the National Museum of
American History, Washington D.C.

CHAPTER 8

SIGNS AND BLESSINGS IN WAR'S AFTERMATH

Glorious indeed has been our Contest: glorious, if we consider the Prize for which we have contended, and glorious in its Issue; but in the midst of our Joys, I hope we shall not forget that, to divine Providence is to be ascribed the Glory and the Praise....I consider it an indispensable duty to close this last solemn act of my Official life, by commending the Interests of our dearest Country to the protection of Almighty God, and those who have the superintendence of them, to his holy keeping.

—George Washington, 1783

It is clear from the previous chapters that God took a most active role during the Revolutionary War, as He repeatedly blessed the American cause through the national covenant. But the blessings certainly did not cease with the end of the conflict. For in the aftermath of war, we see further proof of the Lord's influence over America. This chapter documents some of these evidences at war's end, which lend further credibility to the divinity of America's purposes and to the reality of the American Covenant.

Deeper Connections to the Covenant

The narrative of the Revolution detailed in the past few chapters, culminating at the battle of Yorktown, includes an obvious reflection of the colonists understanding of the covenant relationship between God and America. But at war's end, as the dust finally settled, and as the stories of God's miracles were shared throughout the colonies, Americans began to see how powerful this covenant really was. Many even began to recognize the deeper meaning of what this covenant ultimately promised to all mankind. Such revelatory knowledge amongst the colonists would serve the new nation as it worked to form a righteous government under God. For that reason, this knowledge is counted as one of the great blessings in the aftermath of war.

One example of this greater comprehension of the covenant is witnessed through the words of the Massachusetts minister, David Tappan, who told his congregants that God had brought victory to America for one purpose—"that His [God's] own name might be exalted, that His own great designs...extending the Kingdom of His Son, may be carried into effect."[1]

Other declarations concerning the gospel purposes of America and the Revolution were made by one of the most prominent Christian leaders of the day, Timothy Dwight, who would serve as the president of Yale College. Some years after the Revolution, Dwight prophesied over the meaning of the newly independent America, declaring:

> God brought His little flock hither and placed it in the wilderness, for the great purpose of establishing permanently the Church of Christ in these vast regions of idolatry and sin, and commencing here the glorious work of salvation. This great continent is soon to be filled with the praise and piety of the Millennium. But here is the seed, from which this last harvest is to spring.[2]

Amazingly, Dwight correctly and prophetically recognized that "the seed" of a now free and independent America would usher in a restoration of Christ's church.

On an earlier occasion, in the midst of the Revolution, Dwight made it clear that such "independence and happiness [was] fixed upon the most lasting foundations, and that the Kingdom of the Redeemer... [would be] durably established on the ruins of the Kingdom of Satan."[3]

Furthermore, as one historian pointed out, Dwight knew that the way for America to ensure the advent of this grand restoration was through the "reestablishment of the covenant relationship that their forbears had entered into with God and with one another." It was, after all, Dwight who declared in 1777, just as the Revolution was commencing: "Nothing obstructs the deliverance of America but the crimes of its inhabitants."[4] Dwight confirmed the general recognition in colonial America that success and independence was contingent on living the American Covenant. Now, at war's end, he had seen this covenant largely fulfilled and was now sharing his vision of what this covenant would soon offer the world.

That these inspired Americans presaged the restoration of the gospel as being the ultimate fruit of the Revolution should not be taken for granted. Though they did not necessarily comprehend how or when such a restoration would occur, they certainly were prophetic in their day. What's more, the shared vision of these ministers in post-war America was not the exception but the norm. As one historian explained, "With few exceptions, it seemed to the ministers of America that the Light, which had been brought [to America] by the first Christ-bearers, had at last [with independence now gained] been joined by the glory of his Kingdom come—or soon coming."[5]

Such powerful sentiments regarding God's purposes for the Revolution, particularly as expressed in post-war colonial America, did not stop with religious leaders, but was also expressed by political leaders. One such leader was Sam Adams, whose extraordinary vision of the Revolution's divine purposes prompted him to state that—with independence at last secured—it was now time for America to bring in "the holy and happy period when the kingdom of our Lord and Savior Jesus Christ may be everywhere established, and the people willingly bow to the scepter of Him who is the Prince of Peace."[6] Adams' amazingly accurate statement that the Revolution would usher in an expansion of the gospel is perhaps corroborated by an earlier prophetic idea he put forth in 1776: "[T]he hand of heaven appears to have led us on to be perhaps humble instruments and means in the great providential dispensation which is completing."[7] There is no doubt that Adams saw the emerging power of America as becoming a key factor in this, God's final dispensation.

★ ★ ★ ★

Another revolutionary leader whose understanding seemed to increase in the wake of war was none other than George Washington. Though we know he clearly witnessed, testified of, and believed in the existence of the American Covenant, one wonders how deep his knowledge extended. Did he see or feel at least something of the greater gospel purposes behind that covenant, even as he reflected upon the miraculous American cause through which he said he could so clearly "trace the finger of Providence"?[8] The evidence suggests that he did. Particularly in the years after the war—after having ample time to reflect over its ultimate meaning—it appears he received further light and knowledge.

Washington stated his belief that God works "for wise purposes not discoverable by finite minds."[9]* As Washington knew God had directed the Revolution, he no doubt considered that God quite possibly had His own profound purposes for the Revolution. Without attempting to put his finger directly on the greater purpose, Washington most certainly seemed to have an inspired inkling into

---

* Compare to 1 Nephi 9:5.

what God had in mind. In 1789, while penning a draft of his first presidential inaugural address, Washington wrote the following:

> Can it be imagined...that this continent was not created and reserved so long undiscovered as a Theatre, for those glorious displays of divine Munificence, the salutary consequences of which will flow to another Hemisphere & extend through the interminable series of the ages? Should not our souls exult in the prospect? Though I shall not survive to perceive with these bodily senses, but a small portion of the blessed effects which our Revolution will occasion in the rest of the world; yet I enjoy the progress of human society & happiness in anticipation. I rejoice in the belief that *intellectual light will spring up in the dark corners of the earth.*[10]

Through gospel lenses, we may perhaps see such comments as prophetic allusions to the Restoration. Though the critic might balk at such a suggestion, there is further reason to consider the possibility. According to Washington scholars Michael and Jana Novak, Washington believed that this *intellectual light* was something born out of what the General himself called "the pure and benign light of Revelation."[11] It is possible he saw glimmers of the Restoration forming as a consequence of his Revolution.

Washington first made reference to this *light of Revelation* in what he believed would be his final circular address to Congress. In 1783, on the heals of victory, and with retirement now on his mind, Washington wrote this circular because, as he stated in the address, "I think it a duty incumbent on me to make this my last official communication; to congratulate you on the glorious events which Heaven has been pleased to produce in our favor." But offering congratulations on victory under God was just the beginning. There was another reason he felt so compelled to make this final address. For he said he felt obligated "to offer my sentiments respecting some important subjects." The first (and perhaps most powerful) subject he shared had something to do with the spiritual nature of America.

Washington declared in this address to Congress that the freed Americans were now "to be considered as the Actors on a most conspicuous Theatre, which seemed to be particularly designed by Providence, for the display of human greatness and felicity." He went on to explain that as part of this divine American movement, "Heaven has crowned all [America's] other blessings" with every gift the new nation would need to fill the measure of its creation, and that "above all" these gifts there is one which has a "meliorating influence on Mankind… [which increases] the blessings of society," and this gift he described as "the pure and benign light of Revelation."[12]

Furthermore, upon declaring that this light of America would soon "spring up in the dark corners of the earth," he implied that it would do so thanks in large part to an increase in "freedom of enquiry" (or what the scriptures call "moral agency"). This he knew America would be offering through influence and example to the world.[13]

Though admittedly we can only speculate on what Washington meant by his above statements, it is clear that he knew God was behind America and that God had very significant blessings—even blessings associated with "light" and "revelation"— to offer the world through America. In Washington's words we perhaps see a deeper understanding of the American Covenant and what it would ultimately offer mankind in due time.

A few years before his death, Washington would again speak of the greater purpose of the American cause:

> If it can be esteemed a happiness to live in an age of great and interesting events, we of the present age are very highly favored. The rapidity of national revolutions appear less astonishing, than their magnitude. In what they will terminate, is known only to the great ruler of events; and confiding in his wisdom and goodness, we may safely trust the issue to him, without perplexing ourselves to seek for that, which is beyond human ken; only taking care to

perform the parts assigned to us, in a way that reason and
our own consciences approve of.[14]

That God had some great design planned as the crowning
event of the American Revolution made too much sense for
Washington to ignore. How else could he explain the endless stream
of miracles he had witnessed throughout the cause? Why else would
the Lord be so intricately involved? Indeed, something grand was
on the horizon.

Even though Washington did not seem to know all the
specifics, he did reveal an additional impression that sheds some
light upon his personal testimony. Shortly after independence had
been secured, Washington felt inclined to explain what had
compelled him to fight in the first place. He stated that "[t]he
establishment of Civil and *Religious Liberty* was the motive that
induced me to the field of battle."[15]

From a gospel perspective, Washington's ultimate explanation
for the Revolution seems entirely appropriate. We know that God
inspired the Revolution and secured victory for America in order to
create religious freedom for the restored gospel to take root.
However, this was not obvious during Washington's day. In fact, to
list *religious liberty* as the principal motive for war could scarcely have
been comprehended at the time. To be sure, when the colonists were
planning and justifying their revolution, they created a document in
which they declared their independence and in which they included
a lengthy, perhaps even exaggerated, list of grievances against
Britain (we reviewed these grievances in Chapter 6, and saw how
they were based in political philosophies such as "no taxation
without representation"). This document, of course, is the
Declaration of Independence. Though the Founders attempted to
publically blame the king for everything they could think of and
place the accusations in the Declaration (at one point Jefferson even
made the absurd suggestion to officially blame him for slavery),[16]
nowhere amongst the many complaints against Britain found in the
document will one find a grievance related to religious intolerance

or religious freedom. This fact alone leads us to question why Washington would have placed religious liberty at the forefront of his motives. Perhaps he did know more than he let on. Perhaps he was speaking almost prophetically when he said what he did. As Washington was one of several Founders to make such conclusions (as we will see in later chapters), we will pause briefly here to explain how naming religious freedom as the principal motive for the Revolution in Washington's day would have required some inspired insight.

Admittedly, one might argue that Washington was simply referring to the fact that Great Britain maintained a state religion (the Church of England), which did cause some problems for certain religious minorities. Therefore, his statements about fighting for religious liberty should be obvious and expected. However, Great Britain did not pose an obvious and large-scale threat to religious liberty and, in fact, mostly respected religious freedom. This is evidenced by the many different denominations that were permitted to exist and thrive in America. The Founders themselves belonged to these different denominations and enjoyed their ability to worship freely therein. Had they not been able to worship freely, then complaints of religious persecution against the Crown would have been prominently listed in the Declaration of Independence—not completely ignored, as was the case. Furthermore, Washington himself, along with many other Founders, was an active member of Britain's state church, even the Church of England.[17] Again, any religious intolerance from Britain was mostly directed at certain minority religions and therefore did not conjure up enough outrage at the time to justify war.

This is not to say that Britain, and its interest in government-backed religious establishment, was benign. On the contrary, the British-American relationship had to be severed for the purposes of God. British rule would have given the adversary a tool that could have easily been manipulated to stomp out Joseph Smith and the Restoration. With so much power in the hands of a few—as was characteristic of the monarchy—the adversary would have had little trouble influencing the British elites to choose evil and thus to obstruct God's latter-day work (see Mosiah 29:26). But the colonists could not have known this in their day. Therefore, they would not have been able to easily articulate—at least with human understanding—why religious freedom was a valid justification to fight the British.

Furthermore, churches established in colonial America by the colonists themselves were just as guilty, if not *more* guilty, as the Church of England in their unjust practices toward certain religious minorities. For example, to the great peril of Quakers and Baptists, New England boasted of a state-established and state-sponsored religion—the Puritan religion, later known as the Congregational Church. This America-born church took care to acquire public monies for its support, while denying such monies to other religions. Furthermore, the religious establishment in New England made sure that minority religions were barred from enjoying a fullness of religious freedom. Baptist ministers in New England, for example, were not authorized to conduct marriages, were harassed, and were restricted on where they could preach. And these practices continued well after independence from Britain was gained.[18]

The point is this: as a whole, the colonists did not care that much about the fact that minority religions suffered some persecution. And if religious intolerance over minority sects was not significant enough to solve at home during peacetime, why would it, all of a sudden, be so significant as to warrant war with Britain, the world's superpower? The lack of any significant concern or interest regarding an increase in religious liberty at this point in American history rejects the suggestion that the colonists were willing to go to war over the issue.

But if the revolutionaries were not intentionally fighting specifically for an increase of religious liberty, how do we account for the fact that greater religious liberty was a primary fruit of the Revolution? The answer is simple. As the Americans gained independence and realized that the British could no longer threaten freedoms in America, only then was it brought into sharp focus that

Americans were themselves allowing such persecution domestically. Only then did the plight of religious minorities begin to be more openly recognized and corrected. As one religious history scholar noted, the Revolution made it "difficult for patriots to attack the evils of the Anglican establishment, then turn around and defend the maintenance of an official state church [in America]."[19] Thanks in part to this new perspective, even a new spirit of freedom and a new emphasis on religious liberty, born out of the Revolution, the U.S. Constitution would naturally include protections for minority religions. But this new perspective—though it was an intentional blessing from God, who sees the end from the beginning—was, for the revolutionaries, mostly an unintended consequence.

That Washington saw early on that the Revolution was about the creation of such religious freedom is perhaps evidence of his truly inspired calling. For, based on the arguments presented above, it seems that only by inspiration could one, in Washington's day, point to religious freedom as *the* focal point of the Revolution. Perhaps God's abundant Spirit, which called him to the Revolution and sustained him in war, also dropped revelatory hints about God's ultimate plan. Perhaps such spiritual glimpses encouraged the General to go forward with increasing faith.

Washington's comments about religious freedom being the principal reason for war become even more closely related to God and covenant when we consider that in the same address, just prior to making this statement, Washington first reminds his audience how important it is to "acknowledge publicly our infinite obligations to the Supreme Ruler of the Universe for rescuing our country from the brink of destruction; I cannot fail at this time to ascribe all the honor of our late successes to the same glorious Being." Then, immediately *after* his religious liberty declaration, and upon concluding his address, Washington again shows his understanding of the national covenant by stating that "it now remains to be my earnest wish and prayer, that the Citizens of the United States would make a wise and virtuous use of the blessings, placed before them."[20]

Washington continued to manifest this deeper understanding when he declared in 1790 that the purpose of America was to provide the means by which the religious minority (and he was specifically talking to and about religious minorities) might "sit in safety under his own vine and fig tree, and there shall be none to make him afraid. May the father of all mercies scatter light and not darkness in our paths, and make us all in our several vocations useful here, and in his own due time and way everlastingly happy."[21] Washington was proud that he had, under God's direction, helped create a country abounding with religious freedom, which he said was "unrivalled by any civilized nation of earth." Washington declared that the "bosom of America is open to receive, the oppressed and persecuted of all Nations and Religions, whom we shall welcome to a participation of all our rights and privileges."[22] Washington truly seemed to understand something about how the American Covenant, which he had adhered to so passionately during the Revolution, had created, through that Revolution, a special foundation upon which God could safely bring His work and His glory.

★ ★ ★ ★

The general comprehension of the American Covenant extended even further in post-war colonial America. In addition to understanding the ultimate purposes of the covenant, the revolutionaries at war's end also seemed to gain a deeper understanding about where this powerful covenant had its roots and origin. Many began to understand that the American cause represented a second chance for Israel, even the chance for a new covenant people to work out the purposes of God on earth (as discussed in detail in Chapter 2).

It is a fact, as noted several times throughout this book, that this inspired connection with ancient Israel had repeatedly been made since the earliest colonists landed upon the New World. But at war's end, after having witnessed so much of the fulfillment of this ancient covenant with modern-day Israel, this connection became even more powerful. Many leaders, including congressmen, urged Congress to place the English language aside and make Hebrew the official national language. Though the idea never took hold, many universities did make Hebrew a required course.[23]

The revolutionary and President of Yale University, Ezra Stiles, taught that the ancient covenant of Israel was in fact fulfilled in his America. In 1783, the year America officially gained its independence, he gave a speech entitled, "The United States Elevated to Glory and Honor." In it, he interpreted a prophecy and commandment given by Moses to the Children of Israel. These words of Moses, found in Deuteronomy 30, refer to what LDS students today would call the "gathering of Israel." Stiles explained its connection to latter-day America.

> God determined that a remnant should be saved... recovered and gathered...from the nations whither the Lord had scattered them in his fierce anger...and multiply them over their fathers—and rejoice over them for good, as he rejoiced over their fathers. Then the words of Moses... will be literally fulfilled; when this branch of the posterity of Abraham [who we know, through restored doctrine, to be Ephraim] shall be nationally collected, and become a very distinguished and glorious people under the Great Messiah, the Prince of Peace. He will then make them "high above all nations which he hath made in praise, and in name, and in honor," and they shall become "a holy people unto the Lord" their God.[24]

The Protestant minister George Duffield referred to the newly independent America as the "American Zion" and connected the ancient covenants to the modern ones. He likened Washington of the American Covenant to the Prophet Joshua of the ancient covenant; and he likened the foreigner king of France, who came to the rescue of the American Israelites, to Cyrus, the foreigner who did the same for the ancient Israelites.[25] Declared Duffield:

With Israel of old, we take up our song: 'Blessed be the Lord, who gave us not as prey to their teeth. Blessed be the Lord, the snare is broken and we are escaped'.... Here also shall our Jesus go forth conquering and to conquer, and the heathen be given Him for an inheritance, and these uttermost parts for a possession. The pure and undefiled religion of our blessed Redeemer—here shall it reign in triumph over all opposition.[26]

Washington was also compared on many occasions to the Prophet Moses. Americans sermonized over the notion that the General "has been the same to us, as Moses was to the Children of Israel." One colonial orator declared that "Kind Heaven, pitying the servile condition of our American Israel, gave us a second Moses, who should (under God) be our future deliverer from the bondage and tyranny of haughty Britain." Upon Washington's death, he was eulogized throughout the country well over four-hundred times by varying orators in varying locales. Stunningly, approximately two-thirds of the orations directly connected Washington to Moses.[27] Bruce Feiler explains why the colonists made this comparison, calling the parallels between the two leaders "striking."

Biblical Israel and God's New Israel were formed on the twin shoulders of liberation and law. In both cases, one man was present at both moments. Both men had the unusual combination of skills—leadership and humility, fortitude and diplomacy—that could serve them well in dramatic moments of confrontation as well as years of slowly building a people. Beloved founders, both could have clung to power but resisted the temptation to turn their nations into monarchies. Reticent speakers, both left behind some of the most quoted words ever spoken.[28]

As further witness of this deeper comprehension that existed among the post-war colonists, we turn to the greats of the

Revolution. Benjamin Franklin, for example, proposed that the new American nation should use as its official seal a depiction of Moses freeing Israel from its Egyptian oppressors through the power of God, represented by "Rays from the Pillar of Fire in the Clouds." Thomas Jefferson proposed that the seal depict the Children of Israel being led in the wilderness "by a cloud by day and a pillar of fire by night."[29] In his second inaugural address as president of the United States, Jefferson further connected America's covenant to that of ancient Israel by declaring that in order to ensure the covenant blessings of *prosperity*, he would need "the favor of that Being in whose hands we are, who led our forefathers, as Israel of old...."[30]

And consider this post-war declaration made by Washington:

> May the same wonder-working Deity, who long since delivered the Hebrews from their Egyptian oppressors, planted them in a promised land, whose providential agency has lately been conspicuous in establishing these United States as an independent nation, still continue to water them with the dews of Heaven and make the inhabitants of every denomination participate in the temporal and spiritual blessings of that people whose God is Jehovah.[31]

A gospel perspective informs us of a deep connection between America and Israel; indeed, the scriptures of the Restoration have taught us that America represents a second chance for Israel, even a New Israel—a New Jerusalem.* It represents a second chance for the national covenant. We have already seen how the early settlers and revolutionaries grasped this idea. In post-war America, this idea flourished further. It is no coincidence that the scriptures of the Restoration put forth this principle and that the

---

* Latter-day scriptures that testify of America's place as the host country of the New Jerusalem include 3 Nephi 20:22; Ether 13:3-11; D&C 28; D&C 42:8-9, 30-42; D&C 45:66-67; D&C 52:2, 42-43; D&C 57:1-5; D&C 58:7, 44-58; D&C 84:2-5; Tenth Article of Faith.

settlers and revolutionaries of America applied it to their nation. Through the miraculous wartime events detailed earlier—from Boston to Yorktown—the American Covenant, to include its more profound meanings in connection with Israel, had simply become obvious to the Founders at war's end. It had become obvious to the Founders not only because of what they had witnessed, but also—as Steven Green points out in his book, *The Tribe of Ephraim*—because these Founders "carried that believing blood of Ephraim, cherishing liberty above safety..." and recognizing that "the power of God was with them in their struggle for independence (see 1 Nephi 13:19)."[32]

This deeper comprehension of the covenant was indeed a great blessing to America, for it would serve to guide the newly independent colonies in their quest to build a united nation under God and covenant. Further, it was a witness to God of America's testimony and adherence to the American Covenant; and this guaranteed that the covenant blessings would continue to flow from heaven.

Washington's Sign of the Covenant

In addition to the deeper comprehension of the covenant found in post-war America, there is more to the story. Indeed, there is one powerful event that occurred at war's end that not only emphasized the divine nature of the Revolution, but presented a sign of the American Covenant—a sign offered by that most prominent covenant-maker, General George Washington.

Though America had won its independence, its immediate stability and general happiness was in no way guaranteed. In fact, historical trends forecasted a gloomy immediate future. To be sure, throughout the history of the world, there has been an unfortunate pattern, which seems to dictate how national revolutions are supposed to end. The hero of the revolution, utilizing his victorious armed forces, along with his national popularity, propels himself into power and makes himself dictator over his people. Not only have we seen this pattern in ancient governments—like in ancient

Rome—but also in more modern ones. In the mid-seventeenth century, for example, Oliver Cromwell would lead a popular revolution over the British monarchy only to then purge parliament and rule as king himself. In the late eighteenth century, the French Revolution would also oust the king, only to replace him by other dictators such as Napoleon. The nineteenth century would see countries like Mexico win their popular independence over Spain, only to see military dictators like Santa Ana throw out the constitution and rule according to his personal dictates. In the early twentieth century, the Russian Revolution would result in a series of communist dictators worse than any of the earlier Russian monarchs that had been overthrown. On through the balance of the twentieth century, the world would see a series of the most brutal dictators emerge out of popular, national revolutions: Hitler in Germany, Mao in China, Castro in Cuba, and the list goes on and on.

Such heroes-turned-tyrants would have done well to follow the Lord's warning that "there are many called, but few are chosen."

> And why are they not chosen? Because their hearts are so much upon the things of the world, and aspire to the honors of men....We have learned by sad experience that it is the nature and disposition of almost all men, as soon as they get a little authority, as they suppose, they will immediately begin to exercise unrighteous dominion (D&C 121:35, 39).

And so, the question for the American story would be this: Would Washington fall in line with the rest of the world's revolutionary leaders? The choice would be his alone to make. For, as early as December 27, 1776, Congress had voted to make Washington a virtual dictator over the armed forces (without the luxury of rapid communication technology, Congress had no choice but to give Washington all power).

Upon receiving word back in 1776 that Congress had given him such powers, he immediately responded, stating:

Instead of thinking myself freed from all civil obligations by this mark of their confidence, I shall constantly bear in mind that as the sword was the last resort for the preservation of our liberties, so it ought to be the first thing laid aside when those liberties are firmly established.[33]

By May 1782, this promise would be tested. With independence already "firmly established," the American officers began stirring the hearts of their soldiers against Congress, who had not as of yet made the final payments due to the army. One of Washington's colonels, Lewis Nicola, wrote to Washington and expressed the general sentiments of his men. He offered Washington the opportunity to do that which had always been done by revolutionary heroes: lead a coup on Congress and make himself king of America. (Nicola told Washington that he could use a different title than "king" if he wanted, but in effect, that is what he would become.) After all, who could have stopped Washington? By the end of the war, as McCullough points out, his men would have "follow[ed] [him] through hell."[34] Taking Congress, therefore, would have been easy. Indeed, the only person who could have stopped Washington was Washington. And that is exactly what happened. It was yet another demonstration of the powerful spirit working upon the General.

Shocked and horrified by Nicola's offer, Washington was determined to make good on his word to Congress. As such, he responded to Nicola, shooting back this stinging reply:

With a mixture of great surprise and astonishment I have read with attention the Sentiments you have submitted to my perusal. Be assured Sir, no occurrence in the course of War, has given me more painful sensations than your information of there being such ideas existing in the Army as you have expressed, and I must view with abhorrence, and reprehend the severity. For the present, the communication of them will rest in my own bosom, unless some further agitation of the matter, shall make a disclosure necessary. I am much at loss to conceive what part of my conduct could have given encouragement to an address which to me seems big with the greatest mischiefs that can befall my Country. If I am not deceived in the knowledge of myself, you could not have found a person to whom your schemes are more disagreeable.[35]

So sure was Washington on the matter that he would express years later that God had intentionally barred him from having any children (it is believed he was impotent), so as to prevent any future temptations from them or his countrymen to create a monarchy of his name. "Divine Providence," he would write, "has not seen fit that my blood should be transmitted...by the sometimes seducing channel of immediate offspring." He would state thankfully that there was "no family to build in greatness upon my country's ruins."[36]

Though Washington's refusal to act on Nicola's request had restrained talks of a 1782 coup, within a year, and with things still unresolved with Congress, the officers again began scheming to turn the sword on Congress and take the country by force, even if Washington would not join them. This plot, which was being organized in early 1783 at the army camp in Newburgh, would go down in history as the Newburgh Conspiracy.

When Washington received word of the movement, he at once condemned it and traveled directly to the camp. On March 13, 1783, Washington called a meeting in a large building in the camp known as The Temple. Washington, in a passionate speech, pled with the men not to reverse all the good they had done. The soldiers were still visibly upset and apparently unmoved. Washington then prepared to read a letter from one congressman who expressed his desire to work out a peaceful negotiation with the army. Before reading the letter, Washington took out a pair of glasses, which he had only recently needed and acquired, then stated, "Gentlemen, you will permit me to put on my spectacles, for I have not only grown gray but almost blind in your service." Indeed, Washington, who had begun the conflict while in his early forties, had literally transformed before his soldiers' eyes, and was now tired and aging into his fifties. The reminder of his own personal sacrifice not only melted the anger in the room, but caused a complete change of heart. Many of those present wept openly.[37]

Washington finished his comments and left the officers to make their decision. They called off the coup. Word of the de-escalation arrived just in time to Congress, as it was preparing to declare a preemptive war on the military factions responsible. But thankfully, all would soon be forgiven as a peaceful settlement was at last agreed upon. Washington had once again proven to be the indispensable man.[38]

Thomas Jefferson would appropriately observe that "the moderation and virtue of [Washington] probably prevented the Revolution from being closed, as most others have been, by a subversion of that liberty it was intended to establish."[39] Even King George III, Washington's nemesis (and one who knew a thing or two about political power grabs) declared, upon hearing of Washington's intention to give back all power to Congress, that he must be "the greatest man in the world."[40] And so he was. By Christmas 1783, Washington had retired from public life and began farming quietly at his beloved Mount Vernon.[41]

Though Washington's desire was to at last stay at home, within a few years of his retirement to Mount Vernon, James Madison began pleading with him to enter the public arena once again and head the Constitutional Convention, even that convention which would produce the United States Constitution. Though he attempted to persuade Madison to find somebody else, he knew he was needed. So he arrived at Philadelphia and successfully guided the process.

Then, and again due to no effort on his own part, Washington was elected unanimously as the nation's first president. Though no term limits had been specified at that point in the Constitution, and though he knew he could have remained as president for the duration of his life, Washington vowed to relinquish his position after one term. Unfortunately for him, the voters got to decide (not him), and they voted him in once more. He agreed, but made it clear that it would be his last. And it was.

As president, he would lead the United States down a steady course, always careful to govern under the limits given him by the divinely ordained Constitution. On one occasion, after acting wisely and constitutionally during two crucial moments (putting down the Whisky Rebellion in Pennsylvania, which he physically led, and signing the Jay Treaty, which averted another war with Britain), his political enemies foolishly and erroneously accused him of usurping power and acting like a monarch. Stunned and heart-broken, he emotionally declared, "By God, I had rather be on my farm than be made emperor of the world!"[42]

It was precisely this spirit of humility, derived from an understanding of America's relationship with God, which kept him in check and which made him great. Indeed, his greatness as president stemmed not so much from what he did, but from what he did *not* do. His powerful and divine restraint, even his ability to respect the constitutional harnesses placed upon him as president, had set the example and precedent for good governance.

When he at last was able to retire, his second term complete, he walked off the stage of John Adams' inaugural ceremony, and came face to face with the newly elected vice president, Thomas Jefferson, who was waiting for the former president to precede him through the exit gate. But Washington, in a sign of his recognition of the vice president's authority over his own (he was now a common citizen) insisted with "a firm gesture of command" that Jefferson go first.[43] He was surrendering power and inviting, by example, all his successors to do the same in their turn. Thus far, they all have.

In the end, Washington had indeed proven to be the exception to the rule of world history's revolutionary leaders. At least one revolution and its leader needed to set the example that other nations could follow in ushering in an inspired government in preparation for the arrival of God's gospel restoration. That this standard-bearer was Washington, a principal covenant-maker in the land divinely ordained from its conception, should be of no surprise.

Washington was, after all, fulfilling prophetic utterances pertaining to this chosen land, as issued by the Book of Mormon: "And this land shall be a land of liberty unto the Gentiles, and there shall be no kings upon the land, who shall rise up unto the Gentiles" (2 Nephi 10:11).

Perhaps the crowning moment of the Revolution was when Washington laid his sword before Congress at the end of the great conflict with Britain, thus relinquishing all his power. As he did so, he could not help but invoke the American Covenant one last time, declaring to Congress the following on December 23, 1783:

> Glorious indeed has been our Contest: glorious, if we consider the Prize for which we have contended, and glorious in its Issue; but in the midst of our Joys, I hope we shall not forget that, to divine Providence is to be ascribed the Glory and the Praise....I consider it an indispensable duty to close this last solemn act of my Official life, by commending the Interests of our dearest Country to the protection of Almighty God, and those who have the superintendence of them, to his holy keeping.[44]

Speaking to all Americans in this same spirit and near this same time, Washington declared:

> If in the execution of an arduous Office I have been so happy as to discharge my duty to the Public with fidelity and success, and to obtain the good opinion of my fellow Soldiers and fellow Citizens; I attribute all the glory to that Supreme Being, who hath caused the several parts, which have been employed in the production of the wonderful Events we now contemplate, to harmonize in the most perfect manner, and who was able by the humblest instruments as well as by the most powerful means to establish and secure the liberty and happiness of these United States.[45]

So important was the American Covenant to Washington that he would, before leaving his post, once again impress upon his countrymen the importance of keeping the commandments and thus living the national covenant:

> I now make it my earnest prayer, that God would have you, and the State over which you preside, in his holy protection, and that he would incline the hearts of the Citizens to cultivate a spirit of subordination and obedience to Government, to entertain a brotherly affection and love for one another, for their fellow citizens of the United States at large, and particularly for their brethren who have served in the Field, and finally, that he would most graciously be pleased to dispose us all, to do Justice, to love mercy, and to demean ourselves with that Charity, humility and pacific temper of mind, which were the Characteristiks of the Divine Author of our blessed Religion, and without an humble imitation of whose examples in these things, we can never hope to be a happy nation.[46]

It was in this spirit that the greatest revolutionary war for independence, perhaps in the history of the world, was concluded. It was General Washington's ultimate gift to America. And it was a powerful sign of the national covenant under which the General had been appointed to work.

In light of Washington's actions here, we would do well to consider one piece of undervalued American artwork that captures his covenant experience in a marvelous way. It is a thirty-ton sculpture of the General completed in 1840, and it currently sits in the Smithsonian's National Museum of American History. Entitled simply, *George Washington*, it depicts the General cradling a sheathed sword upon his left forearm and open palm, extending it forward as if to be returning it. It is a symbol of the General's inspired decision to return all power to the people after the war. That this act was part of a greater covenant, made by the great covenant-maker, is also, most astonishingly, represented. First, the statue is full of imagery representing ancient Greece (the first seat of democracy), which reflects the covenant blessing of freedom. Second, Washington is flanked on both sides by small statues—one of a Native American (reminiscent of Manasseh) and one of Columbus (reminiscent of Ephraim). Both figures are depicted in an obvious state of deep meditation. And both figures have obvious connections to the national covenant. That they are present during the depiction of Washington fulfilling the covenant in a powerful way is remarkably fitting. Finally, in a most stunning symbol of the covenant, Washington is depicted sitting upon a grand throne with a robe draped over his right shoulder. While his left arm and hand are returning the sword, his right arm and hand are depicted being raised to the square, with his index finger pointing to heaven.

ENDNOTES

[1] David Tappan, as quoted by Marshall and Manuel, 427.

[2] Timothy Dwight, as quoted by Marshall and Manuel, 427.

[3] Marshall and Manuel, 428.

[4] Marshal and Manuel, 428.

[5] Marshal and Manuel, 427.

[6] Waldman, 88.

[7] Waldman, 42.

[8] George Washington, as quoted in Bennett, *Spirit of America*, 365.

[9] George Washington, as quoted by Novak, *Washington's God*, 130.

[10] Novak, *Washington's God*, 192-193, emphasis added.

[11] Novak, *Washington's God*, 115.

[12] Washington, Circular of 1783 to John Hancock and Congress, as quoted in "The Papers of George Washington," available at http://gwpapers.virginia.edu/documents/constitution/index.html.

[13] Novak, *Washington's God*, 193; Also, the Lord uses the term "moral agency" to describe the freedom of religion, which America and the inspired Constitution would offer "all flesh" (See D&C 101:77-78).

[14] Novak, *Washington's God*, 128.

[15] Novak, *Washington's God*, 111.

[16] McCullough, *John Adams*, 131.

[17] Novak, *Washington's God*, 8, 12.

[18] Waldman, 52, 136, 173.

[19] Waldman, 52.

[20] George Washington, in "Letter to the Reformed German Congregation of New York," available at http://teachingamerican history.org/index.asp?document print=361; also quoted in Novak, *Washington's God,* 130.

[21] Washington, in a letter to the Touro Synagogue in Newport, Rhode Island, August 17, 1790, as quoted in Waldman, *Founding Faith*, 164.

[22] Waldman, 63.

[23] Cleon Skousen, *The Majesty of God's Law,* 23.

[24] Cleon Skousen, *The Majesty of God's Law,* 15-16.

[25] George Duffield (1783), as quoted in Meacham, 80-81.

[26] Duffield, as quoted by Marshall and Manuel, 426.

[27] Bruce Feiler, *America's Prophet, Moses and the American Story* (New York: HarperCollins, 2009), 102-103.

[28] Bruce Feiler, *America's Prophet, Moses and the American Story*, 104.

[29] Waldman, *Founding Faith*, 107.

[30] Jefferson, as quoted by Waldman, 82.

[31] Washington, as quoted by Novak, *Washington's God*, 125.

[32] Greene, 152. Refer to Chapter 2 of this book for evidence of the idea that the blood of Ephraim flowed through the American Founders.

[33] McCullough, *1776*, 286.

[34] McCullough, "The Glorious Cause of America," 47.

[35] Novak, *Washington's God*, 33.

[36] George Washington, as quoted in Gordon S. Wood, *Revolutionary Characters* (New York: Penguin Press, 2006), 51.

[37] Fleming, 183-185.

[38] Fleming, 185.

[39] Novak, *Washington's God*, 34.

[40] Ellis, *His Excellency*, 139.

[41] Joseph J. Ellis, *Patriots, Brotherhood of the American Revolution*, Lectures recorded by Recorded Books, Inc, and Barnes and Noble Publishing: 2004, lecture 7.

[42] Bennett, *America*, 163.

[43] Bennett, *America,* 165.

[44] George Washington, as quoted by Novak, *Washington's God,* 173, 211.

[45] Washington's address at Princeton, August 25, 1783, as quoted by Novak, *Washington's God*, 183.

[46] George Washington, "Circular Address to the States," June 8, 1783, as quoted in William J. Bennett, *The Spirit of America* (New York: Simon and Schuster, 1997), 378-380.

The Great Seal of the United States of America (reverse side).

CHAPTER 9

ANCIENT ORDERS, FOUNDING FATHERS, AND THE TEMPLE OF GOD

[I pray] that the Great Architect of the Universe may bless you and receive you hereafter into his immortal Temple.

—George Washington

In addition to the many evidences we have thus far seen of the Founding Fathers' role as chosen covenant-makers, there is another very unique piece of evidence that has been largely hidden and undervalued within the annals of history. It is a piece of evidence that perhaps ties the Founders to God's covenant and ultimate plan for America in more powerful ways than anything we have yet witnessed. As an introduction to our discussion of this material, we turn our attention to a connection that may appear to be nothing but a coincidence, but in actuality leads us to powerful conclusions relative to God, country, and the Restoration. The connection begins with George Washington, the leader of the latter-day national covenant, and Joseph Smith, the leader of the latter-day priesthood covenant. While it is clear these great men shared a common purpose in sacrificing their lives for the Restoration, they shared even more than most realize—they both participated as high officials in the Masonic Order (also known as Freemasonry or Masonry).

But does this fact carry any real significance? Is it not most easily explained as a mere coincidence? And what possible connection might their participation in Masonry have with the American Covenant and the Restoration? We will now explore the answers to these questions. Our analysis below does not include a comprehensive report on Masonry, nor does it pretend to make any definitive conclusions about it. For Masonic history is lengthy and intricate, and a full analysis of it falls outside of the scope of this study. Furthermore, its history is shrouded in mystery and its origins are largely theoretical. Notwithstanding these obstacles, however, there is enough about this proposed connection to comment on certain evidences—evidences which represent powerful testimony of the American Covenant stemming out of the era of the American Revolution.

The Masonic Order and the Gospel

In order to gain an understanding of how Masonry might connect to the American Covenant, and thus to the purposes of God, we must divert from the subject of America and spend some time discussing certain ideas about what Masonry is and where it came from. *Freemasonry* is defined as a fraternal organization that requires its members to be "of good repute" and possess "a belief in a Supreme Being." It is not a religious organization any more than the Boy Scouts of America is. Its members may belong to any church or no church, as long as they believe in God. Its goal is to inspire its members to "achieve higher standards in life."[1]

In addition to rendering charitable services, the organization participates in an array of ceremonial initiations and rites, which reflect its pursuit for light, knowledge, and progression. These initiations and rites are performed in sacred dwellings called lodges or temples, and they involve the use of the following symbolic imagery and themes: The Almighty God represented by images of the "All-Seeing Eye" and by the letter "G", imagery of the sun, the moon, the stars, the beehive, celestial and terrestrial spheres, angels, and the signs of the compass and the square.[2] Masonic historians specifically define the compass and the square as being ritualistic symbols of Solomon's Temple, symbols whose purpose is to remind the initiate "to square our actions and to keep them within due bounds."[3] Masonry's initiation rites include a ceremonial representation of man progressing through three levels (or what Masons call "degrees"), moving from darker to more enlightened spheres. The third and final level or degree one can attain is that of Master Mason. At each degree, a new name or word is given to the initiate. According to Masonic historians, "Masters are given, at least initially, the name 'Jehovah.' Each of these three words is also accompanied by a particular 'sign,' or placement of the hands, and a particular 'grip,' or handshake."[4] Much of the ceremony revolves around the theme of building or rebuilding God's sacred temple, which is another reason the symbolic use of building tools—like the compass, square, and trowel—figure into the rituals. Different clothing is issued to the participant as he advances through the levels. A symbolic apron is worn as part of the ceremony. Instruction is given and vows are made within a setting of a dramatized narrative. The setting includes a figurative replica of the ancient temple built by King Solomon. There are question-and-answer phases of the ceremony. There is a symbolic knocking at a portal in order to communicate with the officiator. An altar, with scripture laid upon it, plays a symbolic role in these ceremonies. A prayer offered by one kneeling at the altar figures in as well. Often this prayer is offered by another in behalf of the kneeling initiate. And finally, there is an emphasis on the principles of death, resurrection, and the opportunity to return and live with the "Grand Architect of the Universe."[5] All of these rituals are taken seriously and include many ideas and practices that the initiate promises never to divulge or exploit. It should be noted, however, that while these symbolic actions are carried out regularly, the meanings behind them are largely unknown—even to the Freemason.[6]

Many of the above mentioned symbols are found in one form or another engraved or otherwise presented on the exterior walls of the Salt Lake Temple—the hand clasp, the "All-Seeing Eye," the beehive (on the temple doorknobs), the sun, the moon, and the stars.[7] The Nauvoo temple was capped by a weather vane depicting the angel Moroni in priestly robes and cap, carrying a Book of Mormon. Above him hung the signs of the compass and the square.[8] The idea that LDS temple theology appears to share characteristics of Masonic practices,* has led the *Encyclopedia of Mormonism* (produced in large part by Brigham Young University) to suggest that temple ordinances and Masonic rites stem from "a common remote source."[9]

Perhaps this helps explain why the Prophet Joseph Smith and other early Church leaders displayed an interest in Freemasonry, helped establish a Masonic lodge in Nauvoo, and became Master Masons. Brigham Young referred to LDS temple ordinances as "Celestial Masonry." Apostle Willard Richards stated that "Masonry had its origins in the Priesthood. A hint to the wise is sufficient." Apostle Heber C. Kimball added, "There is a similarity of priesthood in Masonry. Brother Joseph says Masonry was taken from Priesthood." Brother Benjamin F. Johnson claimed that Joseph Smith "told me Freemasonry, as at present, was the apostate endowments, as sectarian religion was the apostate religion." The Saints of Salt Lake stated: "Masonry was originally of the church, and one of its favored institutions, to advance the members in their spiritual functions. It had become perverted from its designs." Backing up these claims, Church authorities stated, "The Mormon leaders have always asserted that Free-Masonry was a ...degenerate representation of the order of the true priesthood."[10] The First Presidency even issued a statement at General Conference referring to temple rites and ordinances as "Masonic characters."[11]

---

* Due to the sacred nature of LDS temple services, the only references to them will be those that have been openly discussed in official Church publications or those found in the *Encyclopedia of Mormonism*, which was produced with the support of Brigham Young University.

The commentaries and actions of early LDS Church leaders suggest that true temple practices share a common origin with those of the Masonic Order. A look at what we know about Masonic origins may shed light on this proposed connection. In fact, the most prominent theories suggest the historical roots of Masonry are precisely where we find the true roots of gospel-temple worship. Amazingly, many of the source documents and ideas behind this theory were not discovered or developed until generations *after* early Church leaders made the connections. More amazing still, the Masonic historians who promote this theory have no known or suggested connection to LDS theology or to the statements of early Church leaders regarding Masonry—they are certainly not trying to corroborate ideas put forth by Church leaders. In other words, if the theory is true, we would find independent corroboration to what early Church leaders said and did relative to Masonry. Indeed, we would have further witness that Masons represent a modern era organization that has preserved certain remnants—lost and degenerate though they may be—of gospel truth and temple ordinances.

In fact, these Masonic theorists, in identifying signs and symbols of antiquity, appear to have tapped directly into ancient forms of true priesthood; and they have called them Masonic simply because they believe in no other modern organization or religious practice with whom to associate these signs and symbols. The only reason they are able to connect their ancient findings with modern Masonry is because somehow Masonry was able to preserve, until today, something that ties into antiquity—something that ties into gospel truth. Though the true ordinances existed and were passed down from the beginning, during the Great Apostasy (when these truths were largely hidden) the Masons somehow obtained and preserved parts of them. And this would have powerful and positive consequences for the Restoration and the American Covenant's role in it.

In order to establish the deeper connections between the Masonic Order, the American Covenant, and the Restoration we must understand how and why the Masons ended up with these remnants of truth, and we must comprehend what these truths really were. To that end, we will now examine the Masonic theories of origin. These theories have most successfully been promoted by Masonic historians Christopher Knight and Robert Lomas—also members of the Order—in their book, *The Hiram Key: Pharaohs, Freemasons and the Discovery of the Secret Scrolls of Jesus*. Though their findings are full of conjecture and imaginative interpretations, they do build upon earlier Masonic scholarship and utilize ancient documents and artifacts to make their case. They propose, as do earlier Masonic scholars, that the rites and practices presented through Masonry have been around, in one form or another, since the earliest civilizations—an idea which certainly makes sense if they were, in fact, derived from true priesthood that began with Father Adam.[12] They present ancient Egypt as one of the first identifiable societies to possess the secrets of the Order. They have even identified several Masonic-like rituals performed by ancient Egyptians—to include symbolic resurrection ceremonies—within the walls of their famed temples and pyramids.[13] This could explain why Masonic art and depictions often include Egyptian motifs, particularly those reflecting Egyptian pyramids. Even early nineteenth century Masonic scholarship connects Masonry to Egyptian pyramid practices, by pointing out that, like Masons, ancient Egyptians used the symbolic sign of the square (what ancient Egyptians called the *kan*). According to some scholars, the Egyptian temple practices also coincide with Masonic ritualism in that both emphasize and represent "places of initiation."[14]

But were these Masonic-like rituals in ancient Egypt really just a reflection of true temple worship? LDS scholar Hugh Nibley seems to imply that they were. Utilizing references in Abraham 1:26-27, Professor Nibley points out that the Egyptians indeed imitated true temple ordinances. "The ordinances of the Egyptian temple," concluded Nibley, as recorded in his book, *Temple and Cosmos*, "were essentially the same as those performed in ours."[15] According to the *Encyclopedia of Mormonism*:

> Studies of Egyptian temple ritual...have revealed parallels with Latter-day Saint temple celebrations and doctrine, including a portrayal of the creation and the fall of mankind,

washings and anointings, and the ultimate return of individuals to God's presence. Moreover, husband, wife and children are sealed together for eternity, genealogy is taken seriously; people will be judged according to their deeds in this life, and the reward for a just life is to live in the presence of God forever with one's family. It seems unreasonable to suggest that all such parallels occurred by mere chance.[16]

The *Encyclopedia of Mormonism* also notes the existence of the Egyptian religious practice of "prayer circles."[17]

Professor Nibley further corroborates the idea that gospel truths existed in ancient Egypt by pointing out its religious doctrines of a pre-existence, a council in heaven, the great dispute between two brothers (only one of which was the chosen one), the existence of a Heavenly Father *and* a Heavenly Mother, and Her offspring known as the Great One.[18] Based on this gospel-linked analysis, Egyptian themes and décor in Masonry certainly corroborate the purported statements made by the Prophet and his brethren concerning Masonic origins.

Knight and Lomas connect the ancient religious practices in Egypt to Abraham and the Children of Israel, who spent much time living in and around Egyptian culture.[19] They believe, along with other Masonic scholars dating back to the nineteenth century, that the ordinances from Egypt were taken into the promised land of Israel through Moses and the prophets that followed him. They believe that Israel built their temples, to include Solomon's Temple, with the express purpose of having a venue where these rites and ordinances might be received.[20] This helps explain why Freemasons to this day emphasize and imitate what they believe to be the rites originally performed in, or associated with, Solomon's Temple.[21] Latter-day Apostle, Heber C. Kimball, himself a Freemason, seemed to support this connection when he stated that "the Masonry of today is received from the apostasy which took place in the days of Solomon, and David."[22]

If Masonry is connected to the rites and practices of ancient Israel, then perhaps we have further corroborated once again the idea that so-called "ancient Masonry" is in actuality true gospel in antiquity. We know, after all, that true priesthood and temple ordinances once belonged to ancient Israel. Latter-day Saints of the Kirtland Temple era linked their own washing and anointing ceremonies to those received by the priests of ancient Israel.[23] Furthermore, D&C 124 clearly points out that the Lord had "commanded" ancient Israel to build a temple so that the "ordinances might be revealed which had been hid from before the world was" (verse 38). A few verses earlier, the Lord commanded His Saints in Nauvoo to also build a temple, so that He could "reveal [His] ordinances therein unto [His] people," and so He could reveal "things which h[ad] been kept hid from before the foundation of the world" (verses 40-41). Perhaps all of this sheds light on the conclusions of Knight and Lomas. But more importantly, perhaps all of this connects Masonry to true gospel ordinances, corroborating the ideas of early Church leaders.

The Masonic theorists then point to the idea that Jesus Christ, who had access to the practices of ancient Israel, Himself taught and offered these same Masonic-like rites and ordinances to His disciples while in mortality, and that the original Christian church of Jerusalem was founded upon these rites and ordinances. The Reverend George Oliver, one of the most prolific Masonic writers, placed this idea within a context that Latter-day Saints might fully comprehend. After explaining how Masonry indeed began with Adam, and was passed down through generations of prophets, the reverend explains how it became degenerate "amongst apostate nations." But then, with the advent of Christ, the knowledge of God was "restored," thus elevating Masonry in "vigour and excellence."[24]

Theorists believe they have proof—largely through descriptions found in early Christian writings—that these sacred and symbolic practices were ceremonially carried out by Christ Himself. For example, they point to supposed ancient writings of a second century Christian scholar named Clement, who referenced a supposed lost scripture called the Secret Gospel of Mark. According to this "secret gospel," Christ taught his disciples secret ceremonies that purportedly involved the wearing of white clothing, which is a characteristic consistent with Freemasonry. They point to other early Christian writings originating within a few centuries of the New Testament period, which they believe indicate the existence of ancient Christian resurrection rituals similar to the Masonic Third Degree ceremony. Masonic theorists further point to a Christian sect currently residing in the Middle East, known as the Mandaeans, who were once attached to the ancient Nasorean sect and who trace their roots back to John the Baptist. This sect practices rituals involving handshakes signifying righteousness, and others portraying symbolic resurrections—rituals, again, which coincide with those of the Masons.[25]

If the theorists have correctly traced ancient rites of Masonry to primitive Christianity, then perhaps we have further proof that Masonry is connected to true priesthood. For we know true priesthood ordinances were practiced at this time. We see evidence that these early ordinances were practiced, for example, in The Gospel of Phillip, which was discovered in 1945 among other ancient Christian writings collectively known as the Nag Hammadi Library.* This gospel, which originated from this same early Christian period, speaks of ancient Christian practices and sacraments. While not explaining their meanings, it names them as baptism, anointing (with oil), Eucharist, ransom or salvation, and bridal chamber.[26] Furthermore, it is a fact that the second century Christian writer, Origen, spoke of "higher" doctrines, which allowed the worthy ones to "be boldly initiated in the mysteries of Jesus, which properly are made known only to the holy and pure."[27] LDS scholarship suggests that these higher doctrines are what the New

---

* In 1945, near the Egyptian village of Nag Hammadi, peasants digging for fertilizer stumbled upon a jar containing thirteen leather manuscripts. The manuscripts contained precious early Christian writings dating back to the second century or earlier. See Bart Ehrman, *Lost Christianities: Christian Scriptures and the Battles over Authentication*, Course Guidebook (Chantilly: The Teaching Company, 2002), 21-22.

Testament refers to as the "mysteries" of God and of the kingdom of heaven (see Matthew 13:11; 1 Corinthians 4:1). As recorded in his book, *Temple and Cosmos*, Hugh Nibley quotes Biblical Scholar Morton Smith, who, in his own work, *The Secret Gospel*, speaks to this idea. According to Professor Nibley, "Smith has shown at great length that the word 'mystery,' as used by the early Jews and Christians (taught in secret to the apostles), was nothing else than a series of initiatory ordinances for achieving the highest salvation which today are lost and unknown to the Christian world."[28]

Though some of these early Christian writings are of unknown credibility (some even seem to contradict Christ's core gospel teachings), they have enough truth in them for us to give them consideration. In addition to the temple themes listed above, these lost scriptures include other proposed truths that have been hidden from the world until the Restoration shed light upon them. For example, the Gospel of Phillip implied that Christ was married in mortality. Other Nag Hammadi Christian writings teach the idea that there was a pre-mortal existence and that man was born to earth with a spark of the divine within him. Others teach of three degrees of progression obtainable by mankind. And still others teach that man may return to his heavenly home, not only to his Heavenly Father, but also to his Heavenly Mother.[29]

Knight and Lomas, along with other Masonic theorists, see the primitive Christian era as the pinnacle of Masonry. It seems all of the practices of antiquity—from ancient Egypt to ancient Israel—end here for the historians; for Jesus Christ Himself was leading the Order. What they do not realize, however, is they have perhaps discovered much more than ancient Masonic forms. They appear to have tapped into historical accounts of true priesthood ordinances and temple worship, from which Masonry was later derived. Masonry of today, however, is all they have to compare it to—and so, in their eyes, Masonry takes the credit.

Admittedly, most of the explanations for Masonic history thus far presented—from Egypt to Israel to Christ's primitive church—are based largely on theory. More cautious historians, therefore, explain Masonic origins by pointing to a later era of post-primitive Christianity—an era in which the Orthodox Church (what would become known as the Catholic Church) began to congeal and better record early Christian practices. For example, LDS historian Matthew Brown theorizes in his book, *Exploring the Connections Between Mormons and Masons*, that Freemasonry borrowed many of its practices directly from Christian practices dating mostly between the fifth century and the fifteenth century, or later. In that modern Freemasonry developed in about the fourteenth or fifteenth century, the connection to these early church practices becomes tighter. [30] Examples of these documented Christian practices—which were practiced at different times by different groups of early Christians— that existed in the era leading into the more modern formations of Freemasonry are as follows: altars with scripture laid upon them where one would kneel in prayer; ceremonies that included an advancement through three degrees, each degree more enlightened than the previous; and ceremonial advancements that included the issuance of clothing representing the differing degrees. Also included were dramatizations as part of the ceremony (for early Christianity, this included dramatizations of Adam and the fall). Part of the ceremony sometimes included knocking on a door in order to communicate with other participants in the ceremony. Sometimes they included a question-and-answer exercise between initiate and officiator. These ceremonial practices also included covenant or vow making rituals, the preservation of secrets, the wearing of robes and aprons, the builder's square as a symbol of righteousness, symbolic death and resurrection, and other such symbols. In that the Masons utilized these same symbolic gestures, and in that the earliest official Freemasonic lodges were largely made up of Christians, the idea that they borrowed from orthodox Christianity is simply logical.[31] It should be noted that at this point in history the Great Apostasy was in its prime. And so, it is here where we can see how Masonry perhaps obtained, and then preserved, some semblance of ancient priesthood throughout this dark era lacking in gospel light.

Some Masonic historians, however, searching for additional explanations for the Order's history, and its means and methods of preserving the secret rites and practices, provide other interesting conclusions. For example, Knight and Lomas explain that Christ and/or His disciples deposited the sacred and secret information containing their rites and ordinances into the vaults of Herod's Temple.[32] (Through an LDS perspective, this theory might coincide with the idea that these documents were hidden away from an unworthy world that was fading quickly into the era of the Great Apostasy.) From here, the popular interpretation of Masonic history is employed, in which we are introduced to the Knights Templar. An ancient order of holy warriors, the Templars were organized in 1118 AD, and were given the mission to protect and defend Jerusalem and the Holy Land (mostly from Muslim aggression). They were given this mission after European Crusaders wrested control of the land from Muslim populations. The Templars have been characterized as deeply religious and almost monk-like. They were committed to a life void of sin. They were taught to focus on God and eternal life. They took their name due to the fact that they were assigned to live in a dwelling that laid upon the ruins of Herod's temple. They stabled their horses in the great underground vaults of the Temple Mount. They therefore had unfettered access to what remained of the temple.[33] The theory suggests that they dug under the temple and discovered ancient writings which contained information pertaining to Christ's teachings and ordinances.[34] Interestingly, in 1860, the British Army Engineers excavated portions of the Temple Mount and discovered, and documented, the existence of a deep tunnel system. Inside these tunnels they found Templar artifacts.[35]

In an effort to back the claim that the Templars had found the ancient secrets of Christ, Knight and Lomas present a document they connect to the Templars. Housed in the Ghent University Library is an ancient drawing titled, "Heavenly Jerusalem." It was created sometime during 1119-1121 AD—precisely during the time the Templars walked Jerusalem. The artist was a clergyman named

Lambert of St. Omer, who reportedly had ties to the Templar, Geoffrey de St. Omer. It is believed Geoffrey shared part of the temple find with Lambert, who recorded it in his sketched drawing. The drawing depicts a renewed and rebuilt Jerusalem with twelve towers. Clearly printed on the drawing are the Masonic compasses and squares—sketched five-hundred years before any other such symbols connected to Freemasonry were discovered.[36]

Knight and Lomas further conclude that the Christian scrolls found by the Templars were connected to the famed Qumran (or Essenes) Community, which existed some thirteen miles east of Jerusalem and thrived during the time of Christ. This community was defined by its deep religious vows and ceremonies, which included a Masonic-like ritual requiring the initiate to pass through a figurative death and resurrection to gain admittance to a third degree. Their religious services also involved ceremonial washings and symbolic rites, which the initiate had to swear never to divulge. It was in caves near this community that the Dead Sea Scrolls were discovered in and around 1946; and most scholars believe the scrolls were written and hidden by the members of this community. Knight and Lomas believe this community became part of the early Christian Church founded by Christ and His disciples. One of many problems with this theory is that the Dead Sea Scrolls never mention Christ and in some instances appear to contradict Christ's teachings. However, one of the scrolls, known as the Copper Scroll, describes a treasure, which included additional documents buried in Herod's temple sometime before AD 70 (when the temple was destroyed). Knight and Lomas conclude that these hidden documents were purely Christian and included Christ's mysterious ordinances that he taught his disciples. The theorists claim that it was these documents the Templars found in Herod's Temple.[37]

If the Qumran community knew something of hidden temple rites, then perhaps we should expect that they possessed other temple-related writings. And they did. The Dead Sea collection includes what is called the Temple Scroll, which scholars believe was created between 150 BC and 1 AD. According to BYU Professor

Donald Parry, who has studied the scroll extensively, the Temple Scroll includes a description of temple worship. The scroll speaks of the temple's "holy of holies, chambers, colonnades, mercy seat, cherubim, veil, table, golden lamp, altar, and courtyards." The scroll also describes three courts, where differing levels of rituals represent "three levels of holiness." Professor Parry further states that the scroll describes temple worship in terms of vows, oaths, and priesthood. It also includes laws which emphasize the importance of making oneself pure, so as to be worthy to approach God.[38] It should be noted, however, that there is much in the scroll that seems to have no relation to LDS theology.[39]

One of the more profound aspects of the Temple Scroll is that it was, according to Professor Parry, clearly pointing toward the construction of a future temple—even a temple to be built in the last days.[40] If the theorists are correct about Qumran (along with its Temple Scroll) being connected to the Templars, then the aforementioned "Heavenly Jerusalem" piece becomes more relevant. For "Heavenly Jerusalem," purportedly connected to the Templars and their temple discovery, carries the same theme and vision of a rebuilt Jerusalem/temple of the future, complete with symbolic compasses and squares.

Just as Brown and others show how the familiar rites and practices of early Christian orthodoxy connected to the development of Freemasonry, so the Templar theorists—using an alternate historical route—show how the Templars might have brought this same theology to Freemasonry. In and around 1307 AD, the king of France, backed by the Catholic Church, banned the Templars and began arresting them. It appears as though the Templars were growing too powerful for the reigning political and religious organizations of the day. Having been falsely accused, the Templars were tortured, convicted, and some even executed.[41] Many theorists claim, however, that during this dark time, many Templars fled to Scotland for sanctuary and that they carried with them the secret knowledge and rites of true Christianity. (Those theorists who do not necessarily accept the existence of ancient Christian scrolls buried in the temple, suspect the Templars learned the ordinances any number of ways while in the Holy Land, and then carried them to Scotland.) It is believed that the Templars, for reasons of self preservation against its papal enemy, had remained hidden, passing its secrets on from generation to generation. Due to the Reformation, which reduced papal control during the fourteenth- and fifteenth-centuries, the Templar society reemerged in Scotland and England as the "Freemasons," complete with the rites and practices preserved from antiquity.[42]

As evidence of this theory, historians point to several facts. First, at the time of the Templar's downfall, Scotland was one of the few nations on the earth that possessed a government that could offer safe-haven from the Catholic Church, as Scotland had boldly separated itself from the establishment.[43]

Second, many Templar signs and symbols, dating from the time of the Templar's public demise, have been discovered in Scotland. A church in the Scottish town of Kilmartin, near Loch Awe in Argyll, provides many examples of Templar symbols on gravestones and tombs. This church, along with others nearby, include not only Templar symbols, but also the closely-related Masonic symbols.[44]

Third, Freemasonry definitely stemmed from Scotland. Even historians who balk at the Templar-Mason connection tend to agree that Masonry (wherever it came from) did, in fact, spring from the British Isles beginning in the fourteenth and fifteenth centuries.[45]

Fourth, within a mere four miles of Temple, Scotland (which is generally accepted as the old Templar headquarters), there is a chapel near Edinburgh called Rosslyn.[46] Rosslyn was built in the mid fifteenth-century by the very family—the St. Clair (or Sinclair) family—who largely introduced Freemasonry to Scotland and whose members held the position of Grand Master of Scotland into the late 1700's.[47] Theorists believe Rosslyn was the principal site where the hidden Templars, over many years, morphed into the Freemasons. The chapel décor includes depictions of the sun, the moon, the stars, pyramids, images of Moses, and compasses and squares. It also contains powerful imagery that appears to directly reflect the proposed Templar discovery of the "Heavenly Jerusalem" depiction, complete with its towers and temple imagery. There is also a carving in the wall that clearly depicts a Masonic initiation ritual. Additionally, the tombstone of Sir William Sinclair, who died in 1330, is preserved in the chapel. In bold lettering, the tombstone identifies William as a "Knight Templar." Furthermore, the chapel's floor plan is a clear emulation of the layout of Herod's temple. There is also a small frieze depicting the crucifixion, which makes sense considering the Christian influence over the Templars and their rites. However, some theorists question the Christian origin of the frieze, surmising instead that it represents someone other than Christ. The reason for their hesitation has to do with the one crucial difference between the frieze's depiction of the crucifixion and that of mainstream Christianity—the nails are being driven into the figure's wrists and not his hands.[48] Modern revelation clarifies this discrepancy.

Apart from these physical and geographical indicators of a Templar-Mason handoff, there are other evidences that Masonry was derived from the Templars. These evidences have to do with their shared ideas and practices. For example, the Templars, like the Masons, took vows and wore white clothing and white gloves. Also noteworthy is the fact that Templars wore tight sheepskin undergarments—symbolic of their vows—which they were instructed never to remove. Masons wear white sheepskin aprons, which they are told is "a badge of innocence."[49]

Another powerful connection is their shared vision of building a future temple. We saw this Templar vision in its proposed connection with the Qumran Community and their Temple Scroll, along with the proposed "Heavenly Jerusalem" temple discovery. The Masons also maintain this vision: their rites and rituals clearly point to the building of a temple. The three levels of Masonry even reflect this, in that they represent three degrees of "builders"—the most powerful builder being the Master Mason. This entire ceremony is designed around the symbolic construction and development of Solomon's Temple,[50] a central figure in the ceremony being Hiram Abif—the Temple's chief architect.[51] In fact, the Order's name itself—Masonry—clearly reflects this theme. Some have suggested that Masonry was derived from actual stone mason guilds, while others argue that the references to builders and construction was merely symbolic of loftier ideas.[52] But whether or not actual stonemason guilds ever really represented the true source of the Order, it clearly became an organization of symbolic builders of the sacred—builders dedicated to a vision of the temple.[53]

From Freemasonry's emergence on the British Isles as informal groups or lodges, it slowly grew more organized. The first official Grand Lodge was established in England in 1717. From there, Freemasonic lodges—with their signs and symbols—began to spread throughout Western Europe and America.[54]

As we have outlined these theories of Masonic origins, it is important to note that at the historical points where its practices were identified, the world was, at times, in a state of gospel light, but more often than not, was experiencing general apostasy. This, of course, would account for the fragmented, incomplete, and meaningless versions of what might have at one time been true priesthood ordinances. When modern Freemasonry developed in Europe, whatever practices related to truth that might have existed within it—while sincerely carried by its adherents—were certainly found in their apostate form. Even the theorists agree that whatever the original meanings of the ancient rites and practices were, by the time of the Freemasonic lodge, "the ceremonies were repeated with pride, but [with] no understanding of their origins."[55] Freemasons even admit that many of the "true secrets" have been replaced with "substituted secrets...until such time as they are rediscovered."[56]

★ ★ ★ ★

As pointed out earlier, almost every part of the Masonic theory of origin is surrounded with controversy, debate, and a lack of conclusive data. But regardless of where Freemasonry came from, it all leads us back to Joseph Smith and the Restoration—and not only because of the many parallels between the ancient Order and the gospel. For regardless of which parts, if any, of the above proposed Masonic origins are true, we know what the Prophet and His colleagues said about the ancient Order and we know of their obvious interest in it. It seems very likely that there is something of truth within the Order, which is the only reason any of it becomes relevant to us today. In fact, as we will see, the relevancy to us perhaps stems from the idea that the Prophet learned something in Freemasonry that assisted him in his acquisition and/or dissemination of temple revelations.

Due to similarities in rites and symbols and due to his obvious interest in the Order, many argue that the Prophet simply copied the Masonic ceremony and directly applied it to LDS temple worship. However, the facts do not support the occurrence of any sort of wholesale pilfering and/or full scale adoption of Masonic rites. As Matthew Brown points out at length, Joseph Smith had received an abundance of revelation in preparation for temple restoration well before he became a Freemason. As early as 1823, it was revealed to the Prophet that temples would be restored to the earth.[57] Other temple revelations that occurred long before Joseph was a Mason include those found in the following Doctrine and Covenants selections: D&C 76 reveals the principles of three degrees of glory and of exaltation; D&C 110 reveals how heavenly messengers had delivered temple sealing keys to the Prophet; and D&C 124 reveals that true temple worship would include baptisms for the dead, washings, anointings, solemn assemblies, and endowment—though little more is given in defining these ordinances. Other principles pertaining to priesthood vows, eternal marriage, and other important temple themes had also been revealed before Joseph's Masonic initiation.[58]

Some LDS scholars point to the many glorious temple-related revelations received by the Prophet prior to his becoming a Mason, and from there conclude that he had clearly received *all* there was to receive prior to his membership in the ancient Order.

But among these early revelations, there is no evidence that *every* aspect of the temple ceremony had yet been revealed. The Kirtland Temple, for example, included what was clearly a preparatory service, and did not manifest the fullness of temple blessings.[59] Furthermore, as late as 1841, while in Nauvoo, the Lord told Joseph that he had yet to reveal to him "things pertaining to this house [the temple]" (D&C 124:42). It was not until the Nauvoo Temple era— until after Joseph had become a Mason—that we see a completion of all the familiar symbols, signs, practices, and teaching methods. Such elements, of course, make up a small fraction of the overall temple experience, but they are, nonetheless, present and important. Just because the Prophet had clearly received the bulk of the temple revelation before becoming a Mason, why are we so fast to conclude that he had received it all? Why jump to such conclusions, especially when we know what Masonry meant relative to the priesthood at various historical times, how it was interpreted by the brethren of the Restoration, and especially upon considering the interest in, and timing of, the lodge in Nauvoo?

Indeed, we would do well to examine the interest in, and timing of, the lodge in Nauvoo. On March 15, 1842, the Grand Master of the Illinois Lodge, Abraham Jonas, with the help of his honorary officiator, Joseph Smith (who was not yet a Mason), officially installed the Nauvoo Masonic Lodge. Over the next two days the Prophet participated in Masonic ceremonies. At the end, he had been inducted into the high degree of Master Mason. In the weeks that followed, Joseph participated in or witnessed at least ten induction ceremonies. Then, on May 4, 1842—less than two months after becoming a Master Mason—Joseph revealed for the *first time* the entire temple endowment ceremony to selected Saints.[60] On this May 4th meeting, nine men were chosen to be the first to receive the full temple endowment. Most of these men were mentioned by the Lord in the temple revelation found in D&C 124. And all of them were Masons—most of them Master Masons.[61]

In light of what Joseph and the brethren said of Masonry, and after reviewing the proposed theories put forth regarding its seemingly divine origins, the timing of these events in Nauvoo, far from seeming merely coincidental, seem highly significant. It seems likely that the Prophet's association with Masonry somehow assisted him in receiving and/or disseminating the final revelations, even the final details, of the temple service. This seems especially likely when we ponder over why the Prophet and the brethren—so busy and purpose-driven in their mission under God—would take the time to not only join themselves with this ancient order, but establish their own lodge in Nauvoo. Eleven of the Twelve Apostles had joined the Masonic lodge. Furthermore, by the fall of 1842, there were more Freemasons in Nauvoo than there were in all the other Illinois lodges combined.[62]

Some say it was a simple diversion—a curiosity. But did the brethren really have time to found an entire organization around fun and curiosity? Some argue that it was for political and social security —to build a network of friends. If so, was it just a funny coincidence that the social club also promoted recognizable priesthood truths?

Furthermore, after his initiation as a Master Mason, Joseph thereafter showed very little interest in the lodge.[63] And after the Saints had migrated to Salt Lake, Masonry became practically a dead entity for them. But if it was social security they were seeking—the Saints in Salt Lake still longed for a union with the United States— why not maintain their Masonic ties? After all, the Salt Lake Saints had relied on Masonic connections outside the Church for favors in assisting with convert migrations into Zion, so they obviously knew of the social benefits that an active lodge among them might offer.[64] Yet, it seems that once Joseph had been initiated, he cared little about the lodge, and after the Saints left Nauvoo, they too placed it aside. Perhaps the Order had already served its single purpose in the building up of the kingdom.

That the Order had assisted the Prophet Joseph is an idea supported by Joseph's close friend, Apostle Franklin Richards. Elder Richards stated, "Joseph, the Prophet, was aware that there were some things about Masonry that had come down from the beginning and he desired to know what they were, hence the lodge. Masons knew some keys of knowledge appertaining to Masonry were lost. Joseph enquired of the Lord…and he revealed to him the [temple ceremony]."[65] Joseph Smith biographer, Richard Bushman, concluded that "Joseph turned the [Masonic] materials to his own use. The Masonic elements that appeared in the temple endowment were embedded in a distinctive context—the Creation instead of the Temple of Solomon, exaltation rather than fraternity, God and Christ, not the Worshipful Master. Temple covenants bound people to God rather than to each other."[66]

Dr. Gilbert Scharffs, an LDS Church educator, and the author of *Mormons and Masons,* asserted this same idea:

> When Joseph Smith was exposed to Masonic ritual, he certainly…asked the Lord, "What is this all about? Is there any truth in this?" as he had done with other issues throughout his life. He would have done this especially when he learned that Masons claimed their signs and symbols came from the biblical temple of Solomon. Then revelation from God helped him sort things out and finalize the LDS temple endowment. In the process he discovered that the teaching method of Masonic ritual had great merit, but not the Masonic meanings.[67]

The evidence of the Order's gospel assist in the latter-days continues further. And it continues, oddly enough, with the Prophet Ezekiel of the Old Testament. Ezekiel clearly saw the last days, and as such has been deemed by Latter-day Saint authorities as a true "prophet of the Restoration."[68] In Chapter 2, we pointed out his vision of the Book of Mormon, even that vision of "the stick of Joseph." But his vision of the great latter-day Restoration was extended beyond that, in that he also saw the future of the temple at Jerusalem. Specifically, he saw that it would be restored and rebuilt in the last days (Ezekiel 37:26-28). Latter-day prophets have confirmed that Ezekiel's temple will indeed come to pass, that it will be of God, and that true ordinances will be received therein.[69] This temple, patterned after Solomon's, is clearly connected to the

Restoration; for it is the Restoration, and the building of temples to accompany it, that will eventually lead to the reconstitution of the Jerusalem temple. Furthermore, LDS scholars have linked Ezekiel's proclamation that "the glory of God filled the house" to all temples given by God (Ezekiel 43:5).[70]

We recently discussed the vision held by the Qumran Community—and their Temple Scroll—that the temple would be restored in the last days. Though their details of its structure differ in ways from Ezekiel's description, we know the Dead Sea Scrolls contain Ezekiel's prophetic writings of the latter-day temple.[71] In that Qumran knew of Ezekiel and his temple vision and also preached of a future and latter-day temple, the connections are difficult to ignore. Scholars who describe the Qumran temple vision can scarcely avoid mentioning the obvious connection to Ezekiel's prophecy. If the theorists are correct, the Templars caught this same vision of the temple (presumably from the Qumranians, as per the evidence found in the Copper Scroll), as indicated in part by the proposed Templar find of the "Heavenly Jerusalem" document. We have also discussed other obvious indications that the Templars carried a knowledge of temple practices. That this temple vision continued, and was passed on from the Templars to the Masons, is seen in the obvious Masonic rituals based upon the rebuilding of the temple, as outlined above.[72] Indeed, we have seen how the ritualistic rebuilding of the temple is no casual side note of Masonry. Its Third Degree ceremony even requires the initiate to enter the "temple" from the "east gate" and ascend "seven steps" to the Master's pedestal.[73] These requirements—namely, the "east gate" and the "seven steps"—fully reflect what Ezekiel saw in vision relative to the latter-day temple (see Ezekiel 40:6, 26; 43:1-4). Though we have established Masonic interest in temples, it seems we might add that the interest was not just in temples, but in temples of the future—temples of the Restoration.

The presence of Ezekiel's vision in this case certainly tightens the bond between Masonry and the Restoration. For the Masons not only carried Ezekiel's latter-day temple vision, even acting it out ceremonially, but they also helped fulfill the prophecy—they helped fulfill the ultimate designs of their Order. Indeed, they carried Ezekiel's vision and the tools to make that vision a reality, squarely into the Restoration, delivering the divine gift to a prophet of God. And so, the idea that Masonry played a divine role in the Restoration becomes even more convincing.

Admittedly, the Prophet Joseph's comprehension of matters relating to the Restoration ran deep, and attempting to fully grasp his understanding is difficult at best. That said, it is impossible to determine exactly what role Masonry might have played in the Restoration. Did it really serve to pass information on to the Prophet? Or was it used as a mechanism to teach or ease members into temple worship? Or was there something else that explains the connection? Whatever it was, the evidence above leads us to conclude that Masonry played some role in assisting and supporting the Restoration.

Notwithstanding this conclusion, some understandably balk at the idea that something like Masonry could have had any part in revealing something as sacred and powerful as those things pertaining to temple worship. And yet, they accept the patterns of revelation that support that such a thing might have occurred. Indeed, we have been taught that the purest of revelations can be derived from any good source. If Joseph looked to Masonry for divine guidance, he would only have been following the commandments regulating how revelation is received. "[Y]ou must study it out in your mind," said the Lord, "then you must ask me if it be right" (D&C 9: 8). It was the revelatory pattern with the brother of Jared. Instead of just pouring out all the answers that the brother of Jared requested of the Lord pertaining to lighting his sea vessels, the Lord instead first required work on his part to find a solution (see Ether Chapter 2). Similarly, though the Lord could have revealed a brand new Bible account to the Prophet—as many plain and precious things had been stripped from the current Biblical record (1 Nephi 13:28)—He did not. For it is clear that Joseph took what record he had (the King James Version of the Bible), in the state that it was, and studied it, and then improved upon it as directed by the Lord.[74] As a result we have the Joseph Smith Translation of parts of the Bible. And what about the Book of Abraham? Again, the Lord could have revealed every point and principle to Joseph directly, without the involvement of some other, ancient form of it. And yet it appears that the Lord, directing events from above, took the trouble to inspire the introduction of Egyptian mummies into Kirtland, Ohio, that the Prophet might view them, purchase them, and then translate the papyri attached to them. This is how we received the Book of Abraham.[75] And despite the unusual manner in which Joseph came upon this ancient book, the Lord used it nonetheless to teach Joseph of temple-related principles.[76]

The point is that our Heavenly Father preserves truths of antiquity, sometimes for long periods of time, so that they might be found and utilized later when the time is right. He does this even when He could simply reveal these points of doctrine directly to a prophet when the world is ready to receive them. Perhaps it is His way to allow His children, even those living in the darkness of apostasy, to participate in His grand designs. Sometimes this process involves pure and direct revelation—written on gold plates and hidden away for over one-thousand years—which only requires a prophet and a language translation at the correct and future time. Sometimes it involves the use of priesthood-less monks and scholars who—for over more than one-thousand years—collect and preserve ancient Christian writings (losing some truths along the way), which require a prophet's inspired corrections. Sometimes the ancient message is carried to a prophet attached to a mummy! So why should it be difficult to believe that righteous people from antiquity could provide a gospel assist to the prophet of the Restoration? If God was to trust anyone with this arduous task of preserving truths through the apostasy, why not the Qumran Community? The Templars? The Masons? All were God-fearing people who sought righteousness. And all held sacred the ancient signs, symbols, and practices. Many even promised, under the threat of death, to not reveal or exploit them.

Enter Founding Fathers, American Covenant-makers of the Order

With the rather lengthy premise above, we at last arrive at how all of this is connected to the American revolutionaries and the American Covenant. For if it is true that Masonry was divinely commissioned to carry truths from Christ's primitive church through the Apostasy and on to the latter-day Restoration, then the Founding Fathers of America most certainly fit into the inspired plot. For the Founders were the first Masons in America and, therefore, represent the final link in the divine chain from antiquity that reached out and touched the Restoration. They were relevant players indeed. But a deeper look into the history of Masonry in America makes these American Masons more than just relevant. As we now examine the details of Masonry in America, we will come to more profound conclusions about the Order and the American Founders who carried it. The evidence below offers a powerful witness, not only of the inspired nature of the Order, but of the lofty position held by the Founding Fathers as true American Covenant-makers.

To A Chosen Land; To A Chosen Generation

The first Masonic lodges in America were established in the late 1720s. The first known publicly documented report and advertisement of Freemasonry in America was printed by none other than Benjamin Franklin in 1730, exactly one hundred years before the Church would be organized; and the first lodge in Illinois, which laid the foundation for the Nauvoo lodge, arrived in 1820, the year of the First Vision and ten years before the Church was organized. All of this occurred, perhaps, in just enough time for Masonic principles to congeal and spread throughout America in preparation for the Restoration. Interestingly, many Masonic lodges, including some of the first in America, were traditionally consecrated to God and dedicated to John the Baptist—the great forerunner of the gospel.[77]

Franklin himself joined the Masonic order in 1731 and became the Provincial Grand Master of Pennsylvania by 1734.[78] Franklin testified that "Masonic labor is purely a labor of love."[79] And yet, he was only one of many American revolutionary heroes to help provide and preserve the traditions, practices, and teachings of Freemasonry. The most famous Master Mason in America was George Washington. Washington, who joined the Order in 1753, testified that his participation was largely due to the "private virtue" it promoted.[80] He stated that the Order's grand object was "to promote the happiness of the human race."[81]

Not surprisingly, Washington filled his leading councils of war with his brethren of the Order; half of his generals were Freemasons, and almost every single one of his highest ranking and most trusted commanders were members. Furthermore, Freemasons filled the rank and file of America's revolutionary fighters. A significant portion of these adherents were active participants in famed events such as the Boston Tea Party and the signing of the Declaration of Independence.[82] An astonishing twenty-eight percent of the signers of the Declaration of Independence were most likely members of the Order.[83] (In that all of these signers, along with Washington, participated in the temple miracle at St. George, we might conclude that, while in the temple, they gained deep insight and made profound connections to the Masonic associations they had enjoyed in mortality.)

Though many tend to exaggerate the influence of Freemasonry in the building of the nation, few doubt that the Masonic ideals of "liberty, equality, brotherhood, tolerance [and] the rights of men"—which were in and of themselves revolutionary ideals at the time—helped shape the nation.[84] One prominent sign of its influence is represented in Washington's decision to utilize a Bible from the St. John's Lodge of New York when taking his famous oath of office,[85] described in Chapter 2, with all its deep connections to the American Covenant. Another sign of Masonic influence was witnessed during the ceremonial laying of the cornerstone of the Capitol Building in 1793. Led by Washington dressed in his Masonic regalia, complete with his ceremonial apron and trowel, it was written up as "one of the grandest Masonic processions" ever seen. In the full symbolic and ritualistic character of Freemasonry, the cornerstone was laid, after which a prayer to the Almighty was offered.[86] In the end, with its members consisting of revolutionary heroes like George Washington, Benjamin Franklin, John Hancock, James Madison (the "Father of the Constitution"), James Monroe, Paul Revere, John Jay, John Paul Jones, Marquis de La Fayette, and many others, the Masonic influence can hardly be sidelined.[87]

Though the above narrative may appear on the surface as nothing but a normal and expected introduction of Masonry into a budding nation, there is, in fact, much more to it. To be sure, Masonry in America was unique and powerful in ways that reflect its divine mission. For one thing, Masonry did not just casually appear in the chosen land—it was an explosive import! As one Masonic historian explains, "No one could have foreseen the significance these transplantations [of Masonry in America] would quickly assume."[88] In little time, there would be "more Freemasons in the United States than anywhere in the world."[89] That the Order had received such a positive response in any given nation might be rather unremarkable. But when we consider that the one nation that received it so powerfully was also the one nation given by the scriptures to be the Promised Land and host nation of the Restoration, then we find ourselves lifting an eyebrow. But it gets even more profound. For, as detailed above, the specific American generation that received and developed the Order was not just any generation—it was the very generation mentioned by name in the scriptures, even those Founding Fathers who were raised up by God Almighty to carry the national covenant in preparation for the Restoration (see 1 Nephi 13:16-19; D&C 101:80). Couple these facts with what we know of Masonic origins and the Prophet's interest and probable use of the Order, and we are left with one logical conclusion: the Founding Fathers of the Revolution, in addition to providing the political foundations for the gospel, had also provided another unique gospel assist. In their inspired role as American Covenant-makers, they had also preserved and transferred sacred knowledge in preparation for God's great latter-day work. Not only does this further confirm the divinity of their mission, but it validates the covenant under which they were working.

In making this conclusion, it should be pointed out again that the Lord certainly did not need the Masons or anybody else to preserve His ancient practices in furtherance of the Restoration. That He inspired and encouraged them in this proposed mission, however, does fit His chosen revelatory pattern of allowing remnants of antiquity to be preserved and restored. As the Founders were truly an inspired generation, brought to earth for divine purposes, it makes sense that the Lord would use them in this way. As we consider those who carried the Order from antiquity to the Restoration (i.e., Qumranians, Templars, Scottish Masons) the Founders indeed fit the mold. For like their predecessors, they all took the Order very seriously and connected their preservation of its secrets to God and His purposes.

There are additional reasons why the Founding Fathers might have been divinely appointed to be carriers of the Order. For one thing, the influence of the Order had to be strong enough to spread its knowledge afar and thus draw the attention of a small band of Saints in the western most regions of the country, that they might feel compelled to seek its light. Because of who they were, the Founders offered just this type of influence. Furthermore, the Order needed credibility to withstand the objections of an adversary who knew what it had to offer. A few years before the Church was organized, an irrational and unwarranted wave of anti-Masonic fever filled the nation. Masonic adherents and their families—even their children—were persecuted and denied civil rights. An Anti-Mason Party even developed and managed to win elections.[90] It was a strange time. It seems some dark influence emerged around the year 1830 and wanted the Order discredited and silenced. Perhaps it was that same dark influence that used similar tactics to obstruct the restored Church. If so, it is a witness to Masonry's divine place. But more than that, it shows the important role the Founders had in developing the Order. For they had given it credibility, which allowed it to maintain a strong presence through the persecution, and allowed it to inspiringly endure through to the beginning of the Restoration.

There are other reasons we should not undervalue the connection between the Founders, the Restoration, and the Masonic Order. We recently discussed how Ezekiel's vision of the latter-day temple was carried by the Order through the Apostasy and on to America and Joseph Smith. In that Ezekiel was a prophet who foresaw much concerning the Restoration, perhaps he had seen the chosen Founders as well. Their role in the Restoration had, after all, been foreseen by other ancient prophets.[91] As the first to bring the Order to America, and as the last link in a long chain that endured from the beginning of the Apostasy to the glorious days of the Restoration, theirs was a blessed position. At this great intersection, where symbols and visions became glorious realities, we indeed find the Founders Fathers standing nobly and strong. We might picture, for example, Master Mason George Washington performing the ritualistic temple build within the walls of his lodge, and carrying such ceremony to the laying of the cornerstone of the U.S. Capitol Building. Dressed in his sacred regalia, Washington utilized a special ceremonial builder's trowel on this occasion.[92] This image encourages us to visualize another trowel—one used in the ultimate fulfillment of Ezekiel's prophecy and of Masonry's vision. On April 6, 1853, President Brigham Young, himself a Master Mason, was reflecting over latter-day temple construction, and painted from his memory an inspired mental image of "the great Prophet Joseph, in the stone quarry, quarrying rock with his own hands; and the few men in the Church, following his example of obedience and diligence...while they placed the stone and moved the trowel."[93] The symbolic trowel is used to this day by latter-day prophets in their temple dedicatory services. All of this certainly places

Washington's ideals, actions and vision—along with those of his American brethren—within an enlightened perspective.

Some might question and belittle the relevancy of the American Masons carrying this vision of Ezekiel. However, if they had, in fact, preserved certain symbols and teachings that would assist the Prophet, then their vision of the temple certainly added to the solemnity in which they carried out this mission. They believed in the vision of a rebuilt temple so much so that they acted it out regularly in their ritualistic services. Who can say this did not play into the spirit in which they preserved ancient truths for the Restoration? Like it had been for their predecessors in the Order, this spirit of the temple had likely caused them to hold such things as sacred—things not to be divulged or exploited.

Furthermore, we should be careful before determining the limit of their knowledge. They were, after all, handpicked and sent to America by the Lord. And we have already seen in past chapters how they knew more about God's purposes than historians give them credit for. When it came to their knowledge of what they were working toward, we must remember that not only did they maintain the temple vision, along with the familiar signs and symbols, but they were always in search of loftier ideals, or what they called the "Universal Light." In symbolic representation of this thirst for spiritual knowledge, American Masons added one element to their ceremony: they painted their lodge ceilings, under which they performed the ritualistic temple-building ceremony, blue "to represent the heavens." This is why American Freemasonry is called "Blue Lodge."[94] Indeed, they were seeking further light and knowledge—and this is usually when the Lord responds.

To further shed light on what knowledge lay beneath the Founders' understanding of what they were doing, consider again Washington's prophetic words about what America would produce. Through what he called "the pure and benign light of Revelation," Washington came to understand that from America, "intellectual light [would] spring up in the dark corners of the earth."[95] Washington's revelations are also reflected in a blessing he gave to a

Masonic brother, in which he prayed "that the Great Architect of the Universe may bless you and receive you hereafter into his immortal Temple."[96] Furthermore, among the papers of Washington, preserved for over two hundred years, is a handwritten prayer, attributed to him, which he reportedly recited on Sunday mornings. It reads in part as follows: "I beseech Thee, my sins, remove them from Thy presence…and accept of me for the merits of Thy son Jesus Christ, that when I come into Thy temple, and compass Thy altar, my prayers may come before Thee."[97]

In the end, though speculation abounds among historians and theorists about Masonry, there are certain undeniable facts that have powerful implications relative to the Restoration. One of these facts is that the Order—with all of its signs, symbols, and practices related to the temple—landed powerfully in the chosen land of America. It is also a fact that the Order fell directly into the possession of one of the few generations (of the thousands that have existed) to be directly referenced by scripture—a generation of Founding Americans preordained by God to assist in the Restoration. And finally, it is most definitely a fact that this generation successfully promoted the Order and its temple vision and passed it on to their American sons—one of which was Joseph Smith. These simple facts reaffirm the powerful position held by the Founding Fathers as American Covenant-makers.

Prophecies and Visions of the Order Fulfilled

One piece of evidence that supports the idea that the Founding Fathers were also American Covenant–makers by virtue of the Order, has to do with proposed ancient prophecies and visions stemming from the Order itself. In past chapters, we have reviewed the extensive scriptural prophecies dealing with latter-day America and its divine role. Indeed, the United States of America and its Founders were repeatedly seen in vision by ancient prophets. As such, if the Order is derived from truth, we might expect to see similar prophecies and visions put forth anciently by the Order concerning latter-day America. If so, we would have further reason to believe in the divinity of the Order and its role in God's plan. More importantly, we would have further reason to believe that the Founders' connection to the Order played a role in preparing them to be American Covenant-makers and forerunners of the Restoration.

The proposed American prophecies and visions stemming from the Order begin, once again, with the Qumran community. This ancient temple community, purportedly connected to Masonic-like practices, spoke of a land to the "west" reserved for the righteous, even a land "neither oppressed with storms of rain or snow nor with intense heat." Similarly, the aforementioned Mandaeans—also with links to Masonic-like practices—taught of a sacred land marked with the star they called "Merica." Some Masonic speculators believe this symbolic star to be some sort of prophecy in reference to "A-merica."[98] And rounding it all out, these theorists believe they can corroborate this theory by pointing to Masonic rituals in which newly raised Master Mason's are required to look toward "the morning star." They suggest that the star as an American symbol comes back to such powerful meanings derived of the Order.[99]

The theorists further point to the following question-answer ceremony administered by the Worshipful Master of the Masonic Order:

Brother Senior Warden, Whither are you directing your steps?
Towards the West, Worshipful Master
Brother Junior Warden, Why leave the East to go to the West?
In search of that which was lost, Worshipful Master
Brother Senior Warden, What was that which was lost?
The genuine secrets of a Master Mason, Worshipful Master[100]

Such mysterious and almost prophetic references to a chosen land in the West, perhaps lends something of credibility to the anecdotal account of Washington's vision of an angel anointing

America and setting apart this New World from the old one (see description in Chapter 7).

One thing that might corroborate the existence and proposed meanings of these prophetic-like visions would be historical evidence indicating that members of the ancient Order had received these messages and had taken action—evidence that they had sought for the chosen land to the West. And theorists believe they have found such evidence. They believe that the Templars, after having learned of the prophecies, attempted to find this chosen land, especially after being denounced and sent on the run. They propose that Henry Sinclair (or St. Clair), whose family would promote Scottish Masonry and would build the above-analyzed Templar-Masonic themed Rosslyn Chapel, was one who made the journey to America in the late fourteenth-century (before Columbus ever set sail). These conclusions are based on pieces of evidence, to include letters and maps implying he took the journey to the western lands.[101] In his chapel at Rosslyn, built after his supposed journey, are engravings that date back to approximately 1470 (still years before Columbus' discovery). The engravings include depictions of the aloe cactus and the maize cob—plants which are native to the New World and which were unknown, at the time, to the Old World.[102] Is this proof that the Templars had been some of the first to discover America?

To substantiate this theory, some historians point to a mysterious engraving found in a rock within the small town of Westford, Massachusetts. The engraving depicts what appears to be a knight of the fourteenth-century. Though scholars have made no definitive determination about the origin of the mysterious figure, theorists agree that it is proof of Sinclair's voyage.[103] Further evidence is found in a mysterious tower in Newport, Rhode Island, discovered as early as 1524. It is appropriately called the Newport Tower. To this day, no scientific consensus concerning its origins have been determined. But its twelfth to fourteenth-century European architecture suggests further proof of a Templar-Sinclair voyage.[104] Many scholars, without attempting to stake definitive academic claims on its origin, do agree that the structure is fashioned after ancient European baptisteries.[105] Perhaps Sinclair and the Templars indeed knew of the chosen land. Perhaps they were attempting to hasten its discovery and development for the grand designs of the Order. Unfortunately for them, though their intentions might have been sincere, the time was not right. But the evidence of their attempt does lend credibility to the existence of the ancient prophecies handed down through the Masonic line.

But perhaps what validates these prophecies more than anything else, is the fact that they were fulfilled. For a land in the West *was* discovered, and the secrets of the ancient Order *were*, in fact, imported and developed in this land; and they were put to use in the most powerful of ways. The discovery and use of this land was, astonishingly, foreseen by two separate sources: first, and most credibly, by ancient prophets (as detailed in Part I of this book), and second, by the Order. And both visions, presumably derived from the same divine source, ultimately point to the chosen ones who would fulfill the prophesies and realize the visions—to the Founding Fathers. We thus have further reason to believe in the powerful and foreordained position of the Founding Fathers as preeminent American Covenant-makers.

The Columbus Corroboration

If the Order truly did possess visions and tools of the temple, and if it further possessed prophecies relating to the discovery of a western land where such visions and tools might fill the measure of their design, then perhaps we should expect to see signs of it all in the most significant latter-day discovery of the land America. In other words, perhaps we should take a closer look at Christopher Columbus.

It is an established fact that Columbus married the daughter of a Templar in Portugal. Like Scotland, Portugal was one of the few political safe-havens that protected the fleeing Templars from their political and religious oppressors. In order to conceal their identity, the Templars in Portugal changed their name to the Knights of Christ, and carried on their business under that title well into the sixteenth-century. Apart from his membership in the Order, Columbus' father-in-law was a seaman, and had supplied his son-in-law with maritime charts and diaries. While Columbus and his wife resided on the Portuguese Island of Madeira, they became acquainted with his wife's relatives living there also, one of whom was the grandson of none other than the aforementioned Templar and explorer, Henry Sinclair (of Rosslyn Chapel fame). With so much powerful Templar-maritime influence around him, the speculation, of course, is that Columbus had become converted to the Order's vision of a spiritual quest for the heaven-ordained lands in the West. In that Columbus decided to take his famous journey while residing in Medeira, and in that he hoisted over his American-bound ships the symbol of the Knights' red cross, the speculation becomes more convincing still.[106]

But it is a gospel perspective that shines the most light on the connection between Columbus, the ancient Order, and the decision to seek out the mysteries of the West. For as detailed in Chapter 3, Columbus clearly spelled out his true reasons for exploring the West: "to rebuild the temple [at Jerusalem]," so that his fellow Christians might "go back to the temple to the Holy of Holies."[107] Columbus was in clear possession of the Order's true vision of the temple, so much so that he risked life and limb to see it accomplished. But this was not the only thing he said relative to the Restoration. For, as discussed earlier, he testified that he had been led by the "Holy Ghost"[108] and cited scriptures describing the Restoration—namely, Isaiah 14:1-2, Isaiah 66:19, and John 10:16— scriptures he knew had been fulfilled by his divine mission.[109] And if this were not enough, we would do well to remember that Columbus maintains the rare distinction of being one of the few mentioned in the Book of Mormon who was preordained to assist in the Restoration (see 1 Nephi 13:12).

All of this leads us to powerful conclusions. First, it validates the idea that the Order truly did possess ancient knowledge, not only of future temples, but of the western land foreordained to host these temples. And second, it further validates the idea that the Founders, as American Covenant-makers, had indeed been led by a true vision provided by the Order, and that they had indeed possessed certain ancient truths designed to assist the prophet of the Restoration. This validation comes to us through the recognition of a very unique historical pattern—a pattern which spiritually connects the Order, the Founders, the American Covenant, and the Restoration. The pattern is set by Columbus and his discovery; for in this we witness the Order providing inspiration to one of the few historical characters mentioned in the scriptures (Columbus), and we see how this great man makes statements and takes action based on this inspiration that directly provide a foundation in America for the Restoration. Then, in a completely independent chain of events, we see this same pattern repeated. Indeed, we see the Order provide inspiration to one of the few generations mentioned specifically in the scriptures (the Founding Fathers), and we see how these great men make statements and take action based on this inspiration that directly provide a foundation in America for the Restoration. That this rather intricate historical pattern is repeated twice, and that both examples include powerful experiences that connect the Order to the divine calling and mission of American forerunners of the Restoration, is too unique to be coincidental. It is a powerful pattern that validates and lends credibility to all the variables in it. More specifically, it is a powerful pattern that leaves us convinced not only of the Order's profound place in God's plan, but of the inspired nature of those chosen ones (i.e. the Founding Fathers) who participated in these experiences.

★ ★ ★ ★

As we ponder the role of the ancient Order, which landed squarely into the Founders' generation, which is connected to ancient prophecy concerning the Promised Land, and which is twice represented in the divine narrative surrounding the discovery and founding of this Promised Land, we come to powerful conclusions. First, we gain further proof that the Order had a place in God's plan and that it was much more than just a passing interest. This especially rings true as we add to this equation the fact that the Order, independent of its inspired placement in the historical events recently discussed, is connected in numerous ways to the gospel (symbols, signs, themes, pedagogy, Joseph Smith, etc.). All together, we now have further reason to conclude that the Prophet Joseph's encounter with Masonry was indeed inspired—that there was deep meaning and purpose behind it. And second, in that the Founding Fathers are a major part of the history that links the Order to the gospel, we have further reason to uphold them as the powerful American Covenant-makers they were. They were chosen for the purposes of God, not only to provide inspired political foundations, but also to provide ancient gospel truths.

The Founding Fathers' Symbols of the Covenant

With all this in mind, and with a knowledge of what Freemasonry meant to the Founders of both the country and the restored gospel, we might begin to see the most prominent symbols of America in a much different light. According to Elder Boyd K. Packer, the Lord has proven time and again that He utilizes symbols in teaching His children. When it comes to teaching "spiritual ideals," according to Elder Packer, "it can be done most effectively by using symbols." He further adds that "the most conclusive certification of man's intelligence is his ability to re-create in symbolic form the world in which he lives."[110] That said, if Freemasonry is derived of truth, then the nation indeed offers powerful symbolism (through Freemasonry) in furtherance of our understanding of the American Covenant.

Signs and Symbols

Some of the most powerful examples of gospel symbolism infused into the nation have to do with the signs of the compass and the square. After selecting the land (taken from surrounding states) that would be the new capital, which he did in 1790, George Washington drew up its exact perimeters by connecting two right angles, or symbols of the Masonic square. The four points of the connected squares face directly to the North, South, East, and West, forming a perfectly squared diamond. Though in 1848, part of the federal land was given back to Virginia, any map of the D.C. area will reveal the symbolic power of the two tilted Masonic squares. On April 15, 1791, a Masonic ceremony, to include a prayer to the Almighty, was conducted to lay the symbolic cornerstone of this federal land. Markers were then laid out at every mile around the sacred diamond.[111]

That same year, Congress hired Charles L'Enfant to design much of the city. The compass and the square are seen throughout this design, particularly in the layout of streets and monuments. Any good map of the D.C. area, for example, will reveal the compass patterns of its original design. With the Capitol Building serving as the point of the compass, one easily sees its two legs running down Pennsylvania Ave and Maryland Ave respectively. Of particular interest is the layout of three of the first and most important landmarks: The White House, the Washington Monument, and the Capitol Building. An aerial view of these powerful fixtures shows that together they form the symbol of the square. According to architecture and symbolism expert, David Ovason, "It is almost as though L'Enfant laid upon his virgin parchment the Masonic square as symbol of the spirit of George Washington, and dedicated its three points to the founder of the nation."[112] The many artistic renditions of Washington, along with other Founders, wearing ceremonial aprons and carrying the symbolic signs of the compass and square reflect this same spirit. Such art can be found, among other places, displayed inside the Capitol Building.[113] In light of more profound meanings and connections, are these not powerful symbols? Considering how these symbols reflect temple worship (these symbols, for example, were placed over the roof of the Nauvoo Temple),[114] and considering how America and its covenant were established to support true temple worship, the fact that America openly connects itself to these signs and symbols truly emphasizes the power and veracity of the American Covenant. These are truly signs and symbols of the American Covenant.

If these are in fact symbols of the national covenant, then their meaning is strengthened by the idea that some of these very symbols were already in the land before the settlers of America arrived. To be sure, for well over one hundred years historians and archeologists have logged their many findings, which link the mysterious signs of Masonry to Native American culture. For example, in his book, *Mormonism and Masonry*, E. Cecil McGavin points out several anecdotal accounts of early settlers coming into contact with Native American tribes who clearly practiced Masonic-like rituals, to include Masonic hand grips and ceremonies involving three degrees. The settlers were awestruck and asked the Natives where they had learned such things. "The Great Spirit," they were told, had revealed it.[115]*

Archeologists have likened Native American symbols and traditions to those found in Egypt, Israel, and Freemasonry.[116] Others have identified familiar engravings on ancient American seashells—engravings which date back to over eighteen-hundred years ago (back to the days when Nephite generations were living in righteousness), and which include clear depictions of the compass and the square.[117] Upon witnessing such symbols, some early

---

* That the "Great Spirit" does reveal such things from time to time is evidenced by a latter-day account of Elder Parley P. Pratt. In his autobiography, Elder Pratt records that on one evening in the fall of 1830 (years before the temple ordinances had been revealed by the Prophet), he was walking home alone from a missionary meeting. He was pondering the greatness of the Restoration he was now a part of when his attention was diverted to "a sudden appearance of a brilliant light which shone around me, above the brightness of the sun. I cast my eyes upward...when I perceived a long chain of light extended in the heavens." The chain of light then formed three very distinct patterns above him, which he described as "a horizontal position," "an exact square," and "a compass." Declared Elder Pratt, "I fell upon my knees in the street, and thanked the Lord for so marvelous a sign." See Parley P. Pratt, *Autobiography of Parley P. Pratt* (Salt Lake City: Deseret Book, 1985), 31.

American Masons (of the Colonial Era) took it as a sign from God, and felt compelled to promote and grow the lodge system in America.[118]

Such accounts are too numerous to fully review in this study, but their obvious existence certainly adds to the power of the symbols put forth by the Founders. For it corroborates the idea put forth in Chapter 2, that there was a covenant transfer of sorts from Manasseh of old (Native Americans derived from Book of Mormon peoples) to Ephraim in the latter-days. That Ephraim displays, within the modern capital of America, the same sacred gospel symbols used by his ancient brother Manasseh, lends credibility to the power of such symbols. We are reminded from where such symbols were originally derived.

The Great Seal of the United States

In light of how symbols play a powerful role in the pedagogy of God, we might turn to one of the most prominent symbols of the Promised Land: the Great Seal of the United States of America. Commissioned by Congress on that spiritual and historic day of July 4, 1776, the seal contains both a front and reverse side.[119] Both sides of the seal are displayed today on the back of the one dollar bill. We will first examine the reverse side. The prominent figure on the reverse side is a pyramid with thirteen steps, presumably representing the thirteen colonies. The All-Seeing Eye (symbol of God the Father) is also depicted. The All-Seeing-Eye (the same one found engraved on the exterior of the Salt Lake Temple) is surrounded by glorious rays and hovers above the pyramid. The Secretary of Congress, Charles Thompson, was commissioned to finalize the seal project. Not insignificantly, Thomas was a Biblical scholar who had translated the Greek Bible into Latin. A moral man, he was known as the "Soul of Congress."[120] Naturally, Thompson commented on the seal's symbolism in terms that clearly reflect the American Covenant:

The pyramid signifies strength and duration: The eye over it and the motto, Annuit Coeptus [translation: "God Has Favored Our Undertakings"], allude to the many interventions of Providence in favour of the American cause. The date underneath is that of the Declaration of Independence, and the words under it, Novus Ordo Seclorum [translation: "A New Order of the Ages"], signify the beginning of the new American era in 1776.[121]

And yet the pyramid has a much deeper meaning that has been all but lost to America. According to Ovason and others, "the pyramid has remained something of an enigma" and has been largely "unknown because it has not been understood."[122] Perhaps Masonry sheds light on the true meaning. We have already reviewed the idea, based on Masonic theory and scholarship, that ancient rites and practices have been transmitted, or at least been reflected, by and through ancient pyramid builders and passed on to Freemasonry. In that so many Founders were Freemasons, that this symbolic motif in the seal was placed by influence of the ancient Order makes sense.

Furthermore, the only prominent structures in or near the capital that include pyramid imagery are clearly Masonic: The House of the Temple (Masonic lodge), The Alexandria Lodge and Memorial (Masonic lodge), and The Washington Monument (more on its Masonic connections later). All of these Masonic structures are capped with a pyramid, which reflects the image in the seal. By coupling the connections between the pyramid and Masonry with the connections between Masonry and true temple theology (along with LDS scholarship which presents the pyramid as an ancient form of temple worship), we have added insight. In light of how the national covenant ultimately facilitates temple blessings, perhaps the national sign of a pyramid (a temple allusion) on the seal provides yet another very powerful symbol of the American Covenant.

Supporting this idea is the truncated form the seal's pyramid takes—indeed, it is an unfinished pyramid. According to the Treasury Department, this unfinished pyramid was the designers' way to portray the message "that there was still work to be done" in America.[123] In that America and its national covenant were but a foundation for greater things to come under God, particularly those things related to the temple, the symbolism of an unfinished pyramid being watched over by the All-Seeing Eye becomes even more powerful. Furthermore, the All-Seeing Eye is actually depicted inside the capstone of the pyramid—the part that is yet to be placed onto the pyramid itself. This seems to portray that whatever finishes the pyramid (i.e. true temple worship) will be something holy and fully consummated by God the Father. The symbolic power grows further in light of what Masonic historian H. Paul Jeffers says about the All-Seeing Eye and the unfinished pyramid: "[It] conveys the immortality of the soul and that in eternity a Mason will complete the capstone of his earthly labors according to the designs of the Supreme Architect of the Universe."[124]Adding even more to the gospel-connected symbolism is the idea put forth regularly by historians that the pyramid also represents the Christian theology of the Godhead: the three points remind us that we are governed by the Father, the Son, and the Holy Ghost.[125]

The truncated pyramid takes on additional meaning upon considering that some speculative historians believe there is a connection between this modern American symbol and ancient American civilizations. The connections are based in the idea that ancient American structures also included marvelous truncated pyramid structures. And though little evidence is provided to show how these ancient American forms somehow influenced the modern American symbol, the similarities might still have profound meaning, if we believe that all truth goes back to the same divine source. These truncated pyramid forms were built anciently to supply a platform whereupon Native American temples were placed. We see this pattern in both the more prominent Mayan structures (in Mesoamerica) as well as those lesser known structures of the Mound Builders (in North America), who built truncated pyramids of earth and placed temples upon them.[126]*

Relating these structures to the seal's pyramid would be to repeat the implication stated earlier that its truncated pyramid is a symbolic proposition that a temple is the crowning experience of America—an idea consistent with the purpose of America and its covenant. As Ovason records, those writers who subscribe to this notion believe the Masonic idea that "at the completion of this Temple [the seal's pyramid], the present era will come to an end, and be succeeded by a more splendid spiritual era."[127] We have already reviewed at length how the Masons did, after all, promote as their ultimate goal to rebuild God's temple in the last days. In light of the obvious LDS/Book of Mormon connection to ancient America —and by extension its temple-pyramids—and the already established idea that ancient Egyptian pyramids were a form of temple worship, the pyramid as a gospel symbol grows further still. And when that pyramid symbol is attached to the modern Promised Land as well, whose responsibility it is to provide a base and foundation for the temple, the symbol's meaning becomes almost overwhelming.

A discussion of the symbolic power of the pyramid in America is incomplete without an analysis of the Washington Monument, whose obelisk structure is capped with perhaps the most well-known American pyramid. Though L'Enfant had chosen the sight for the monument when designing the city, the cornerstone was not laid until July 4, 1848. And the fact that this dedicatory service was wholly Masonic only emphasizes the above-mentioned temple symbolism and thus connects the monument to this theology.

---

* One fascinating piece of ancient artwork from South America is a "heavy golden plate" (the ancients *did* use golden plates!) depicting a "thirteen-stepped pyramid" (just like America's pyramid) with a face surrounded by glorious rays hovering over its top (similar to the All-Seeing Eye). Running along the base of the pyramid are symbols in the fashion of "Proto-North Semitic linear writing." See Figure 5.5 in Robert Hieronimus, *Founding Fathers, Secret Societies* (Rochester: Destiny Books, 2006), 131. The similarities between this artifact and the American seal's pyramid—not to mention the obvious connections to Book of Mormon themes—is astounding.

The Masonic grandmaster who laid the stone even used the same trowel, apron, and sash Washington used and wore in the Capitol's cornerstone ceremony in 1793. The compass and square were even included on a plaque which was affixed to the monument.[128] Interestingly, depictions of pyramid-capped obelisks, like that of the monument, are found in Masonic imagery dating back well before the construction of the monument.[129] Furthermore, the monument's original designers, which included Freemason architect Robert Mills, put forth many ideas for the monument—but the pyramid cap was included in all of them. The pyramid symbolism was clearly intentional.[130] Its symbolism should therefore be significant to us today—indeed, we should recognize that the pyramid connects to a sacred Order of the past, characterized by priesthood and temple ordinances.

But the temple themes in the monument do not stop there. For the monument also includes inscriptions of prayers for the well-being of the nation, and placed inside its cornerstone is a Bible. Furthermore, engraved upon the monument are the words so often connected to latter-day temples: "Holiness to the Lord." And upon the capstone of the Monument, facing ever-symbolically to the East, in a place where perhaps only Heaven can see, is the Latin inscription *Laus Deo*, which literally means "Praise be to God."[131] In that this inscription would be completely unseen to any mortal eye, we must recognize to whom the monument was directed and dedicated. It is an invocation of the American Covenant. Indeed, throughout the whole of the Washington Monument, symbols of the American Covenant ring loud and clear.

The more popular front side of the seal is less Masonic, yet still connects to the American Covenant in powerful ways. The prominent figure is an eagle clutching arrows in one talon and an olive branch in the other. The eagle is being defended by a shield. The American Covenant ideal of peace through strength and defense is clearly portrayed. Furthermore, above the eagle's head are thirteen stars arranged into the pattern of the Seal of Solomon, also known as the Star of David—another reminder of where the national covenant was originally derived. The eagle itself, however, has been deemed by historians an "open mystery."[132] Some propose that the seal's designer, Charles Thompson, apparently received the idea for the eagle from an earlier proposed design that included a phoenix. But where it ultimately stemmed from is unknown. In fact, it was so unknown that Benjamin Franklin questioned its relevance and use as a national symbol.[133]

As mentioned above, Thompson was a lover of morals and the Bible. He also had a profound affection and appreciation for Native Americans. He had even been adopted into a Native American tribe and given the name Wegh-wu-law-mo-end, or Man Who Tells the Truth. His connection to the Natives have left many wondering if he borrowed from them ideas for the seal. And it is here where the eagle may have its origins.[134] One group of Natives with whom Thompson reportedly associated was the Iroquois League, a confederation of five North American Indian nations. The Iroquois League broke the mold of Native Americanism by establishing peace through law set forth on principles of equality, justice, and division of power. Their politics obviously intrigued the Founding Fathers, who were working to similarly confederate the thirteen colonies. Benjamin Franklin and John Adams, among others, publically acknowledged the Iroquois as fine examples deserving of influence over the budding American republic.[135] The Iroquois were also among those groups whose religious practice had been identified with signs and symbols of the Masonic Order.[136] So impressive and influential were the Iroquois, that some believe Thompson borrowed directly from them in writing a significant portion of American policy.[137] In that the eagle is the prominent symbol of the Iroquois, perhaps Thompson borrowed that, too.

If the eagle did come from the Iroquois, it becomes more significant as a symbol of the American Covenant. For the Iroquois eagle reflects the principles found in that book of scripture which, more than any other, promotes the American Covenant—even that book of scripture written quite possibly by the very ancestors of the Iroquois. Indeed, within the context of the great symbol of the

Iroquois, the eagle finds itself in the middle of Book of Mormon ideals. Front and center in the Iroquois League's national symbol is a tree, known as the Great Tree of Peace—the ultimate Iroquois ideal. We might compare this tree to the Book of Mormon's Tree of Life, which represents the peace and salvation provided by the pure love of God (see 1 Nephi 11:25). Beneath the Iroquois tree is the symbolic placement of a weapon of war which, according to one historian, "symbolized the burial of weapons of war because hostilities between the five nations ended in their union."[138] We might compare this obvious Book of Mormon theme to the recorded actions of the people of Anti-Nephi-Lehi, who buried their weapons of war as a sign to God that they intended to keep peace at all costs (see Alma 24: 16-18).

And then the sign of the national covenant: hovering above the Iroquois tree is an eagle. As one historian of the Iroquois explains, "The eagle atop the tree symbolized watchfulness and a need to be ever vigilant and farseeing, and to stand guard to defend liberty, the peace, the union, and the constitution."[139] We might compare the eagle to the power of the national covenant promised to the peoples of the Book of Mormon—that their gospel and religion (even that most prized possession represented by the Tree of Life) would be ever-protected and ever-preserved. Beginning in October 1775, the American fleet (whose job it was to intercept British supplies coming into Boston), carried a flag with a single tree and the motto: "An Appeal to Heaven." Notwithstanding alternate explanations for it, some believe it was derived from the influence of the great Iroquois symbol. There is reason enough to theorize that Thompson did the same with the eagle and applied it to the Great Seal of the United States.[140] If he did, he was serving as a transmitter of American Covenant symbols, from the ancient covenant to the modern one. And if he did, the eagle on the seal today represents in every way the American Covenant—a defender and protector of the rights and principles that directly sustain the gospel of Jesus Christ, even a defender and protector of the Tree of Life. With this proposed concept, will we ever look at the American Eagle the same way again?

The Lord has repeatedly proven that He speaks to us through symbols. The fact that these symbols are at times veiled or indirect should not deter us from thinking they are true and of divine origin. After all, gospel symbols revealed in temple services and elsewhere make it clear that the Almighty does not always intend to make symbolic meanings obvious. And just as He speaks to us through temple symbols, perhaps He has also spoken to us through the symbols of that chosen land and country He specifically created for His purposes. Perhaps there is a powerful message He longs for us to grasp. Perhaps we should pay greater attention.

Conclusion: From Mortal Visions to Eternal Realities

Throughout this chapter we have seen how ancient visions and ancient tools of the Order assisted in the Restoration. More specifically, we have seen how ancient *temple* visions and ancient *temple* tools of the Order have assisted in the Restoration. As beneficiaries of temple blessings today, we should not fail to recognize those Founders who made the sacrifice to carry these visions and tools. They entered the national covenant; and by so doing, they provided for the Restoration in that they offered an inspired political foundation and a significant Masonic gospel assist —both of which laid a path for the restoration of temple worship. To be sure, all the Founders did under God ultimately points to the temple. This is a witness to the power and truth of the American Covenant and of those Founders who sacrificed so much working under it.

In light of how the temple has so effectively been supported by the national covenant and by the Founders of the Revolution, it is only fitting that we conclude this chapter by pondering over perhaps the most powerful connection we know of between the Founders and the temple. It is a connection based in the fact that the Lord had granted these chosen ones special access to the ultimate fruits of their labors—He had granted them access to the temple. And through reviewing this connection, we will receive yet one more witness to all of the above—one more witness to the American Covenant. The scope of this study does not permit a comprehensive review of every Founder's journey from mortal hopes and visions of the temple to eternal realities of the sacred dwelling. But we will follow the spiritual journey of one man who, more than any other, embodied the true spirit of revolutionary America and all that it meant to the gospel—George Washington.

In early December of 1799, only two years after having retired from public life, a happy and healthy Washington was fulfilling his quiet dream of farming his beloved Mount Vernon. He suddenly caught what appeared to be a common cold. Then, to the shock of his family and the entire nation, within twenty-four hours of becoming ill, he was dead. (Perhaps due to a premonition of sorts, shortly before becoming ill, Washington had given specific instructions on the construction of his tomb.) While on his deathbed, and with Martha at his side, he declared, "I die hard...But I am not afraid to go."[141] And why should he fear? This was, after all, the man who seemed to walk with God throughout his life, even stating himself that "No Man has a more perfect Reliance on the alwise, and powerful dispensations of the Supreme Being than I."[142] Furthermore, it was Washington who stated years before his death that when the "curtain of separation shall be drawing, my last breath will, I trust, expire in a prayer for the temporal and eternal felicity of those who...extended their desires to my happiness hereafter, in a *brighter world.*"[143]

Upon his death, his beloved Martha would submit, saying "Tis well, all is now over. I shall soon follow him! I have no more trials to pass through."[144] She, too, was a woman of great faith, a converted Christian well-versed in the scriptures.[145] She was always willing to suffer with the suffering and pray for their wellbeing.[146] Within two years, she would join him in death. And what a reunion it would be! Though they were a private couple, they could not hide the fact that they were "soul mates." George would often write to her during the war of his longing to be near her, even inviting her when he could, to stay with him at his ever-changing military headquarters. And she would always come. Furthermore, he loved her children (from a previous marriage), and adopted them as his own, which certainly endeared him to her all the more.[147]

The "brighter world," which Washington said he looked forward to beyond the veil, grew even brighter as he was introduced to, and accepted, the restored gospel of Jesus Christ, as administered through and by the Church of Jesus Christ of Latter-day Saints. For he was recorded as present in the spirit at the St. George Temple in August 1877, where his temple work was done at his own request. This "brighter world" was perhaps made even brighter in light of the fact that his beloved Martha was also among the choice spirits whose work was done pursuant to the miraculous visitation at St. George.

If Washington had not yet learned what his great sacrifice to God and country had meant in mortality, he most certainly did now. In mortality, he had knowingly entered the national covenant, he had walked with God on the battlefields of war, he had felt His presence, he had incessantly pleaded with the Father on behalf of the nation, and he had repeatedly called his fellow citizens and soldiers to the covenant. Moreover, he had strongly expressed his deep belief that America was part of God's divine plan and that it was meant to secure religious freedom, and he had shown a willingness to put his life on the line time and again for these principles under God. Furthermore, he was privy to the Order that provided him with sacred practices and ideals dealing with temple worship; and he had applied these ideals in his life in hopes that "the Great Architect of the Universe may bless [him] and receive [him] hereafter into his immortal Temple,"[148] and that the Father would forgive him his sins "and accept of me for the merits of Thy son Jesus Christ, that when I come into Thy temple, and compass Thy altar, my prayers may come before Thee."[149]

To be sure, regardless of what he comprehended in mortality, all of this most assuredly came together for him as he stood in God's true temple. There is no doubt that a full comprehension of what he and his colleagues had done in mortality supported his impassioned plea to the Apostle in the St. George Temple, which plea was recorded as follows by Elder Woodruff himself: "You have had the use of the Endowment House for a number of years, and yet nothing has ever been done for us. We laid the foundation of the government you now enjoy, and we never apostatized from it, but we remained true to it and were faithful to God."[150]

Washington was certainly justified in these sentiments. For without him and the work he gave himself to, there may not have been a St. George Temple in the first place. Yet, thanks to his faithfulness, there he was, making covenants that would lead him and his family to eternal life in the Celestial Kingdom of Heaven. And not only was Martha's work done at this same miraculous time, but, according to the temple records of Wilford Woodruff, the work was also performed for Washington's family, to include his father, Augustine; his mother, Mary Ball; his grandfather, Lawrence; his great-grandfather, John; his brother, Lawrence, and his wife, Anne Fairfax; several members of Martha's family; and Washington's beloved step-children and step-grandchildren.[151]

With this restored gospel perspective pertaining to the death and after-life of Washington, perhaps there is something very inspired about certain events and reactions surrounding his passing into immortality—particularly as these events and reactions pertain to the temple. For example, just before his burial, a ceremonial apron was placed upon his body along with a sprig from an acacia tree, which is a symbol of the resurrection.[152] Also symbolic of Washington's temple experience is the famous monument which bears his name. Indeed, in light of the above, the powerful temple themes that are so pervasive throughout the monument should be powerful reminders of what Washington and his cause under the covenant were really all about. We might also reconsider the aforementioned grand sculpture in the Smithsonian entitled, *George Washington* (1840), which depicts the president returning power to the people (giving up his sword), with a robe draped over his right shoulder and his arm raised to the square. The covenant connections to both Columbus and to Native Americans make their artistic presence in this sculpture all the more profound.[153]

But perhaps the most astonishing restored gospel allusion related to Washington is gloriously painted onto the ceiling of the grand rotunda of the U.S. Capitol Building. The work is called *The Apotheosis of Washington.* It is a 4,664 square foot fresco that consumes the entirety of the rotunda's massive canopy. The outlaying areas of the fresco are adorned with several scenes reminiscent of the American Covenant. For example, one scene depicts a mythological-type figure that, with raised sword, is destroying other figures representing "tyranny and kingly power." Watching over the victorious freedom fighter is a fierce bald eagle—even that powerful symbol of the covenant—carrying thunderbolts and arrows. The covenant blessings of *liberty* and *protection* are easily seen within this scene. Other scenes show heavenly messengers (represented by goddesses) providing wisdom to great Americans like Benjamin Franklin, teaching and showing them how to progress in science, commerce, and agriculture. The covenant blessings of *prosperity* are clearly depicted.[154]

Reaffirming the covenant-based symbolism of this work is the fact that other powerful pieces of art depicting great American Covenant moments are also displayed within the grand rotunda. These include the oil-on-canvas paintings entitled *Landing of Columbus, Embarkation of the Pilgrims,* and *Baptism of Pocahontas* (whose symbolic connections to the American Covenant are described in Chapter 4). Other paintings in this chain of art enveloping the Rotunda's interior include depictions of subsequent moments—some of the most powerful moments—of American Covenant history. There is *Discovery of the Mississippi,* reminding us of the prominent place this river would play in the Restoration as a principle mode of transportation for the gathering of Zion at Nauvoo. Also present are paintings depicting two of the greatest victories of the Revolutionary War, which, as detailed previously, were won by miracles under the American Covenant: *Surrender of*

General Burgoyne (at Saratoga) and *Surrender of Lord Cornwallis* (at Yorktown). We see depicted another powerful sign of the covenant in the painting *General Washington Resigning His Commission*. And finally, we see the famous painting of the famous signers in *Declaration of Independence*. It is nothing short of Nephi's vision of Ephraim and latter-day America, as recorded in 1 Nephi 13, dramatically played out around the interior of the Capitol's rotunda.

These giant works seem to support the symbolic power presented by *The Apotheosis of Washington*, not only due to the related and powerful themes carried in all the artistic wonders, but also due to the paintings' position relative to the larger and more prominent work emblazoned upon the canopy. Indeed, the paintings sit upon the base of the rotunda walls, seemingly in support of the canopy on which we see *The Apotheosis of Washington*.

But these symbolisms do not even scratch the surface of the power behind *The Apotheosis of Washington*. For the real power of this work is seen portrayed in a scene placed climactically at the middle of the masterpiece: a depiction of George Washington himself, dressed in white robes, ascending on a cloud to heaven with the covenant symbol of a rainbow arch at his feet. Flanking Washington are the goddess Victory and the goddess Liberty, and surrounding him are thirteen maidens, representing the colonies.[155] The principal word in the artwork's title, *apotheosis*, literally means "elevation to the status of a god."[156] It comes from the ancient Greek: *apo*—"to become," and *theos*—"God." To be sure, the scene is nothing less than a depiction of Washington receiving his exaltation—becoming like his Heavenly Father.

The symbolism of it all is almost overwhelming to those with a testimony of the restored gospel. Throughout this book, we have documented how Washington was responsible for laying a foundation which would allow for the existence of temples on the earth. And we know that these temples exist so that mankind might access what is needed to gain exaltation with the Father—even to become like God. And so to stand in the most prominent place of the U.S. Capitol Building and take in what clearly depicts Washington—

even he who helped make possible our access to exaltation—attaining his own exaltation is simply breathtaking. Then, to see this imagery of Washington supported by so many additional artistic allusions of American Covenant principles, we are presented with the whole picture. We see a full depiction of how America and her covenant truly serve to elevate man to his highest potential—even eternal life and exaltation. Seen in this light, the U.S. Capitol Building truly becomes a temple—perhaps the most important temple—of the American Covenant.

As we consider the artwork in the Capitol Building and the miraculous events that occurred to Washington and his family in the St. George Temple, we can appreciate the full account of this most prominent American Covenant-maker. As a leader of a nation, he made a covenant to bring about *liberty, protection,* and *prosperity.* As a patriarch of a family, and with the support of this national covenant, he made another, more powerful, covenant to bring about exaltation. George Washington's life is the anecdote that fully tells the story of the American Covenant.

ENDNOTES

[1] Matthew B. Brown, *Exploring the Connection Between Mormons and Masons* (American Fork: Covenant Communications, 2009), 13-14.

[2] "Secrets of the Masons," *US News and World Report: Mysteries of History: Secret Societies*, Collectors Edition, (2008), 32.

[3] E. Cecil McGavin, *Mormonism and Masonry* (Salt Lake: Bookcraft, 1956), 60.

[4] Michael Baignet and Richard Leigh, *The Temple and the Lodge* (New York: Arcade Publishing, 1989), 127.

[5] Brown, *Exploring the Connection Between Mormons and Masons*, 12-18, 44, 49-51, 55-56; Christopher Knight and Robert Lomas, *The Hiram Key: Pharaohs, Freemasons and the Discovery of the Secret Scrolls of Jesus* (New York: Barnes and Noble Books, 1996), 1-18; Michael Baignet and Richard Leigh, *The Temple and the Lodge* (New York: Arcade Publishing, 1989), 127; David Ovason, *The Secret Architecture of Our Nation's Capital* (New York: HarperCollins, 2000), 235.

[6] Christopher Knight and Robert Lomas, *The Hiram Key: Pharaohs, Freemasons and the Discovery of the Secret Scrolls of Jesus* (New York: Barnes and Noble Books, 1998), 4-5.

[7] Gerald Hansen Jr., *Sacred Walls: Learning From Temple Symbols* (American Fork: Covenant Communications, 2009), 75-81.

[8] H. Paul Jeffers, *The Freemasons in America* (New York: Citadel Press, 2006), 88; see also http://www.ldschurchnews.com/articles/54236/Another-angel.html.
[9] Daniel H. Ludlow, ed, *Encyclopedia of Mormonism* (New York: Macmillan, 1992), 2:528.

[10] Brown, *Exploring the Connection Between Mormons and Masons*, 167, 180-1.

[11] From the First Presidency, issued at General Conference on April 9, 1911, as referenced in Gilbert Scharffs, *Mormons and Mason* (Orem: Millennial Press, 2006), 34.

[12] McGavin, *Mormonism and Masonry*, 49-53.

[13] Knight and Lomas, *The Hiram Key,* chapters 6-8.

[14] W. Kirk MacNulty, *Freemasonry: A Journey Through Ritual and Symbol* (New York: Thames and Hudson, 1991), 67; David Ovason, *The Secret Architecture of our Nation's Capital* (New York: HarperCollins, 2000), 231, 235.

[15] Hugh Nibley, "The Meaning of the Temple," *Temple and Cosmos* (Salt Lake: Deseret Book, 1992), 26-7.

[16] Daniel H. Ludlow, ed, *Encyclopedia of Mormonism* (New York: Macmillan, 1992), 1:37; see also Matthew Brown, *Exploring the Connection Between Mormons and Masons,* 160; BYU Professor Andrew Skinner points out LDS temple theology reflected in ancient panel art found in an ancient Egyptian temple. Professor Skinner's analysis is found in Andrew Skinner, *Temple Worship* (Salt Lake: Deseret Book, 2007), 63-65.

[17] Daniel H. Ludlow, ed, *Encyclopedia of Mormonism* (New York: Macmillan, 1992), 2:528.

[18] Hugh Nibley, "The Expanding Gospel," *Temple and Cosmos* (Salt Lake: Deseret Book, 1992),179-182.

[19] Christopher Knight and Robert Lomas, *The Hiram Key*, 96, 122.

[20] Christopher Knight and Robert Lomas, *The Hiram Key*, 167-169; see also McGavin, *Mormonism and Masonry,* pp. 38-39.

[21] Baignet and Leigh, *The Temple and the Lodge*, 124-127.

[22] Heber C. Kimball, as quoted by Brown, *Exploring the Connection Between Mormons and Masons*, 153.
[23] Brown, *Exploring the Connection Between Mormons and Masons,* 130.

[24] McGavin, *Mormonism and Masonry*, 53.

[25] Knight and Lomas, *The Hiram Key*, 42, 67-70, 74-75.

[26] See Bart D. Ehrman, *Lost Christianities* (New York: Oxford University Press, 2003), 126; and Bart D. Ehrman, *Lost Scripture* (New York: Oxford University Press, 2003), 38

[27] As quoted by Tad Callister, *The Inevitable Apostasy* (Salt Lake City: Deseret Book, 2006), 250; (see also pages 248-251).

[28] Hugh Nibley, "The Meaning of the Temple," *Temple and Cosmos*, 28.

[29] See Dan Burstein, ed., *Secrets of the Code* (New York: CDS Books, 2004), 13, 68-69; see also the Nag Hammadi book called Gospel of Truth, as described in Andrew Skinner, *Temple Worship* (Salt Lake: Deseret Book, 2007), 63; see also the course guidebook to Bart Ehrman, *Lost Christianities: Christian Scriptures and the Battle over Authentication* (Chantilly: The Teaching Company, 2002), 25.

[30] Brown, *Exploring the Connection Between Mormons and Masons*, 26.

[31] Brown, *Exploring the Connection Between Mormons and Masons,* 42-46, 49-52, 56.

[32] Knight and Lomas, *The Hiram Key*, see Chapters 4-5 and Chapter 12.

[33] Michael Haag, *The Templars* (New York: Harper , 2009), 97-102.

[34] Knight and Lomas, *The Hiram Key*, Chapter 3.

[35] See http://www.robertlomas.com/Freemason/Freemason.html; For details about the excavation, see Christopher Knight and Robert Lomas, *The Second Messiah* (UK: Century Books Limited, 1997).

[36] Knight and Lomas, *The Hiram Key*, 267-269.

[37] Knight and Lomas, *The Hiram Key*, 58, 191, 196-7, 220, 252.

[38] Donald Parry, "The Dead Sea Scrolls Bible: Puzzles, Mysteries and Enigmas" *BYU College of Humanities Alumni Magazine,* Spring 2009, 9-11.

[39] See Andrew Skinner, "The Dead Sea Scrolls and Latter-day Truth," *Ensign*, February 2006, 44-49.

[40] Donald Parry, "The Dead Sea Scrolls Bible: Puzzles, Mysteries and Enigmas," 10 .

[41] Haag, *The Templars*, 217-238.

[42] Knight and Lomas, *The Hiram Key*, 326-328

[43] Knight and Lomas, *The Hiram Key*, 297-299.

[44] Knight and Lomas, *The Hiram Key*, 295-301.

[45] Brown, *Exploring the Connection Between Mormons and Masons*, 30.

[46] Haag, *The Templars*, 325.

[47] Knight and Lomas, *The Hiram Key*, 313.

[48] Knight and Lomas, *The Hiram Key*, 305, 178 (see photographs following this page); see also http://www.robertlomas.com/Freemason/Freemason.html.

[49] Knight and Lomas, *The Hiram Key*, 34; Michael Haag, *The Templars, The History and the Myth* (New York: Harper, 2009), 101.

[50] Baignet and Leigh, *The Temple and the Lodge*, 126-127.

[51] Knight and Lomas, *The Hiram Key*, 10-11.

[52] McGavin, *Mormonism and Masonry,* 197-8.

[53] Knight and Lomas, *The Hiram Key*, 200-201; Ovason, *The Secret Architecture of Our Nation's Capital*, 235; Baigent and Leigh, *The Temple and the Lodge*, 127.

[54] Ridley, *The Freemasons*, 33.

[55] Knight and Lomas, *The Hiram Key*, 328.

[56] Knight and Lomas, *The Hiram Key: Pharaohs, Freemasons and the Discovery of the Secret Scrolls of Jesus*, 4-5.

[57] Brown, *Exploring the Connection Between Mormons and Masons,*87.

[58] Brown, *Exploring the Connection Between Mormons and Masons,* Chapter 5.

[59] Brown, *Exploring the Connection Between Mormons and Masons,* 93.

[60] Brown, *Exploring the Connection Between Mormons and Masons,* 74-77.

[61] Brown, *Exploring the Connection Between Mormons and Masons,* 107-112.

[62] Richard Bushman, *Joseph Smith, Rough Stone Rolling* (New York: Alfred A. Knopf, 2005), 450 .

[63] McGavin, *Mormonism and Masonry,* 90.

[64] McGavin, *Mormonism and Masonry,* 184.

[65] Gilbert W. Scharffs, *Mormons and Masons* (Orem: Millennial Press, 2006), 23.

[66] Bushman, *Joseph Smith, Rough Stone Rolling*, 450.

[67] Gilbert W. Scharffs, *Mormons and Masons* (Orem: Millennial Press, 2006), 23-24.

[68] *Old Testament Student Manuel : 1 Kings-Malachi*, second edition (Salt Lake City: The Church of Jesus Christ of Latter-day Saints, 1982), 279.

[69] *Old Testament Student Manuel : 1 Kings-Malachi*, second edition (Salt Lake City: The Church of Jesus Christ of Latter-day Saints, 1982), 284-287.

[70] *Old Testament Student Manuel : 1 Kings-Malachi*, second edition (Salt Lake City: The Church of Jesus Christ of Latter-day Saints, 1982), 285-287.

[71] Peter R. Davies, George J. Brooke and Phillip R. Callaway, *The Complete World of the Dead Sea Scrolls* (New York: Thames and Hudson, 2002), 129, 156-7, 165.

[72] Knight and Lomas, *The Hiram Key*, 200-201; Ovason, *The Secret Architecture of Our Nation's Capital*, 235; Baigent and Leigh, *The Temple and the Lodge*, 127.

[73] Knight and Lomas, *Hiram Key*, 180.

[74] That Joseph used the King James Version of the Bible to derive the new inspired form of it is discussed in Richard Bushman, *Joseph Smith, Rough Stone Rolling* (New York: Alfred A. Knopf, 2005), 132.

[75] John Gee, *A Guide to the Joseph Smith Papyri* (Provo: BYU/FARMS, 2000), 1-4.

[76] Brown, *Exploring the Connection Between Mormons and Masons,* 132.

[77] Baigent and Leigh, *The Temple and the Lodge*, 202-203; Brown, *Exploring the Connection Between Mormons and Masons,* 12-13; H Paul Jeffers, *The Freemasons in America* (New York: Citadel Press Books, 2006), 43.

[78] Baigent and Leigh, *The Temple and the Lodge*, 202.

[79] Franklin, as quoted by Jeffers, *The Freemasons in America,* 25.

[80] Jeffers, *The Freemasons in America*, 21.

[81] Robert Hieronimus, *Founding Fathers, Secret Societies*, 42.

[82] Jeffers, *The Freemasons in America*, 21; Baigent and Leigh, *The Temple and the Lodge,* 225, 227.

[83] Jeffers, *The Freemasons in America*, 24.

[84] Baigent and Leigh, *The Temple and the Lodge,* 252.

[85] Baigent and Leigh, *The Temple and the Lodge,* 261.

[86] Jeffers, *The Freemasons in America*, 30-33.

[87] Jasper Ridley, *The Freemasons, A History of the World's Most Powerful Secret Society* (New York: Arcade Publishing, 2001), 108-9; Jeffers, 30.

[88] Baigent and Leigh, *The Temple and the Lodge,* 201.

[89] Jeffers, *The Freemasons in America*, xiii.

[90] Jeffers, *The Freemasons in America*, Chapter 7.

[91] Refer to 1 Nephi 13, D&C 101:80, and other references throughout this book.

[92] Jeffers, *The Freemasons in America*, 35.

[93] Brigham Young, quoted in McGavin, *Mormonism and Masonry*, 149; also in *Journal of Discourses* 2:31.

[94] Jeffers, *The Freemasons in America*, xiii.

[95] Novak, *Washington's God*, 115.

[96] Washington (January 1792), as quoted in Waldman, 62.

[97] Connell, 34-35.

[98] Knight and Lomas, *The Hiram Key*, 75-77.

[99] Knight and Lomas, *The Hiram Key*, 76.

[100] Knight and Lomas, *The Hiram Key*, 74-76.

[101] See Steven Sora, *The Lost Colony of the Templars* (Rochester: Destiny Books, 2004), special consideration should be given to Chapter 4, particularly pp. 136-142; see also Tim Wallace and Marilyn Hopkins, *Templars in America* (Boston: Weiser Books, 2004).

[102] Knight and Lomas, *The Hiram Key*, 76-79.

[103] Knight and Lomas, *The Hiram Key*, 288-289; Wallace and Hopkins, *Templars in America*, 125-135.

[104] Wallace and Hopkins, *Templars in America*, Chapters 10-11.

[105] Sora, *The Lost Colony of the Templars*, 169-171; Wallace and Hopkins, *Templars in America*, 141.

[106] Michael Baigent, Leigh and Lincoln, *Holy Blood, Holy Grail* (New York: Bantam Dell, 2004), 78; Sora, *The Lost Colony of the Templars*, Chapter 6.

[107] Hugh Nibley, *Temple and Cosmos* (Salt Lake City: Deseret Book Company, 1992), 31.

[108] Columbus, as quoted by Jacob Wasserman, *Columbus, Don Quixote of the Seas,* translated by Delno C. West, and August Kling (Gainesville, FL: 1991); and as quoted in Greene, *The Tribe of Ephraim*, 117.

[109] Ibid, 113; See Chapter 3 of this book.

[110] See Boyd K Packer, *The Holy Temple* (Salt Lake: Bookcraft, 1981), 38-41.

[111]David Shugarts, *Secrets of the Widow's Son* (New York: Sterling Publishing, *2005),* 112-113.

[112] David Ovason, *The Secret Architecture of our Nation's Capital* (New York: HarperCollins, 2000), 253.

[113] Ovason, 72-74.

[114] Jeffers, 88; see also http://www.ldschurchnews.com/articles/54236/Another-angel.html.

[115] McGavin, *Mormonism and Masonry*, 160, 174; Robert Hieronimus, *Founding Fathers, Secret Societies*, 29.

[116] McGavin, *Mormonism and Masonry*, 77; see Timothy Jenkins, *The Ten Tribes of Israel* (1883) (Colfax: Hay River Press, 2005), produced by the Ancient American Archeological Foundation.

[117] McGavin, *Mormonism and Masonry*, 71-72.

[118] McGavin, *Mormonism and Masonry*, 182.

[119] Michael Haag, *The Templars, The History and the Myth* (New York: Harper, 2009), 275-276.

[120] Robert Hieronimus, *Founding Fathers, Secret Societies*, 91.

[121] Michael Haag, *The Templars, The History and the Myth*, 276.

[122] Ovason, 220, 225-226.

[123] Jeffers, 103.

[124] Jeffers, 101.

[125] Ovason, 226.

[126] http://en.wikipedia.org/wiki/List_of_Mesoamerican_pyramids; http://en.wikipedia.org/wiki/Pyramid; http://en.wikipedia.org/wiki/Mound_builder_(people).

[127] Ovason, 235.

[128] Jeffers, 35; David A Shugarts, *Secrets of the Widow's Son* (New York: Sterling, 2005), 134-136.

[129] W Kirk MacNulty, *Freemasonry: A Journey Through Ritual and Symbol*, 67.

[130] Ovason, 125-129.

[131] Newt Gingrich, *Rediscovering God in America* (Nashville: Integrity House, 2006), 38.

[132] Ovason, 218.

[133] Ovason, 218-221.

[134] Hieronimus, 91-92.

[135] Hieronimus, 11-20.

[136] McGavin,159-160.

[137] Hieronimus, 91.

[138] Hieronimus, 9.

[139] Hieronimus, 9-10.

[140] Hieronimus, 9-10.

[141] Washington, as quoted by Novak, *Washington's God*, 207.

[142] Novak, *Washington's God*, 61.

[143] Novak, *Washington's God*, 190.

[144] Martha Washington, as quoted in Novak, *Washington's God,* 208-209.

[145] Meacham, 13.

[146] Marshall and Manuel, 404.

[147] Novak, *Washington's God,* 26.

[148] Washington (January 1792), as quoted in Waldman, 62.

[149] Connell, 34-35.

[150] *Journal of Discourses,* 19:229, September 16, 1877.

[151] Vicki-Jo Anderson, *The Other Eminent Men of Wilford Woodruff* (Cottonwood: Zichron Historical Institute, 1994), preface and pp. 411-413.

[152] Shugarts, 194.

[153] Refer to Chapter 8 for a full description of this sculpture.

[154] The facts, descriptions and interpretations of *The Apotheosis of Washington*, as described in this book, can be verified at the following government official website: www.aoc.gov/cc/art/rotunda/apotheosis; also available at http://en.wikipedia.org/wiki/The_Apotheosis_of_Washington.

[155] Ibid

[156] Waldman, 56.

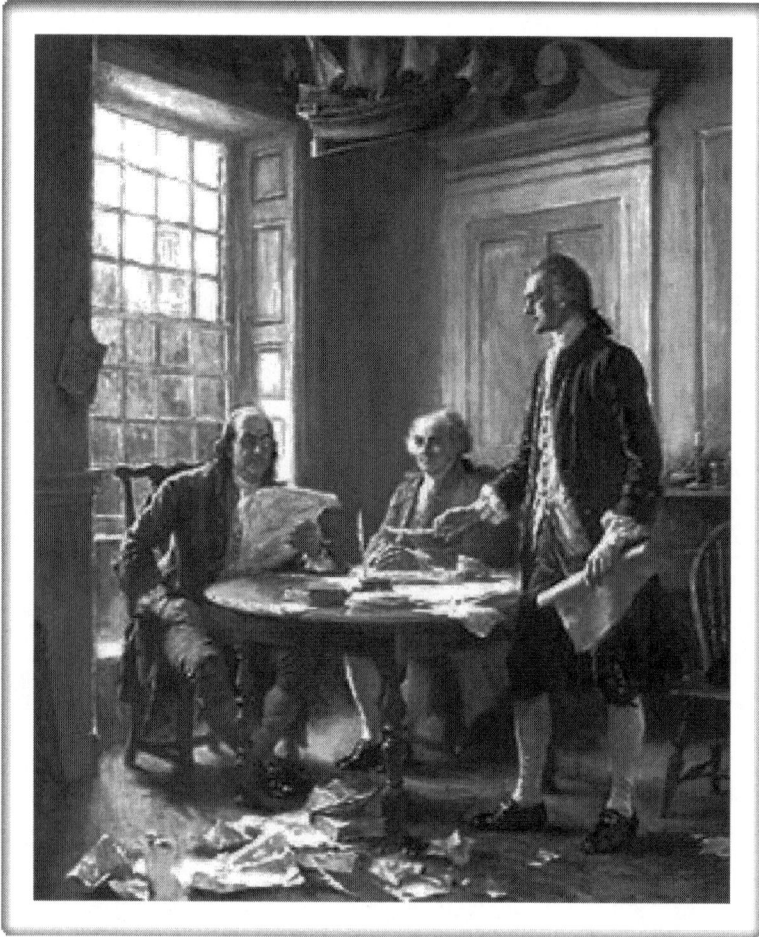

Writing the Declaration of Independence, by Jean Leon Gerome.
(Franklin, Adams, Jefferson)
Courtesy of The Library of Congress.

CHAPTER 10

THE DECLARATION OF INDEPENDENCE AS COVENANT

[Independence Day] ought to be commemorated as the Day of Deliverance by solemn acts of devotion to God Almighty.

—John Adams

And for the support of this Declaration, with a firm reliance on the protection of Divine Providence, we mutually pledge to each other our Lives, our Fortunes and our sacred Honor.

—Thomas Jefferson

In the previous chapters, we have corroborated our claims regarding the American Covenant and validated the scriptures which support this covenant, by showing how God truly intervened in the American Revolution both spiritually and physically. If we are to believe that God was the source of inspiration and power behind the Revolution, then should we not expect to discover His hand in the supporting documents of this movement? Furthermore, if the

Founding Fathers were types and shadows of prophets, should we not expect them to have left us with types and shadows of scripture? We can answer affirmatively to both these questions and point to the Declaration of Independence to support this affirmation. The Declaration is a gift and covenant of God, a true representation of the American Covenant. In proving that the Declaration is part and parcel of the American Covenant, we will find yet another witness that the ancient prophecies of this covenant have been fulfilled, thus proving the reality of this covenant and the truthfulness of its divine purpose.

National Scripture

 A principal reason for connecting the Declaration to the national covenant is that the document itself, like most scripture as we know it, reads like a covenant with God. It recognizes the fight for American independence as the work of God. It also recognizes that America's success hangs on its citizens' willingness to obey God. It is no wonder that Samuel Adams, upon signing the document, declared, "We have this day restored the Sovereign to whom men alone ought to be obedient. He reigns in heaven...from the rising to the setting of the sun, His kingdom come."[1] Whether he understood it or not, Adams' statement would prove prophetic, as the Declaration did, in many ways, usher in God's kingdom, even His restored gospel. And Sam Adams knew he was not alone in implying that the Declaration was scripture-like. Referring to the Declaration, Adams pronounced, "The people...recognize the resolution as though it were a decree promulgated from heaven."[2]

That the Declaration is tightly connected to God and covenant is evidenced by the fact that God is referenced in the Declaration at least four times and given the titles of *Lawgiver, Creator, Judge,* and *Providence.* The historian and author, Michael Novak, placed these references together, along with their accompanying text within the Declaration, to show how this language reads like a covenant-based prayer.

Creator, who has endowed in us our inalienable rights, Maker of nature and nature's laws, undeceivable Judge of the rectitude of our intentions, we place our firm reliance upon the protection of divine Providence, which you have extended over our nation from its beginning.[3]

Furthermore, a careful read of the Declaration plainly reveals that, throughout its entirety, it is an invocation of the very blessings of the American Covenant—the blessings of *liberty, protection,* and *prosperity.* The document clearly states America's intention to "secure" for America the "inalienable rights" of "Life, Liberty, and the Pursuit of Happiness," thus invoking the blessings of *liberty.* The document further states America's intention to create and maintain "Safety and Happiness," thus invoking the blessings of *protection.* It also puts forth an economic plan, which includes the power to independently regulate its own trade, its own taxes, and its own geographic expansion of its territories, thus invoking the blessings of *prosperity.* Furthermore, these blessings are recognized as being accessible to America only through "a firm reliance on the protection of Divine Providence." The Declaration is a true reflection of the American Covenant as put forth by the Old Testament prophecies of Jacob to Joseph and by the Book of Mormon prophecies foretold by Lehi and the Nephites.[4] To be sure, the Declaration is a direct fulfillment of these prophecies. And, again, these blessings of the American Covenant, if received and applied, have the ultimate effect of developing and protecting God's gift of agency to man—a gift that is necessary for man's eternal progression.

Such a perspective is backed by one of our most inspired presidents, John Quincy Adams, who—as the child of one of our greatest revolutionaries—was a first hand witness of the American Revolution. Asked Adams, "Is it not that the Declaration of Independence first organized the social compact on the foundation of the Redeemer's mission upon the earth? That it laid the cornerstone of human government upon the first precepts of

Christianity?"[5] Not only does Adams recognize the covenant (or "compact") nature of the document, but clearly connects its purposes to those of the true gospel of Christ. (It is worth noting that John Quincy Adams was one of the chosen spirits who, along with his family, was given the special opportunity in the St. George Temple to receive his Priesthood covenants.)[6]

Another allusion to the Declaration's connections to God and the national covenant is witnessed—yet too often overlooked—by thousands of visitors and tourists of the United States National Archives in Washington D.C., which houses and displays the original Declaration. Upon entering the building, all one has to do is look on the floor to see an impressive bronze engraving of the Ten Commandments—the most famous example of God's covenant with a nation.[7] It is not a coincidence that such a display welcomes visitors as a preface to the Declaration of Independence.

Further proof of the Founders' intention and inspiration to create the Declaration as a covenant, with blessings contingent upon national worthiness, can be found though analyzing the historical background and context in which the Declaration was written and issued. Shortly after the Declaration was signed, America experienced severe hardships, including Washington's defeat at New York and the poor harvest of that year. Though the Declaration had clearly recognized God's supremacy and indispensable role in America, this was evidently not enough to invoke the full blessings of Heaven. Perhaps America's obligation in this covenant with the Almighty needed to be better understood and applied. The Declaration, which was directed at Britain, would require an appendage of sorts, directed at America alone, that its citizens might better adhere to their covenant. It was in this spirit that the Congress, just months after signing the Declaration, issued a national decree for a Day of Fasting and Repentance to take place on December 11, 1776. This document stated the following:

> WHERAS, the war in which the United States is engaged
> with Great Britain, has not only been prolonged, but is

likely to be carried to the greatest extremity; and whereas, it becomes all public bodies, as well as private persons, to reverence the Providence of God, and look up to him as the supreme disposer of all events, and the arbiter of the fate of nations; therefore,

RESOLVED, that it be recommended to all the United States, as soon as possible, to appoint a day of solemn fasting and humiliation; to implore of Almighty God the forgiveness of the many sins prevailing among all ranks, and to beg the countenance as assistance of his Providence in the prosecution of the present just and necessary war.

The Congress do also, in the most earnest manner, recommend to all the members of the United States, and particularly the officers civil and military under them, the exercise of repentance and reformation; and further require of them the strict observance of the articles of war, and particularly, that part of the said articles, which forbids profane swearing, and all immorality, of which all such officers are desired to take notice.[8]

This congressional action truly validates and embodies the American Covenant, even to the extent that it reflects certain truths touching the covenant language of restored scripture: "Inasmuch as they shall keep my commandments they shall prosper in the land" (2 Nephi 4:4; Alma 50:20); for "I, the Lord, am bound when ye do what I say; but when ye do not what I say, ye have no promise" (D&C 82:10). The fact that this document was issued by the same group of statesmen who had only recently issued the Declaration—and inasmuch as they issued it in support of that same cause of independence—it is difficult not to see how it functioned as an appendage to the Declaration. Like the Declaration itself, it was a powerful invocation of the national covenant. (And let us not forget the many other like-minded invocations of the covenant given by Congress throughout the conflict, as explained in earlier chapters.) Fortunately, in the end, America adhered to this covenant and thus received those blessings required for victory—and required for the establishment of a national foundation in support of God's latter-day work and glory.

In sum, the Declaration was issued in God's name; it specifically spelled out the covenant blessings; it was tightly connected to the Founders' understanding of a covenant with God; and finally, through faithfulness to this document, and through general obedience to God, these covenant blessings of the Declaration were received in preparation for the Restoration. All of this leaves us with a powerful witness. It is a witness that the Declaration was, in fact, part and parcel of the American Covenant. Add to that witness the many spiritual manifestations accompanying the revolutionaries, along with the many battlefield miracles that supported the cause of independence, and the Declaration's place as national scripture and covenant becomes overwhelmingly secure.

A Miraculous Confirmation

The scriptures teach us that from time to time the Lord offers His children signs from Heaven in order to convey messages to them. Sometimes the purpose of such a message is to convey disappointment and to inspire change. Such was the case with the Nephites, for example, who suffered through droughts, earthquakes, wars, and other tragedies, so that they might remember the Lord. Other times the purpose of such a message is to convey approval or to confirm a promise or covenant. Such was the case with the sign of a rainbow given to the Prophet Noah as a confirmation of a covenant with God. Such was the case with signs given to ancient America, including the star in the sky and a night without darkness, to confirm the advent of Christ.

In the previous chapters, we have seen many examples of such miraculous messages given to America. These included miracles performed on the battlefields of war, which are proof of God's covenant with America and His desire to make this covenant known. However, there is one sign having to do with America's covenant that has not yet been mentioned. This particular sign from God is a miraculous event that places a seal of approval on the American revolutionary cause and confirms the Declaration of Independence as a covenant with the Almighty. And, as the Declaration is but an appendage of the American Covenant, this final miracle of the Revolution only confirms once again the validity of the American Covenant itself. However, in order to fully comprehend this sign from Heaven dealing with the divinity of the Declaration, we must first understand something about the two most important actors in the creation of the Declaration. Fittingly, they are the same principal actors involved in the miracle. They are John Adams and Thomas Jefferson. And so, before providing the details of this miracle, we will first briefly discuss these two men and their connection with the Declaration, God, and the American Covenant.

John Adams: The Voice of Independence

John Adams was born into a good, religious, middle-class family in Massachusetts. Adams had toyed with the idea of following the example of his father and joining the clergy, but instead became a successful attorney in and around Boston. Adams was married to his best friend, Abigail, and found himself, throughout his twenties and thirties, practicing law, farming his land, raising his children, and getting involved in local politics. In 1774, on the eve of turning forty, Adams was elected by his countrymen to represent them in Philadelphia at the Continental Congress, which had been designed as a national venue to discuss, among other things, the emerging conflict with Britain.

Though Adams had arrived at Philadelphia as unassuming and as normal as any of the other delegates, he found himself rising to his feet and taking the floor of the congressional convention so powerfully and so often that he soon made a name for himself. His speeches in favor of independence from Britain would be recognized as some of the most persuasive and powerful in the history of Congress. They were even described as being spiritually moving.[9]* Adams was also responsible for influencing Congress to appoint Washington as Commander-in-Chief. When considering the divine and critical nature of Washington's role in the Revolution, such a call by Adams was not only inspirational, but perhaps prophetic. After nominating Washington, Adams predicted that the "appointment will have great effect in cementing and securing the union of these colonies." He further prophesied that Washington would become "one of the most important characters in the world."[10] So trusted and respected was Adams among his fellow delegates, that he was repeatedly chosen to sit on the most important committees. He was, according to David McCullough, "the leading committeeman of the Massachusetts delegation, perhaps indeed of the whole Congress."[11] "It was John Adams," according to McCullough, "more than anyone, who had made [independence] happen."[12] He would appropriately become known as the *Voice of Independence*.

In light of his influence in the spiritually charged cause of American independence, we can assume that much of what Adams accomplished was inspired by the Spirit and that he was a direct instrument in the hands of God. His personal religion—he was a devout Christian—makes such a claim easy to accept. Adams' regular scripture study, church attendance, and regular observance of the Sabbath (including a reluctance to travel on Sunday),[13] are evidence of his spiritual character. He said of Christianity that it is "the brightest of the glory and the express portrait of the character of

---

* According to one anecdotal account of events surrounding the signing of the Declaration of Independence, a mysterious man's voice was heard by several of the delegates above all the vitriolic debate of the Convention. The voice declared loudly, "God has given America to be free!" Unable to identify the source of the voice from within Independence Hall, several took it as a heavenly sign to forget themselves and finish the work of the Convention. While some LDS speculators attribute the incident to one of the Three Nephites, others believe that the voice heard was but a legendary interpretation of one of those famous and spiritually moving speeches by John Adams. Refer to Robert Hieronimus, *Founding Fathers, Secret Societies* (Rochester: Destiny Books, 1989), 135; Michael J. Hunter, *Mormon Myth-ellaneous* (American Fork: Covenant Communications, 2008), 98-99.

the eternal, self-existent, independent, benevolent, all powerful, and all merciful creator, preserver, and father of the universe." Adams' personal religion was made complete by his dear companion, Abigail. He remembered the testimony she bore to him on the day they met: "Men and woman are here to serve God and humanity. We are made in the image of God, and must fulfill our promise or we are a blasphemy to God. An hour wasted is an hour's sin." Declared Adams, "She makes me so happy...her Christian beliefs make her ever a joy to know."[14]

There are also other indications that Adams was a chosen disciple with a deeper than normal sense of gospel truth. For example, he recognized that he lived during a time of religious apostasy. When in Philadelphia, he was known for attending as many different churches and church services as possible, presumably to seek out further gospel light. He was often disappointed at what he found. For example, he expressed sadness at the churches' over-emphasis in their art of the agony of his Savior on the cross.[15] Furthermore, the popular post-apostolic, false doctrine that it is by grace *alone* that man is saved, regardless of his works in this life, was, according to Adams, "detestable" and "hurtful." He further expressed disdain for the similarly false doctrine that mankind is inherently punished for Adams' transgressions.[16]

Another doctrinal problem which Joseph Smith and the Restoration would have solved for Adams (but at the time locked him in a state of disappointment and frustration) was the popular theological proposition that if one does not accept Christ in mortality, even if not given the opportunity, then he or she is consigned to hell for eternity. In a letter to Jefferson, Adams explained that nine-tenths of the world had not heard of Christ and would, according to that doctrine, thus suffer forever. Adams rhetorically asked why God would permit "innumerable millions to make them miserable forever." He explained that the only answer to that question given him by the churches was "For his Own Glory," which for Adams was an unacceptable and sickening explanation.

"Is he vain?," asked Adams, "Tickled with Adulation? Exulting and triumphing in his Power and Sweetness of his Vengeance? Pardon me, my Maker, for these Aweful Questions. My Answer to them is always ready: I believe no such Things."[17]

Adams' insight into gospel truth is also reflected in a declaration he made, which echoes revelations found in Doctrine and Covenants, Section 122. Commenting on the difficult trials that lay ahead for America and her revolution, Adams asserted the following:

> It may be the will of heaven that America shall suffer calamities still more wasting and distresses yet more dreadful. If this is to be the case, it will have this good effect, at least: it will inspire us with many virtues which we have not, and correct many errors, follies and vices, which threaten to disturb, dishonor and destroy us....The furnace of affliction produces refinements in states, as well as individuals.[18]*

Though his spiritual sensitivity brought him personal revelation, Adams did, in fact, live in the era of gospel apostasy. All he could do was the best he could with what he had. Lacking the fullness of the gospel, he shunned the many denominational nuances and returned to the basics. He wrote to Jefferson: "The Ten Commandments and The Sermon on the Mount contain my Religion."[19] Until he was given more, that would have to suffice.

And so we see that Adams had incredible spiritual insight into gospel truths and into the world's misinterpretation of these truths. This insight certainly reflects his inspired nature—an attribute that God would utilize for His purposes. Adams understood that these divine purposes revolved around achieving

---

* "....if the very jaws of hell shall gape open the mouth wide after thee, know thou, my son, that all these things shall give thee experience, and shall be for thy good" (D&C 122:7).

liberty under God for the United States of America. Whether or not he comprehended that his success in this cause would eventually pave the way for his most pressing religious frustrations to be solved—as his political achievements provided the foundation whereupon God could send His Restoration—it is impossible to know. However, we might conclude that he knew at least something of the divine purposes underlying the American cause. He himself declared, "It is the will of heaven that the two countries [America and Great Britain] should be sundered forever."[20] Adding to his testimony that God was in the Revolution, Adams declared his belief that it was God that placed him at the forefront of the American cause. "By a train of Circumstances, which I could neither foresee nor prevent," declared Adams in October 1775, "I have been called by Providence to take a larger share in active Life, during the Course of these struggles, than is agreeable either to my Health, my Fortune or my Inclination."[21]

So strongly did he feel about his calling having come from God that, as President of the United States, he prayed for a similar mantle to fall upon his successors. Etched into the fireplace mantle of the State Dining Room in the White House is his prayer, which reads: "I pray to heaven to bestow the best of blessings on this house [referring to the White House] and all that hereafter inhabit it. May none but the honest and wise men ever rule under this roof."[22]

Furthermore, he seemed to understand what his and his successors' role in achieving an independent and secure America, under God, was ultimately all about: religious freedom. Years before the Revolution, Adams seemed to see such purposes behind his country, when he declared the following in an article on political philosophy: "Let the pulpit resound with the doctrine and sentiments of religious liberty...Let us see delineated before us the map of man. Let us hear the dignity of his nature, and the noble rank he holds among the works of God, and that God Almighty has promulgated from heaven, liberty, peace and good-will to man!"[23]

Whether or not Adams was implying or prophesying at this early date that America should or would be the guardian of religious freedom, he seemed sure about it in his twilight years. In 1815, Adams expressed to a friend in a private letter that religious freedom contributed "as much as any other cause" to the fight for independence. He even recognized this sentiment as having "aroused the attention...of the common people."[24] This was, of course, a very visionary, and thus risky, proposition (and perhaps explains why he only expressed it in a private letter); for, as discussed in previous chapters, religious freedom did not even make it on the long list of official reasons to go to war with Britain.[25] But Adams had been at the center of the storm, and by 1815 (some thirty years after the Revolution), when he made this statement, he had had plenty of time to ponder the Revolution's more eternal purposes. Adams was ultimately correct about what the Revolution was all about. For religious freedom was exactly what God intended to extract from the Revolution. Indeed, the Almighty knew that this would become the issue of greatest importance once the Restoration commenced. Adams' prescient insight on the matter seems to manifest his truly inspired soul.

It might even be argued that Adams' foresight went even deeper. Perhaps he knew something of the forthcoming gospel restoration; and perhaps this knowledge was reflected in his personally expressed belief that the very settlement of America represented "the opening of a grand Scene and Design of Providence, for the illumination of the ignorant...."[26] Adding to this sentiment, Adams declared, in the middle of the devastations of the Revolutionary War, that "through all the gloom I can see the rays of ravishing light and glory. I can see the end is worth more than all the means."[27] Perhaps he spoke prophetically.

Whatever Adams understood by his vision of "the opening of a Grand Scene of Providence" or by the "rays of ravishing light and glory," is ultimately speculative. What is sure, however, is that Adams had a clear insight into the existence and power of the American Covenant. He believed, as implied in the previous chapters, that the American revolutionary movement was one that was to be supported by a covenant with God. In support of the many aforementioned national decrees, proclamations, circulars, etc., which invoked and re-invoked the American Covenant, Adams was always among those at the forefront to promote them. It was not uncommon for Adams to make comments like the following, which he made at the commencement of the war: "Millions will be upon their knees at once before their Great Creator, imploring His forgiveness and blessing; his smiles on American Councils and Arms."[28] In an even more direct commentary concerning the American Covenant, Adams had this to say about the success of the Revolution: "I have seen all my life such selfishness and littleness even in New England. I sometimes tremble to think that, although we are engaged in the best cause that ever employed the human heart, yet the prospect of success is doubtful not for want of power or wisdom but of virtue." Adams further believed, as discussed above, that any defeat upon the Americans might be God's way to cleanse the nation of its "vicious and luxurious and effeminate appetites, passions and habits." He ultimately believed, as he declared to a friend, that the American colonists would only be victorious "if we fear God and repent our sins."[29]

Adams' wife and most trusted advisor, Abigail, served to support and augment her husband's belief in the American Covenant. Even during the earliest days of conflict, Abigail wrote to her husband:

> I feel no anxiety at the large armament designed against us. The remarkable interpositions of heaven in our favor cannot be too gratefully acknowledged. He who fed the Israelites in the wilderness, who clothes the lilies of the field and who feeds the young ravens when they cry, will not forsake a people engaged in so righteous a cause, *if we remember His loving kindness.*[30]

Adams' feelings toward the Declaration of Independence, which he had been so instrumental in developing, also reflect his belief that that document was—like the Revolution itself—deeply attached to God and His purposes. So powerful was this connection for Adams that he even suggested, almost immediately after the Declaration had been passed in Congress, that Independence Day "will be celebrated by succeeding generations as the great anniversary festival." He then instructed those succeeding generations that "[i]t ought to be commemorated as the Day of Deliverance by solemn acts of devotion to God Almighty."[31]* Adams' suggestion that Independence Day should be celebrated in reverence to God convinces us further that he understood that America and her blessings of liberty were given by a national covenant and required national observance.

His love and passion for the independence of mankind was also reflected in his deep hatred of slavery, which he called "an evil of colossal magnitude."[32] Though he would not see the eradication of this evil in his lifetime, he would help set his nation on the right path towards the acceptance and application of greater liberties— liberties which would one day reach the most oppressed people in America. As will be discussed in Volume II, without the complete eradication of slavery, the American Covenant would never be able to fill the measure of its creation. Perhaps Adams understood this.

Upon analyzing Adams, there is little question as to his inspired role in founding America and establishing the American Covenant. He did this most powerfully through creating and carrying out the Declaration of Independence for the purposes of God. We have seen evidence of his inspired calling in our analysis above. We have outlined his religious nature, his almost innate ability to discern gospel truths while living during the apostasy, his recognition that the cause of America was the cause of God, and his clear understanding that America's national covenant with the Almighty would bring both victory and the promise of greater

---

* In this same statement, Adams suggested that these solemn acts of devotion to God should include "Pomp and Parade, with Shows, Games, Sports, Guns, Bells, Bonfires and Illuminations from one End of the Continent to the other from this Time forward forever more." See Joseph Ellis, *First Family* (New York: Alfred A. Knopf, 2010), 53. As we celebrate the Fourth of July today in the fashion Adams so presciently foresaw, let us heed his counsel to direct these celebratory activities to God Almighty.

blessings to come. And finally, we have witnessed his ability to take all of the above and masterfully apply it to the fight for independence, thus becoming one of the most important revolutionaries in American history. Why would this man, who was as closely involved in the making of the Declaration as any other, say and do the things he did unless he understood that this document represented a calling, a mission, even a covenant from God? Though Adams would go on to serve as ambassador to France and Britain, as well as the first vice president and the second president of the United States, his role as the *Voice of Independence* would continue to represent his most lasting contribution to America and her national covenant with the Almighty. For it was Adams, more than all the others, who influenced the decision to declare independence;[33] and this independence, once achieved, led to the liberties responsible for supporting the Restoration. Adams once stated that "I must study politics and war that my sons may have liberty to study mathematics and philosophy."[34] He might have just as well added that he studied politics and war that the Prophet Joseph might have the liberty to bring forth God's gospel. The idea, after all, is the same. Adams and his colleagues had indeed laid the groundwork of liberty upon which the gospel might flourish.

Thomas Jefferson: The Pen of Independence

One of Adams' most important colleagues in the cause of America, and in the creation of the Declaration of Independence, was Thomas Jefferson. Early in his career, before entering politics, the highly educated Jefferson spent his time in Virginia as a planter, lawyer, husband, and father. As a member of the Virginia House of Burgesses, still in his early thirties, Jefferson was dispatched to represent his state at the Continental Congress. There, he was befriended by John Adams. It was Adams' influential voice that proposed that the young Jefferson, known for his eloquence in writing, be tasked with composing the Declaration. This proposal was backed by a congressional mandate that Adams and Benjamin

Franklin form a committee to help Jefferson in drafting the document.[35] If Adams was the "Voice" of independence, then Jefferson was the "Pen."

With such an important role in this American cause under God, we might assume that, like Adams, Jefferson also shared a connection with God as he worked under divine influence. Though this certainly was the case, Jefferson was much more private when it came to his personal religion. It is a fact that Jefferson called himself "a real Christian...a disciple of the doctrines of Jesus;"[36] and that he testified that "[t]here is only one God, and He is perfect, and to love God with all thy heart and thy neighbor as yourself is the sum of religion."[37] However, Jefferson also made it clear that his personal religion should not be speculated upon, for "it is known to my God and myself, alone."[38]

Many secularists point to Jefferson's criticism of religion as proof that he was no believer. However, serious study of the matter reveals that Jefferson's apparent criticisms of religion were more a reflection of his recognition of the religious apostasy under which he lived than anything else. Like Adams, he had serious misgivings about the direction of religious thought in America. And as the restored gospel informs us, he was ultimately right most of the time. Therefore, his criticism of religion should not be seen as anti-religious, but instead should be seen as inspired. For example, Jefferson's recognition of the apostasy was absolute and unequivocal: "But a short time elapsed after the death of the great reformer of the Jewish religion," stated Jefferson, "before his principles were departed from by those who professed to be his special servants, and perverted into an engine for enslaving mankind, and aggrandizing their oppressors in church and state." Jefferson specifically pointed out the Council of Nicaea as having been especially damaging. The council members' attempt to define God was, according to Jefferson, a "mere Abracadabra of the mountebanks calling themselves the priests of Jesus."[39]

His disdain did not end with Catholic doctrines, but was also directed at the falsehoods invented and spread by subsequent

Christian-based religious movements. Like Adams, Jefferson hated the idea that man is saved by grace alone and that his works before God mean nothing. The man who invented such a doctrine, according to Jefferson, "was indeed an atheist... [who] worshiped a false God."[40]

Jefferson, one of the greatest scientific minds in his day, even weighed in on a religious debate raging today: evolution verses intelligent design. Balancing both the spiritual and scientific, Jefferson landed squarely on the side of intelligent design, giving credit for creation to "an eternal pre-existence of a creator, rather than in that of a self-existent Universe."[41]

With so much religious falseness pervading his world, however, Jefferson did not know exactly where to draw the line between fact and fiction. This confusion, understandably, caused him to question certain miracles wrought, as reported in the New Testament. He would ask himself, *Had the churches invented those too?* But in the end, his "clear love of Jesus,"[42] along with his inspired insights into the earth's state of religious apostasy, combine as powerful evidence that Jefferson was an inspired man.

Further proof of the inspiration that flowed through Jefferson was the fact that he believed—notwithstanding the state of religious apostasy in which he lived—that God would shortly bring forth a restoration of truth. Stated Jefferson:

> The religion-builders have so distorted and deformed the doctrines of Jesus, so muffled them in mysticisms, fancies and falsehoods, have caricatured them into forms so monstrous and inconceivable as to shock reasonable thinkers....Happy in the prospect of *a restoration of primitive Christianity*, I must leave to younger athletes to encounter and lop off the false branches which have been engrafted into it by mythologists of the middle and modern ages.[43]

On another occasion, Jefferson implied his desire for a restoration of the gospel when making the following observation: "Had the doctrines of Jesus been preached always as pure as they came from his lips, the whole civilized world would now have been Christian."[44]

Jefferson's vision of the Restoration was so sure in his own mind that, on yet another occasion, he confirmed it once again, stating: "The genuine and simple religion of Jesus will one day be restored; such as it was preached and practiced by Himself. Very soon after His death it became muffled up in mysteries, and has been ever since kept in concealment from the vulgar eye."[45] Jefferson further explained:

> I hold the precepts of Jesus, as delivered by himself, to be the most pure, benevolent, and sublime which have ever been preached to man. I adhere to the principles of the first age; and consider all subsequent innovations as corruptions of this religion, having no foundation in what came from him...*if the freedom of religion, guaranteed to us by law in theory, can ever rise in practice* under the overbearing inquisition of public opinion, *truth will prevail* over fanaticism, and the genuine doctrines of Jesus, so long perverted by his pseudo-priests, *will again be restored to their original purity*. This reformation will advance with the other improvements of the human mind, but too late for me to witness.[46]

Coincidentally (or not!), Jefferson wrote these words in 1820 —the same year that the Father and the Son appeared to the Prophet Joseph to commence that very restoration of gospel truth.[47] Equally amazing are the allusions to the American Covenant found within these words. For Jefferson clearly recognizes that Christ's gospel would "again be restored to [its] original purity" once the then relatively new law of "freedom of religion" (i.e. the Constitution) advanced from "theory" and "r[o]se in practice." Per the stipulations of the American Covenant, Jefferson felt that the Restoration was contingent on the success of America's divinely inspired governmental foundations. It is also noteworthy that these words reflect Jefferson's prophetic insight that, though this gospel restoration was on the horizon, it would come "too late for [him] to witness." Jefferson passed away some four years before the Church of Jesus Christ of Latter-day Saints was officially organized.

It seems Jefferson knew that his role in establishing the laws of America would set the stage for the gospel restoration, which he sought. Not only did he clearly state, as just quoted, that American law would usher in such a religious restoration, but it was he who, more than anybody, promoted the divine principles behind this inspired law. Indeed, he promoted the very political foundations that the Lord required for His Restoration, namely civil and religious freedom. So powerful were his inclinations toward such moral agency, that he openly rebuked himself as a slaveholder and declared, in his famous *Notes on the State of Virginia*, that slavery is "the most unremitting despotism on the one part, and degrading submissions on the other."[48] In reference to the slaves, Jefferson concluded, "Nothing is more certainly written in the book of fate than that these people are to be free."[49] As early as 1769, Jefferson even supported a Virginia bill to emancipate slavery.[50]

His belief in moral agency is further reflected in his authorship of the Virginia Statute for Religious Freedom. It was this law that paved the way for a righteous division between church and state. This division inspiringly barred the government from oppressing or otherwise interfering with man's right to worship God. One of the greatest lines Jefferson wrote into the statute was, "Truth is great and will prevail if left to herself."[51] This Statute, written in the midst of the Revolutionary War, shows how Jefferson, like Adams, was inspired and visionary in his belief that America's goal should be the protection and preservation of religious freedom. As pointed out in previous chapters, this was not seen as a major issue in revolutionary America.[52] In fact, America was not yet ripe for such truth to take hold, as evidenced by the fact that Jefferson's statute was initially shelved by the state legislature and not revisited until well after the war, when the country began catching up to Jefferson's vision. Only then would another inspired founder, James Madison, resurrect it and see it passed.[53] Jefferson's forward-looking and inspired vision of America surely emphasizes his spiritually connected nature. When his statute was finally implemented, it not only affected Virginia law, but also influenced the Constitution of the United States.

Even at the end of his life, Jefferson possessed the inspired and correct understanding about what America was ultimately all about. Weeks before his death, Jefferson had been asked to draft a message to be read at the Fourth of July festivities for the celebration at the nation's capital. Jefferson wrote of the importance to use the Fourth of July celebration to "forever refresh our recollection of these rights, and an undiminished devotion to them." One scholar asked rhetorically, "What rights was he referring to? The pursuit of happiness? No taxation without representation? In these weeks before his death, those were not the rights Jefferson was thinking of most." What he had on his mind was religious freedom![54] Again, the Declaration never specifically addresses religious freedom, as religious freedom was not initially given by the colonists as a primary reason for revolution. However, this is what it was ultimately designed, by God, to provide. This is what the inspired and forward-looking Jefferson saw as the take-home message of the Fourth of July : "the free right to the unbounded exercise of reason and freedom of opinion."[55]

So important was moral agency to Jefferson that he would go to his grave believing that his contributions to such liberty summed up his most important work. Of his countless accomplishments and titles achieved in mortality, he ordered that only three be mentioned on his tombstone: his authorship of the Declaration of Independence, his authorship of the Virginia Statute for Religious Freedom, and his founding of the University of Virginia.[56] As explained above, the first two on the list were directly connected with the development of moral agency. The third, his founding of the university, is also connected to liberty. As Jefferson stated: "If a nation expects to be ignorant and free…it expects what never was and never will be."[57] It is no coincidence that Jefferson's self-decided greatest accomplishments were in line with God's preparatory work to usher in the restoration of His gospel.

Beyond possessing a life-long, deep understanding of the importance of moral agency in America, Jefferson seemed to also comprehend that gifts such as liberty and agency were connected to God and covenant. When entering the Jefferson Memorial in Washington D.C., one gets this sense upon reading his words engraved upon the memorial's panels: "Almighty God hath created the mind free...All attempts to influence it by temporal punishments or burthens...are a departure from the plan of the Holy Author of our religion...all men shall be free to profess and by argument to maintain, their opinions in matters of religion."[58] Engraved upon an adjacent panel are these similarly relevant words from Jefferson: "God who gave us life gave us liberty. Can the liberties of a nation be secure when we have removed a conviction that these liberties are the gift of God?"[59]

Also engraved within the memorial are Jefferson's words from the Declaration of Independence, complete with his reference to God as the Creator who endowed us with the inalienable rights of liberty. We would do well to further consider the deep roots connecting the Declaration, not only to the blessings of *liberty*, but also to those other American Covenant blessings of *protection* and *prosperity*. As explained above, the Declaration recognizes all three covenant blessings as being "supported" and "protected" by "Divine Providence." In light of the fact that Jefferson was the principal author of the Declaration, his role as American Covenant-maker becomes all the more convincing.

That Jefferson believed in the American Covenant is evidenced by more than the mere implications he made, as cited above, that since these blessings come from God we are obliged to Him for them. To be sure, he laid out America's covenant relationship with God in even clearer terms. In his first inaugural address, Jefferson reminded his fellow-Americans that we should be "acknowledging and adoring an overruling Providence, which by all its dispensations proves that it delights in the happiness of man here and his greater happiness in the hereafter."[60] He would again invoke the American Covenant when later telling the nation that America's peace and prosperity should be credited to the "smiles of Providence."[61] His belief that America was under covenant is further supported by his warning that if America does not work towards national worthiness, to include efforts toward repenting of its sin of slavery, then God would punish them. "For God is just," declared Jefferson, while commenting on the wickedness of slavery, "and his justice cannot sleep forever."[62]

Jefferson drew the connection between his nation and God's covenant even closer by alluding to the idea (detailed in Part I of this book), that the ancient national covenants with Israel, to include *prosperity* under God, were connected to those covenants of latter-day America. During his second inaugural address, he declared, "I shall need, too, the favor of that Being in whose hands we are, who led our forefathers, as Israel of old, from their native land and planted them in a country flowing with all the necessaries and comforts of life."[63] Promoting a similar message, Jefferson proposed that the official seal of the United States include a depiction of the "Children of Israel in the wilderness led by a cloud by day and a pillar by night."[64]

Jefferson's sentiments on the relationship between Israel's covenant and the American Covenant take on an even fuller meaning upon considering the fact that he, as president of the United States, purchased for America—from France—the vast western territories stretching from the Mississippi River to the Rocky Mountains. Known as the Louisiana Purchase, this single inspired move brought certain sacred lands, connected with modern Israel, squarely under the protection of God's America and thus squarely under the protection of the American Covenant. These lands include Jackson County, Missouri, which is the site of the New Jerusalem and the Center of Zion. They also include the true location of the Garden of Eden and Adam-ondi-Ahman, where a great council of prophets will one day occur. Just as God brought sacred lands to ancient Israel by a national covenant, so He did it once again, this time for modern Israel under the American Covenant—and all for the same gospel purpose. The significance of these lands for God's kingdom on the earth is immeasurable, and so their placement by Jefferson within the nation God created under the covenants of Israel is truly inspired.

Furthermore, and in connection with the Louisiana Purchase, Jefferson commissioned the famous Lewis and Clark Expedition, which explored the lands recently purchased and also the territories further west. This move proved to be inspired, as the maps and reports that came out of this expedition were utilized by Joseph Smith and Brigham Young in planning and prophesying over the Church's western settlements.[65] Additionally, the exploration and development of these new territories would one day add great economic *prosperity* to the nation, thus further fulfilling promises of the American Covenant. Considering all these blessings flowing from the Louisiana Purchase, it is only natural to recognize the inspired nature of Jefferson, even he who the Lord utilized to make the acquisition, exploration, and development of these lands possible.

Finally, in one of Jefferson's most powerful quotes, which is memorialized in a unique position within the Jefferson Memorial—it spreads elegantly around the interior of the dome—Jefferson again alludes to the national covenant. He does so by offering the covenant imagery of "the altar of God" as it relates to the sacrifice required for America's true eternal purposes. His immortalized words are as follows: "I have sworn upon the altar of God, eternal hostility against every form of tyranny over the mind of man."[66] With his covenant imagery, Jefferson sums up the American Covenant; for he explains in powerful simplicity that there are evil forces that would thwart our moral agency (forces that began their quest in the pre-mortal existence, as the gospel informs us). But Jefferson also suggests here that God has offered us a covenant that we make upon His altar, to ensure through our actions, and His blessings, that moral agency—even that most precious pre-requisite for exaltation—be secured on this earth. Jefferson was certainly an inspired man whose knowledge, foresight, and wisdom in the Lord ran deep.

Upon analyzing Jefferson's life, we have proven his inspired nature by pointing out his spiritual roots firmly attached to Christ, his divine insights into the religious apostasy pervading his world, and his testimony that a gospel restoration was forthcoming. Most importantly, we have seen how, through this inspiration, Jefferson invoked America's national covenant with God by seeking out those most important national covenant blessings of *liberty, protection,* and *prosperity*. There is no doubt that Jefferson, like Adams, was a true American Covenant-maker who laid the foundation for gospel restoration. Also like Adams, Jefferson's career was long and distinguished. In addition to being a famous architect, scientist, and inventor, Jefferson served as a state legislator, governor of Virginia, ambassador to France, first secretary of state of the United States, second vice president of the United States, and third president of the United States. However— and again, just like Adams—none of these high positions overshadow his singular role as the author of the Declaration of Independence. He would fight tooth and nail for the rest of his life in defense of those Godly principles of liberty unto salvation, as laid out in the Declaration. His role as the *Pen of Independence* contributed as much or more to the American Covenant and to the purposes of God than any of his other vast accomplishments.

The Confirming Miracle

Through reviewing the inspired lives and accomplishments of the two most prominent actors in the birth of the Declaration of Independence, we are now prepared to delve into the details surrounding the miraculous event which confirms and seals the Declaration (and by extension, the American Covenant) as a true covenant from God. For we have established not only that Adams and Jefferson were the force behind the Declaration, but also that they were perhaps more connected to gospel truth and the national covenant than any of their colleagues (Washington excepted). With this understanding, we can see the significance in God's decision to make them the principal players in this miracle; and we can see how, with them as the principal players, the Lord has blessed this miracle, and the eternal purposes this miracle represents, with powerful credibility.

The scene of this historic miracle opens at the sunset of Adams' and Jefferson's lives. These two old and fading revolutionaries had been through much together. As the best of friends, they had served together during the Revolution (first in Congress, then on the committee to draft the Declaration of Independence, and then as ambassadors to France). However, upon returning home to an independent United States, they became the bitterest of enemies, disagreeing over the direction the new country should take. Their personal conflict culminated when they confronted each other in one of the most vitriolic, hate-filled, and mud-slinging presidential elections in U.S. history. As political enemies, their close connection had been severed. Indeed, they would refuse to even speak to each other for years. Both men, and their families, were heartbroken at this prospect, for they had been, at one time, so very close. For example, when Jefferson had joined Adams as a fellow diplomat in France, the Adams family had invited Jefferson to live with them in their home. Adams, at one point, even conceded to Jefferson that Adams' son—John Quincy —"was as much your son as mine."[67] When the Adamses departed France to work in London, Jefferson confessed that he was "in the dumps" and that "my afternoons hang heavily on me." Then, after Adams fulfilled his diplomatic mission and returned home (leaving Jefferson in Europe), Jefferson declared that, without Adams on his side of the Atlantic, "I now feel widowed."[68] Such bonds, when severely broken years later, had produced deep sorrow indeed.

But now, as old and weary men, their differences did not seem so important. After what seemed like a lifetime of silence between them, the two fading revolutionaries began to rekindle their old friendship through a series of letters—Adams writing from his home and farm outside of Boston and Jefferson from his Virginia estate, Monticello. These two men had outlived almost every other Founding Father of the revolutionary era. Now, all they had was each other, and so they reminisced about the glory days, about politics, and about those sacred things most important to them.

One of these most sacred subjects they discussed was prompted by the death of Adams' best friend and truest confidante —his wife, Abigail. Adams' love and devotion to his wife, and their bond together (which endured so much, with Adams being absent from her for a total of ten years during the revolutionary period) has become legendary. Abigail was everything to Adams, as documented by the many letters he wrote to her in his absence. She was his truest love, his truest political ally, and his truest friend.[69] Adams once referred to their fifty-four years of marriage as a "love feast."[70] And she clearly felt the same way towards him. "When he is wounded, I bleed," she once told a friend.[71] Understandably, the old man Adams was inconsolable upon the death of his life-long partner. After leaving her deathbed in tears, he exclaimed, "I wish I could lie down beside her and die too."[72]

Jefferson, seeing an opportunity to express his feelings about eternal things, reminded Adams that hope was not lost and that God certainly had an eternal plan which would one day banish the pain forever. Jefferson, too, had lost his dear wife, Martha. And as an expression of hope in dealing with that death, Jefferson had the following epitaph engraved upon his wife's tombstone: "In the melancholy shades below, The flames of friends and lovers cease to glow, Yet mine shall sacred last; mine undecayed. Burn on through death and animate my shade."[73]

In an effort to transfer such hope to Adams and to reassure his old friend—and perhaps himself—that a glorious reunion with their wives was not far away, he wrote the following in one of those legendary communications:

> The public papers, my dear friend, announce the fatal event of which your letter of October 20 had given me ominous foreboding. Tried myself, in the school of affliction, by the loss of every form of connection which can rive the human heart, I know well, and feel what you have lost, what you have suffered, are suffering, and have yet to endure....altho' mingling sincerely my tears with yours, will I say a word more, where words are vain, but that it is of some comfort to us both that the term is not very distant at which we are to deposit, in the same cerement, our sorrow and suffering bodies, and to ascend in essence to an ecstatic meeting with the friends we have loved and lost and whom we shall still love and never lose again. God bless you and support you under your heavy affliction.[74]

"I have always loved Thomas Jefferson,"[75] the elderly Adams would say of his old friend. No doubt this letter improved upon his sentiments.

Adams returned his own feelings and thoughts of that glorious eternity, which was rapidly approaching. His mind still upon his recently deceased Abigail, Adams wrote the following to Jefferson:

> I know not how to prove, physically, that we shall know each other in a future state; nor does revelation as I can find give any positive assurance of such felicity [remember, Adams lived during a gospel apostasy, where the lack of scripture or lack of correct scriptural interpretation, blocked much gospel light]. My reasons for believing it, as I do most undoubtedly, are that I cannot conceive such a being as the human, merely to live

and die on this earth. If I did not believe in a future state,
I should believe in no God...And, if there be a future
state, why should the Almighty dissolve forever the
tender ties which unite us so delightfully in this
world....[76]

All this talk of life after death certainly had these two old
revolutionaries thinking about the eternities. One year before his
death, Jefferson, in a seemingly reflective moment, wrote about
how mortality is a proving ground for greater things to come and
how we, as mortals, can and should prepare. Advising the son of
a friend, the weary Jefferson counseled: "Adore God. Reverence
and cherish your parents. Love your neighbor as yourself, and
your country more than yourself. Be just. Be true. Murmur not at
the ways of Providence. So shall the life into which you have
entered, be the portal to one of the eternal and ineffable bliss."[77]
Jefferson's own portal to the eternal bliss was opening up, even
as he wrote these words.

Then came the miracle: John Adams and Thomas Jefferson,
virtually the last of the prominent surviving signers of the
Declaration of Independence, died. Why was this so miraculous?
Because their deaths—which occurred for reasons unrelated to
each other, and which took effect at their respective homes some
five states away from each other—happened on the same day,
within hours of each other. What makes this event particularly
miraculous was the date—July 4, 1826: the fiftieth anniversary of
the Declaration of Independence. Two revolutionaries dying on
the same day might be a curiosity. But two revolutionaries who
were so connected with God and His national covenant, and two
revolutionaries who were the most prominent in achieving
independence—even the "Voice" and "Pen" of the Declaration of
Independence—dying on the same day, of unrelated causes, is
more than that; indeed, it is more than mere coincidence. And
finally, that this all happened on the fiftieth anniversary of the

Declaration of Independence only seals the entire event as a singular act of God, to seal and symbolize their joint sacrifice in His work.*

It was a sign to the world that the American Covenant, embodied in so many ways by the Declaration itself, was true, living, and divinely administered. This was a covenant sign, as real as Noah's rainbow or as the Nephites' days without night. And though the Adams-Jefferson miracle has sadly become all but lost to current generations of Americans, it was fully comprehended by those early Americans who experienced it.

Adams' son, John Quincy, wrote in his diary that the miraculous nature of Adams' and Jefferson's twin deaths was a "visible and palpable mark ...of Divine favor, for which I would humble myself in grateful and silent adoration before the Ruler of the Universe."[78] Not insignificantly, John Quincy Adams was the president of the United States when the miracle occurred, thus making his sentiments even more profound, as he was (by position) a living head of the American Covenant. Another leading

---

* There is additional reason to believe that this Adams-Jefferson experience was an intentional sign from Heaven, and it has to do with events surrounding their reunification. The person responsible for bringing them back together in their old age was the prominent revolutionary, Benjamin Rush (who was also a participant in the St. George Temple miracle). Rush was a dear friend to both Adams and Jefferson. He approached Adams in 1809 (when Adams and Jefferson were still not speaking to each other) and told him about a dream he had recently had. In the dream, Rush was blessed to see a history book of the future. The history book he read told of the tumultuous relationship between Adams and Jefferson. But it also told of a great reconciliation between the two. It told of a series of letters they wrote to each other at the end of their lives. In the letters, they discussed (in the words of the dream's history book), "many precious aphorisms [truths], the result of observation, experience, and profound reflection." According to the book, "It is to be hoped the world will be favored with the sight of [the letters]." The book then stated: "These gentlemen sunk into the grave nearly at the same time, full of years and rich in the gratitude and praises of their country." Rush's dream prompted Adams to extend the olive branch to Jefferson through the first of many letters. But nobody could have predicted that what would follow would directly fulfill Rush's dream. It was inspired. It was prophetic. See David Barton, *Benjamin Rush, Signer of the Declaration of Independence* (Aledo: WallBuilders, 1999), 198-200; Joseph Ellis, *Founding Brothers* (New York: Alfred Knopff, 2001), 220.

statesman of the day was Daniel Webster, who, while eulogizing Adams weeks after his death, echoed John Quincy, declaring the Adams-Jefferson miracle to be "proof" from the Almighty "that our country, and its benefactors, are objects of His care."[79]

The passing of Adams and Jefferson, in and of itself, was a deeply significant sign from Heaven. Yet this miracle becomes even more profound as we follow these two revolutionaries beyond the veil. In doing so, we witness what they and their fellow patriots had lived for; we come to better understand what the Declaration of Independence and the American Covenant really meant.

The death scene at the Adams home in Quincy, Massachusetts, was recalled by several eyewitnesses. Days before Adams' death, he was asked what message he might have to be read as a toast for Quincy's upcoming Fourth of July celebration. "I will give you," replied Adams, "Independence forever."[80] Then, on the day of his death, even in the final moments leading up to his death, a semi-conscious Adams shifted in his sleep and, in a voice strong enough for several witnesses present to understand, said, "Thomas Jefferson survives."[81] Adams then passed away; the time was approximately six-twenty in the evening. A few hours earlier, at approximately one o'clock in the afternoon, Thomas Jefferson had passed away at his Monticello estate.[82] There is only speculation as to why Adams would utter these words in reference to Jefferson as his dying refrain. However, as is the case with our assumptions surrounding the meaning of Brigham Young's dying words of "Joseph! Joseph! Joseph!,"* it is reasonable to conclude that Adams, in his final moment, saw the spirit of his old friend Jefferson, who—having only just passed away himself—had come to accompany Adams home. Daniel Webster might have approved

---

* Brigham Young's dying words were "Joseph! Joseph! Joseph!" Zina Young, Brigham's daughter, witnessed the event and stated that her father's final words, together with "the divine look in his face seemed to indicate that he was communicating with his beloved friend, Joseph Smith, the Prophet." This statement from Zina Young is quoted in *Church History in the Fulness of Times* (Salt Lake City: The Church of Jesus Christ of Latter-day Saints, 2000), 419.

of such an interpretation, for he declared that "on our fiftieth anniversary...while their own names were on all tongues, [Jefferson and Adams] took their flight together to the world of spirits."[83] John Quincy added that while "the mortal vestments" of his father and Jefferson were "sinking into the clod of the valley, their emancipated spirits were ascending to the bosom of their God!"[84]

In the moments leading up to this joyous spiritual reunion, a strange yet fitting weather pattern occurred. Hours before Adams' final departure, a violent thunderstorm struck—"The Artilleries of Heaven," as some later called it.[85] Then, almost at the moment of Adams' death, as witnesses recalled, there was a final crashing thunder, which seemed to stop the storm. The rain ceased and the sun, which had just begun to set, broke through. John Marston, who was an eyewitness of the event, explained that the sunlight began "bursting forth...with uncommon splendor at the moment of his exit...with a sky as beautiful and grand beyond description."[86]

At that splendid moment, we might imagine Adams and Jefferson passing together into the Spirit World. And as we picture them entering the spiritual realm, we might consider again how these two kindred spirits had made it clear in mortality that they had sought gospel truth throughout their lives. We might further ponder the fact that the most important gospel truth they hoped for (as indicated in their final correspondence to each other) was an eternal reunion with their respective wives. Their testimonies of these things in mortality make what followed for them all the sweeter. For, we know today that Adams and Jefferson found and accepted the true gospel of Jesus Christ in the Spirit World. Indeed, John Adams and Thomas Jefferson were recorded as present in the spirit during the miracle that occurred at the St. George Temple. Their temple work was done. But a fuller blessing of the Restoration would also be theirs. For the work on behalf of their respective wives—Abigail Adams and Martha Jefferson—was also performed at the same time, all pursuant to the grand vision received by Wilford Woodruff. They all received their Priesthood covenants at the hands of a true apostle of God.[87]

This leads us to the powerful and vital point: Adams, Jefferson, and all their colleagues did what they did in life so that a foundation might exist whereby they, along with all mankind, might participate in just such an event of eternal magnitude. In the pages above, we have detailed how it was under God and covenant that these two Founding Fathers laid such a foundation for the gospel. The increase of religious freedom in America that they initiated with their Declaration of Independence, and later with the Constitution, had prepared the way so that God might call a prophet to restore the keys of the priesthood. Those keys would facilitate temple ordinances unto eternal life. This religious freedom would likewise provide the necessary tools to protect the administration of these temple ordinances. What is more, this restoration of gospel blessings would include the recommencement of the work for the dead, thus making eternal life available to Adams, Jefferson, and all of God's children in the Spirit World—all of His children from all dispensations of time. Because of what these revolutionaries and founders did in mortality, they were able to stand where they were in immortality. And because of what they did in mortality, the rest of us can stand in such temples as well. Under the American Covenant, they had established the foundation that would allow everyone access to eternal life through the restored gospel of Jesus Christ.

At the time of their miraculous deaths, this gospel had already taken root. In fact, in the very year that Adams and Jefferson passed away, the Angel Moroni was in the middle of his yearly visits to the Prophet Joseph on the Hill Cumorah, preparing him to bring forth the Book of Mormon. Instead of focusing his efforts on the Founders (as he had, for example, reportedly done in the camps of Washington), Moroni was now tutoring the next generation—the generation of the prophets. The Founding Fathers' mission was complete, and they were at last given leave to return to the Father. The deaths of these last remaining Founding Fathers seem to represent a sort of symbolic passing of the torch. The next generation and their divine mission regarding the Restoration could now be played out. The era for the fullness of the gospel had at last come forth! From the time of the Adams-Jefferson deaths, it would only be a matter of a few short years before the principles and ordinances of the gospel would be fully restored.

Before their deaths, Jefferson had written to Adams that it was his hope that they might meet again in heaven "with our ancient colleagues and receive with them the seal of approbation, 'Well done, good and faithful servants.'"[88] Certainly, as they stood together in the temple with their loved ones, both men knew that their much anticipated day had arrived. Regardless of how much they knew in mortality, upon their deaths, all was surely revealed to them. They had come to know that the restoration of temple blessings, which they at last had embraced, had always been the ultimate purpose of their life missions. They gained tremendous perspective on the eternal purpose of their Declaration of Independence and how it worked as a reflection of the American Covenant in furthering God's work. We, too, should internalize this perspective and live accordingly. It was for this purpose, after all, that God sent us the Adams-Jefferson miracle in the first place.

Conclusion

We have seen ample historical evidence that the Declaration of Independence is an embodiment and representation of the American Covenant. It ultimately corroborates the ancient prophecies of the American Covenant and, thus, validates the notion that this covenant and its purposes are true and divine. As we have seen, the Declaration truly reflects the national covenant, not only through the covenant principles found within the text of the document, but also through the endless invocations to Heaven, and the miraculous responses from Heaven, surrounding this document.

As we now conclude our discussion of the American Revolution, let us not forget to add to this equation the many other declarations, invocations, actions, inspirations, tokens, signs, and miracles we have detailed in the last several chapters. These too, along with the spirit of the Declaration, provide proof of the existence of the American Covenant during the period of the Revolutionary War. Throughout these last chapters dealing with this war, we have certainly witnessed God's will for America and have seen His workings pertaining to this land and its covenant. We have seen His intentions for latter-day America through reading the words of His prophets. We have seen His Old Testament prophets outline the American Covenant, as given to the tribe of Joseph, and renewed again through the Book of Mormon prophets of the same bloodline. And we have seen how these scriptural prophecies directly apply to latter-day America and the American Revolution. We have also read the words of His modern-day prophets, who confirmed the Lord's will and covenant for latter-day America, particularly in relation to the Revolution.

Though we will not revisit all these scriptural and prophetic statements here, as they have been documented in earlier chapters, let us refresh our memory with Nephi's words pertaining to his vision of revolutionary America. Speaking of the latter-day settlers of America, and in direct reference to the American Covenant, Nephi declared that "the power of the Lord was with them" *only after* they "did humble themselves before the Lord." Only then were they "delivered by the power of God out of the hands of all other nations" (see 1 Nephi 13:16-19). Also in the Book of Mormon is a similar American Covenant prophecy issued by the Savior Himself. As He stood among the Nephites, the resurrected Lord, in direct reference to latter-day Americans, prophesied that "they should be established in this land, and be set up as a free people by the power of the Father, that the covenant of the Father may be fulfilled which he hath covenanted with his people, O house of Israel" (3 Nephi 21:4). These two samples represent the many prophecies of, and references to, the American Covenant. They place latter-day America and the American Revolution in the forefront of God's plans.

And then, in powerful fulfillment of these prophetic declarations, we have seen in the last several chapters how the thoughts and actions of that chosen generation of Founders played directly into the American Covenant. With their miraculous understanding of the covenant, they were able to embrace it and use it in bringing to pass God's will. We have witnessed all this through their spiritual conversions and preparatory experiences relating to the American cause; through their testimonials of God's hand in the conflict; through their Declaration of Independence; through their inspired foresight into God's truest purposes for America; through their remarkable declarations connecting their land and covenant to ancient Israel; through their endless stream of both informal and official invocations to God; through their humble recognition that only through their national obedience would they be blessed with victory; and through their equally humble recognition of the many miracles performed by God—both on and off the battlefields of war —which they knew had secured their ultimate success. In compliance with the covenant, they had sufficiently obeyed and served the Almighty, for which they were blessed to the fullest. All of this points to the reality of the American Covenant.

With the exception of ancient Israel, to include that branch consisting of Book of Mormon peoples, this American story stands unique within the annals of world history. Few other people in history have been surrounded by such powerful prophecy and fulfillment of prophecy. But perhaps this should be expected. For, in many ways, this American story is but an extension of these earlier Old Testament and Book of Mormon accounts and covenants.[89] Such is the eternal nature and grand purpose behind the American Covenant.

Thanks to a restored gospel perspective, we can see clearly the importance of God's work in fulfilling this covenant, particularly through the American Revolution. As explained in Chapter 5, the Revolution brought three indispensable fruits in support of God's work and glory. First, it rid America of a dangerous monarchical regime which would have obstructed God's latter-day Restoration; second, it showered America with a spirit of liberty, which would eventually inspire the creation of a new government espousing and protecting this liberty, and thus providing the political foundations for the Restoration; and third, it made America an ensign to the world, inspiring other nations to join America in turning away tyranny and oppression in exchange for the freedom required for the Restoration. With such critical gospel fruits at stake in the Revolution, it is no wonder God backed this inspired era of history with the American Covenant.

We must always recognize—and never forget—the power of this covenant and what it has provided to all mankind. It is the lifeblood of America and a powerful support to the gospel. Our American problem is that we *have* forgotten this story. However, as we grow to more fully recognize the divine within our history, we will feel compelled to more fully adhere to the American Covenant —as did our forefathers—by living righteously and serving God. Thus, we will secure from Him the blessings of *liberty, protection,* and *prosperity.* Only then will such blessings be perpetuated in support of God's kingdom on the earth.

In a final historical account related to the Revolution, we see the powerful presence of God and covenant once more. With the knowledge we have gained through examining the Revolution's history from a gospel perspective, this account will now carry with it a much deeper significance. Shortly after the war, Charles Thompson, secretary of the Continental Congress—and the same aforementioned Founder who, as discussed in the previous chapter, inspiringly designed the United States Seal, complete with gospel allusions—proposed an idea to Washington. He wanted the two of them to collaborate on writing their memoirs of the entire war experience. After all, Thompson had been present during all the congressional actions, while Washington could account for the battles. Between the two of them, they could tell the entire story. However, upon outlining the project, they realized how the results simply did not add up. For no combination of America's congressional actions and/or military maneuverings could explain the American victory. By all accounts, the British should have won. Because of this, they decided against the memoir. The renowned historian of the American Revolution, Thomas Fleming, explains the decision: "It would be too disillusioning if the American people discovered how often the Glorious Cause came close to disaster." Fleming concludes his brief narrative, explaining that Washington and Thompson "jointly agreed that the real secret of America's final victory in the eight-year struggle could be summed up in two words: Divine Providence."[90]

ENDNOTES

[1] Sam Adams, as quoted in H.L Richardson, "A Most Uncivil War," *California Political Review*, January/February 2006, Vol. 17, No.1, 25.

[2] Sam Adams, as quoted by Marshall and Manuel, 391.

[3] This idea and prayer is inspired by Michael Novak, *On Two Wings*, 18.

[4] Refer to Part I of this book.

[5] John Quincy Adams, as quoted by Newt Gingrich, *Rediscovering God in America* (Nashville: Integrity House, 2006), 30.

[6] Vicki-Jo Anderson, *The Other Eminent Men of Wilford Woodruff* (Cottonwood, Zichron Historical Institute, 1994), preface and pp. 411-413.

[7] Gingrich, *Rediscovering God in America*, 27.

[8] "Fast Day Proclamation of the Continental Congress, December 11, 1776," Worthington C. Ford, Gaillard Hunt, et al., eds., *The Journals of the Continental Congress, 1774-1789* (Washington, D.C.: Government Printing Office, 1904-37), vol. 6, 1022; also quoted in Novak, *On Two Wings*, 18.

[9] The details and background of Adams' speeches and influence over Congress can be found in McCullough, *John Adams*, 126-129; details on Adams' influence can also be read in Chapter 6 of this book, under the subheading, *The Conversion of the Founders*.
[10] David McCullough, *1776* (New York: Simon and Schuster, 2005), 43.

[11] McCullough, *John Adams,* 88-89.

[12] McCullough, *John Adams*, 129.

[13] McCullough, *John Adams*, 20, 41.

[14] John C. McCollister, *God and the Oval Office* (Nashville: W Publishing Group, 2005), 11-12.

[15] McCullough, *John Adams*, 84.

[16] Waldman, 35.

[17] Adams, as quoted in Waldman, 184.

[18] Adams, as quoted in Marshall and Manuel, 391.

[19] Adams, as quoted by Michael Winder, *Presidents and Prophets* (American Fork: Covenant Communications, 2007), 17.

[20] Adams, as quoted in McCullough, *John Adams*, 130.

[21] James Grant, *John Adams, Party of One* (New York: Farrar, Straus and Giroux, 2005), 157.

[22] Gingrich, 114.

[23] John Adams, as quoted in Michael Novak, *On Two Wings: Humble Faith and Common Sense at the American Founding* (San Francisco, Encounter Books, 2002), 78.

[24] Waldman, 40.

[25] Refer to Chapter 8 of this book, under the subheading *Deeper Connections to the Covenant.*

[26] Adams, as quoted by Waldman, 37; full quote by Skousen, *The Five Thousand Year Leap*, 304.

[27] John Adams, as quoted by Marshall and Manuel, 392.

[28] John Adams, as quoted by Waldman, 108.

[29] Adams, as quoted by Waldman, *Founding Faith*, 70.

[30] Abigail Adams, as quoted in Marshall and Manuel, 382 (emphasis added).

[31] McCullough, *John Adams*, 130.

[32] McCullough, *John Adams*, 134.

[33] We refer again to McCullough's statement: "It was John Adams more than anyone who had made [independence] happen," as quoted in McCullough, *John Adams*, 129. Also, refer to the accounts of Adams' great power in influencing the decision to declare independence, as detailed in Chapter 6 of this book, under the subheading, *The Conversion of the Founders.*

[34] Adams, as quoted by Mac and Tait, 303.

[35] McCullough, *John Adams*, 119-120.

[36] Waldman, 77.

[37] McCollister, 20.

[38] Jefferson, as quoted by Winder, 21.

[39] Waldman, 73-74.

[40] Waldman, 74.

[41] Waldman, 83-84.

[42] Waldman, 80.

[43] Jefferson, as quoted by Tad Callister, *The Inevitable Apostasy* (Salt Lake: Deseret Book, 2006), 217-218.

[44] Jefferson, as quoted by Waldman, 80.

[45] Winder, 22.

[46] Jefferson, as quoted by Callister, *The Inevitable Apostasy*, 106.

[47] Winder, 22; Callister, 106.

[48] McCullough, *John Adams*, 331.

[49] Jefferson, as quoted in Gingrich, *Rediscovering God in America,* 46.

[50] John J. Stewart, *Thomas Jefferson, Forerunner to the Restoration* (Bountiful: Horizon Publishers, 1997), 80.

[51] Waldman, 124-125.

[52] Refer to Chapter 8 of this book, under the subheading *Deeper Connections to the Covenant.*

[53] Waldman, 124-125.

[54] Waldman, 91.

[55] Jefferson, as quoted by Waldman, 91.

[56] John Stewart, *Thomas Jefferson and the Restoration of the Gospel of Jesus Christ* (Mercury Publishing Company, 1959), 5.

[57] Jefferson, as quoted by Stewart, *Thomas Jefferson and the Restoration of the Gospel of Jesus Christ*, 57.

[58] Jefferson Memorial quotes, as quoted in Gingrich, *Rediscovering God in America*, 45-46.

[59] Gingrich, 46.

[60] Waldman, 81.

[61] Waldman, 82.

[62] McCullough, *John Adams*, 331.

[63] Jefferson, as quoted by Waldman, 82-83.

[64] Waldman, 107.

[65] John J. Stewart, *Thomas Jefferson, Forerunner to the Restoration* (Bountiful: Horizon Publishers, 1997), 78-79.

[66] Jefferson, as quoted by William J. Bennett, *America The Last Best Hope*, Vol. 2 (Nashville: Nelson Current, 2007), 219.

[67] Joseph Ellis, *First Family* (New York: Alfred A. Knopf, 2010), 115.

[68] Joseph Ellis, *First Family*, 121, 136.

[69] The vast correspondence between John Adams and Abigail can be found in William J. Bennett, *The Spirit of America* (New York: Simon and Schuster, 1997), 105-107, 109-11, 112-115, 134-138.

[70] McCollister, *God in the Oval Office,* 12.

[71] Abigail Adams, as quoted by Bennett, *Spirit of America*, 137.

[72] Joseph Ellis, *First Family*, 244.

[73] Callister, 430, n. 330; Jefferson borrowed these words from Homer's *Iliad*.

[74] Letter from Jefferson to Adams, as quoted by Waldman, 186-187.

[75] Adams, as quoted by Bennett, *America, the Last Best Hope,* Vol. 1, 219.

[76] Adams, as quoted by Michael Winder, *Presidents and Prophets* (American Fork: Covenant Communications, 2007), 17.

[77] Waldman, 186.

[78] John Quincy Adams, as quoted by Richard Brookhiser, *What Would the Founders Do?* (New York: Basic Books, 2006), 6.

[79] Daniel Webster, as quoted in McCullough, *John Adams*, 648. It is worth noting that Daniel Webster, along with John Quincy Adams, were among the eminent men of Wilford Woodruff to have their temple work done, pursuant to the grand vision at the St. George Temple. fittingly participated in the miracle at the St. George Temple. See Vicki-Jo Anderson, *The Other Eminent Men of Wilford Woodruff* (Cottonwood, Zichron Historical Institute, 1994), preface.

[80] McCullough, *John Adams,* 645.

[81] McCullough, *John Adams*, 646.

[82] McCullough, *John Adams*, 646.

[83] Webster, as quoted in Mac and Tait, 305.

[84] John Quincy Adams, as quoted in Mac and Tait, 306.

[85] McCullough, *John Adams*, 646.

[86] McCullough, *John Adams*, 647.

[87] Vicki-Jo Anderson, *The Other Eminent Men of Wilford Woodruff* (Cottonwood, Zichron Historical Institute, 1994), preface and pp. 417-418.

Another interesting connection between the revolutionary era and the gospel of Jesus Christ comes through the sentiments of yet another signer of the Declaration, Benjamin Rush, who was also recorded as present in the spirit at the St. George Temple with his revolutionary colleagues. As a dear friend of Adams and Jefferson, it was Rush who facilitated the reconciliation of Adams and Jefferson, thus instigating the final and revealing correspondence between the two. It is thus all the more profound that the eternal reunification of Adams and Jefferson with their respective wives was also what Rush hoped for and believed in as the ultimate gift for himself and his own wife. Rush wrote the following about his wife, Julia:

> And when my mortal part shall lay
> Waiting in hope, the final day,
> Who shall mourn o'er my sleeping clay,
> My Julia.
> And when the stream of time shall end,
> And the last trump, my grave shall rend,
> Who shall with me to Heaven ascend?
> My Julia.

These poetic lines are quoted in Callister, *The Inevitable Apostasy*, 204.

[88]Thomas Jefferson in a letter to John Adams, as quoted in Meacham, 232.

[89] See Part I of this book.

[90] Thomas Fleming, "Unlikely Victory," *What If? The World's Foremost Military Historians Imagine What Might Have Been* (New York, Penguin Putnam Inc, 1999), 186.

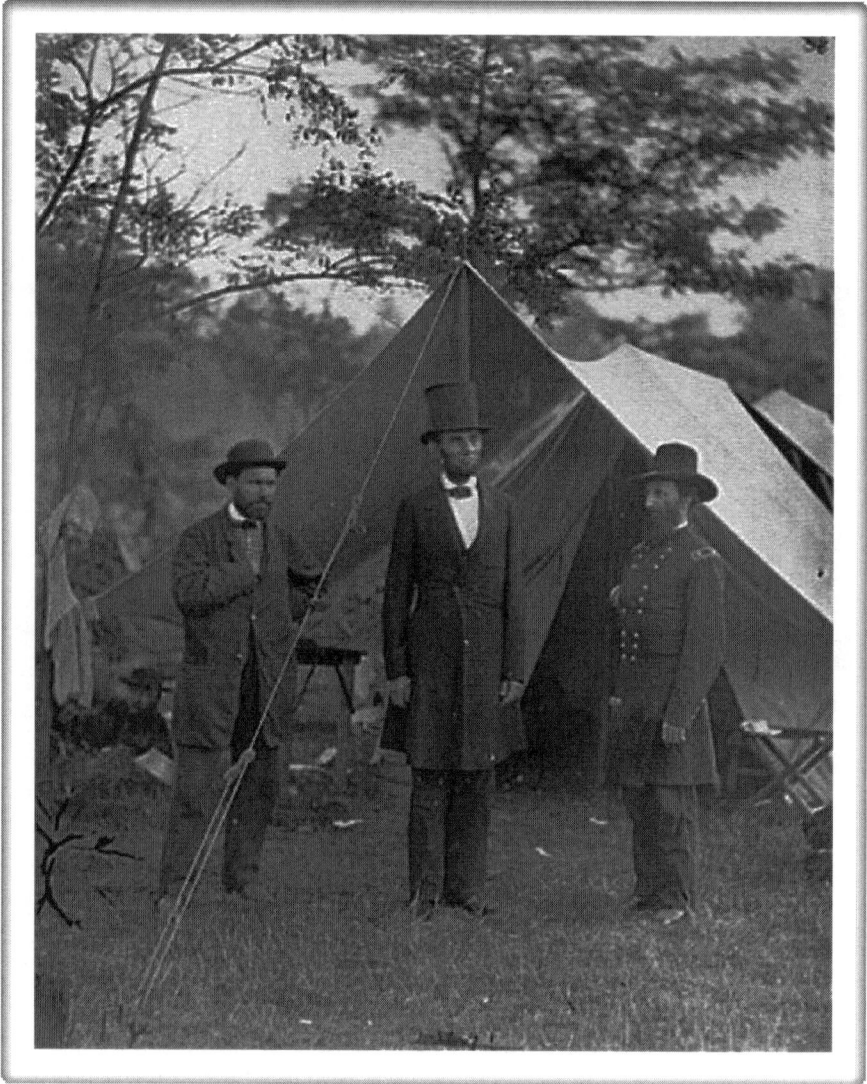

Lincoln at Antietam, by Alexander Gardner.
Courtesy of the Library of Congress.

EPILOGUE

The covenant had been firmly established. In fact, by the end of the revolutionary period, the covenant was shining gloriously, as if on fire. However, in many ways, the American Covenant story had only just begun. For, the time of implementing the promises of Heaven into the new nation —the time of inserting the covenant's principles into constitutional foundations—was only just descending upon the Founders. Furthermore, the nation's first real test pertaining to its willingness and ability to live the now codified covenant was still pending....though fast approaching.

As these crucial events transpired in God's Promised Land, the American Covenant story continued to unfold. It is a story of triumph and tragedy—of spiritual highs and demonic lows. It is a story that places presidents on stage with prophets. It is a story that fulfills ancient and modern prophecies in a way few have openly recognized. It answers questions like: *Why was James Madison the chosen one to bring forth the Constitution? Why did Joseph Smith love this document so much that he was willing to die for it? And why did the Prophet of the Restoration feel compelled to run for the presidency of the United States? What deep connection did the Prophet share with Abraham Lincoln, and what powerful relationship did Lincoln establish with the God of this land? Was the Civil War really a reflection of the covenant relationship? Why did Lincoln seek out a Book of Mormon during the darkest days of his presidency? What evidence exists that his purported reading of the Book of Mormon influenced his conversion to the American Covenant? Was the Union's General Order #11 really a direct fulfillment of Joseph Smith's prophecy? And did the Prophet really know—and did Lincoln and his people come to learn—that this national calamity would restore the national covenant and build up the Kingdom of God? What other historical figures (even in our more modern-day history) were profoundly connected to God's covenant and purposes? And finally, Where do we stand today as a nation under this covenant?*

These, and many other, questions lack any sort of answer stemming from the revolutionary period. However, their answers will be provided, discussed, and fully developed in *The American Covenant: One Nation Under God, Volume II: The Constitution, the Civil War, and Our Fight to Preserve the Covenant Today.*

BIBLIOGRAPHY

SCRIPTURES

The Bible. 1986. Salt Lake City: The Church of Jesus Christ of Latter-day Saints. Authorized King James version with explanatory notes and cross references to the standard works of The Church of Jesus Christ of Latter-day Saints.

The Book of Mormon: Another Testament of Jesus Christ. 1986. Salt Lake City: The Church of Jesus Christ of Latter-day Saints.

Doctrine and Covenants of The Church of Jesus Christ of Latter-day Saints (abbreviated in this work as D&C). 1986. Salt Lake City: The Church of Jesus Christ of Latter-day Saints.

The Pearl of Great Price. 1986. Salt Lake City: The Church of Jesus Christ of Latter-day Saints.

BOOKS AND ARTICLES

Ambrose, Stephen. *To America, Personal Reflections of an Historian.* New York: Simon and Schuster, 2002.

Anderson, Vicki Jo. *The Other Eminent Men of Wilford Woodruff.* Malta: Nelson Book, 2000.

Baigent, Michael, Richard Leigh, and Henry Lincoln. *Holy Blood, Holy Grail.* New York: Bantam Dell, 2004.

———. *The Temple and the Lodge.* New York:

Barton, David. *Benjamin Rush, Signer of the Declaration of Independence.* Aledo: WallBuilders, 1999.

Bennett, William J. *The Spirit of America.* New York: Simon and Schuster, 1997.

———. *America, The Last Best Hope.* Nashville: Nelson Current, 2006.

Benson, Ezra Taft. "The Lord's Base of Operations." *The Improvement Era* 65, no. 6. 1962. 454-56

Bowman, John. *The History of the American Presidency.* North Dighton: World Publication Group,1998. (Revised edition 2008.)

Brookhiser, Richard. *What Would the Founders Do?* New York: Basic Books, 2006.

Brown, Matthew B. *All Things Restored.* American Fork: Covenant Communications, 2000.

———. *Exploring the Connection Between Mormons and Masons.* American Fork: Covenant Communications, 2009.

Brough, R. Clayton . *They Who Tarry.* Bountiful: Horizon Publishers, 1976.

Burstein, Dan, ed. *Secrets of the Code.* New York: CDS Books, 2004.

Bushman, Richard L. *Joseph Smith: Rough Stone Rolling.* New York: Alfred A. Knopf, 2005.

———. "1830: Pivotal Year in the Fulness of Times," *Ensign.* September 1978, 9.

Butler, Jon. *Awash a Sea of Faith: Christianizing the American People.* Cambridge: Harvard University Press, 1992.

Callister, Tad. *The Inevitable Apostasy and the Promised Restoration.* Salt Lake City: Deseret Book, 2006.

Childress, David Hatcher. *The Lost Cities of North and Central America.* Kempton: Adventures Unlimited Press, 1998.

Church History in the Fulness of Times. Salt Lake City: Church of Jesus Christ of Latter-day Saints, 2000.

Columbus, Christopher. *Libro de las profecias.* Translated by Delano C. West and August King. Gainesville: University of Florida Press, 1991.

Columbus, Ferdinand. *The Life of Admiral Christopher Columbus by His Son Ferdinand Columbus.* New Brunswick: Rutgers University Press, 1959.

Connell, Janice T. *The Spiritual Journey of George Washington.* New York: Hatherleigh Press, 2007.

Cowley, Mathias F. *Wilford Woodruff: History of his Life and Labors.* Salt Lake City: Bookcraft, 1964.

D'Souza, Dinesh. "Created Equal: How Christianity Shaped the West," *Imprimis,* Volume 37, Number 11, November 2008, 4.

Davies, Peter R., George J. Brooke, and Phillip R. Callaway. *The Complete World of the Dead Sea Scrolls.* New York: Thames and Hudson, 2002.

Delaney, Carol, "Columbus's Ultimate Goal: Jerusalem." *Comparative Studies in Society and History,*48, 2006, pp 260-292.

E.D., Partridge, "An Experience of One of Columbus' Sailors," *The Improvement Era.* Vol. 12, June, 1909.

Edwards, Lester. *The Life and Voyages of Vespucci.* New York: New Amsterdam Books, 1903.

Ehrman, Bart. *Lost Christianities: Christian Scriptures and the Battle over Authentication.* Chantilly: The Teaching Company, 2002.

———. *Lost Scripture.* New York: Oxford University Press, 2003.

Ellis, Joseph J. *His Excellency.* New York: Alford A. Knopf, 2004.

———. *Patriots, Brotherhood of the American Revolution.* Lectures recorded by Recorded Books, Inc, and Barnes and Noble Publishing: 2004. Study Guide

———. *First Family.* New York: Alfred A. Knopf, 2010.

———. *Founding Brothers.* New York: Alfred Knopf, 2001.

Evans, Michael D. *American Prophecies.* New York: Warner Faith, 2004.

Faust, James E. "The Restoration of All Things,". *Ensign,* May 2006, Vol.5, No.5, 62.

Feiler, Bruce. *America's Prophet: Moses and the American Story.* New York: HarperCollins, 2009.

Ferling, John. *Adams vs. Jefferson: The Tumultuous Election of 1800.* New York: Oxford University Press, 2004.

Fleming, Thomas. "Unlikely Victory," *What If? The World's Foremost Military Historians Imagine What Might Have Been.* New York, Penguin Putnam Incorporated, 1999, 162-163.

Ford, Worthington C. and Gaillard Hunt, eds, "Fast Day Proclamation of the Continental Congress, December 11, 1776,"*The Journals of the Continental Congress, 1774-1789* .Vol.6. Washington, D.C.: Government Printing Office, 1904-37, 1022.

Foster, Marsha, and Mary Elaine Swanson. *The American Covenant, The Untold Story.* Thousand Oaks: The Mayflower Institute, 1981.

Francis, Richard. *Judge Sewall's Apology.* New York: Harper Collins Publishers, 2005.

Gee, John. *A Guide to the Joseph Smith Papyri.* Provo: BYU/FARMS, 2000.

Gingrich, Newt. *Rediscovering God in America.* Nashville: Integrity House, 2006.

Givens, Author Terryl. *By the Hand of Mormon.* Oxford: Oxford University Press, 2002.

Grant, James. *John Adams, Party of One.* New York: Farrar, Straus and Giroux, 2005.

Greene, Steven D. *The Tribe of Ephraim.* Springville: Horizon Publishers, 2007.

God Bless America: Prayers &Reflections For Our Country. Grand Rapids: Zondervan, 1999.

Haag, Michael. *The Templars, The History and the Myth.* New York: Harper, 2009.

Hall, Timothy L. *Separating Church and State*. Chicago: University of Illinois Press, 1998.

Hall, Verna M. *The Christian History of the Constitution of the United States of America*. San Francisco: Foundation for American Christian Education, 1975.

Hansen, Gerald Jr. *Sacred Walls: Learning From Temple Symbols*. American Fork: Covenant Communications, 2009.

Henry, William Wirt. *Patrick Henry: Life Correspondence and Speeches*. Vol. 1. 1891.

Hieronimus, Robert. *Founding Fathers, Secret Societies*. Rochester: Destiny Books, 2006.

Hinckley, Gordon B. *Standing for Something*. New York: Times Books. Random House, Incorporated, 2000.

———. "An Unending Conflict, A Victory Assured," *Ensign*, June 2007.

History of the Church, 1834-1837, Vol. II (Salt Lake City: Deseret Book Co., 1978), 104-105.

Holland, Matthew S. *Bonds of Affection*. Washington D.C.: Georgetown University Press, 2007.

Hosmer, William."Remember Our Bicentennial—1781," Foundation for Christian Self-Government *Newsletter*. June 1981, 5.

Hunter, Howard W. "The Gospel—A Global Faith," *Ensign*, Nov. 1991.

Hunter, J. Michael. *Mormon Myth-ellaneous*. American Fork: Covenant Communications, 2008.

Hyde, Orson. "Celebration of the Fourth of July," *Journal of Discourses*, 6:368.

Irving, Washington. *The Life and Voyages of Christopher Columbus*, Vol. 6. New York: Peter Fenelon Collier, 1897.

Isaacson, Walter. *Benjamin Franklin, An American Life*. New York: Simon and Schuster, 2003.

Jeffers, H. Paul. *The Freemasons in America*. New York: Citadel Press, 2006.

Jenkins, Timothy. *The Ten Tribes of Israel*. Colfax: Hay River Press, 2005. Produced by the Ancient American Archeological Foundation. (Originally published 1883).

Jensen, De Lamar. "Columbus and the Hand of God," *Ensign*, October 1992.

Journal of Discourses, 26 vols. London: Latter-Day Saint Book Depot, 1854-86.

Kengor, Paul. *God and Ronald Reagan*. New York: Regan Books, 2004.

Knight, Christopher, and Robert Lomas. *The Hiram Key: Pharaohs, Freemasons and the Discovery of the Secret Scrolls of Jesus.* New York: Barnes and Noble Books, 1996.

Leidner, Gordon. *Lincoln on God and Country.* Shippensburg: White Mane Books, 2000.

Lester, Edward. *The Life and Voyages of Americus Vespucius.* New York: New Amsterdam Book Company, 1903.

Let Freedom Ring, The Words That Shaped Our America. New York: Sterling Publishing Company, Incorporated, 2001.

Lossing, Benjamin. *Signers of the Declaration.* New York: J.C. Derby Publisher, 1856.

Ludlow, Daniel H., ed. *Encyclopedia of Mormonism.* New York: Macmillan, 1992.

Lund, John. *Mesoamerica and the Book of Mormon.* Salt Lake: The Communications Company, 2007.

Lund. Gerald N. *The Coming of the Lord.* Salt Lake City: Deseret Book, 1971.

Mac, Toby, and Michael Tait. *Under God.* Minneapolis: Bethany House, 2004

MacNulty, W. Kirk. *Freemasonry: A Journey Through Ritual and Symbol.* New York: Thames and Hudson, 1991.

Madsen, Truman. *Joseph Smith, The Prophet.* Salt Lake City: Deseret Book, 2008.

Mann, Charles. *1491-New Revelations of the Americas Before Columbus.* New York: Alfred A. Knopf, 2006.

Marshal, Peter, and David Manuel. *The Light and the Glory.* Grand Rapids: Revell, 2009.

Mathisen, R. *The Role of Religion in American Life.* Washington D.C.: University Press of America.

McCollister, John C. *God and the Oval Office.* Nashville: W Publishing Group, 2005.

McConkie, Bruce R. *Mormon Doctrine.* Salt Lake City: Bookcraft, 1995. (Originally published 1966.)

McCullough, David. *1776.* New York: Simon and Schuster, 2005.

———. "The Glorious Cause of America," *BYU Magazine* , Winter 2006, 48-49.

———. *John Adams.* New York: Simon and Schuster, 2001.

———. "What the Fog Wrought," *What If? The World's Foremost Military Authorities Imagine What Might Have Been.* Edited by James Cowley. New York: Penguin Putnam, Incorporated, 1999.

McGavin, E. Cecil. *Mormonism and Masonry.* Salt Lake: Bookcraft, 1956.

Meacham, Jon. *American Gospel: God, the Founding Fathers, and the Making of a Nation.* New York: Random House, 2006.

Nathanial Greene to Nicolas Cooke, Jan. 10, 1777. *The Papers of General Nathanial Greene.* Vol. 2. Showman, Richard K., and Dennis Conrad, ed. Chapel Hill: University of North Carolina Press, 1980.

Nibley, Hugh. *Temple and Cosmos.* Salt Lake City: Deseret Book Company, 1992.

Novak, Michael, and Jana Novak. *Washington's God.* New York: Basic Books, 2006.

Novak, Michael. *On Two Wing: Humble Faith and Common Sense at the American Founding.* San Francisco: Encounter Books, 2002.

Old Testament Seminary Student Guide. Salt Lake City: The Church of Jesus Christ of Latter-day Saints, 2002.

O'Reilly, Bill and Martin Dugard. *Killing Lincoln.* New York: Henry Holt and Company, 2011.

Ovason, David. *The Secret Architecture of our Nation's Capital.* New York: HarperCollins, 2000.

Packer, Boyd K. *The Holy Temple.* Salt Lake: Bookcraft, 1981.

Parry, Donald. "The Dead Sea Scrolls Bible: Puzzles, Mysteries and Enigmas" *BYU College of Humanities Alumni Magazine,* Spring 2009, 9-11.

Porter, Bruce, and Rodney Meldrum. *Prophecies and Promises: The Book of Mormon and the United States of America.* Mendon. NY: Digital Legend, 2009.

Prince, Gregory, and Wm. Robert Wright. *David O. McKay and the Rise of Modern Mormonism.* Salt Lake City: The University of Utah Press, 2005.

Richards, LeGrand. *A Marvelous Work and a Wonder.* Salt Lake City: Deseret Book Company, 1976. Richardson, H.L. "A Most Uncivil War," Vol. 17, No. 1. *California Political Review,* Jan/Feb 2006.

Ridley, Jasper. *The Freemasons: A History of the World's Most Powerful Secret Society.* New York: Arcade Publishing, 2001.

Scharffs, Gilbert W. *Mormons and Masons.* Orem: Millennial Press, 2006.

Schweikart, Larry, and Michael Allen. *A Patriot's History.* New York: Sentinel, 2004.

Sergeant, R. "Battle of Princeton," Vol. 20. *Pennsylvania Magazine of History and Biography,* 1896, 515-16.

"Secrets of the Masons," *US News and World Report: Mysteries of History: Secret Societies,* Collectors Edition, 2008, 32.

Seely, David Rolph. "Words 'Fitly Spoken,' Tyndale's English Translation of the Bible," *Prelude to the Restoration.* Salt Lake City: Deseret Book Company, 2004.

Shugarts, David. *Secrets of the Widow's Son.* New York: Sterling Publishing, 2005.

Sheldon, H., Robert T. Handy, and Lefferts A. Loetscher Smith. *American Christianity, An Historical*

Skinner, Andrew C. "Forerunners and Foundation Stones of the Restoration," *Prelude to the Restoration.* Salt Lake City: Deseret Book Company, 2004.

————. *Temple Worship.* Salt Lake City: Deseret Book, 2007.

————. "The Dead Sea Scrolls and Latter-day Truth," *Ensign*, February 2006, 44-49.

Skousen, W. Cleon. *The Five Thousand Year Leap.* Washington D.C.: The National Center for Constitutional Studies, 1981.

————. *The Majesty of God's Law.* Salt Lake City: Ensign Publishing, 1996.

Interpretation with Representative Documents. Vol.1: 1607-1820. New York: Charles Scribner's Sons, 1960.

Smith, Joseph Fielding. *Doctrines of Salvation.* Compiled by Bruce R. McConkie. 3 vols. Salt Lake City: Bookcraft, 1954-56.

————. *Gospel Doctrine.* Salt Lake City: Deseret Book, 1986.

————. *The Progress of Man.* Salt Lake City: Deseret News Press, 1952.

Snow, Erastus. *Journal of Discourses* 23:186-187, May 6, 1882.

Sora, Steven. *The Lost Colony of the Templars.* Rochester: Destiny Books, 2004.

Sorenson, John L. *The Geography of Book of Mormon Events*, Provo: FARMS, BYU, 1990.

Stewart, Chris, and Ted Stewart. *Seven Miracles That Saved America.* Salt Lake: Shadow Mountain, 2009.

Sweet, Leonard, "Christopher Columbus and the Millenial Vision of the New World, *The Catholic Historical Review,* 1986, pp. 72, 3.

Teachings of President's of the Church: Spencer W. Kimball. Salt Lake: The Church of Jesus Christ of Latter-day Saints, 2006.

Talmage, James. *The Great Apostasy.* Salt Lake City: Deseret Book Company, 1978.

The Great Prologue: A Prophetic History and Destiny of America. Salt Lake City: The Church of Jesus Christ of Latter-day Saints, 1976.

Thompson, Kenneth W. *The U.S. Constitution and the Constitutions of Latin America.* New York: University Press of America, 1991.

Utah Genealogical and Historical Magazine, Vol.11. July 1920, 107.

Vespucci, Amerigo. *Mundus Novus.* Translated by George Tyler Northrup. New Jersey: Princeton University Press, 1916.

Waldman, Steven. *Founding Faith: Politics, Providence and the Birth of Religious Freedom in America.* New York: Random House, 2008.

Wallace, Tim, and Marilyn Hopkins. *Templars in America*. Boston: Weiser Books, 2004.

Wardle, Lynn D. "The Constitution as Covenant," *BYU Studies* 27, no. 3. 1987.

Wasserman, Jacob. *Columbus, Don Quixote of the Sea*. Translated by Delno C. West, and August Kling. Gainesville, FL: 1991.

Watts, Pauline Moffat. "Prophecy and Discovery: On Spiritual Origins of Christopher Columbus' Enterprise to the Indies," *American Historical Review* Feb.1985, 95.

Webster's College Dictionary. New York: Random House, 2000.

Weems, Mason Locke. *A History of the Life, Death, Virtues and Exploits of George Washington*. Philadelphia: Lippencott, 1918.

Widtsoe, John A. *Discourses of Brigham Young*. Salt Lake City: Deseret Book Company, 1954.

Wilbur, William H. *The Making of George Washington*. DeLand: Patriotic Education, Incorporated, 1970.

Winder, Michael. *Presidents and Prophets*. American Fork: Covenant Communications, 2007.

Winthrop, John. "A Model of Christian Charity". *Winthrop Papers, 1498-1649*. Vol. 2. Boston: The Massachusetts Historical Society, 282-295.

Wood, Gordon S. "Evangelical America and Early Mormonism," *New York History* 61. October 1980.

———. *The Creation of the American Republic: 1776-1787*. Chapel Hill: The University of North Carolina Press, 1969.

———. *Revolutionary Characters*. New York: Penguin Press, 2006.

Woodruff, Wilford. *Wilford Woodruff's Journal, 1833-1898*. Typescript. Edited by Scott G. Kenney. Midvale, Utah: 1985.

———. Recorded in *Journal of Discourses*. Salt Lake City: LDS Church, 1877.

SPECIAL COLLECTIONS AND ONLINE SOURCES

Papers from the Continental Congress, from the Library of Congress *American Memory Collection*—memory.loc.gov/ammem/collections/continental/bdsdcoll2.html.

The George Washington Papers, from the Library of Congress *American Memory Collection*—lcweb2.loc.gov/ammem/gwhtml/gwhome.html.

The Writings of George Washington, Volume 4, Electronic Text Center, *University of Virginia*—http://etext.virginia.edu/toc/modeng/public/WasFi04.html.

The Papers of George Washington—http://gwpapers.virginia.edu/documents/constitution/index.html.

The Avalon Project at Yale University—www.yale.edu/lawweb/Avalon/.

The Church of Jesus Christ of Latter-day Saints—www.lds.org

Journal of Discourses, 26 vols. Liverpool, Eng.: FD Richards, 1855-86.

Joseph J. Ellis, *Patriots, Brotherhood of the American Revolution.* Lectures recorded by Recorded Books, Inc, and Barnes and Noble Publishing: 2004.

Truman G. Madsen, *The Presidents of the Church,* recorded lecture series (Salt Lake City, Bookcraft).

About the Author

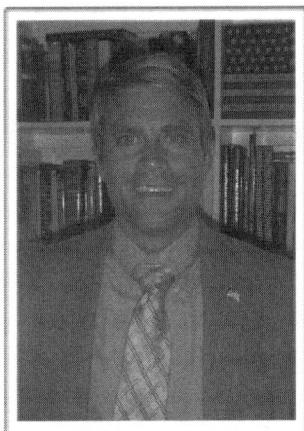

TIMOTHY BALLARD

After completing a Church mission to Chile, Timothy Ballard graduated Cum Laude from Brigham Young University in Spanish and Political Science, then went on to receive a MA (Summa Cum Laude) in International Politics from the Monterey Institute of International Studies.

Tim has worked for the Central Intelligence Agency and is currently a Special Agent for the Department of Homeland Security, where he spends time as an overseas operative to dismantle crime rings threatening the United States. For the last eight years, he has worked as an adjunct professor in American and International Politics at San Diego State University and at Imperial Valley College. Tim is also a book reviewer for The Association for Mormon Letters.

A frequent youth and fireside speaker in matters dealing with national and spiritual security, Tim lives in Southern California with his wife and six children.

For more information, visit **www.theamericancovenant.com**

* *The views and opinions expressed in this book are those of the author and do not necessarily represent the views of the Department of Homeland Security or the United States government.*